WALES IN
BRITISH POLITICS
1868–1922

WALES IN
BRITISH POLITICS
1868–1922

BY

KENNETH O. MORGAN

CARDIFF
UNIVERSITY OF WALES PRESS
1991

First published, 1963
Second edition, 1970
Third edition, 1980
First paperback edition, 1991

British Library Cataloguing in Publication Data

Morgan, Kenneth O. (Kenneth Owen)
Wales in British politics 1868–1922.
I. Title
320.9429

ISBN 0708311245

First printed at The University Press, Oxford
Paperback edition printed in Great Britain
by Dynevor Printing Company, Llandybïe, Dyfed

TO MY
FATHER AND MOTHER

PREFACE

IN November 1868 Henry Richard, a native of the village of Tregaron in Cardiganshire, but internationally celebrated after thirty years of strenuous activity on behalf of the various causes of transatlantic radical dissent, addressed the newly enfranchised electors of Merthyr Tydfil. Even shorn of the rhetoric of an election campaign, it was a startling appeal that he had to convey. For Richard was openly challenging, in the name of Welsh-speaking nonconformists, the claims to authority made by the English-speaking landed gentry who had dominated the social and political life of Wales for over three centuries.

> The people who speak this language [i.e. Welsh], who read this literature, who own this history, who inherit these traditions, who venerate these names, who created and sustain these marvellous religious organizations, the people forming three fourths of the people of Wales—have they not a right to say to this small propertied class. . . . We are the Welsh people and not you? This country is ours and not yours, and therefore we claim to have our principles and sentiments and feelings represented in the Commons' House of Parliament.[1]

Richard's emotional eloquence found a ready response among the radical electors of Merthyr and Aberdare, with their old associations with Chartism and early trade unionism, and he was triumphantly returned at the head of the poll. More, the forces that his campaign dramatically symbolized and helped to release were in the next half-century to transform the face of authority in Wales, and indeed to develop nationalist overtones far beyond anything Richard himself visualized. Henceforth, Wales was to attain a new status and a new recognition in the wider political unit of which it formed a part. The decades following the 'great election' of 1868 have come to be regarded since as a kind of national awakening in Wales, a political and indeed a cultural renaissance, a rekindling of the flame of national consciousness after centuries of isolation and neglect. Even today, when so many of the passions of late-nineteenth-century Wales have died away, the impetus of the national revival, such as it was, still reverberates throughout the daily life of Wales. The emotions aroused by the threat to the Welsh Sunday Closing Act of 1881 and

---

[1] *Aberdare Times*, 14 Nov. 1868.

to the federal structure of the University of Wales, both products of the political agitation of the years after 1868, stem ultimately from an uncertain but real awareness that both are in some sense surviving testimony to the unity and the nationality of Wales.

Yet it is remarkable that no real attempt has been made to analyse the nature of this political transformation that took place in Wales in the half-century following the 1868 election. It is unnecessary to subscribe to some of the more idealized interpretations of those years to recognize that something very fundamental was taking place within Wales at that time. Yet the period still lingers in a vague twilight of nostalgic recollection, hovering indeterminately between history and myth. Indeed, remarkably little has been written on the history of Wales subsequent to the Act of Union in 1536, as though somehow a change in the superstructure of political authority implied that Wales had lost its individual identity. The study of recent Welsh history is still being conducted in schools, extra-mural classes, and university colleges from a scanty number of secondary sources. As we approach the nineteenth century this dearth becomes still more apparent. Professor David Williams's great study of the social and economic structure of early nineteenth-century Wales remains almost alone in the field.[1] Much of the valuable and detailed inquiry that is now being conducted into social and political aspects of this period has yet to be published. Even more, the latter half of the nineteenth century and the early part of the present century, with their marked regeneration of Welsh public life, have still to find their historian. A large number of biographical *cofiannau* have come down to us, but they are of varying merit. Useful at times in illuminating the 'climate of opinion', they are largely romanticized and partisan. Among those that I have found useful, I may mention the biographies of Thomas Gee (1913), of Thomas Edward Ellis by his son, Mr. T. I. Ellis (1944–8), of Sir Herbert Lewis (1958), and of Bishop Owen of St. David's (1958–61),[2] but these few are distinguished exceptions. If Welsh historians have been strangely remiss in penetrating the recent history of their native land, historians outside Wales have, understandably no doubt, been even more negligent. The study and teaching of British history in schools and universities is still overwhelmingly dominated by a preoccupation with the affairs of England, not to say of London. There persists a kind of 'metropolitan provincialism'

---

[1] David Williams, *The Rebecca Riots* (Cardiff, 1955).
[2] These are indicated in section E of the Bibliography.

towards the major trends in recent British history: even the 'Irish question' is all too often presented simply as a study in the convolutions of policy by the government at Westminster. Yet we have recently seen how new depth may be revealed in a movement such as Chartism by treating it as a study in regional diversity.[1] The growth of the Labour Party is another subject that might fruitfully be investigated in the same manner. As the 'Namier revolution' has demonstrated for the eighteenth century, we may discover new truths about the nature of society and the struggle for political authority by turning away from the centre to the periphery. In particular, a study of modern Wales, and of modern Scotland as well, by pointing the contrast with England, might shed new light on the political characteristics of contemporary Britain, in which the rebirth of a sense of a local, regional, or national community has been an important theme. As the writings of Hardy or of Housman illustrate the new awakening of the social and cultural diversity of later Victorian England, so too the national movement in Wales, no less than that in Ireland, is an essential, though hitherto neglected facet of the evolution of modern Britain.

The purpose of this book is, therefore, twofold. First it is an attempt to meet what appears to be a marked deficiency in the historiography of modern Wales. It tries to illustrate the nature and the limitations of the political nationalism that arose in Wales in the last century, and to investigate its impact upon Welsh politics and society. But it is secondly an attempt to deal with a far wider theme. I have tried to outline and to explain the growing awareness of opinion outside Wales of the distinctive needs of the Principality, as the indifference if not the contempt of mid-Victorian Britain gradually gave way to a more intelligent, if sometimes still patronizing, understanding. Of necessity, this is primarily a political story. The advance of democracy after 1867 made political activity the major channel for asserting the individuality of Wales and for articulating that growing self-awareness that had been welling up throughout the nineteenth century. Welsh nonconformity turned from social to political action, as the way to national liberation seemed to lie through the ballot box. I have tried then to analyse the attitudes of the British political parties towards Welsh affairs, the presuppositions they and their leaders and supporters held about Wales, and the policies they adopted as these assumptions were confirmed or rejected. The initial and terminal

[1] Asa Briggs (ed.), *Chartist Studies* (London, 1959).

points of the story seem to me to be clearly dictated by the evidence. It was the aftermath of the election of 1868 that compelled British political parties for the first time to formulate an attitude towards Welsh questions, particularly towards the disestablishment of the Church in Wales. Conversely, by the end of the First World War the major themes had worked themselves out. The Welsh Church had been irretrievably disestablished; the land and education controversies had seemingly lost their urgency; the Speaker's Conference on home rule had reported with little apparent effect. The administration of the Welsh Prime Minister, Lloyd George, indicated the emergence of a new phase, to be dominated in Wales itself by the Labour Party, in which the interests of Wales were once again to become virtually indistinguishable from those of the other nations. Between 1868 and 1922, therefore, when Lloyd George left office for the last time, a cycle can be traced, the rise and decline of political nationalism. Naturally, the period cannot be delineated too precisely: national sentiment in Wales did not erupt spontaneously in 1868, nor did it disappear in 1922. It is still an active force today. But it was, I believe, in the period covered in this work that the affairs of Wales formed a major political issue. The 'Welsh question', no less than the more spectacular 'Irish question', had been a political reality. In this sense the period from 1868 to 1922 has a unity of its own.

Many difficulties confront the historian of this complex theme. The physical difficulties alone are formidable: the immediate reaction is perhaps to echo Lytton Strachey's verdict on the nineteenth century as a whole and to say that its history will never be written because we know too much about it. There is a vast abundance of material, manuscript and printed sources, all hitherto scarcely examined. The voluminous correspondence of many of the leading Welsh political figures in these years is available: only the papers of Lloyd George are still unfortunately denied to the researcher. One of my major difficulties has been the absence of detailed research into so many important aspects of my subject. To mention but a few, the growth of nonconformity, the nature of Welsh agriculture from 1850 onwards, the character of the *Cymru Fydd* movement, and the rise of the Labour movement in Wales—all these have still to be investigated, and much laborious but important inquiry remains to be undertaken. No more has been attempted here than to establish a general political framework, which I hope may perhaps encourage others to launch themselves into this fascinating field, with the enthusiasm that scholars show in penetrating some of the more remote aspects of the history of Wales.

The emotional difficulties assailing the historian of this subject are still more pressing and real. The optimism and the later disillusion that the national movement aroused are still very much of a reality in Wales: as one who has lived mainly in England, I am perhaps all the more conscious of the immediacy of the recent past in Wales, when so much inquiry into contemporary problems is nostalgic in tone. On the one hand, the Welsh national movement still retains much of the romantic quality of folk-myth, the uprising of *y werin* against their clerical oppressors, with such men as Tom Ellis and Lloyd George assuming an unreal and heroic stature. On the other hand, the cynicism and despair of numerous Welsh writers since the 1890's, their feeling that so many of the achievements of the years since 1868 have somehow become insignificant and irrelevant, this too has its repercussions today. The search for the 'guilty men' who betrayed the tradition they inherited has been intense. The inquiry into the incomplete nature of the Welsh nationalist movement, which has preserved a Welsh community but failed to produce a Welsh state, is still avidly being conducted. Never has the alleged 'schizophrenia' of the Welsh people towards themselves and their English neighbours been more amply displayed. Yet surely the task of countering these emotions and attempting a more detached assessment of modern Wales is not an impossible one. In recent years, Irish historians have been able to treat with scholarly objectivity such controversial questions as the Great Famine, the fall of Parnell, and the Dublin rising. It should be possible now, with the sectarian and nationalist passions of the years before 1914 becoming increasingly remote, to appraise with equal detachment the recent history of Wales. Only thus can the dignity and the vigorous reality of Welsh nationality in the mid-twentieth century be sustained and fostered.

My researches into this subject have been conducted in two stages, first as an advanced student at Oxford University and then in the History Department of the University College of Swansea. In each case, I have much cause to be grateful for guidance and encouragement in my work. Mr. R. B. McCallum, Master of Pembroke College, Oxford, supervised my initial researches to my great benefit. Professor Glanmor Williams of Swansea has read the whole of the work in manuscript: his scholarship and thoroughness, together with many other kindnesses, great and small, place me deeply in his debt.

Professor David Williams of Aberystwyth has been constant in his kindly interest and advice over the years. In different ways, I am grateful also to my colleagues, Mr. Ieuan Gwynedd Jones and Mr. N. C. Masterman, and to Dr. Gwyn A. Williams of Aberystwyth: I am particularly indebted to Mr. Jones for generously allowing me access to his unpublished study of the election of 1868. Needless to say I cannot inflict responsibility on these friends and advisers for the conclusions I have drawn or for any errors that doubtless remain. Among those whose personal recollections of the period have been of value to me, I must thank the Rt. Hon. James Griffiths, M.P., the late Dr. Thomas Richards, Mr. W. W. Price, Aberdare, Mr. T. J. Evans, Carmarthen, and Mr. H. Llewelyn Williams, Q.C. I am also indebted to Professor and Mrs. Idwal Jones for their generous hospitality and for full and free access to the valuable papers of Sir Herbert Lewis at Plas Penucha. Miss Eluned E. Owen kindly sent me transcripts of material from the Bishop Owen Papers. Among the many library staffs which have been helpful to me, I wish to thank the Manuscripts Department of the National Library of Wales at Aberystwyth and Mr. T. J. Hopkins of the Cardiff Central Library for their unfailing courtesy and assistance over the past few years. The University College of Swansea assisted the later stages of my research with grants from its research fund. I must conclude by thanking the University of Wales Press for coping so ably with the transatlantic problems of publication. KENNETH O. MORGAN

Columbia University, New York City, Christmas, 1962

PREFACE TO SECOND EDITION

In this second edition, I have taken the opportunity to correct misprints and minor errors: I am very grateful to reviewers and readers (especially to Dr. T. I. Ellis) for pointing them out. I have also made some additions to Chapter VII to take account of developments since 1962 when I completed the writing of the first edition. A further note has been appended to the bibliography to indicate some primary and secondary sources that have become available during the past eight years, in the hope that this will assist others in their research. Otherwise, I have not thought it necessary to make changes in the text, or to modify the general conclusions put forward in the first edition. K. O. M.

Oxford, July 1970

This new edition contains no major changes from its predecessor. The discussion of more recent political developments in Chapter VII has been left at the same point of time as in the second edition, namely the general election of June 1970. This is partly because a more extended account of Welsh political change between 1970 and 1978, including the whole debate over devolution and nationalism, would seriously unbalance a book which focuses primarily on the period down to 1922. In addition, I have recently completed a lengthy general survey of Welsh history since the 1880s for the university presses of Wales and Oxford, in which the politics of the very recent past are given extensive treatment. I have appended a further note to the bibliography, to take account of works published since 1970. Otherwise, I have nothing to add, save that I still believe the main arguments developed in this book (and originally conceived nearly twenty years ago) to be broadly correct.

K.O.M.

Oxford, July 1979

AUTHOR'S NOTE TO PAPERBACK EDITION

For material published since 1980 the reader should consult *A Bibliography of the History of Wales* edited by Philip Henry Jones and available on microfiche (University of Wales Press, 1989).

K.O.M.

Aberystwyth, July 1991

ABBREVIATIONS

Add. MSS.   Additional Manuscripts.
Bangor   Library of the University College of North Wales, Bangor.
B.M.   British Museum.
Cardiff   Cardiff Central Library.
L.S.E.   Library of the London School of Economics.
N.L.W.   National Library of Wales, Aberystwyth.
Trans. Hon. Soc. Cymm.   *Transactions of the Honourable Society of Cymmrodorion.*

NOTE ON
NONCONFORMIST DENOMINATIONS

THE Welsh nonconformist denominations are referred to by their Welsh appellations throughout. Thus the Calvinistic Methodists are termed 'Methodists', the Congregationalists are referred to as 'Independents', and the Wesleyan Methodists as 'Wesleyans'.

ACKNOWLEDGEMENT

I WISH to acknowledge permission granted by the Cabinet Record Office for me to consult the records of the Gladstone ministry of 1892–94, contained in the Gladstone Papers in the British Museum (Add. MSS. 44648).

CONTENTS

I

WALES AND BRITISH POLITICS BEFORE 1868

(i) *The Growth of Radicalism*

In the summer of 1854 George Borrow went on a circuitous and picturesque journey in search of Wales, from the Vale of Llangollen in the north down to Newport in the far south. Borrow was a sympathetic observer, an enthusiast for Celtic folk-lore and romance.[1] Yet, in *Wild Wales*, in which he later described his adventures, he portrayed for his English readers an unfamiliar land, alien in speech and primitive in customs. Even Borrow was to confirm widespread 'Saxon' preconceptions of a region intellectually backward and politically dormant. Among his English public, the idea that this comparatively remote hinterland might be elevated to the status of a separate nationality, in the same way as Scotland and Ireland, with characteristics of its own and interests that might diverge from those of England, was indeed seldom put forward. That these regional peculiarities should be preserved or even encouraged, remained the chimera of a few eccentrics. When, a decade later, Matthew Arnold was invited to the Chester *Eisteddfod* of 1866, and subsequently urged the injection of Celtic mysticism as an antidote to the 'Philistinism' of the Anglo-Saxon and 'the despotism of fact', his remarks were widely deplored.[2] In *The Times*, Delane commented that the Welsh language was 'the curse of Wales', a lingering obstacle to the mid-Victorian march of intellect and prosperity.[3]

In later years, Welsh publicists and politicians tended to look back on this period as one of social and political decadence, ultimately brought to an end by the national liberation of the election of 1868. 'The political subjection of Wales was complete. . . . It had no voice in Parliament, no advocate in the Press, no valorous friend to do

[1] See René Fréchet, 'George Borrow and the Celts', *Trans. Hist. Soc. Cymm.*, 1960, pp. 65–76.

[2] Matthew Arnold, 'The Study of Celtic Literature' (1867), printed in J. Bryson (ed.), *Matthew Arnold: Poetry and Prose* (London, 1954), pp. 469–88.

[3] *The Times*, 8 Sept. 1866. The controversy surrounding Arnold's views continued in *The Times*, until 17 Sept. *The Times* succinctly summarized its own view on 14 Sept. when it described Wales as 'a small country . . . with an indifferent soil and inhabited by an unenterprising people'. A contemporary work echoing this view is H. L. Spring, *Lady Cambria* (London, 1867).

B

battle for its honour outside its borders, no one to meet enemies in the gate.' Thus wrote Tom Ellis in 1894, looking back with satisfaction on a quarter century of emancipation.[1] To Henry Richard, these were years of 'feudalism', of a patriarchal society in which 'clansmen battled for their chieftains'.[2] He complained that until the 1880's there were no parliamentary papers relating to the needs of Wales.[3] When he arose in the House of Commons in 1869 to draw attention to the political evictions that had recently shocked the Principality, he alleged 'that no question relating to Wales had occupied the attention of Parliament in the memory of man'.[4] Not merely was separate treatment for the affairs of Wales unknown; even in its accepted role as twelve of the more westerly counties of England (Monmouthshire being invariably regarded as English) or as four remote dioceses in the province of Canterbury, Wales found meagre recognition. In the *Daily News*, a Welsh journalist was to deplore the isolation of 'Neglected Wales'.[5]

In retrospect, it is clear that many of these later charges were much exaggerated—those by Henry Richard indeed are factually untrue. They often over-emphasized the isolation of Wales for polemical purposes. In reality, Wales had long developed a great diversity of contacts with England and the outside world. From the later eighteenth century, tourists were penetrating the mountain barriers in search of coastal bathing places, while a host of topographical guides flooded the market. Culturally, there was intimate communication between Welsh Augustan scholars of the Morrisian circle and their English counterparts, through such bodies as the Honourable Society of Cymmrodorion, founded in 1751. The Romantic movement stimulated writers in Wales as elsewhere, Iolo Morganwg prominent among them. There were close links between religious and philanthropic movements such as the Methodists and the Society for Promoting Christian Knowledge, while the impact of English dissenting academies was indirectly to permeate to every level of Welsh society. Most striking of all, the growth of industry was

---

[1] Tom Ellis, 'Wales and the Local Government Act, 1894', *Speeches and Addresses* (Wrexham, 1912), p. 182.

[2] Henry Richard, *Letters on the Social and Political Condition of Wales* (London, 1867), p. 80.

[3] Henry Richard, *Letters and Essays on Wales* (London, 1884), p. 185. This is, of course, a totally inaccurate statement.

[4] *Parl. Deb.*, 3rd ser., vol. cxcvii, p. 1295.

[5] 'Neglected Wales', three articles by 'Adfyfr' (T. J. Hughes), in the *Daily News*, 12, 27 Oct., 16 Nov. 1887.

intensifying the connexions which bound Wales to the economic life of England. If the industrialization of the northern counties was in decline by mid-century, in Glamorgan and Monmouth the successive penetration of the valleys, down to the opening up of the Rhondda in the 1860's, was to make South Wales an area of intense economic activity and the greatest coal-exporting area in the world. The spread of communications, roads, canals, and railways, was rapidly opening up the inland valleys. By 1850 there were fourteen railways already completed, reaching to Swansea in the south and to Holyhead in the north, linking up Wales with the markets of industrial England and beyond.

Yet, in spite of this over-emphasis, there remains an important element of truth in later charges of isolation and neglect. The factors of geography and the pattern of cultural life lent to Welsh society a rhythm and a development of its own. Geographical remoteness helped to delay the expansion of industry and the growth of communications. Railways extended haphazardly and served to underline the growing division between the coalfield and the rural hinterland. Roads were erratic in distribution under the turnpike system which provoked the wrath of the Rebecca Rioters, and their poor quality brought condemnation from suffering travellers until recent times.[1] Most of the country remained a land of marginal agriculture, with few towns of any size. Finally, Welsh educational development was unusually retarded. In spite of the achievements of Griffith Jones of Llanddowror and his successors in the extension of circulating schools during the eighteenth century, there remained scant provision for either primary or higher instruction. Not until the middle decades of the nineteenth century were the nonconformist churches, so active elsewhere, roused from their hostility towards secular aid for education. The Education Commissioners of 1847, who produced the notorious *Llyfrau Gleision* (Blue Books), largely nullified the effect of their report through their mass indictment of the culture, social conditions, religion, and morals of the people of Wales, but the existence of widespread educational backwardness, illiteracy, and ignorance remained plain to see, until reform later in the century.

Nowhere was this tendency towards insulation more evident than in the political development of Wales. In the political life of the United Kingdom, Wales had played an insignificant role since Tudor

---

[1] A. Griffith-Boscawen, *Memories* (London, 1925), p. 55. For the turnpike system, see David Williams, *The Rebecca Riots* (Cardiff, 1955), ch. vi.

times. The great controversies of the industrial age, the debate over
the revolutionary movement in France, the struggle for Catholic
emancipation and for parliamentary reform, the campaign for the
recognition of working-class movements, all affected Wales to only
a marginal extent. It is true that the years of economic upheaval and
social distress after 1815 saw in Wales signs of a political ferment of
a new and revolutionary nature.[1] There was growing pressure by the
nonconformist churches through such bodies as the Dissenting
Deputies and the Protestant Society, for the repeal of the legal disabilities to which nonconformists everywhere were subject: in 1828,
over 150 petitions reached the House of Commons from Wales alone,
in support of repeal of the Test and Corporation Acts. Again, in
some areas of industrial Glamorgan there was a mounting agitation
for extension of the franchise, particularly by the local 'shopocracy'
in Merthyr Tydfil. In these areas can be found the early crystallization
of that radical tradition which was ultimately to transform the face
of authority in Wales in the years after 1868. Yet these pressures,
significant though they were, were localized and intermittent, and
left only a slight impression on Wales as a whole. This was an inevitable consequence of physical and cultural remoteness. In a society
in the early stages of industrialization and widely unfamiliar with the
English language, political radicalism found slender roots and political controversy was largely muted.

Since the Union with England in the reign of Henry VIII, Welsh
politics and society had been dominated by the gentry, landowners
with rent rolls up to £3,000 a year, bound to the great magnates
such as Powis or Dynevor by 'connexion' and to each other by a network of inter-marriage. In a variety of guises, as lords-lieutenant,
commanders of the county militia and, above all, justices of the peace,
they dominated the life of the country-side. 'They interpreted the
law at Petty Sessions, they were responsible for all local administration at Quarter Sessions, they constituted, in fact, a ruling caste',
writes an apologist.[2] As a reflection of the authority of the *Plasty*
over local affairs, parliamentary representation fell completely

---

[1] For the growth of radicalism in the early nineteenth century, see Ieuan Gwynedd
Jones, 'Wales and Parliamentary Reform', *Wales through the Ages*, vol. ii (Llandebïe,
1960), pp. 132–9, and 'The Liberation Society and Welsh Politics, 1844–1868', *Welsh
History Review*, vol. i, no. 2 (1961), pp. 193–224; Gwyn A. Williams, 'The Making of
Radical Merthyr, 1800–1836', ibid., pp. 161–92; Islwyn David, 'Political and Electioneering Activity in South West Wales, 1820–1851' (unpublished M.A. thesis, University of Wales, 1959), ch. iii.

[2] H. M. Vaughan, *The South Wales Squires* (London, 1926), p. 3.

under their control, a process facilitated by the single-member representation of Welsh counties which continued down to 1832. In Wales, the civil wars had taken the form of private family disputes rather than declarations of principle, and the upheavals of the seventeenth century left the power of the gentry beyond challenge.[1] Families such as the Bulkeleys in Anglesey, the Mostyns in Flintshire, the Vaughans of Trawscoed in Cardiganshire, the Vaughans of Golden Grove in Carmarthenshire, and the Morgans in Monmouthshire maintained their undisputed authority for decades.[2] Most powerful of all, the Wynns of Wynnstay first established themselves in the Denbighshire seat in 1716 and rapidly extended their influence into neighbouring Montgomeryshire and Merioneth. A Wynn represented Montgomeryshire from 1799 to 1880, while the dynasty of 'Old Sir Watkin' survived economic and political pressures in Denbighshire until 1885.[3]

Thus arose the two main peculiarities of parliamentary representation in Wales—its remarkable continuity of membership and its domination by Welsh members. Unlike the Irish gentry, Welsh landlords were usually not alien in race. They generally bore traditional Welsh names. They lived on their home farms and preserved customarily good relations with their tenants. But, if they were Welsh by birth and tradition, in outlook they were increasingly anglicized. Since the later Middle Ages they had gradually become English in tongue and education, often English by intermarriage and custom, dependent upon English land law of entail and primogeniture for the building up of their estates. By the eighteenth century, such names as Corbet, Pennant, Assheton-Smith, Cawdor, and Bute testified to the extent of English and Scots penetration. Gradually, therefore, the landlords of Wales became separated from the life of the community amongst whom they lived. English and Scots agents helped to transform this growing estrangement with a new bitterness. The *uchelwyr* who had patronized Welsh bards were succeeded by descendants English in speech, and increasingly marked off from

[1] See A. H. Dodd, 'The Pattern of Politics in Stuart Wales', *Trans. Hon. Soc. Cymm.*, 1948, pp. 51–90.

[2] For Welsh parliamentary representation, see W. R. Williams, *The Parliamentary History of Wales, 1541–1895* (Brecknock, 1895), and G. P. Judd, *Members of Parliament, 1734–1832* (New Haven, Conn., 1955). The general principles involved are discussed in relation to one county by Glyn Roberts, 'Political Affairs, 1536–1900', Sir J. E. Lloyd (ed.), *History of Carmarthenshire*, vol. ii (1939), pp. 1–80.

[3] For an example of the survival of the Wynn influence and mystique into the present century, see Alwyn D. Rees, *Life in a Welsh Countryside* (Cardiff, 1950), pp. 151–9.

the community by a growing gulf in class and language, and soon in religious and political affiliation. By the mid-nineteenth century, this division was almost complete.

It was these conditions which helped to produce the paradoxical nature of Welsh society and of the Welsh national movement which was to spring from it. The very factors which emphasized the separateness of Wales—geographical remoteness and cultural division—resulted in Wales being bound administratively ever more closely to England. The result of cultural isolation was political assimilation. It was this that gave nationalism in Wales its peculiar character. Welshmen could only assert their national needs and differences by rebelling against their isolation and involving themselves more and more closely in the affairs of England. Only by challenging the dominance of the landowning classes which had governed their society for three centuries could Welsh needs be adequately recognized, and Wales accepted as something more than a geographical expression. For nationalism in Wales, therefore, unlike nationalism in Ireland, separatism would be fatal.

The difference in status between Wales on the one hand, and Ireland and Scotland on the other, became more acute as the nineteenth century progressed. The existence of a distinct Irish nation was undeniable, even if unwelcome to English eyes. The simple fact of the physical separation of Ireland by the Irish Sea was an argument easily understood, and later used in extending disestablishment of the Church to Ireland while denying it to Wales. The political union with England dated only from 1800, while the basic dilemma of Irish government remained. Throughout the nineteenth century, from O'Connell to Parnell, the obvious existence of a distinct social structure, a fundamental cleavage in religious affiliation, a nationally articulate public opinion, and a tragically insoluble problem of economic subsistence was to make Irish nationality a central theme in British political life.

Again, the separate nationhood of Scotland was equally clear. The Union dated only from 1707, while distinctive Scottish institutions were maintained in the legal system, in the Kirk, and in education. In an aristocratic age, Scottish landowners, unlike their counterparts in Wales, were themselves the most powerful advocates of Scottish national sentiment, with a romantic attachment to the Stuart cause. Intellectually and culturally, the vigorous tradition of Scots 'intellectual Calvinism', the influence of Adam Smith and

Carlyle, of Scott, the *Edinburgh Review*, and the metaphysical philosophers, were universally recognized. Young Scotsmen travelled forth to London in the eighteenth century with the clear impress of a national environment, with the long sanction of tradition and of popular sentiment. They preserved their pride in being Scots, in inheriting a superior national culture, and in England they maintained an unmistakable national identity.

But in the case of Wales it was very different. Here there was no O'Connell or Walter Scott to bludgeon or beguile English opinion from its apathy. The extent of Wales was in itself a cause of speculation: it contained no accepted capital, and the boundary with England was artificial, if it existed at all. Here the Act of Union with England was of so remote a date as to seem an ineradicable part of the political scene. Indeed, the Act of 1536 had itself claimed to be merely confirming a union that had always existed. Recollections of a previous age of independent statehood in the days of Llewelyn or Glyndwr had to be conjured up by ingenious antiquaries from the fragmentation of Welsh medieval development. Further, the union with England had been followed by a systematic process of administrative uniformity down to the abolition of the Court of Great Sessions in 1830, itself a creation of the Act of Union. From Tudor times, it had been governmental policy to extinguish the language and cultural expression of the Welsh people for official purposes, in the interests of centralization, although in fact by authorizing the use of Welsh in Church services the Tudors themselves had helped to ensure the survival of a native culture. In Scotland, an independent legal profession had become the 'bearers and defenders of nationality'.[1] In Wales, barristers had to make their way on English circuits. In Ireland, a dual system of administration between Westminster and Dublin Castle testified to the separate role of Ireland in public policy. In Wales, the Home Office and the Court of Chancery made no distinction between Welsh and English problems. In Scotland, the Kirk remained a representative assembly of a Scots community: the Schism of 1843 which split the Presbyterian Kirk asunder was a dispute above all between Scotsmen. In Wales, the Church had long begun to shed its national characteristics, and no Welsh-speaking bishop had been consecrated since the reign of Anne. Already, the rising tide of nonconformity was looking

---

[1] Richard Pares, 'A Quarter of a Millennium of Anglo-Scottish Union', *History*, vol. xxxix (Oct. 1954), p. 238. This stimulating article is valuable for implicitly pointing the contrast with Wales.

back to some distant horizon before the Norman Conquest, when the Church was truly Celtic and truly independent. In all aspects of public policy, the trend towards assimilation and uniformity was consistent, testimony to the notorious directive in the *Encyclopaedia Britannica*: 'For Wales—see England'.

Yet this was never a complete picture. In spite of all administrative efforts, the separate existence of a Welsh community was maintained. In two respects above all, Wales continued to be recognized and accepted as a different place from England, however unwelcome this might appear.

First there was the continued survival of the Welsh language. In spite of all official discouragement, there seems little doubt that Welsh continued to serve as the normal medium of communication for people in most parts of Wales at least until the growth of the public education movement after 1870. The Blue Books of 1847 left no doubt on this point. Indeed, during the eighteenth century, Welsh as a literary medium had made notable progress. Interest had revived in imaginative literature, in local *eisteddfodau* and in the folk-lore and archaeology of the past, this despite the declining prestige of Geoffrey of Monmouth as an historian.[1] The growth of nonconformity in the early years of the nineteenth century was a great stimulus to the use of Welsh as a medium of education, exhortation, and persuasion, particularly through the Sunday schools: in 1867 it was estimated that 70,000 Welsh Bibles were sold,[2] and the sufferings of Mari Jones of Llanfihangel-y-Pennant in the quest for a Bible in her native tongue passed into popular tradition. More powerful still was the growth of a popular press for the expression and moulding of Welsh opinion.[3] The Baptists and Independents were active from the early years of the nineteenth century: the Baptist *Seren Gomer*, first published in Swansea in 1814, was the first Welsh-language newspaper to be issued. It was shortly to be joined by such influential organs as the Independent *Dysgedydd* (1821) and *Diwygiwr* (1835), and the Methodist *Drysorfa* (1831). The middle decades of the century were a period of massive expansion for Welsh periodicals and newspapers, with the

---

[1] See A. O. H. Jarman, 'Literature and Antiquities', *Wales through the Ages*, vol. ii, pp. 110–16.

[2] Henry Richard, *Letters on the Social and Political Condition of Wales*, p. 37.

[3] For the growth of the Welsh press, see *Bibliography of the History of Wales* (Cardiff, new ed., 1962), pp. 223–6. See also *The Times*, 20 Dec. 1887 ('Letters from Wales, IX'); R. D. Rees, 'Glamorgan Newspapers under the Stamp Acts', *Morgannwg*, iii (1959), pp. 61–94, and 'South Wales Newspapers under the Stamp Acts', *Welsh History Review*, vol. i, no. 3 (1962), pp. 37–60.

growth of conscious social and political attitudes transcending denominational barriers, and with greater freedom afforded by the repeal of the Stamp Acts in 1855 and the abolition of Paper Duties in 1861. By 1866 it was estimated that there were in Welsh five quarterlies, twenty-five monthlies, and eight weeklies, with a combined circulation of 120,000.[1] They were from the first overwhelmingly nonconformist. In 1883 Archbishop Benson lamented to Gladstone that only one of twenty-five publications was Anglican—'and it dies this week'.[2] The growth of the Welsh press and its early association with the outlook of nonconformists was a fundamental factor in shaping the outlook and sensibilities of people throughout Wales. As in Ireland, the credulity of a peasant population was susceptible to the influence of the written word. The press became the vehicle for every effective popular leader from Gwilym Hiraethog to David Lloyd George, and a powerful medium for invigorating and extending the Welsh language.

The second respect in which Wales remained quite distinct from England was in the structure of its society. Welsh society was quite different from English society, with a different network of class relationships. It rested on the economic basis of Welsh agrarian society, 'the prevalence of a large number of small, separate farms of what may be described as the peasant and family type'.[3] This system differed equally from the large commercial farms of England and from the myriad, sub-divided holdings of Ireland and the crofting districts of Scotland. The spread of English land law and of the inclosure system had resulted in the virtual extinction of the leaseholder in favour of tenancy-at-will, on a year-to-year basis. The inclosure of mountain uplands during the French Revolutionary Wars greatly advanced this process, creating a network of small farms of less than 100 acres, with few labourers and most of these indoor. Tenure became less and less secure, leaving the tenant without protection against arbitrary eviction and extortionate increases in rent. The prices of holdings in sales were driven ever upward in an ever more competitive market. Superimposed on this simple economic division between the landowning and occupying classes was a growing divergence in social attitudes: the owners remained Church, Tory, and English-speaking, while their tenants to an ever-increasing

---

[1] Henry Richard, *Letters on the Social and Political* . . ., p. 36.
[2] Archbishop Benson to Gladstone, 23 July 1883 (B.M., Add. MSS., 44109, f. 40). This is, presumably, a reference to *Y Llan*, which, in fact, survives to the present day.
[3] *Royal Commission on Land in Wales and Monmouthshire, Report* (1896), p. 148.

degree were becoming nonconformists, and radical, as well as Welsh. This combination of economic instability and cultural division was to divide every village and valley into two communities. From this clash of two societies, modern Wales was to be forged.

At the turn of the nineteenth century, two more profound forces were to transform Welsh society and to create these individual characteristics into forces of political significance. These were the growth of industrialism and the expansion of religious nonconformity. Between them, they produced an upheaval of society and of ideas which in speed and in extent sharply divide off the subsequent history of Wales and create a pattern recognizably modern.

The advance of industrialization lent a new complexity to the economy and society of the country.[1] It divided Wales anew into two distinct cultures and created new connexions with England. An initial expansion from the 1780's in the metallurgical industries, iron from Hirwaun to Abergavenny, copper at Swansea and Neath, was followed by rapid penetration down the hill-side into the inland valleys. After 1840 the coal industry was revolutionized. A local traffic to nearby coastal areas was transformed on a world-wide scale, with a massive expansion of output and the development of great ports such as Cardiff and Barry to link the growth of South Wales to international demands. The population of Glamorgan and Monmouth swelled from 116,465 in 1801 to 389,267 in 1851 and on to 968,314 by 1891, with a vast rate of immigration from the rural hinterland and from outside. For the first time, Wales had become a land with large towns. In the present century commentators have dramatized the contrast between urban and rural Wales, between what Sir Alfred Zimmern termed 'Welsh Wales' and 'American Wales'.[2] The relative failure of Welsh political nationalism is often explained on these grounds. Yet the Welsh character of the new industrial population was apparent from the first.[3] Many of the later industrialists,

[1] For the growth of industrialization in general, see Sir Frederick Rees, 'How South Wales became Industrialized', *Studies in Welsh History* (Cardiff, 1948), and A. H. John, *The Industrial Development of South Wales* (Cardiff, 1950). For the coal industry, see J. E. Morris and L. J. Williams, *The Coal Industry in South Wales, 1841–1875* (Cardiff, 1958); E. D. Lewis, *The Rhondda Valleys* (London, 1959); and Eric Wyn Evans, *History of the South Wales Miners* (Cardiff, 1961). For the iron, steel, and tin-plate industries, see J. P. Addis, *The Crawshay Dynasty, 1765–1867* (Cardiff, 1957); W. E. Minchinton, *The British Tinplate Industry* (Oxford, 1957); Madeline Elsas (ed.), *Iron in the Making. Dowlais Iron Company Letters, 1782–1860* (London, 1960).

[2] A. Zimmern, *My Impressions of Wales* (London, 1927), p. 37.

[3] This case is presented somewhat differently by Brinley Thomas, 'Wales and the Atlantic Economy', *Scottish Journal of Political Economy*, Nov. 1959, pp. 169–92. He goes so far as to argue that it was industrialization that saved the Welsh language.

particularly the coalowners and their managers—men like David Davies and Samuel Thomas—were Welsh in speech and nonconformist by religion, preserving an intimate, personal relationship with their employees, with whom they could combine against the anglicized squires who ruled Welsh society. In the half-century after 1860, 320,000 people migrated into the coalfield from the Welsh countryside, bringing with them the outlook, the speech, and the institutions of the rural peasantry. Eisteddfodau and the *Cymanfa Ganu* flourished in rural and urban areas alike. The very dispersal of much of Welsh industry, isolated by barren mountains, encouraged the growth in industrial villages of Welsh chapels, newspapers, societies, and voluntary activities. Not simply by mere increase of numbers but also by the opportunity for co-operative association afforded by an industrial community, the South Wales coalfield retained for long a national as well as a cosmopolitan character. It was this that was to lend to Welsh radicalism in the later nineteenth century a nation-wide quality.

More fundamental still was the rise of nonconformity, initially influenced by the English followers of Whitfield, but soon to become an indigenous institution. Not until after 1800 did nonconformity become predominant: as late as 1775 there were said to be only 171 chapels in Wales, mainly Baptist or Independent.[1] The secession of the Methodists from the established Church was a slow movement: Howell Harris, Daniel Rowland, Williams of Pantycelyn lived and died as members of the Church. Not until 1811 did Thomas Charles lead a definite secession and form the Calvinistic Methodists, the only church of Welsh origin. Even in 1834 John Elias proclaimed at the Bala *sasiwn* his fidelity to the Thirty-nine Articles of the Church of England. But events were rapidly outstripping the cautious leaders of dissent. From the beginning of the century, nonconformity and industrialization proceeded side by side. The itinerant methods of the sects proved far more adaptable than the static parochial system of the Church, and far more suitable for provision for the rapidly growing industrial population. Their very fragmentation was a sign of strength. Above all, it was the Welsh character of nonconformity in its services and Sunday schools which ensured its dominance, a marked contrast to the inadequate attention paid by the Church to

[1] Henry Richard, *Letters on the Social and Political . . .*, p. 20. See the statistics provided in Thomas Rees, *History of Protestant Nonconformity in Wales* (London, 2nd edition, 1883), pp. 259 ff.

the linguistic question for over a century.[1] As a class, nonconformist ministers were invariably men of humble origin, self-taught and powerful through their native eloquence. The distribution of the various denominations became somewhat localized, Methodism flourishing above all in northern and western Wales, Baptism and Congregationalism in the south. But their mystique and methods of organization transcended doctrinal variations and lent to nonconformity a distinctively Welsh character. Church leaders such as Dean Edwards of Bangor were to comment how chapels of every denomination had sprung up on every hill-side, shaping the lives and the outlook of their flock in society and at the hearth.[2]

The numerical preponderance of nonconformity was later an issue much contested during the prolonged and bitter campaign over disestablishment of the Church. Church and chapel alike exerted much ingenuity towards proving their own superior numbers. Churchmen provided only the totals of Easter communicants and assumed that all who were not professed dissenters and Romanists were *ipso facto* members of *Yr Hen Fam* (the old mother) which fostered all religion and ministered to all. Nonconformists generally provided their own figures of communicants and also of 'adherents', which included both regular and irregular members and also children, and were of little statistical accuracy. They were on firmer ground in quoting the number of places of worship and the totals of voluntary contributions, both of which were shown to be far in excess of those of the Church. But the decisive figures of those in attendance at actual places of worship remained in dispute, aggravated by the reluctance of nonconformists to countenance a religious census lest religious indifference should bolster up the cause of the Church. But what evidence there was seemed to indicate an overwhelming nonconformist majority. Horace Mann's census of 1851 showed a rough preponderance of 80 per cent. throughout Wales in attendance at nonconformist chapels on 31 March 1851, although equally significant is the fact that 47·67 per cent of the population remained unclaimed by any denomination.[3] The impression, in a field where evidence of any kind is indeterminate, is that this affords a roughly accurate picture at this stage. In terms of absolute numbers, the major impact of nonconformity was

[1] But see also below, Chapter II, p. 32, n. 2.

[2] *Report of the Nineteenth Annual Meeting of the Church Congress at Swansea, 1879* (London, 1880), pp. 354–8.

[3] *Census of Great Britain, 1851. Religious Worship, England and Wales. Report and Tables* (1853), pp. 122–5.

still to come. The year 1859 brought perhaps the most dramatic of all Welsh religious revivals, beginning in the Ystwyth valley in Cardiganshire and galvanizing all religious bodies throughout Wales. It was these years that saw the dramatic extension of the nonconformist press, and the development of new forms of political and other organization. In the years up to 1868 the expansion of nonconformity and the rise of popular radicalism as a political creed went hand in hand.

By mid-century the growth of nonconformity had come to create a fundamental line of division within Welsh life, polarizing opinion in different areas in a way that class affiliations were not able to do. Nonconformity, not industrialism, was to form the basis of Welsh social and political development. As the gentry withdrew from national life, nonconformist ministers became indisputable popular leaders, dominating press and pulpit. In a real sense they came to form a national religion, extended to the masses and founded, in the traditional phrase, 'on the pence of the poor'. The democratic basis of nonconformity has, no doubt, been exaggerated. Its articulate leaders tended to feel themselves segregated from *y dosbarth gweithiol*. Their attitude towards trade unions and other working-class movements was uniformly hostile.[1] Deacons more often than not were chosen from farmers rather than from their labourers: in great conurbations such as Merthyr Tydfil the articulate spokesmen of dissent came from solicitors and the 'shopocracy' rather than from ironworkers and colliers. Even so, as the attraction of industry brought in tens of thousands of short-distance migrants from the rural hinterland, nonconformity rapidly penetrated throughout all classes in the coalfield. Even in the fast-expanding coastal towns of Cardiff and Newport, which had both been predominantly English in language and outlook until the early decades of the nineteenth century, a growing number of Welsh-language chapels was founded from the 1830's onwards. In great urban centres and tiny villages alike, nonconformity gave to Welsh society its own characteristic ethos, social equality accompanied by denominational rivalry, a vivid popular literature beside a repression of artistic experiment. In all its essential characteristics, the communal life of Wales came to be uniquely centred in the Zions, Bethels, and Bethesdas which sprang up and flourished along hill-sides and valleys.

[1] The only religious body to give support to Chartism in Wales was the Unitarian. The Independent *Diwygiwr*, Feb. 1839, pp. 58–60, gave a general welcome to the Charter, but it opposed the threat of violence and disorder.

The development of political consciousness in Wales followed on directly from this transformation of religious life. There seemed at first no essential reason why the growth of nonconformity should encourage the rise of a specifically Welsh attitude, or indeed generate political activity of any kind. During the French Revolution the great mass of Welsh dissenters had remained loyalist and quiescent. Those Welsh nonconformists who joined with the Dissenting Deputies in the protest against the Test and Corporations Acts in the years up to 1828 were more of a pressure group, in the tradition of their brethren of the early eighteenth century, than an independent political machine.[1] Great popular preachers such as John Elias and Christmas Evans warned against intervention in political affairs, in transgressing the boundary between the realm of Caesar and the Kingdom of God. Dissenters were ranged emotionally on the side of the Reform Bills of 1831–2, but, save in Merthyr Tydfil, in activity they were cautious.

The effect of the great Reform Act on Wales, indeed, was a limited one. In county seats, the hold of the gentry remained unimpaired, if not more powerful, with great families less and less anxious to risk an expensive contest. The Wynns, the Morgans, the Mostyns, the Pryses, the Bulkeleys, the Owens, and the Douglas-Pennants continued largely as before. In borough constituencies, the enfranchisement of the £10 householder had some effect—industrialists such as Sir John Guest at Merthyr and Lewis Weston Dillwyn at Swansea demonstrated that there were more varied forms of influence beyond that of the landed families.[2] In Glamorgan, representation came to be shared between the Talbots of Margam and industrial families such as the Vivians of Swansea. But on a parliamentary level, the political life of Wales pursued its tranquil and undistinguished course for thirty years to come.

The years following the Reform Act, however, were to see a gradual change in the outlook of Welsh nonconformity. On the surface, their quiescent political attitude remained unchanged. The events which saw the formation of a coherent working-class movement in Wales from the Merthyr rising in 1831 down to the Chartist rising at Newport in 1839 encouraged the leaders of the main denominations,

---

[1] On this, see Ieuan Gwynedd Jones, 'The Liberation Society and Welsh Politics', *Welsh History Review*, vol. i, no. 2, pp. 193–200.

[2] Although Gwyn A. Williams has argued forcibly that the significant feature of Guest's tenure of the Merthyr seat is the extent to which he was the prisoner of the middle-class radicals of the town between 1832 and 1837 (op. cit., pp. 179–87).

the Methodists in particular, to warn their flock of the dangers of subverting worldly authority. The violence of the Rebecca Rioters between 1839 and 1843 lent substance to their exhortations. But events were beginning to overtake them, producing a gulf between the leadership and the rank and file. It was indisputable that Chartism and the Rebecca Rioters had close links with nonconformity and with the agrarian hinterland: far more was at stake than the mere tangible tyranny of the tollgates.[1] Welsh nonconformity was beginning to rediscover its links with English dissent, and to emulate its political activity. Just as Miall was founding the *Independent* in England, so the Rev. David Rees of Llanelly was using *Y Diwygiwr* to further radical reform. Using O'Connell's slogan 'Agitate! Agitate!', he linked the traditional grievances of dissent—Church rate, tithe, the burial laws, religious tests—with a more general programme of radical protest.[2] Publicists such as Samuel Roberts ('S. R.') of Llanbryn-mair were forcing Welsh dissent into the campaign against the Corn Laws, economic and religious protest being merged, since the Corn Laws and the tithe would, it seemed, stand or fall together.[3] In a multitude of ways, there was emerging a great crisis of conscience among the nonconformists and for the first time a submerged political movement was evolving that was both radical in its scope and national in its aspirations.

The 1840's are a great divide in the formation of popular radicalism in Wales. Techniques of agitation were developed which were to have permanent influence over the course of events in the next half-century. In many ways the developments followed a parallel course in Wales as in England. Dissenters everywhere shared the same grievances and inherited the same philosophy. Their campaigns against the Church Rate and the Tithe Commutation Act of 1836 sprang from similar causes wherever there was an articulate dissenting community. In Wales, as in England, there was being forged a middle-class self-consciousness alongside and in opposition to the tendency to working-class co-operation shown during the period of the Chartists and Rebecca. But the nature of Welsh society and its distinctive

[1] On these points, see David Williams, *John Frost* (Cardiff, 1939); *The Rebecca Riots*; and 'Chartism in Wales', in *Chartist Studies* (ed. Asa Briggs, London, 1959).
[2] *Y Diwygiwr*, Apr. 1838, p. 122 (*Cynhyrfer! Cynhyrfer!*). Even a politically conscious journal like the *Diwygiwr*, however, devoted only a small portion of its space to political affairs.
[3] For Samuel Roberts, see the *Dictionary of Welsh Biography*; Glanmor Williams, *S. R.* (Cardiff, 1950); and Wilbur Shepperson, *Samuel Roberts, a Welsh Colonizer in Civil War Tennessee* (Knoxville, Tennessee, 1961).

class division lacking a vigorous urban bourgeoisie,[1] gave these controversies a quite separate character. The numerical majority of nonconformists made them in some sense the spokesmen of a nation. The campaign of Lewis Edwards and 'S. R.' against the Corn Laws became transformed slowly into a challenge to the hegemony of parson and squire which remained the fundamental feature of Welsh society. The dissenting campaign for social equality gradually evolved into a wider struggle for national equality which was to penetrate every layer of communal life.

Two landmarks stand out in this process. First there was the nation-wide revulsion created by the Report of the three Education Commissioners in 1847. An inquiry that had begun with a campaign by William Williams, M.P. for Coventry, to remedy the under-provision and under-endowment of education, became the most effective starting-point for a revival of Welsh national self-consciousness.[2] The indictment made by the Commissioners of the illiteracy and ignorance of the Welsh country-side was clothed with a mass condemnation of the literature, language, and religion of the people. No episode did more to rouse nonconformist bodies from their political quietude. The 'treachery' of the Blue Books was to be handed down in oral tradition as the censure of a nation, the Glencoe and the Amritsar of Welsh history. More than any other factor, it stamped the character of national feeling in Wales, a struggle against contempt rather than physical oppression, a campaign for national recognition. In the formation of a radical movement, it had the decisive effect of associating the disabilities of nonconformists with the status of Wales as a nation. It is true that many Anglicans were as vocal as the sects in their condemnation of the *Llyfrau Gleision*: Dean Cotton of Bangor and the later Dean H. T. Edwards were especially vehement. But increasingly the protest came to assume a nonconformist character, and gave to the journals of Lewis Edwards and William Rees ('Hiraethog') a new impetus. In addition, the Blue Books went far

---

[1] There were the scattered elements of a middle class in Wales, but they rarely formed a large group and were largely located in the more anglicized southern and eastern counties. They generally comprised professional rather than mercantile classes—clergymen, lawyers, schoolmasters. Cf. Nesta Evans, *Social Life in Mid-Eighteenth Century Anglesey* (Cardiff, 1936), pp. 143–7.

[2] For the controversy surrounding the Blue Books, see Daniel Evans, *Life and Work of William Williams, M.P.* (Llandyssul, 1940), pp. 165–285. For hostile contemporary comment, see *Y Diwygiwr*, Jan. 1848, pp. 30–34, and Mar. 1848, pp. 94–97; also the analysis of the Report by Lewis Edwards in *Y Traethodydd*, Jan. 1848, pp. 110–35. For Thomas Gee, see *Dictionary of Welsh Biography* and the valuable biography by T. Gwynn Jones, *Cofiant Thomas Gee* (Denbigh, 1913).

towards removing denominational barriers. Until the 1840's the 'older dissent' of Baptists and Independents had provided the spearhead of political agitation. Now the sense of outrage created by the Report roused Methodists as well, and helped to impel them towards political radicalism. New Methodist leaders were emerging to challenge the traditional quiescence of older men such as John Elias. In particular, Thomas Gee of Denbigh was to become the most effective and polemical publicist of his day, and his *Baner ac Amserau Cymru*, established in 1859, the most influential of all radical journals.

Secondly, the Blue Books controversy came at a time when Welsh nonconformity was evolving a new coherent machinery and techniques of organization which were ultimately to play a fundamental part in the election triumph of 1868. The Liberation Society, founded in 1844, was initially an English movement, but in Wales it was to become a national organization. Throughout the 1850's Liberationist cells were formed throughout the country, initially in centres of local industry, but later to spread to the remotest of villages. For the first time, Welsh dissent possessed an intelligible political creed and an efficient machinery. The basic issue of disestablishment embraced all the lesser disabilities and humiliations to which nonconformists as a class were subject. More, a system of pressure and of financial organization was created which provided an outlet for so many grievances inarticulately expressed. A new phase began in 1862, when a great assembly at Swansea, convened to commemorate the martyrs of the Clarendon Code, was addressed by leading members of the Society, Miall, Richard, Carvell Williams from London, together with such familiar local personalities as the Rev. David Rees and the Rev. John Thomas. Henceforth, the Society directed a national campaign in Wales to put pressure on Parliament to repeal the legislation which denied nonconformists full civic equality.[1]

Individual campaigns were conducted against the Church rate and the burial laws. Electoral statistics were compiled and registration programmes completed. In 1867 Registration Leagues were formed in South Wales and later in the North to collate electoral details throughout the area. By 1868, therefore, Welsh nonconformists possessed the nucleus of coherent political organization, well financed, with a constant stream of speakers and of political literature. Without this organizational basis, Welsh radicalism would have remained subdued and ineffective.

[1] This paragraph is based largely on Ieuan Gwynedd Jones, op. cit.

The Liberation Society was significant also in its stimulus to collective activity in other fields. Gee led combined protests against religious tests and denominational education.[1] More and more, Welsh politics assumed a denominational form, since, Whig or Tory, Welsh members of Parliament in no way reflected the outlook of their constituents. Liberationists pointed out that two Welsh members alone, Dillwyn, the Liberationist member for Swansea, and C. R. M. Talbot (Glamorgan), voted for Irish disestablishment in 1856. Only twelve members out of thirty-two voted against Church rates in 1861. Between 1832 and 1868, one solitary dissenter, Walter Coffin (member for Cardiff District, 1852–7) represented a Welsh constituency, and his support rested on his industrial rather than his religious position. In any case, Coffin proved to be an ineffective member and never addressed the House.[2] The ferment of agitation within Wales towards reform was concealed by an anachronistic political structure, reflecting a stage of social development that was rapidly passing away.

In the middle years of the century, this growth of an articulate radical movement merged into a number of other forces which made these years a time of particular excitement. This surge of activity of revivalist nonconformity was in part stimulated by a gradual renaissance on the part of the Church. The appointment of two distinguished administrators, Connop Thirlwall at St. David's and Alfred Ollivant at Llandaff, encouraged a revival in organization and in evangelical enthusiasm after a century of tranquillity.[3] In the 1850's an extensive programme of Church building was begun and from this time dates the spread of many of those 'National' schools which were to prove such a crucial problem half a century later. The Oxford Movement also had some impact on Wales, causing disproportionate alarm among nonconformists. Isaac Williams, a distinguished poet and the friend of Pusey and Keble, made Llangorwen church near Aberystwyth a centre of Ritualism in the heart of Calvinistic Wales. It was this consciousness of a reawakening in the established Church itself which intensified and embittered nonconformity now in its most active phase of expansion.

Economic factors also contributed to the turmoil of these years. From 1857 industrial Wales suffered an increasing number of inter-

---

[1] T. Gwynn Jones, op. cit., p. 172.
[2] For Coffin, see E. D. Lewis, op. cit., pp. 40–44.
[3] There are two useful articles on Bishops Thirlwall and Ollivant in J. Vyrnwy Morgan (ed.), *Welsh Political and Educational Leaders in the Victorian Era* (London, 1908), pp. 91 ff.

ruptions to the flow of mid-Victorian economic growth. In Merthyr Tydfil in particular, the home of the riots of 1831 and a last strong-hold of Welsh Chartism which still maintained active roots there, there were periods of recession and of unemployment. After the conclusion of the American Civil War in 1865, depression was more prolonged and new tendencies towards collective union developed among ironworkers and colliers. Wage reduction and the introduc-tion of the double-shift system were to play their part alongside denominational issues in the critical election of 1868.

In the rural areas the years after the repeal of the Corn Laws were a period of relative prosperity and the violence of Rebecca died away. But basic problems of land exhaustion and of land hunger remained, and agricultural life continued to be precarious. A solution much canvassed in these years was that of emigration overseas.[1] An early venture by 'S. R.' in eastern Tennessee in 1857 disintegrated amid general recrimination. However, a more ambitious attempt to create an isolated cultural community on the Chubut River in Patagonia, sponsored by the Rev. Michael Daniel Jones in 1865, survived in spite of all hardships. As with Ireland, so Wales on a smaller scale was developing a world-consciousness. Welshmen in many thousands poured into the United States to operate the mines of Pennsylvania or the iron foundries of Ohio. In economic terms, this migration was of limited significance and the number of immigrants has often been exaggerated. But, in general tradition, the idea of a small Welsh com-munity preserving its culture and fighting successfully for its status overseas intensified and heightened the struggle at home. Michael Daniel Jones, in particular, the early apostle of land nationalization and of Welsh home rule, became the spokesman of a distinctively Welsh cultural radicalism that links the days of the *Llyfrau Gleision* with the campaigns of Tom Ellis and *Cymru Fydd* in later years.

Finally, these decades were a time of intense cultural activity. The contemptuous censure of the Blue Books gave a new significance to literary and artistic activity. The religious revival of 1859 provided a unique stimulus for the composers of choral music.[2] Newspapers and pamphlets flooded Wales as never before, drawing inspiration

---

[1] For Welsh emigration to the United States and elsewhere, see R. Berthoff, *British Immigrants in Industrial America* (Cambridge, Mass., 1953); Wilbur Shepperson, *British Emigration to North America* (Oxford, 1957); and Alan Conway, *The Welsh in America* (Cardiff, 1961). For Michael Daniel Jones, see *Dictionary of Welsh Bio-graphy*; and E. Pan Jones, *Oes a Gwaith Michael Daniel Jones* (Bala, 1903).

[2] Cf. D. H. Lewis, *Cofiant John Thomas Rees* (Llandyssul, 1955), p. 15.

from European nationalist movements with pointed emphasis. The *eisteddfod* became from 1858 a truly national festival for the first time, transcending sectional barriers, though also to fall more and more under nonconformist domination. Above all, in education it was a period of great advance. The indictment of the Blue Books and the rival stimulus of the Church schools lent substance to Hugh Owen's famous appeal to the sects in 1843 on behalf of general education. It aroused especial enthusiasm from the Methodists of Northern and Western Wales; as a result, the British and Foreign Society was able to organize the rudiments of a basic undenominational primary education system for the first time. More ambitious schemes were considered. After the Swansea *Eisteddfod* of 1863, the idea of a national university was mooted, and a national committee appointed with Hugh Owen and George Osborne Morgan as joint secretaries. In education, as in religious institutions, the appeal to voluntary enthusiasm was immediately effective.

This background of political, economic, and cultural upheaval made the 1860's a period of increasingly intense ferment. More and more, these varied forces tended to merge into the same kind of movement, with nonconformist radicalism as its spearhead, since in every case the way to national liberation lay through the ballot-box. In the press, in vestry meetings, on the eisteddfodic platform, and in the schoolroom, nonconformists were bidding for leadership. The recognition of Welsh individuality in one direction would encourage further demands in another, and thus even essentially non-political issues such as university education were to become matters of party controversy. Even here, the fundamental question was the attitude to Welsh nationality.

Tension built up throughout the decade. A violent controversy was aroused in 1859, when the Wynne representative in the Merioneth constituency was challenged unsuccessfully by David Williams, a Liberal landowner from Penrhyndeudraeth, with acknowledged nonconformist support. The first of a notorious sequence of evictions followed when several tenants on the Rhiwlas estate were evicted for voting against the landlord W. W. E. Wynne. The alleged predilection of Wynne towards Anglo-Catholic ritualism embittered the controversy still further. Nearly forty years later, Tom Ellis, whose uncle was one of the victims in 1859, testified how the evictions had sent 'a thrill of horror' throughout the country-side.[1] The mother of

---

[1] *Land Commission Evidence*, vol. i (1894), qu. 16,912.

Michael Daniel Jones, a widow, was another victim. With the rise of the Liberation Society, opposition in subsequent years became sharper. In the next election in 1865, a majority of avowed Whigs or Liberals was returned for the first time, while nonconformists such as David Davies of Llandinam and Dr. Thomas Price actively took part in contests.[1] In this, as in other ways, Victorian Britain was taking a different course. The rise of militant nonconformity in Wales coincided with the economic crisis which saw the collapse of Overend, Gurney, and other banking houses, with turbulent reform meetings in Hyde Park and with the ideological excitement provided by the Northern victory in the American Civil War, all contributing to a new temper in society. Less spectacular, but of fundamental influence for Wales itself, was the appearance in the early months of 1866 of a series of articles in the *Morning* and *Evening Star* by the Rev. Henry Richard, born in Cardiganshire and risen to eminence internationally through the Peace and Anti-Slavery Societies.[2] Richard's analysis of 'The Social and Political Condition of Wales' was a call to arms, to terminate the age-long overlordship of the gentry. *Trech gwlad nag arglwydd* (a land is mightier than its lord) was its rallying-cry, and it stirred fundamental passions in Wales. Years later, at the Mold *Eisteddfod* in 1873, Gladstone was to testify how these remarkable articles had first opened his eyes to the neglect of Welsh affairs.[3]

Yet all these pressures would have remained ineffective without an extension of the franchise. It was this that gave Disraeli's Reform Act of 1867 a unique importance in Wales. Liberals in the House were divided over their attitude: in addition to the intransigence of Lowe's 'Adullamites', Disraeli's adroit concessions divided radical back-benchers from Gladstone and the more cautious leadership. An influential voice among radicals in committee was that of Dillwyn, member for Swansea District, and nowhere was the effect of the Bill to be more striking than in Wales. The constituencies were left virtually unimpaired, save for the important change that Merthyr Tydfil was henceforth to return two members. The change in the county franchise was negligible—£12 rating rather than £50 rental was to be the basic requirement. But the enfranchisement of urban

---

[1] Ivor Thomas, *Top Sawyer* (London, 1938), pp. 120–8. B. Evans, *Cofiant y diweddar Barchedig T. Price M.A., Ph.D., Aberdâr* (Aberdare, 1891), pp. 169–70.

[2] They appeared in the *Morning* and *Evening Star* between Feb. and May 1866, and were published in the form of the *Letters* in 1867. For Richard, see C. S. Miall, *Henry Richard M.P.* (London, 1889).

[3] *The Times*, 20 Aug. 1873.

householders, even when hedged about by a multitude of qualifications, suggested a dramatic change in political control. Nowhere was
this demonstrated more dramatically than in Merthyr Tydfil, where
the electorate increased at a bound from 1,387 to 14,577, an increase
of 1,000 per cent. and ten times the national average.[1] Elsewhere in
Wales, the increase was less notable, though still above the average
for England. The provisions of the Act were less of direct effect than
in indicating a process that might continue indefinitely as mobility
in urban areas increased. Under these new and revolutionary political conditions, the new machinery and unity of purpose among nonconformist radicals in Wales found a unique opportunity to disturb
the political balance of centuries.

(ii) *The Great Election of 1868*

In Britain as a whole, the elections of November–December 1868
provided a clear mandate for Gladstone's 'call' for the disestablishment of the Church of Ireland. But in Wales the election has always
been regarded as a national awakening. To Lloyd George forty years
on, 'it woke the spirit of mountains, the genius of freedom that fought
the might of the Normans. . . . The political power of landlordism in
Wales was shattered as effectively as the power of the Druids.'[2]

Sober analysis somewhat demolishes the Chancellor's rhetoric,
and yet returns in Wales were indeed a remarkable testimony to the
social and political changes that were taking place. Even in rural
areas, where the increase in the franchise had been modest indeed,
the age-old domination of many landed families was rudely inter-
rupted. In Carmarthenshire the Independents were active at the poll,
with the result that E. J. Sartoris, a landowner of radical leanings,
headed the poll, surpassing even John Jones of Llandovery, the Tory
Deputy Lieutenant of the county. In Carmarthen District, too, a
Whig, Cowell-Stepney, gained the seat for the Liberals. More striking still were results in remote Cardiganshire and Caernarvonshire.
In Cardiganshire, the Vaughans of Trawscoed were ousted by Evan
Matthew Richards, a nonconformist industrialist from Swansea,
who triumphed where David Davies of Llandinam had narrowly

---

[1] Cf. Ieuan Gwynedd Jones, 'Franchise Reform and Glamorgan Politics, 1832–67',
Morgannwg, ii (1958), pp. 60–61.
[2] Speech by Lloyd George at Queen's Hall, 23 Mar. 1910; quoted in *Better Times*
(London, 1910), p. 296. For a more general account of the 1868 election, see H. J.
Hanham, *Elections and Party Management: Politics in the Time of Disraeli and Glad-
stone* (London, 1959), pp. 209 ff.

failed in 1865. More astonishing still was the defeat of the powerful
Penrhyn interest in Caernarvonshire. Thomas Love Jones-Parry,
a buccaneering landowner of unorthodox social and moral outlook,
carried the day in this stronghold of nonconformity, owing much to
the advocacy of popular ministers such as the Rev. Herber Evans of
Caernarvon. In Merioneth, David Williams of Penrhyndeudraeth,
unsuccessful in 1865 and in 1859, was returned without opposition.

Equally striking was the campaign in Denbighshire, where the
personality of Thomas Gee dominated the contest in both shire and
borough. The North Wales Reform League had been active in the
area for over two years, and much care was taken in the choice of
candidates. In the shire the man selected was George Osborne Morgan, a forceful personality who had had an unusually brilliant career
at Oxford before turning to the Bar with success. Morgan was the
son of the vicar of Conway, but in early manhood he turned to
political radicalism and was soon active in the Liberation Society.
Unlike most other Welsh county seats, Denbighshire was a two-
member constituency. Sir Watkin Williams Wynn, member since
1841, was quite invincible, but in the second seat, Morgan ousted
the 'Adullamite' Whig, Col. Biddulph of Chirk Castle. A feature of
the campaign was the emphasis laid by *Y Faner* on the tenurial
vulnerability of the tenant farmer alongside his religious grievances.
In Denbigh District, where Liberal Denbigh and Ruthin were poised
against the Conservatism of Holt and Wrexham, there was a clear
Liberal gain, Watkin Williams, a prosperous barrister, defeating
Mainwaring, the Conservative incumbent, by 374 votes. Here again
was a clear triumph for Gee and the Liberation Society. Williams
had written to Gee before the campaign that it was a contest not of
personalities but of principles, in itself a striking breach with traditional ideas of individual influence. 'If the Welsh people are really
favourable to religious equality, they have now a fair chance of
proving it to the world.'[1] It was an opportunity for extending to
Wales the same measure of equality that Gladstone was proposing
for Ireland. Once returned, Williams at once began to campaign to
this end.

The most remarkable result of all, however, came in the constituency most spectacularly affected by the expansion of the electorate
in 1867, Merthyr Tydfil.[2] The whole character of the constituency

---

[1] Watkin Williams to Gee, 4 July 1868 (N.L.W., Gee MSS., 8309c, 385).
[2] I am indebted to Mr. Ieuan Gwynedd Jones for access to his unpublished survey

had been transformed. At the beginning of 1868 there seemed to be little obstacle to the return of the sitting member, Henry Austin Bruce, colliery proprietor, magistrate, educationalist, with a traditional background of support from nonconformity in an area almost totally under nonconformist control. The other seat seemed likely to fall to Richard Fothergill, a professed Liberal whom Dr. Thomas Price supported, an employer on whose whim 20,000 people directly depended, and a noted philanthropist who contributed to many nonconformist activities. But a new element had been introduced into the campaign by the arrival of the Rev. Henry Richard, on the invitation of the local nonconformist committee, under the chairmanship of C. H. James, later to be Richard's colleague in Parliament. From the first, Richard combined the essential qualities likely to appeal to the electorate of Merthyr and Aberdare. He was one of the most articulate nonconformist spokesmen of the day, a pillar of the Liberation Society and of the Peace Society. He had still preserved his links with Wales: he was remembered as one of the most effective critics of the Blue Books of 1847, while his recent articles in the *Star* had circulated widely. Richard stressed his Welshness in his speeches, although on nonconformist rather than on nationalist grounds. Above all, Richard claimed to show more sympathy with the economic problems of a working-class electorate. He claimed to be the workers' candidate, laying stress on his poverty, and ex-Chartists appeared on his platform. On such burning controversies as the double-shift and the sub-inspectorate system, he adopted the miners' standpoint, and in areas such as Dowlais and Mountain Ash he polled strongly. On all these grounds, Richard easily topped the poll with 11,683 votes. Fothergill came second with 7,439—an interesting instance of local influence. Bruce, rapidly losing ground as Churchman, an Englishman, and an employer with a dubious record in industrial disputes, came third, with 5,776, and when appointed the new Home Secretary in Gladstone's ministry had thus to seek refuge in Renfrewshire. In essence, local factors had determined the campaign in Merthyr—Gee's attacks on Bruce from long range seem to have missed their mark.[1] The combination of actively organized dissent with working-class associations in industry formed the basis of Richard's triumph. It

of the Merthyr Tydfil election of 1868, upon which I have drawn heavily. Mr. Jones has summarized his conclusions in 'The Election of 1868 in Merthyr Tydfil: a Study in the Politics of an Industrial Borough in the mid-Nineteenth Century', *Journal of Modern History*, vol. xxxiii, no. 3 (Sept., 1961), pp. 270–86.

[1] See *Baner ac Amserau Cymru*, 12 June–12 Aug. 1868.

pointed the way to the extension of the radical tradition throughout South Wales and provided that tradition with its most powerful spokesman.

To John Griffiths, *Gohebydd*, writing in *Y Faner*, the triumph at Merthyr seemed to i..troduce a new era in the history of Wales.[1] But the election results as a whole showed far less clearly a breach with the traditional pattern. Twenty-three members returned claimed attachment to the Liberal Party, but in almost every case they were representative of the Whig element, which was to remain so powerful in the party for twenty years more. Particularly was this true in the smaller borough constituencies. A Stanley in Beaumaris District, a Lloyd in Cardigan District, a Hanmer in Flint District, a Crichton-Stuart in Cardiff District continued as before. Of the thirty-three Welsh members, twenty-four were landowners, including all ten Conservatives returned. Seven Liberals and four Conservatives were the sons or grandsons of peers. More significant still, no less than thirty of the thirty-three were communicants of the Anglican Church, and three members only, Henry Richard, Evan Matthew Richards (Cardiganshire), and Richard Davies (Anglesey) represented directly the nonconformist majority. The shift in the balance of power was at best partial and localized.

It was the aftermath of the election, as much as the results themselves, which helped to make 1868 a landmark in popular memory in later years. The unwise retaliation by some Tory landlords as reprisal for the defection of many of their tenants at the polls added greatly to the tension of the country-side. In many parts of Wales, and especially in Caernarvonshire, Carmarthenshire, and Cardiganshire, farmers were evicted for having voted Liberal and having thus challenged the structure of local authority. For decades to come, a vivid impression remained among the farming community. So notorious had the evictions become that on 6 July 1869 Henry Richard rose to draw attention to them in the House of Commons.[2] He quoted with powerful effect attested cases of persecution, together with details of more subtle pressure, such as that exerted by Lord Willoughby d'Eresby on the Gwydir estate in Caernarvonshire. Many Welsh and English members supported him, and Bruce, as Home Secretary, promised careful attention. The events in Wales played their part in the appointment of a Select Committee under the

---

[1] Richard Griffiths, *Cofiant y Gohebydd* (Caernarvon, 1905), p. 55.
[2] *Parl. Deb.*, 3rd ser., vol. cxcvii, pp. 1295 ff.

chairmanship of Lord Hartington, himself briefly a Welsh member (for Radnor District in 1868–9), to inquire into the conduct of elections. Six witnesses were called from Wales and many accounts of evictions put forward. It was alleged that 200 notices to quit had been served in Cardiganshire alone. The most effective witness was the Rev. Michael Daniel Jones, who gave detailed evidence of increased rents and arbitrary evictions which had been the lot of tenants up and down Wales. 'In the next election we shall lose ground, if the witnesses have no protection', he had written.[1] In all, there were noted forty-three proven cases of eviction in Cardiganshire and twenty-six in Carmarthenshire, with innumerable other suspected instances of pressures on farmers, and an alleged dismissal of eighty quarrymen in the slate quarries of Lord Penrhyn.[2] Tory witnesses countered with charges against the 'chapel screw'. This evidence from Wales played an important part in the successful attainment of a secret ballot. In the House in 1871, Henry Richard reminded members on the Third Reading of the Ballot Act of the cases of hardship and oppression in Wales which had led up to it.[3]

The evictions of 1868 were an important episode in the growth of political consciousness. They afforded to radicals and nonconformists of all shades a cause for common action. The campaign in Wales for the relief of homeless tenants, which raised the sum of £20,000 in voluntary contributions and made a nation-wide impact in the English press, drew Welsh Liberal members closer together. The debate in the Commons was a portent also. As *Gohebydd* remarked, there had been Scottish and Irish debates in abundance, but never before had there been a Welsh debate.[4] It suggested to Welsh members and their supporters the possibilities of political pressure, though many years were to pass until this lead was followed up decisively.

Most important of all, the evictions of 1868 created a new popular martyrology. They added a new dimension to the social divisions of rural and industrial Wales. For half a century, the memory of the homeless victims of 1868 powerfully stimulated the radical cause on

[1] *Report of the Select Committee on Parliamentary and Municipal Elections*, 1869, qu. 6,541–6,816 (Michael D. Jones's evidence). Michael D. Jones to Henry Richard, 13 Apr. 1869 (N.L.W., Richard MSS., 5504B).

[2] *Yr Herald Cymraeg*, 24 Oct. 1868.

[3] *Parl. Deb.*, 3rd ser., vol. ccviii, pp. 1131–7.

[4] *Baner ac Amserau Cymru*, 25 Aug. 1869. This statement by *Gohebydd* is, of course, far from being strictly accurate. To note but two instances, there had been lengthy debates on the abolition of the Courts of Great Sessions in 1830 and on the South Wales Turnpike Trust Act of 1844.

the platform and in the press. As late as 1910 elderly farmers would denounce their oppressive landlords of years gone by from Liberal platforms, with often an improbable wealth of detail. Radicalism in Wales had been provided now with a grievance more tangible than the contempt of the Blue Books, with the direct spur of physical injustice, without which no popular movement can thrive. Preserved and relived in the oral tradition of the country-side, the myth and the reality of 1868 created passions which were to transform the injustice of a class into the indictment of a nation.

II

FROM RADICALISM TO NATIONALISM
1868–1886

(i) *Disestablishment—Irish and Welsh*

THE triumphant elections of 1868 were widely acclaimed as symbolizing the awakening of the Welsh nation. Yet they represented an assault on privilege not essentially different in quality from that of radicalism throughout Britain as a whole. It was Liberalism, if not Liberationism, that had been vindicated at the polls in Wales. There is little evidence that any contest was determined by nationalist sentiment. When Henry Richard emphasized his Welsh origins before the voters of Merthyr Tydfil, it was to his nonconformity that he was drawing attention. 'the nonconformists of Wales were the people of Wales'. Osborne Morgan, the other spectacular victor in 1868, can be found shortly after his election stressing the essential unity of Wales and England: 'I have never in all my life heard of an Act of Parliament being passed for Wales which did not extend to England also.'[1] Welsh and English Liberals alike subscribed to the same philosophy and to the same radical tradition. Yet, in the subsequent two decades, this backwoods radicalism was to become the source of a new awareness of Wales as a nation. The ill-formed and half-expressed aspirations entertained by Welsh nonconformists in 1868 gradually became transformed into a national programme. By 1886, when the Liberal schism over Irish home rule created new opportunities for the radical spokesmen of Wales, the transition from radicalism to nationalism was largely complete.

However, in 1868 it was more general questions that claimed immediate attention. The general election had provided, above all, a clear-cut mandate for the disestablishment of the minority Church of Ireland, and this was the first major measure Gladstone introduced. After some delay by the Lords, which was resolved by the intervention of the Queen herself, the Bill received the Royal Assent on 26 July 1869. The new temper of the Welsh members was soon demonstrated: they voted by eighteen to nine in favour of the Third

[1] *Baner ac Amserau Cymru*, 1 Sept. 1869.

7

Reading. A striking feature of the discussions of the measure in the Lords was a speech in support by Connop Thirlwall, Bishop of St. David's, a solitary episcopal rebel at this time, as he was when voting for the repeal of the Corn Laws in 1846.[1] Thirlwall believed that 'the stream of tendency' was running hard against all established churches, and that intelligent compromise was inevitable.[2] But he went out of his way to deny that there was any possible analogy between the Church in Ireland and the Church in Wales. 'Does anyone believe that if the Irish Church had not existed the anomalies of the Church of England in Wales—considerable and in one respect similar as they are—would have served the same purpose? Bright's speech at Liverpool, I think, shows that they neither would nor could.'[3] Thirlwall scorned the argument that disendowment was a 'robbery of God'.[4] However, in later years his intellectualized and sophisticated arguments were to be given an embarrassing prominence.

The Liberation Society clearly regarded the triumph in Ireland as a mere preliminary for further expansion. To Henry Richard, Gladstone's measure established a number of important fundamental principles.[5] The fallacious claim for a 'collective state conscience' had been exploded. The position of an established church which claimed the adherence of only a small fraction of the community was recognized as an anomaly. Finally, he maintained, it had been shown that ecclesiastical property was national property, which could lawfully be diverted to secular ends. In every case, the analogy with Wales was heavily underlined. Indeed, the Church membership here was believed to consist of an even smaller percentage of the population than in the case of the Irish Church. Inevitably, therefore, Wales became the next subject of debate. Arguments by Gladstone, Thirlwall, and others that Ireland was a peculiar and unique case were little heeded. For the first time in recent political history, a Welsh issue came to be a cause of acute party controversy, the issue of Welsh disestablishment.

Disestablishment of the 'Church of England in Wales', *Eglwys*

[1] *Parl. Deb.*, 3rd ser., vol. cxcvi, pp. 1820–8. John Connop Thirlwall, *Connop Thirlwall, Historian and Theologian* (London, 1936), pp. 142, 252 ff.

[2] Thirlwall to the Bishop of Argyle, 27 Apr. 1868 (quoted in Dean Perowne and the Rev. L. Stokes (eds.), *Letters Literary and Theological of Connop Thirlwall* (London, 1881), p. 285).

[3] Thirlwall to Lord Arthur Hervey, 18 June 1868 (quoted, Perowne and Stokes, op. cit., p. 294).

[4] *Parl. Deb.*, loc. cit., pp. 1821–2.

[5] Henry Richard, 'The Established Church in Wales', *British Quarterly Review*, Jan. 1871; reprinted in *Letters and Essays on Wales* (London, 1884), pp. 129–84.

Loegr, had been a contentious subject in Wales since 'S. R.' 's famous diatribe against established churches in 1834. David Rees and 'Brutus' had belaboured one another on this theme in the days of Rebecca. But not until after 1868 did the cause find its champion at Westminster. On 5 August 1869 Watkin Williams, newly returned as member for Denbigh District, gave notice of a motion calling for the termination of the establishment of the Church in Wales, and for the application of its endowments to an undenominational system of education.[1] Although an Anglican and long resident in England, Williams had laid stress on the disestablishment question during the recent election campaign. The Welsh people had an opportunity for 'carrying out for Wales the same measure of religious equality Gladstone proposed for Ireland'.[2]

However, the circumstances in which this motion arose reveal clearly the confusion surrounding the issue in Wales, and the rudimentary nature of collective action among the Welsh members of Parliament. In embryo, the latent conflict between liberalism and nationalism was foreshadowed.

From the first, Williams had proved a difficult colleague in the Commons. He rarely associated with his fellow Liberals.[3] His decision to move his disestablishment resolution was taken quite independently without consulting even his closest associates. Osborne Morgan first learnt of it in the morning newspapers.[4] Many members were loud in their protests. Henry Richard thought the action most ill-advised. He would have preferred a settlement of the ballot issue first, with a commission of inquiry later to collect definite data on the position of the Welsh Church.[5] Osborne Morgan thought it 'ill-timed and premature', following so closely on Irish disestablishment. It would drive the Tories into further evictions of tenants, while the Liberals would be divided.[6] The two experienced Glamorgan members, Vivian and Dillwyn, the latter a prominent Liberationist, were much offended by Williams's failure to consult them.[7]

In Wales also, there was much angry comment. In *Y Faner,* Gee

[1] *Baner ac Amserau Cymru,* 11 Aug. 1869.

[2] Watkin Williams to Gee, 25 May 1868 (N.L.W., Gee MSS., 8309c, 378).

[3] 'Gohebydd' (John Griffiths) to Gee, 11 Aug. 1869 (N.L.W., Gee MSS., 8310e, 507).

[4] Osborne Morgan to Henry Richard, 20 Aug. 1869 (N.L.W., Richard MSS., 5505b).

[5] Richard to Gee, 17 Aug. 1869 (N.L.W., Gee MSS., 8308c, 297).

[6] Osborne Morgan to Henry Richard, 20 Aug. 1869 (N.L.W., Richard MSS., 5505b).

[7] 'Gohebydd' to Gee, 13 Aug. 1869 (N.L.W., Gee MSS., 8310e, 508).

warmly welcomed Williams's initiative. The 'Rip van Winkle' of non-conformity was rousing himself from deep slumber. The fact that Williams was an Anglican made him all the more suitable as an advocate.[1] But in the columns of the same journal, its most effective correspondent, *Gohebydd*, thought the motion premature and Williams's motives dubious.[2] Privately, he doubted whether Williams had any genuine sympathy with Liberalism at all.[3] A vigorous correspondence in *Y Faner* found many protagonists for each view. 'S. R.' of Llanbryn-mair, the doyen of Welsh journalism, now returned from his unhappy stay in America, castigated Williams for imperilling Welsh Liberalism, so soon after the glorious triumphs of 1868.[4]

Beneath and beyond these disputes over strategy lay a more profound divergence over general principles. Williams, Gee, and a growing number of Welsh Liberals believed that Wales should be treated as a separate entity over disestablishment, as Ireland had been. But, even in Wales, this opinion was much contested. Osborne Morgan maintained that it was no more feasible to deal separately with the Church in Wales than in Yorkshire or Cornwall. Wales was an integral part of England and disestablishment would have to be tackled as a whole.[5] *Gohebydd* wrote that a local majority of nonconformists in Wales had no firmer case for demanding separate treatment than a similar body would have in Cornwall.[6] Above all, the Liberation Society, the organizational machinery of Welsh Liberals, and of which Henry Richard was a leading spokesman, refused to support Williams's move. There had been inadequate campaigning and publicity beforehand. The Welsh members would be divided and Gladstone driven into positive hostility. Above all, the Welsh Church could not be disestablished separately. The establishment should be attacked as a whole, and Wales used 'as a platform for attacking it in a special way'.[7] Carvell Williams, the Society's Welsh secretary, in the *Liberator*, and Miall in the *Nonconformist* condemned Williams outright.[8]

---

[1] *Baner ac Amserau Cymru*, 11 Aug. 1869.
[2] 'Llythyr y Gohebydd', ibid., 18 Aug. 1869. This attitude was shared by *Yr Herald Cymraeg*, 13 Aug. 1869, which advocated a Royal Commission.
[3] 'Gohebydd' to Gee, 11 Aug. 1869 (N.L.W., Gee MSS., 8310E, 507).
[4] Letter by 'S. R.' in *Baner ac Amserau Cymru*, 13 Oct. 1869.
[5] Speech at Wrexham, ibid., 1 Sept. 1869.
[6] 'Yr Eglwys yng Nghymru: Goleu newydd ar y pwnc!', ibid., 3 Nov. 1869.
[7] Carvell Williams to Gee, 25 and 30 Sept. 1869 (N.L.W., Gee MSS., 8311D, 583, 584).
[8] Letter by 'Elihu', *Baner ac Amserau Cymru*, 2 Feb. 1870.

There is no doubt that the prevailing temper of the political parties made the moment unpropitious for Williams's motion. Conservatives were on their guard against a further spread of Liberationist contagion, while Liberals generally viewed disestablishment as a closed issue. Gladstone himself, according to Matthew Arnold, was 'in a much more Anglican mood' in 1870.[1]

Yet it was in February 1870 that Gladstone himself made a striking departure in policy towards the Church in Wales. Its anglicized character had increasingly come to be recognized as a major weakness. As early as 1836 a motion had been introduced urging that Welsh-speaking clergy be appointed to Welsh sees and benefices, but it had failed, in spite of the support of the youthful member for Newark, W. E. Gladstone.[2] Bishop Thirlwall had acquired sufficient fluency and confidence to be able to preach in Welsh,[3] but he remained exceptional. The episcopate was especially a cause for much criticism: since the reign of Anne no Welsh-speaking bishop had been appointed, and in the eighteenth century many ardent churchmen, such as Erasmus Saunders, had been vehement in their strictures. When, therefore, Bishop Vowler Short resigned from the see of St. Asaph in 1870, Gladstone devoted much time and energy to the problem of his successor. 'I think it beyond doubt most important, amidst this singularly susceptible population . . . to consider thoroughly whether any man can be found who is not only a native Welshman, but a practical, efficient and impressive preacher in the Welsh tongue.'[4] He told the Archbishop of York: 'I have not since taking my present office felt more strongly the gravity of any matter requiring to be done than this of the Welsh bishopric.'[5]

Gladstone sought and received advice in abundance. The Welsh bishops themselves were not very helpful. Ollivant of Llandaff main-

[1] J. L. Garvin, *Life of Joseph Chamberlain*, vol. i (London, 1932), p. 106, note.

[2] *Parl. Deb.*, 3rd ser., vol. xxxv, pp. 150 ff. This motion, introduced by J. Jervis (Chester) on the committee stage of the Established Church Bill, led, however, to a clause being included in the Bill which directed the Ecclesiastical Commissioners to prevent the appointment of clergymen unable to speak Welsh in Welsh benefices where the majority of the inhabitants did not speak English (6 & 7 William IV, c. 77). This provision was later repealed in the Pluralities Act, 1838 (1 & 2 Victoria, c. 106), and a new clause introduced empowering bishops to refuse appointments to Welsh benefices in similar circumstances. It remained virtually a dead letter (see Ivor Bowen, *The Statutes of Wales* (London, 1908), pp. cxii–cxv, 251–3; T. I. Jeffreys-Jones, *Acts of Parliament concerning Wales, 1714–1901* (Cardiff, 1960), nos. 2446 and 2448, p. 306).

[3] John Connop Thirlwall, op. cit., p. 121.

[4] Gladstone to the Bishop of St. David's, 12 Jan. 1870 (B.M., Add. MSS., 44424, f. 88).

[5] Gladstone to the Archbishop of York, 12 Jan. 1870 (B.M., Add. MSS., 44424, f. 90).

tained that the inferior social position of the wife of one possible candidate ruled him out.[1] Bruce, the Home Secretary, knew of no Welsh clergyman suitable for the appointment. The most able men were all Englishmen or Englishmen settled in Wales, such as Campbell, recently appointed by Lord Derby to Bangor.[2] On the other hand, the aged Lady Llanover protested vehemently and often illegibly in favour of a 'genuine Welsh bishop'. Thirlwall was very learned, but 'as a Welsh bishop he might as well be in New Zealand'.[3] Nonconformists such as Gee and Richard were also prolific with advice, while Dean Edwards of Bangor, himself a strong candidate, as he well knew, alleged that English bishops were 'an outrage on the national sensibility of the Cymric peoples'.[4] A dozen candidates were put forward, all with their partisans and detractors. Gladstone complained wearily after a month of feverish correspondence: 'If you read in the papers some morning that I have been carried to Bedlam and that a straight waistcoat is necessary, please to remember that it will be entirely owing to the vacancy in the see of St. Asaph.'[5]

Eventually, the problem was resolved, and the Rev. Joshua Hughes, rector of Llandovery, was appointed. This was far from being a universally popular selection. Hughes was distinguished neither for scholarship nor for administrative ability. He had the embarrassment of informing Gladstone after his appointment that his degree was B.D. (Lampeter) and not B.A. (Cantab.), as recorded in Crockford.[6] To his horror, Gladstone had appointed a non-graduate to the episcopal bench. But overriding every other factor was the appointment of a Welsh-speaking Welshman, the first for 150 years, and immense satisfaction was shown in Wales itself. More, the importance of the question of nationality in Church questions in Wales was a principle of wider application. An important precedent had been laid down. Although Gladstone's intentions were practical rather than sentimental, the Church question could not be allowed to rest there.

Shortly after Hughes's consecration, Watkin Williams introduced

---

[1] Bishop of Llandaff to Gladstone, 14 Jan. 1870 (B.M., Add. MSS., 44424, f. 97).

[2] Bruce to Gladstone, 8 Jan. 1870 (B.M., Add. MSS., 44424, ff. 196–8).

[3] Lady Llanover to Gladstone, 24 Jan. 1870 (B.M., Add. MSS., 44424, ff. 166–71).

[4] In his *Church of the Cymry: a Letter to the Rt. Hon. W. E. Gladstone, M.P.* (Caernarvon, 1870), pp. 52–57. Reprinted in his *Wales and the Welsh Church* (London, 1889). For Dean Edwards, see the *Dictionary of Welsh Biography*.

[5] Gladstone to Bruce, 18 Jan. 1870 (B.M., Add. MSS., 44086, f. 123).

[6] Joshua Hughes to Gladstone, 20 Mar. 1870 (B.M., Add. MSS., 44425, f. 291). Cf. G. Hartwell Jones, *A Celt looks at the World* (London, 1946), p. 51.

his motion in a well-attended House.[1] Gee's advocacy had swayed many in Wales in support of the motion, but English opinion, already inflamed over the education controversy, was intransigent. Williams claimed that a cabinet minister had already given his private blessing to his motion,[2] but it was with the certainty of a heavy defeat that he rose to move his resolution. As he said later, by making a moderate statement, he won a fair hearing.[3] He rested his case on history, on the nepotism and corruption that had characterized the Church in Wales in the past, its remoteness from Welsh life, and its supersession by nonconformity. Osborne Morgan, who had agreed to second Williams, also dwelt on the anti-national nature of the Church, although he prefaced his remarks with a desire for disestablishment in general.

The main significance of the debate lay in Gladstone's attitude, and he spoke with an uncompromising rigidity that was later to cause him acute embarrassment. He admitted certain resemblances between the Welsh and Irish Churches. But in Wales there was neither such hostility to the Church in the past, nor the deep doctrinal cleavage that lay between Catholicism and Protestantism in Ireland. In Wales, the real schism from the Church dated only from 1800. Under the Tudors and early Stuarts, the 'Welsh Church was entirely acceptable to the Welsh people',[4] and only after 1688 was the alienation from it of the great mass of the people evident. He admitted the neglect of the eighteenth century, but claimed that there had been a great advance in the last thirty years. Above all, and this he stressed in particular, the Welsh Church could not be isolated. It possessed 'a complete constitutional, legal and . . . historical identity with the Church of England'.[5] The real question at issue was that of English disestablishment, and this he emphatically rejected.

Williams's motion was supported by forty-seven members (including the tellers), all Liberals, twenty-eight English, eight Scots, four Irish, and seven Welsh. The majority were acknowledged Liberationists. The response among the Welsh members was poor. Apart from Williams and Osborne Morgan, Richard and Fothergill (Merthyr), R. Davies (Anglesey), Dillwyn (Swansea), and Col. H.

---

[1] *Parl. Deb.*, 3rd ser., vol. cci, pp. 1274 ff.
[2] Williams to Gee, 11 Aug. 1869 (N.L.W., Gee MSS., 8309c, 400). He is presumably referring to John Bright (President of the Board of Trade) who did in fact vote for his motion.
[3] Williams to Gee, 11 June 1870 (N.L.W., Gee MSS., 8309c, 405).
[4] *Parl. Deb.*, loc. cit., p. 1295.   [5] Ibid., p. 1297.

Edwardes (Haverfordwest) supported the resolution. Perhaps the most surprising name is that of Edwardes, Vice-Lieutenant of Pembrokeshire and heir presumptive of the Irish temporal peer and Pembrokeshire landowner, Lord Kensington, but he had voted for Liberationism on previous occasions. Sixteen Welsh members, eight Conservatives and eight Liberals, voted against Williams's motion. These last included Samuel Holland, whose election address at the Merioneth by-election in January 1870 had included a general theoretical belief in disestablishment, but had denied that the Welsh Church could be treated on a separate basis.[1] This must have been an attitude general among many of his colleagues. Ten Welsh members were absent or abstained, including the nonconformist E. M. Richards and E. J. Sartoris (Carmarthenshire), who had been warned not to vote for the motion lest he put his seat in jeopardy.[2] In all, 211 voted against the motion, and it failed by 164 votes.

Williams's initiative was thus an isolated episode. In Wales, disestablishment was still an issue to make Liberals pause: Sir Robert Cunliffe specifically refused to commit himself in the Flint by-election in 1872.[3] On the other hand, support for disestablishment in general was growing. Ten Welsh members voted for each of Miall's motions in 1871 and 1873.[4] Reactions to the debate in Wales were mixed. *Yr Herald Cymraeg* and the Methodist *Goleuad* considered it a failure.[5] But *Y Faner* prophesied that Gladstone would 'eat his words' in this, as in so many other respects, and events were to bear this judgement out.[6]

In England the debate evoked little interest. *The Times* studiously adopted an air of contempt. The *Church Times* displayed patronizing moderation, but drew the correct moral that the Church should show more sympathy towards Welsh sentiment and culture.[7] The Liberal Party, apart from the nucleus of Liberationists who were more vocal than effective, regarded disestablishment as a dead issue. Gladstone did publicly admit in 1871 the weakness of the Church in Wales,[8] but disestablishment remained anathema to him. Osborne

---

[1] Election address published in *Baner ac Amserau Cymru*, 5 Jan. 1870.

[2] 'Gohebydd' to Gee, 11 Aug. 1869 (N.L.W., Gee MSS., 8310E, 507). In fact, Sartoris did lose his seat in 1874.

[3] Sir Robert Cunliffe to Gee, 6 Sept. 1872 (N.L.W., Gee MSS., 8305C, 22).

[4] Debates of 9 May 1871 and 16 May 1873.

[5] *Yr Herald Cymraeg*, 3 June 1870, again urged the appointment of a royal commission. *Y Goleuad*, 4 June 1870, strongly criticized Watkin Williams's speech.

[6] *Baner ac Amserau Cymru*, 1 June 1870.

[7] *The Times*, 25 May 1870; *Church Times*, 3 June 1870.

[8] *Parl. Deb.*, 3rd ser., vol. ccxvi, p. 44.

Morgan believed that it was his own advocacy of disestablishment which cost him the office of Solicitor-General in 1873, in favour of Harcourt, while James was appointed Attorney-General.[1] In brief, the idea of separate legislation for Wales in matters ecclesiastical was not yet accepted by either political party. However, the continued striking growth of Liberationism in Wales during the seventies suggested that the debate of 1870 was merely an initial skirmish in a lengthy campaign.

(ii) *Separate Laws for Wales*

One of the immediate results of the 1868 election was the growth of a new cohesion among the Welsh members at Westminster. The first example was the debate on the political evictions in Wales, in July 1869, to which reference has already been made in the previous chapter. The campaign for the redress of injustices and for the passage of a secret ballot went on in Wales for another two years, financed by wealthy English sympathizers such as Samuel Morley. As E. M. Richards wrote: 'When I first entered the House, I felt it was desirable to merge Welsh and English together, and that some mischief might result from a Welsh party: I have now modified my views *to some extent* and I now see the advantages of Welsh members holding together.'[2]

As has been seen, this nascent unity of action among Welsh members did not extend to the disestablishment motion of 1870, although there was a strong feeling that Watkin Williams was acting in an unconventional manner in not consulting his colleagues. 'It was a breach of the confidence which ought to exist between us', wrote Osborne Morgan, and he summoned a formal meeting of Welsh members to outline 'some common plan of action',[3] although clearly with little effect.

A more effective opportunity came in 1872 over the long-felt grievance over the appointment of English judges to Welsh-speaking areas. Welshmen were especially sensitive on this point in view of the destruction of the last remnants of a distinctively Welsh legal structure in 1830. Of the first five judges appointed to the five Welsh Circuits in 1847, four had been Welsh-speaking,[4] but in recent years very few had

---

[1] Osborne Morgan to Gee, 10 Mar. 1873 (N.L.W., Gee MSS., 8307c, 195).

[2] E. M. Richards to Gee, 10 July 1869 (N.L.W., Gee MSS., 8308c, 306).

[3] Osborne Morgan to Henry Richard, 20 Aug. 1869 (N.L.W., Richard MSS., 5505B).

[4] They were A. J. Johnes (North Wales), E. L. Richards (Mid-Wales), J. Johnes (Carmarthen, Pembroke, Cardigan), J. M. Herbert (Monmouth), all appointed in 1847.

been Welsh even by birth. When the Lord Chancellor, Hatherley, appointed Homersham Cox to the Mid-Wales circuit, which was mainly a monoglot Welsh area, many protests followed. In March 1872 Osborne Morgan drew attention in the Commons to the anomaly whereby a judge was not conversant with the everyday language of (it was claimed) four-fifths of the population, and no regular interpreter was provided.[1] He quoted Gladstone's appointment of Bishop Hughes of St. Asaph in 1870 as a parallel. Many Welsh members rose to support him, though Henry Richard was careful to disavow any intention of 'Welsh Home Rule'.[2] Bruce was conciliatory: in private he admitted that Hatherley 'had gone much too far on Welsh legal appointments'.[3] On 11 March, a resolution advocating Welsh-speaking judges was carried without debate. It was, said the *Daily News,* 'a victory all down the line'.[4]

However, the grievance remained without redress, and Osborne Morgan rose again in the new Parliament of 1874, complaining that his resolution had remained a dead letter.[5] He received unexpected support from, among others, C. W. Wynn (Montgomeryshire), a Conservative, but the new Home Secretary, R. A. Cross, was less sympathetic, and the question continued to irritate Welsh national sentiment for another thirty years, with 'English Judges' joining 'English Bishops' as a target for attack.[6]

In spite of this activity, at the general election of February 1874 the Liberal cause lost ground in Wales. As in the United Kingdom as a whole, the Liberals suffered from the disunion of their own supporters over such issues as the Education and Licensing Acts, and from the revived cohesion of their Conservative opponents. Nineteen Liberals and fourteen Conservatives were returned in Wales and Monmouthshire, a net Liberal loss of four seats. The strength of the Liberal Party remained in the borough constituencies, of which they retained twelve, though with much difficulty in many cases. In Flint District, Peter Eyton, a Liberationist, won a three-cornered contest by only four votes; in Cardiff District Crichton-Stuart defeated Hardinge Giffard (years later to become Lord Chancellor, as Lord

---

[1] *Parl. Deb.*, 3rd ser., vol. ccix, pp. 1648 ff.

[2] Ibid., p. 1655.

[3] Bruce to Mrs. Bruce, 9 Mar. 1872 (quoted in *Letters of Lord Aberdare* (London, 1902), vol. i, p. 335).

[4] Emily Morgan to Gee, 9 Mar. 1872 (N.L.W., Gee MSS., 8307c, 205).

[5] *Parl. Deb.*, 3rd ser., vol. ccxx, pp. 524 ff.

[6] The question is discussed in two articles by T. R. Roberts ('Asaph') in *Young Wales,* Jan. and Feb. 1900.

Halsbury) by nine;[1] while Watkin Williams got home in Denbigh over a popular opponent, the Hon. George Kenyon, by thirty. But in the county constituencies, with their more restricted franchise and their more stable class relationships, there were several Conservative gains. In Wales, as in England, the influence of the landed gentry was powerful on the Conservative side. It was significant that Liberals were ousted in those areas where rural intimidation had been most notorious after 1868. The Ballot Act seems to have been imperfectly understood, and to have made little impact at this stage.[2] Viscount Emlyn of Golden Grove, heir to the 70,000 acres of the Cawdor estates, captured the second Carmarthenshire seat, while Carmarthen District also fell to the Conservatives. T. E. Lloyd, a squire who farmed a mere 4,500 acres, regained Cardiganshire. Most powerful, the Penrhyn 'prevailing interest' reasserted itself in Caernarvonshire, and the heir to the estate, the Hon. George Douglas-Pennant, was returned. After the poll the Rev. Herber Evans walked sadly home through the gaslit streets of Caernarvon, tears on his cheeks.'Civilization', he lamented, 'is at an end.'[3]

Even so, the election returns were not wholly discouraging to the radical element of the Liberal Party. The Whig element was gradually being eliminated, Hanmer (Flint), Stanley (Beaumaris), and Sir T. D. Lloyd (Cardigan District) all disappearing from the parliamentary scene. Three more nonconformists were returned, Eyton, the town clerk of Flint, Morgan Lloyd, a Methodist barrister (Beaumaris), and David Davies of Llandinam (Cardigan District), the railway pioneer, who had now turned to the exploitation of the coal deposits of the Rhondda Valley.[4] Two more were to be returned at by-elections before the Parliament of 1874 was prorogued, John Roberts (who succeeded Eyton in Flint District), a Methodist timber merchant, and Benjamin Williams (Carmarthen District), a Unitarian barrister

[1] The *South Wales Daily News*, 14 Feb. 1874, reported, without comment, that forty-five votes had been invalidated for incorrect marking of the ballot forms!

[2] *Royal Commission on Land in Wales and Monmouthshire, Report* (1896), p. 168. Thomas Gee pointed out that, whereas borough electors had had two years' experience of the ballot procedure in municipal elections, county electors were quite unfamiliar with it ('Cymru a'r Etholiad', *Baner ac Amserau Cymru*, 18 Feb. 1874). Cf. *Y Goleuad*, 21 Feb. 1874.

[3] H. Elvet Lewis, *Cofiant y Parch. E. Herber Evans* (Wrexham, 1901), p. 92. Douglas-Pennant's strength was in the northern part of the county, including Bangor, Llandudno, and the quarrying areas of Bethesda and Llanberis, where the Penrhyn interest prevailed.

[4] Both Morgan Lloyd and David Davies appear in the *Dictionary of Welsh Biography*. Also, for David Davies see Ivor Thomas, *Top Sawyer* (London, 1938), and E. D. Lewis, *The Rhondda Valleys*.

and Queen's Counsel. An election introducing a different theme in 1874 was that in Merthyr Tydfil, where Thomas Halliday, general secretary of the Amalgamated Association of Miners and the key figure in the bitter strikes in the coalfield in 1871–5, was defeated by the sitting members, Richard and Fothergill. Political nonconformity and industrial paternalism were still the most important factors in the political structure of the valleys, although Halliday's strikingly high poll of 4,912, as against Richard's 7,606 and Fothergill's 6,908, was a portent for the future.

The years 1874–80 were tranquil ones for Wales at Westminster, and little response was found from the Beaconsfield government towards such issues as reform of the Burial Laws or the endowment of Welsh higher education which were raised by Welsh members. The calm, however, was deceptive, and concealed a great ferment of political activity and organization within Wales itself. This was fully brought out in the election of 1880, when the Liberals almost swept the board. Radical journals had devoted immense trouble towards explaining the ballot procedure for their readers,[1] and the Hon. G. Douglas-Pennant had to make a specific avowal to a hostile audience at Criccieth that no intimidation would follow the poll.[2] The result was that nine seats were gained, and all save four of the thirty-three Welsh seats fell into Liberal hands. Osborne Morgan attributed the results to the anger of Welsh nonconformity over the Burial Acts.[3] Others testified to the impact of the agricultural depression on the farming community, and to the influence on pacifist sentiment of Gladstone's Midlothian campaign, not without a trace of anti-semitism towards the Jewish premier.[4] In Montgomeryshire, the Liberal candidate, Stuart Rendel, was urged to begin his speeches with the Eastern Question, continue with the Game Laws and disestablishment, and conclude with the Burial Laws 'as you will have the audience here completely with you'.[5] The need for conciliating nonconformity with liberal subscriptions was also emphasized: '£1 now will be worth £100 in election expenses.'[6]

---

[1] See, for example, the editorials in *Baner ac Amserau Cymru*, 31 Mar. 1880, and *Yr Herald Cymraeg*, 24 Mar. 1880.

[2] *Yr Herald Cymraeg*, 31 Mar. 1880.

[3] Letter in *The Times*, 15 Apr. 1880.

[4] See, for example, the article in *Baner ac Amserau Cymru*, 31 Mar. 1880, by 'Rhen Ffarmwr' (William Rees).

[5] A. C. Humphreys-Owen to Stuart Rendel, 11 Apr. 1878 (N.L.W., Rendel Papers, xiv. 12).

[6] Humphreys-Owen to Rendel, 19 Apr. 1878 (N.L.W., Rendel Papers, xiv. 13).

This contest in Montgomeryshire was the most remarkable of the entire election. For the first time since 1799, a Wynn had been defeated. Rendel, the victorious Liberal, proved to be an excellent fighting candidate. An Englishman and an Anglican, he placed Welsh disestablishment on his programme, laying stress in his speeches on the anti-national aspects of the established Church in Wales.[1] The contest was exceptionally turbulent and unusually expensive, with expenditure still largely unaffected by the series of Corrupt Practices Acts. It was believed to have cost Rendel £12,000 and Wynn £20,000.[2] The constituency was largely divided along linguistic lines, the Welsh-speaking western areas being solidly Liberal, the more anglicized eastern half Church and Tory. Rendel's meetings were broken up in the Church stronghold of Welshpool, while Sir Watkin Williams Wynn was assaulted in Welsh Llanidloes. In spite of the combined influence of Wynnstay, Powis Castle, and Plas Machynlleth on the other side, Rendel was returned by 191. His appeal to nationality at a time when most Welsh members were indifferent or hostile to disestablishment, carried him to a great victory. In later years, Rendel's services to the causes of Welsh Liberalism were to be considerable. It was he who was primarily the creator of a distinct Welsh Party in the Commons, and the author of its programme. With his charm, his tact, and his wide connexions (particularly his friendship with Gladstone himself), Rendel was to do more than any other man to make Wales a force in political life.

The results in 1880 bore out the changing character of Welsh Liberalism. Only a small minority of the twenty-nine members returned represented the Whig element, while there were now eight nonconformists.[3] The trend towards professional and mercantile members continued: nine were industrialists or manufacturers, and a further eleven were barristers or solicitors. The legal profession was already beginning to serve as a channel for the training of Welsh political leaders. The pattern of representation laid down in 1880 was to remain largely constant in rural and industrial districts alike for nearly forty years more. Party attitudes towards Welsh affairs became

---

[1] There is a vigorous *ex post facto* account by Rendel in F. E. Hamer (ed.), *Personal Papers of Lord Rendel* (London, 1931), pp. 289–91.

[2] J. M. Robertson to Mrs. T. E. Ellis, 16 June 1912 (N.L.W., Daniel Papers, 34).

[3] They were: Richard Davies (Anglesey), David Davies (Cardigan Bor.), John Roberts (Flint Bor.), Morgan Lloyd (Beaumaris), all Methodists; C. H. James (Merthyr) and B. T. Williams (Carmarthen Bor.), Unitarians; William Davies (Pembrokeshire), Henry Richard (Merthyr), Independents.

hardened. While the Conservative Party became increasingly hostile to Welsh demands, whether .overtly political or not, the Liberal Party was subjected to growing pressure for special treatment over a wide range of policy. In Wales, as in Britain as a whole, the content and ideology of Liberalism were in flux.

The election results and the return of a Liberal administration again revived the trend to collective action that had been apparent among Welsh members in the Parliament of 1868–74. They were bolder now in their assertion of the special claims of Wales. It was pointed out that Wales was regarded as a distinct unit for a number of administrative purposes—by the Registrar-General in making statistical returns, by the Home Office for factory and mining regulations, and by the Court of Chancery in disposing of charitable trusts. Even military developments encouraged nascent national sentiment in this most anti-military of nations: Cardwell's reforms of 1870–1 by localizing regiments in the districts where they were originally raised helped to imbue the Welsh artillery regiments and the ten Welsh infantry regiments with a patriotic aura. While the Zulu Wars of 1879 were generally unpopular with Welsh opinion, the courage of the 24th Welsh at Rorke's Drift and Isandhlwana was widely applauded. Analogies were drawn with the men of Leonidas at Thermopylae.[1] Not for the first or last time in Welsh history, patriotism and pacifism were in irrational harmony.

An episode which had a particularly stimulating effect on Welsh feeling was the appearance of Gladstone at the Mold *Eisteddfod* of 1873. Although the attendance was small, owing to the wet weather, Gladstone's eloquent defence of Welsh nationalism aroused immense enthusiasm. He upheld the Welsh language as a 'venerable relic of the past' and lauded the 'ancient history, the ancient deeds and the ancient language of your country, the Principality of Wales'. He referred warmly to Henry Richard's articles in the *Star* which, he said, had first opened his eyes to the character of Welsh society. As earlier in 1866, *The Times* regarded the occasion with scorn and contempt. It ridiculed Gladstone's theory that 'the continued prevalence of the Welsh language is chiefly due to the misguided and ungenerous policy of the British government', and hoped that, now national honour had been satisfied by the appointment of a Welsh bishop, the Welsh

---

[1] Speech by Sir Hussey Vivian, *Parl. Deb.*, 3rd ser., vol. ccxlvii, pp. 1151–2. Cf. Alan Conway, 'Welsh Soldiers in the Zulu Wars', *National Library of Wales Journal*, summer 1959, pp. 86–98.

'would consent to learn the language which is necessary to make them well-informed members of society'.[1] But the contempt of the Thunderer had already a somewhat dated ring. Ideas were changing, and the long unbroken attachment of Wales to the venerable and venerated Liberal leader had been forged.

These different currents merged into the remarkable passage of the Welsh Sunday Closing Act of 1881. Welsh nonconformists, like their co-religionists elsewhere, had long pressed for temperance reform and the recent passage of an Irish Sunday Closing Act, as previously with Irish Disestablishment, provoked the demand for similar treatment for Wales. Petitions had been signed in Wales by 267,000 people who favoured such a measure. It had figured prominently in the 1880 election campaign, and even a number of Conservative candidates for rural constituencies had pledged support for Sunday Closing on their election addresses.[2] In 1880, therefore, John Roberts (Flint) moved a bill to close public houses on Sunday in the twelve Welsh counties. There was insufficient time to take it further during that session, but in 1881 it was reintroduced and the Second Reading was carried easily by 163 votes to 17.[3] During the debate some remarkable assertions were made. Morgan Lloyd (Beaumaris) claimed that Wales had as much right as London to departmental legislation. Osborne Morgan stated the 'people should understand that in dealing with Wales you are dealing with an entirely distinct nationality',[4] more distinct than Scottish or Irish because of the additional barrier of language. In Wales, he said, crime was as little known as Conservatism.[5] Above all, Gladstone intervened with powerful effect. He noted how little attention had been paid to Welsh opinion in the past. 'Where there is a distinctly formed Welsh opinion upon a given subject, which affects Wales alone . . . I know of no reason why a respectful regard should not be paid to that opinion.'[6] Even this

---

[1] *The Times*, 20 Aug. 1873.

[2] Notably the Hon. G. Douglas-Pennant (Caernarvonshire) and A. M. Dunlop (Merioneth).

[3] *Parl. Deb.*, 3rd ser., vol. cclx, pp. 1748 ff.   [4] Ibid., p. 1761.

[5] A claim made frequently by Welsh nonconformists—Wales as the 'Land of the White Gloves' (*Gwlad y Menyg Gwynion*). There is an interesting correspondence on this between Henry Richard and Lord Aberdare in N.L.W., Richard MSS., 5503B. See particularly Aberdare to Richard, 4 Nov. 1875.

Lleufer Thomas's *Appendix* to the *Report* of the Land Commissioners in 1896 showed (p. 300) that, for the period 1874–93, crimes in Wales averaged 176 per 10,000 population and in England, 196 per 10,000. On the other hand, in crimes of violence, crimes against morality and, significantly, crimes of drunkenness (Wales, 711; England, 539), the Welsh totals were the higher for the same period.

[6] *Parl. Deb.*, loc. cit., p. 1772.

characteristically ambiguous phrase was later to cause him grievous embarrassment.

The Bill, supported by twenty-eight Welsh members out of thirty (excluding Monmouthshire), passed through all its stages with ease and received the Royal Assent on 27 August 1881. An attempt to include Monmouthshire within the operation of the Act was, however, negatived by the Attorney-General, Sir Henry James, on the debatable ground that Henry VIII had created Monmouthshire as an English county in 1542.[1] Despite this setback, the Act created enormous interest in Wales. Its operation was to remain a matter of some controversy. The Commissioners who investigated the problem in 1889 tended to approve in general, but to criticize in detail.[2] There were suggestions that the Act was most effective in those areas where the strength of nonconformity made it least necessary. The 'dry' Sunday remains a fundamental feature of Welsh life to this day, and inviolable until the Licensing Act of 1961.[3] The local option polls in November 1961 clearly revealed the continuing support for the principle of Sunday closing in the most strongly nonconformist and Welsh counties of northern and western Wales. But the significance of the Act lay in its underlying principle rather than in its operation. For the first time in history, the Imperial Parliament had sanctioned separate legislative treatment for Wales. There had been 'Welsh Acts' in abundance in the past—the South Wales Turnpike Act of 1844 was a recent example. But never before had a distinct legislative principle been applied to Wales, as distinct from England.[4] Never before had Wales been treated as in some sense a national unit. Some Anglican clergymen refused to sign petitions in support of the Act.[5]

[1] Ibid., vol. cclxii, pp. 615–16. A controversial claim (cf. David Williams, *Modern Wales* (London, 1950), p. 41).

[2] *Report of the Royal Commissioners appointed to enquire into the operation of the Sunday Closing (Wales) Act, 1881* (c. 5994, 1890).

[3] One of the difficulties confronting the defenders of the Welsh Sunday Closing Act in 1961 was that, whereas the Act of 1881 was based solely on the opinion of the people of Wales, the new Act of 1961 placed them in the position of appearing to deny the expression of Welsh opinion at the polls. The preamble of the Sunday Closing Act (44 & 45 Victoria, c. 61) makes a point of emphasizing that 'the people of Wales are desirous that in the principality of Wales those provisions (i.e. licensing) be extended to the other hours of Sunday'.

[4] An exception, perhaps, was the Act for the Propagation of the Gospel in Wales, 1650. But it was allowed to expire in 1653; cf. Thomas Richards, *Puritan Developments in Wales, 1639-53* (London, 1920), pp. 79–89.

[5] Owen Thomas and J. Machreth Rees, *Cofiant y Parch, John Thomas* (London, 1898), p. 405. This point is also stressed by Daniel Rowlands, 'Cynnigiad Mr. John Roberts A. S.' *Y Traethodydd*, 1880, pp. 117–32.

They greeted it with apprehension, foreseeing, correctly, that the principle enshrined in it could be applied elsewhere.

(iii) *The Education Movement*

It was, however, in a quite different field that was seen most striking evidence of the new vitality in Welsh public life after 1868, the field of education. In some respects, the issue of public education was a social, religious, and intellectual controversy that affected the United Kingdom as a whole. Particularly was this true of elementary education, where the position of those voluntary schools, most of which belonged to the established Church, was bitterly contested wherever there was an active nonconformist community. The centre of opposition to the Forster Education Act of 1870 was Birmingham, where Chamberlain and Morley made the National Education League the spearhead of political dissent.

But in Wales there was particular tension, since here the position of the Church was felt with especial keenness. In the early part of the century, while Welsh nonconformists had often been apathetic towards educational reform, Church 'National' Schools had penetrated into many rural areas, often with the moral and financial support of local nonconformists. By 1880 there were 223 Church Schools in St. David's diocese alone, with an average total attendance of 19,000 pupils.[1] In addition, of the twenty-seven grammar schools endowed under the Endowed Schools Act of 1869, two-thirds of the pupils were Anglican.[2] The grant aid afforded to National Schools by Forster's Act thus aroused particular resentment in Wales.

Another controversy ushered in by the Act of 1870 was that of religious instruction in schools, over which nonconformists themselves were divided. A conference of Welsh nonconformist leaders at Aberystwyth in January 1870 decided in favour of permissive Biblical instruction, with denominational teaching outside school hours. Led by Gee, they sent a deputation to Gladstone and Forster in March, and their outlook was largely reflected in the subsequent 'Cowper-Temple clause'.[3] However, a vigorous body of Welsh nonconformists, especially among the Independents, advocated the removal of all religious teaching from the schools, and a completely secular system. Their views were voiced by Henry Richard during the

[1] J. Vyrnwy Morgan (ed.), *Welsh Political and Educational Leaders in the Victorian Era*, p. 113.
[2] T. I. Ellis, *The Development of Higher Education in Wales* (Wrexham, 1935), p. 37.
[3] T. Gwynn Jones, op. cit., p. 309.

Second Reading on 18 March.[1] He pointed out the absurdity of having a conscience clause which applied to the great mass of the population, and of instruction in the catechism for nonconformist pupils. There could be no conscience clause for ratepayers. Welshmen, he claimed, favoured the exclusion of all religious education from the schools, and leaving it to the Sunday Schools, a truly national institution in Wales. In the Lords, Earl Russell championed this view. On 20 June 1870 Richard moved that the grants to denominational schools be not increased, and that education should be entirely secular. However, this motion was lost by 421 to 60, the minority including ten Welsh members.[2] Dixon's resolution against endowed denominational instruction in March 1872 also failed by 355 to 94, the Welsh members present voting in favour by fourteen to twelve. Thus a dual system of Church and Board School education continued side by side.

As in England, Welsh School Board elections were essentially trials of strength between different denominations, with minorities given exaggerated influence through the cumulative vote system. The results bore testimony to the religious complexion of Wales. The Cross Commission inquiring into the educational system in 1886–8 found that while England contained only seven secular School Boards, in Wales there were no less than fifty.[3] A Church spokesman in 1899 stated that, of 320 School Boards in Wales, 62 had no religious instruction, 118 taught the Bible without comment, and almost all had no religious examination.[4]

But the bitterness of nonconformists towards Church schools could not be assuaged by these statistics. Education in Wales, like most other public issues, was fundamentally permeated by the religious divisions that rent society. While Board Schools penetrated widely, especially in industrial towns such as Cardiff and Newport,[5] in hundreds of rural parishes the Church retained its monopoly of primary

[1] *Parl. Deb.*, 3rd ser., vol. cc, pp. 263 ff.

[2] Ibid., vol. ccii, pp. 495 ff., and see the comments of *Yr Herald Cymraeg*, 24 June 1870. Cf. A. W. W. Dale, *The Life of the Rev. R. W. Dale of Birmingham* (London, 1903), pp. 278–80. The ten Welsh members were Dillwyn, Richard, Fothergill, Osborne Morgan, Col. Edwardes, Jones-Parry, Sartoris, Crichton-Stuart, Watkin Williams, E. M. Richards.

[3] *Final Report of the Commissioners appointed to inquire into the Elementary Education Acts*, 1888, p. 113.

[4] Speech by Lord E. Cecil, *Parl. Deb.*, 4th ser., vol. lxviii, p. 89.

[5] Cf. C. T. Whitmell, *Elementary Education, Cardiff District* (1886). The 'Undenominational' (i.e. nonconformist) candidates succeeded in controlling the Cardiff School Board for the entire period from 1873 to 1902 (Cardiff MSS., 4,488, Scrapbooks of Henry Allgood, secretary of Cardiff Liberal Association). See also the evidence before the Education Commissioners in 1887 by Lewis Williams, chairman of Cardiff School Board, *Evidence*, vol. II, qu. 39,400 ff.

education. There were, it was claimed, over 300 'single school areas', where parish schools catered for a nonconformist community. Schools which nonconformists had helped to build, they claimed, compelled their children to learn the catechism, and debarred non-conformist pupil teachers. Lloyd George and O. M. Edwards were themselves rebellious products of such schools. In several counties, Brecknockshire, Denbighshire, Flintshire, Montgomeryshire, Pembrokeshire, and Radnorshire, voluntary schools, almost entirely Anglican, remained in a majority down to 1902.[1] Not only was their system of instruction obnoxious to nonconformists, but often their structure and sanitation were sadly deficient, owing to the paucity of Church endowments, and the absence of rate aid which nonconformists themselves rejected. Often, local landowners, bulwarks of the Church, exerted their influence against the construction of Board Schools. The other divisions in Welsh communal life were intensified by the duality of a system of education which saw Board and voluntary schools rise up side by side in countless areas. Able young nonconformists such as the future Sir Henry Jones were to complain of the proselytizing of Anglican schoolmasters.[2] In a multitude of ways religious antagonism diverted the zeal of the Welsh people for a national system of elementary education.

It was, however, in the field of higher education that a distinctively Welsh question emerged, and the clear deficiency of Wales in this respect evoked sympathetic response from both political parties.[3]

The first approach came in an interview with Gladstone on 28 May 1870 by Henry Richard and Osborne Morgan, with the object of securing government aid for a proposed University College of Wales.[4] The Welsh University Committee formed in 1863 had been exceptionally active, under the leadership of Sir Hugh Owen. Thousands of pounds had been subscribed in a national appeal, and a site had been obtained in the form of a disused railway hotel on the seafront at Aberystwyth. Gladstone was sympathetic, and admitted the need for an undenominational Welsh college. But he had already refused grants to several English colleges, and could hardly make an

[1] *List of Public Elementary Schools in Wales on 1 August 1906* (Cd. 3640, 1907).
[2] Sir Henry Jones, *Old Memories* (London, 1923), pp. 31, 84.
[3] The growth of Welsh higher education is very clearly dealt with in J. R. Webster, 'The Place of Welsh Secondary Education in Welsh Society, 1800–1918' (unpublished University of Wales Ph.D. thesis, 1959) and also in T. I. Ellis, op. cit. The best account of the university movement is D. Emrys Evans, *The University of Wales* (Cardiff, 1953). See also T. I. Ellis (ed.), *Letters of Thomas Charles Edwards* (Aberystwth, 1952–3).
[4] Minutes of Interview (N.L.W., MS. 5509c).

exception now, though significantly he conceded that 'it was impossible to place Wales, with its clearly marked nationality and its inhabitants divided from England by a strong line of demarcation, both of race and language, upon the same footing as an English town or district'.

Richard persisted and wrote again on 8 April 1871.[1] But Gladstone felt that he could not persuade his colleagues to offer financial aid. It would raise the religious issue, and would commit the state to a new principle in aiding colleges from the exchequer on the basis of their teaching only 'an undenominational education'. He shrewdly remarked that Richard himself had opposed Forster's Act on this account. After declining to support Owen's College, Manchester, the government could not aid Aberystwyth. Even so, in October 1872 the 'University College of Wales' was opened at Aberystwyth with twenty-five students, with most of the £10,000 purchase money still owing. For many years it had to struggle hard for survival.

The future of a Welsh college was made more uncertain by the absence of any organized schooling above the elementary level, and it was to draw attention to the 'deficiencies of higher education in Wales' that H. Hussey Vivian, the Swansea copper magnate who sat for Glamorgan, rose in the Commons on 1 July 1879.[2] Many authors had recently written on Welsh higher education.[3] In particular, much indignation had been aroused by the proposal of Principal Harper of Jesus College, Oxford, to throw open the endowments and scholarships of the College to general competition. The potential influence of Jesus had not been fully realized, owing in part to its strong association with the Anglican Church and in part to the inferior quality of undergraduates from Wales.[4] Since 1854 half the fellowships had been open to Englishmen, and the inadequacy of Welsh grammar schools led to Harper's new scheme, which would have virtually deprived Welsh education of £10,000 of endowments annually, mainly from the Meyricke Trust. All shades of opinion in Wales protested, and there were few who followed Lord Aberdare in maintaining that open competition for Welsh awards would raise academic standards. The belligerent Dean H. T. Edwards of Bangor led the protests, and it was his attacks that led to Vivian's motion.[5]

[1] Gladstone to Richard, 14 Apr. 1871 (N.L.W., Richard MSS., 5504B).

[2] *Parl. Deb.*, 3rd ser., vol. cclxvii, pp. 1141 ff.

[3] For example, D. L. Lloyd, *The Missing Link* (1876); T. Marchant Williams, *The Educational Wants of Wales* (1877).

[4] *Report of the Committee appointed to inquire into the condition of Intermediate and Higher Education in Wales* (C. 3047, 1881), p. xxii.

[5] Dean Edwards to Henry Richard, 6 Mar. 1879 (N.L.W., Richard MSS., 5503B).

Vivian referred to unmistakable grievances. While Ireland had 1,634 university students (1:3,121 of the population), and Scotland boasted the proud total of 4,000 (1:840), the total number of Welsh students enjoying higher education of any kind, at Jesus College, at Lampeter College (an Anglican college which had been granted the right to confer the B.A. degree by a charter in 1865), and at the struggling college at Aberystwyth amounted to a mere 189. Intermediate secondary education was almost non-existent. The twenty-seven Welsh grammar schools were largely situated away from the large urban centres; they shared £6,531 annually, and their students numbered less than 4,000.

The main interest of this debate lies in the attitude of the political parties. It was a bi-partisan motion, the seconder being Sir John Puleston (Devonport), a Conservative resident in North Wales.[1] Several Welsh Conservatives also supported Vivian, as did many of his Liberal colleagues. Most notable of all, Gladstone himself intervened, and demonstrated how far his outlook had advanced since 1870. He based his case simply on the proven nationhood of Wales, as shown by its language, religious life, and culture. By this brief speech he consolidated his hold on the devoted affection of the Welsh people.[2] But the Conservative government failed to respond. Lord George Hamilton, Vice-President of the Council, saw no reason why the consolidated fund should be applied to Welsh, any more than to Cornish education. The facilities that did exist were the subject of so much local controversy that the government felt reluctant to devote money to them. He saw no reason for a Welsh university: Welsh parents would always prefer to send their sons to the older universities. Sir Stafford Northcote, in similar vein, warned against the dangers involved in the unnecessary multiplication of universities. The fifty-five supporters of the motion included all twenty-two Welsh members present, Liberal and Conservative, but it failed by fifty-one votes.

Nevertheless, the debate was an important landmark: it made Welsh higher education a political issue for the first time. The question was much discussed in the electoral campaign and many candidates of both parties committed themselves in their addresses to support a state grant. When Gladstone returned to power, he immediately sanctioned the appointment of a Departmental Committee to inquire into higher education in Wales and Monmouthshire,

---

[1] He was to become Constable of Caernarvon Castle, 1890–1908.
[2] *Parl. Deb.*, loc. cit., p. 1160.

with Lord Aberdare, who had originally proposed the inquiry, as chairman. It was a most able body. Nonconformists complained that they had only one representative—Henry Richard—against four Churchmen—Lord Emlyn, Professor Rhŷs, Lewis Morris, and Canon Robinson, and Mundella had urged Gladstone in vain to enlarge the Committee.[1] But criticism soon evaporated. The Committee acted with dispatch and efficiency, and in August 1881 its Report appeared. Nothing could have less resembled its notorious predecessor, the Blue Books of 1847. Despite the anglicized preponderance of the Committee, the preamble sympathetically emphasized the distinct nationality of Wales, its flourishing literature, its deep religious convictions, and its zeal for education.[2] Wales was entitled to accommodation for 15,700 pupils. In fact, it existed for only 4,000. A meagre 1,540 enjoyed grammar-school education, while a further 2,496 were at private and proprietary schools, mainly Anglican.[3] Educational charities in Wales amounted to only £14,281.

The Report recommended the creation of a new system of intermediate schools, run by elected governing bodies. Endowments should be more widely distributed to aid existing schools, while the new schools should be supported by a halfpenny rate and a parliamentary grant on a pound-for-pound basis. Exhibitions to higher intermediate schools should be awarded to the more able pupils at elementary schools. Finally, two colleges should be set up, one in South Wales, and one in the North, at Aberystwyth, Bangor, or Caernarvon preferably, with a grant of £4,000 a year each. Lampeter College should be affiliated to them. No recommendation was made over Jesus College, nor over the teaching of the Welsh language.

Thus this remarkable Report came out boldly in favour of a Welsh education system, more advanced than that of England. It was the first comprehensive survey of Welsh higher education, and party policies towards Welsh education for the next twenty years were largely concerned with implementing its recommendations.

The first proposal to be acted on was the creation of two colleges. The major stumbling-block at first was that of finance. Mundella,

---

[1] Mundella to Lord Spencer, 21 Aug. 1880 (Ministry of Education records). Quoted in Sir Ben Bowen Thomas, 'Establishment of the Aberdare Departmental Committee, 1880. Some notes and letters', *Bulletin of the Board of Celtic Studies*, May, 1962. I am grateful to the author for permission to consult the proofs of this article. Another criticism made was the lack of familiarity of the Commissioners with Welsh society: cf. Webster, op. cit., p. 330: 'they saw Welsh educational problems essentially through English eyes'.

[2] *Report*, pp. xlvi ff. [3] Ibid., p. xvi.

the new Vice-President of the Council in Gladstone's second ministry, was faced with the objections of Courtney and Spencer among his colleagues towards the proposed award of £8,000 a year.[1] In 1882, however, a start was made when Aberystwyth College, which had largely surmounted its initial difficulties through the crusading of Sir Hugh Owen and the munificence of David Davies of Llandinam, was granted £4,000 a year. In 1883 the grant to the Welsh colleges was raised to the specified £8,000 although, according to Mundella, 'only with the very greatest difficulty—and by Gladstone's imperative decision'.[2]

Negotiations also began over the sites of the proposed colleges. Each occasioned intense local rivalry and jealousy. In South Wales the adjudicators preferred the more anglicized Cardiff to Swansea, doubtless being influenced by a grant of £10,000 from the Marquis of Bute. The new college opened in October 1883 with as its first principal, J. Viriamu Jones, formerly principal of Firth College, Sheffield, and still only twenty-seven years of age. By March 1884 it had 152 students.[3]

The northern college was still more contentious. Despite the wide fervour it had stimulated, Aberystwyth College was considered by many too remote to serve the needs of North Wales.[4] Thirteen other towns were canvassed, while Gee promoted his own scheme for a network of half a dozen local colleges. Finally, in August 1883, the adjudicators under Lord Carlingford selected Bangor, bitterly opposed by many nonconformists as 'the only Conservative town and the only Church City in North Wales'.[5] They feared cathedral influence on the students in so typically Welsh an area.[6] More apprehension was aroused by the appointment of (Sir) Harry Reichel as the first principal, a High Churchman and 'an Irish Tory, blackest shade of Toryism in its native state', in the words of one angry patriot.[7] These fears soon evaporated. The new principal proved an excellent choice, though fears of 'Reichel the Orangeman' continued

[1] Lord Carlingford to Mundella, 26 June 1882 (B.M., Add. MSS., 44258, ff. 188–9).
[2] Mundella to Gladstone, 22 Oct. 1889 (B.M., Add. MSS., 44258, f. 264). Also cf. Rendel to Humphreys-Owen, 15 Dec. 1883 (N.L.W., Glansevern MSS., 132).
[3] Viriamu Jones to Richard, 13 Mar. 1884 (N.L.W., Richard MSS., 5504B). For Viriamu Jones, see *Dictionary of Welsh Biography*; K. Viriamu Jones, *J. Viriamu Jones* (London, 1915); Neville Masterman, *J. Viriamu Jones, 1856–1901: pioneer of the modern university* (Llandebïe, 1958).
[4] Humphreys-Owen to Rendel, 20 Apr. 1883 (N.L.W., Rendel Papers, xiv. 165).
[5] Herber Evans to Gee, 'Friday' 1883 (N.L.W., Gee MSS., 8310E, 440).
[6] W. Evans to Gee, 10 Aug. 1883 (N.L.W., Gee MSS., 8305C, 66).
[7] W. Evans to Gee, 18 May 1884 (N.L.W., Gee MSS., 8305C, 68).

to rankle.[1] Shortly it was the Conservative press which was complaining of the assistance given to Lloyd George by Bangor students in the Caernarvon election of 1892.[2]

A new controversy concerned the older college at Aberystwyth. An attempt to secure Aberystwyth as the college of North Wales had failed, and its grant had been transferred to Bangor.[3] Although Lord Carlingford had advised against a grant to a third college, efforts were now made to put Aberystwyth College on a similar footing to the new colleges at Bangor and Cardiff. Under its remarkable principal, Thomas Charles Edwards, Aberystwyth had served as the symbol of the national passion for education. Already in its brief ten-year existence a remarkable group of students had been attracted there, among them several men who were to shape the national life of Wales profoundly in later years, scholars such as John Edward Lloyd, educationalists such as T. F. Roberts, political leaders such as Samuel Evans, Ellis Jones Griffith, and above all Thomas Edward Ellis. At Oxford, former students of Aberystwyth proudly formed a society to preserve an integrated community of Aberystwyth men, the 'A.C.C.', forerunner of the better-known 'Cymdeithas Dafydd ap Gwilym'. In Aberystwyth in these years can be seen developing the idea of an organic relationship between a university and society in Wales, which was later to issue in the cultural and political revolution of *Cymru Fydd*.[4]

It was inevitable, therefore, that when Stuart Rendel moved a resolution in the Commons in 1884, to preserve Aberystwyth College, that he should receive very wide support.[5] Welsh Conservatives such as Lord Emlyn, and the Liberal historian James Bryce (Tower Hamlets), who took a close interest in Welsh education, defended Aberystwyth with passion, while several Conservative front benchers, notably Lord Claud Hamilton and R. A. Cross, took the opportunity to harass the government for their dilatory handling of Welsh education. The result of the debate was indecisive, but the government had been shaken by the feeling shown, perhaps to an exaggerated degree. Mundella wrote afterwards to Henry Richard: 'I wish you would

[1] J. Arthur Price to John Edward Lloyd, 4 Dec. 1902 (Bangor, Lloyd Papers, MSS. 314, 455). For Reichel, see J. E. Lloyd (ed.), *Sir Harry Reichel* (Cardiff, 1934).
[2] *The Times*, 2 Sept. 1892. These educational controversies are dealt with in W. H. G. Armytage, *A. J. Mundella, 1825–1897* (London, 1951), pp. 215–17.
[3] Lord Aberdare to Richard, 19 Aug. 1883 (N.L.W., Richard MSS., 5503B).
[4] For accounts of Aberystwyth in these years, see T. I. Ellis, *Thomas Edward Ellis: Cofiant*, vol. i (Liverpool, 1944), *passim*, and David Williams, *Thomas Francis Roberts* (Cardiff, 1961), pp. 13–19.   [5] *Parl. Deb.*, 3rd ser., vol. cclxxxv, pp. 1589 ff.

come and see me about Aberystwyth. We had better settle this question before you turn us out, as the Tories will not help you. If we
subsidize a third College, we must do it on the same conditions as the
other two.'[1]

In subsequent negotiations, much depended on the extent to which
Rendel could persuade the recalcitrant Childers at the Exchequer.
Eventually, the grant to the Welsh colleges was revised. The new
colleges at Bangor and Cardiff were each granted their £4,000, while
Aberystwyth received £2,500. Some educationalists criticized this on
grounds of inadequacy, but Mundella had had the greatest difficulty
in persuading his colleagues to accept this amount.[2] An agitation
then began to gain the equivalent grant for Aberystwyth. Rendel
approached Childers and Gladstone in 1884, but as late as April
1885 Mundella was 'not at all encouraging' over the balance of
£1,500.[3] It was the succeeding Conservative Salisbury ministry which
raised the Aberystwyth grant to £4,000 also, in August 1885.[4] A
later Salisbury administration in September 1890 granted the University College at Aberystwyth its charter, thus giving it completely
equal status with Bangor and Cardiff. Thus, successful lobbying of
both political parties achieved, and more than achieved, the first
recommendation of the Aberdare Committee, and in less than
a decade there were three University Colleges in Wales.

But the success of these colleges depended largely on the implementation of the other major recommendation of the Committee of 1881,
a system of intermediate schools. As long as Welsh intermediate
education remained negligible, there would be few able Welshmen to
benefit from higher instruction. Of the 313 students who entered
Aberystwyth College up to 1880, 70 were under sixteen years of age.[5]

Here the Gladstone ministry was slow to act. Mundella gave up the
attempt to legislate in 1882, and in March 1883 he still found it
'a difficult task'.[6] In July 1883 twenty-seven Welsh Liberal members
signed a memorandum in favour of an intermediate education bill
during the session.[7] But crises in Ireland and in the Empire delayed

---

[1] Mundella to Richard, 17 Mar. 1884 (N.L.W., Richard MSS., 5505B).
[2] Rendel to Humphreys-Owen, 15 Dec. 1883 (N.L.W., Glansevern MSS., 132).
[3] Humphreys-Owen to T. C. Edwards, 1 Apr. 1885 (T. I. Ellis (ed.), *Letters of
Thomas Charles Edwards* (Aberystwyth, 1953), p. 239).
[4] Rendel to T. C. Edwards, 25 Aug. 1885 (ibid., p. 251).
[5] D. Emrys Evans, op. cit., p. 24, Also a large number of students tended to return
home after only one or two terms (David Williams, op. cit., p. 15).
[6] Mundella to Richard, 13 Mar. 1883 (N.L.W., Richard MSS., 5505B).
[7] N.I.W., MS. 5509C.

other legislation, while the Franchise and Redistribution Bills occupied much of the session of 1884–5. After much delay, Mundella introduced a measure on 21 May 1885 which foreshadowed the Act of 1889.[1] A halfpenny rate would be levied, backed by an equivalent treasury draft, to finance a network of intermediate schools. The new local authority would be a county education committee, consisting of members of Parliament, with additional members elected by municipalities. All endowments would be devoted to intermediate education, while a new commission would replace the Charity Commissioners, as in Scotland. There was obviously little chance of the measure becoming law. It was introduced in an empty house, which was almost counted out on the whim of an eccentric Irishman.[2] The Bill had received only the formal First Reading when the government fell in June. The succeeding Salisbury ministry, a minority administration, ignored the Bill, and when the Liberals took office again in January 1886 Ireland excluded legislation on other domestic issues. In March Playfair, Mundella's successor, informed the Hon. G. T. Kenyon (Denbigh District, Conservative) that the Bill was being delayed pending the report of the Select Committee inquiring into the Endowed Schools Act. The government fell in June, with the question still in abeyance.

This caused much disappointment in Wales, where Professor Henry Jones now led a vigorous public campaign.[3] The Liberals had implemented only a part of the Aberdare recommendations. Even so, sufficient had been accomplished up to 1886 to make education in Wales the major force in transforming the regional vitality of 1868 into consciousness of nationhood.

(iv) *The Collapse of Agriculture*

A totally new element was added to this complex fusion of political, religious, and cultural attitudes in Wales by the disastrous depression that struck the agricultural community from the autumn of 1879.[4] An international slump in the prices of foodstuffs coincided

---

[1] *Parl. Deb.*, 3rd ser., vol. ccxcviii, pp. 1136–9.

[2] Armytage, op. cit., p. 227.

[3] Sir Henry Jones, op. cit., pp. 180–1.

[4] The basic source for a study of Welsh agriculture in the later nineteenth century is the Royal Commission on Land in Wales and Monmouthshire, in 1893–6; *Evidence*, vols. i and ii (1894); vols. iii and iv (1895); vol. v, *Report and Appendices, Index* (1896). For an interesting discussion of the international political consequences of the agricultural depression, see 'A pessimist's view of agriculture', *Spectator*, 25 Feb. 1893.

with catastrophically bad harvests to produce a quarter of a century of depression and misery in the country-side. This, of course, was an international phenomenon and not one peculiar to Wales. The flood of cheap imports from overseas, refrigerated meat products from Australia and the Argentine, grain from the American Mid-West and the Russian steppes, shattered most European economies, not just that of Wales. As so often in recent economic history, there was greatest poverty at a period of greatest opportunity. At a time when farming had reached an unprecedented level of mechanization and of mobility, and when millions of acres were being opened up in the American West, smallholders in the French Midi, peasants on Italian *latifundia*, cultivating squires in Prussia and Pomerania, occupying freeholders in Minnesota, Wisconsin, and Iowa were being driven to desperate lengths of collective self-defence. From Scandinavia to the American Far West, agriculturists, traditionally a conservative element in society, were turning to radical political activity to express their discontents. The forms which resistance took varied with the social and economic structure. In Germany, Junker landowners created the Agrarian League, the most powerful of German pressure-groups on Bismarck's government. In Ireland, Davitt's Land League of peasant occupiers threatened to overturn the whole system of land ownership, with its myriad sub-divisions. In Denmark, there were striking experiments in co-operative farming and limits imposed on the aggregation of land holdings. In the American Mid-West, farmers bid for power both at the local and at the national level, in the Granger movements and the Populist Party, with its panacea of free silver. But in Wales the depression had especial significance. It added an economic element to the enduring and pervasive social cleavage between landlord and tenant. A new and powerful impetus was provided for the development of a coherent and militant nationalism.

The effect of the depression on Welsh dairy farmers was catastrophic. Thousands of holdings were deserted, and the population of countless rural villages was sharply diminished. Between 1881 and 1891 the population of eight Welsh counties declined, in Montgomeryshire by as much as 11·68 per cent., as able-bodied young Welshmen sought employment elsewhere.[1] Some emigrated to the United States, where 100,000 native-born Welshmen were recorded in the 1890 census.[2] Others crossed the border into England, where

[1] *Land Commission, Report*, p. 47.
[2] R. Berthoff, *British Immigrants in Industrial America*, p. 7.

already over 228,000 Welsh-born were resident.[1] But the great majority found opportunity within Wales itself, 87,200 migrating into industrial Glamorgan and Monmouth in the decade, 1881–91. In all,
in the period 1851–1911 a net loss of 388,000 out of rural Wales was
counterbalanced by an inward migration of 366,000 into the Welsh
coalfield.[2] In this way, Wales was saved from the worst effects of
rural depopulation and poverty that so seriously disrupted the social
development of Ireland.

Under these conditions, however, the basic problems of insecurity
of tenure, high rents, land hunger, and land exhaustion in Wales were
felt the more keenly, and government legislation proved inadequate.
The Duke of Richmond's Agricultural Holdings Act of 1875 had
been the first act to recognize the principle of compensation for improvements made by a tenant, and the first real interference with the
sacred 'freedom of contract' between landlord and tenant. But it
seems to have had little effect in Wales, few tenants in a largely monoglot Welsh community appearing to appreciate its effects, and few
landlords being anxious to explain them.[3] To these economic hardships were added the more traditional and subtle social difficulties
caused by the lack of sympathy between landlords and tenants in
general. The Land Commissioners of 1896 shrewdly noted that complaints of excessive rents were most vocal in the strongly nonconformist and Welsh-speaking areas. In anglicized Brecknockshire
and Radnorshire, complaints were few.[4]

As in so many other Welsh questions, there was little information
available on the Welsh land question, and little to indicate that it
might take a different form from that of England. The Royal Commission on Agricultural Interests (1879–82), presided over by the
Duke of Richmond, had examined over 200 witnesses, but only nine
dealt at all with Wales. Five of these nine were land agents, and
a sixth was Lord Penrhyn himself. It is not surprising that the Report
of the Assistant Commissioner for Wales, Doyle, a former Poor Law
Inspector who knew no Welsh, gave a very inadequate picture of
conditions.[5]

At the general election of 1880 the land question played a prominent part. In many contests, compensation for improvements,

[1] *Land Commission, Report*, pp. 50 ff.
[2] Brinley Thomas, 'Wales and the Atlantic Economy', *Scottish Journal of Political Economy*, Nov. 1959, pp. 169 ff.
[3] *Land Commission, Report*, pp. 900 ff.
[4] Ibid., p. 420.   [5] Ibid., Appendix A, pp. 61–64.

abolition of the laws of settlement and of entail to facilitate land transfer, and a radical revision of the game laws were prominent proposals in the Liberal platform. What Hanham terms the 'kinship of outlook between landlord, farmer and villager'[1] was much less evident in Wales where there were other, more profound social and cultural factors making for division. It was notable that it was the most anglicized parts of Wales which were most susceptible to landlord influence—the Vale of Glamorgan, where the influence of Dunraven and Bute was powerful on the Conservative side, in Radnorshire, where Lord Ormathwaite by custom enjoyed the 'prevailing interest' and in southern Pembrokeshire, where the Cawdors maintained a traditional supremacy. On the other hand, the revulsion of Welsh tenant farmers against landowners must not be exaggerated at this stage. The Whig magnate could be a useful ally even in rural Wales. Watkin Williams in Caernarvonshire and Samuel Holland in Merioneth benefited in 1880 from the benevolent patronage of the influential family of Glynllifon,[2] and its scion, Lord Newborough, while Lord Sudeley in Montgomeryshire, and Lord Kensington and the Philippses of Picton in Pembrokeshire, gave valuable assistance to the victorious Liberal candidates in both shire and borough seats. In many a local Liberal machine, a landowner took the leading part, as Arthur Humphreys-Owen of Glansevern was Stuart Rendel's chief support in Montgomeryshire. Rendel was told that 'the squires in Montgomeryshire are personally liked by the voters, so far as is compatible with the wide difference in politics and religion'.[3] While appearing to reject the traditional structure of social authority in theory, Welsh Liberals were often to embrace it in practice.

After 1880 the debate on the Welsh land question became more intense. The Farmers' Alliance, a movement strongest in eastern England, which attempted to combine tenant farmers and labourers in one unified organization, had some influence in Wales, where 'there was not that distinction between (Welsh farmers) and the cottagers which exists in the large farm English counties'.[4] In addition to urging a simplified system of ownership through the abolition of entails and the partition of joint tenancies, the Alliance veered towards compulsory compensation for outgoing tenants. It had support in high places. For example, Homersham Cox, the unpopular 'Eng-

[1] Hanham, op. cit., p. 32.
[2] Yr Herald Cymraeg, 31 Mar., 7 Apr. 1880.
[3] Humphreys-Owen to Rendel, 15 Jan. 1882 (N.L.W., Rendel Papers, xiv. 123).
[4] Humphreys-Owen to Rendel, 11 Apr. 1878 (N.L.W., Rendel Papers, xiv. 12).

lish judge' of 1872, was, as Humphreys-Owen complained to Rendel, 'a doctrinaire radical in land matters'.[1] An additional factor was the Irish Land Act of 1881, which created a judicial tribunal to regulate the rental of tenant holdings, encouraging a growing demand for similar legislation in Wales. Clearly, a radical breach with traditional ideas was required to alleviate the growing distress in the Welsh country-side. The new Agricultural Holdings Act of 1883 was little more effective than its predecessor of 1875. Although it established in embryo the principle of compulsory compensation for temporary as well as for permanent improvements, it was of little value to poorer tenants and scarcely understood at all in Welsh-speaking areas.

In 1885 the crisis on the land was a major political question in Wales. In West Carmarthenshire, W. R. H. Powell, a Liberal land-owner from Maesgwynne, Deputy-Lieutenant and master of fox-hounds, defeated the Cawdor representative, the popular Lord Emlyn, in an election fought largely, it was stated, on the Agricultural Hold-ings Act of 1883.[2] Every one of the thirty Liberal members returned included proposals for land reform in his election address. The cry of 'fair trade', euphemism for a nascent protective tariff system, made some headway in Montgomeryshire, where it was 'headed by a manu-facturer whose followers are farmers; not as elsewhere by land-owners',[3] and where the great landowners, Wynn, Lord Powis, and R. E. Jones, kept aloof. Chamberlain's Unauthorized Programme, with its suggestions of a land purchase system, alarmed Humphreys-Owen as an attempt to prejudice the electorate against the land-owner,[4] but it aroused wide support in Wales. Gee, in particular, was its enthusiastic advocate in *Y Faner*. Moreover, Chamberlain had begun to show a vague appreciation that there was a distinct prob-lem in Wales. In a speech at Ipswich during the 1885 election he had said that the Irish Land Act could not be applied to England because English farmers did not want fixity of tenure if it implied throwing the responsibility for improvements on to their shoulders, and find-ing the necessary capital. 'English farmers are prejudiced into sup-porting the Tory demand for protection'.[5] But, he went on, 'in Wales no doubt it is different and probably the question there may be

---

[1] Humphreys-Owen to Rendel, 29 Sept. 1881 (N.L.W., Rendel Papers, xiv. 106).
[2] Land Commission, *Evidence*, vol. 3, qu. 42,661 (H. A. Jeremy's evidence).
[3] Humphreys-Owen to Rendel, 31 Dec. 1884 (N.L.W., Rendel Papers, xiv. 245). This is a reference to Colonel Pryce-Jones, later M.P. for Montgomery Boroughs, 1885-6 and 1895-1905.
[4] Humphreys-Owen to Rendel, 3 Feb. 1885 (N.L.W., Rendel Papers, xiv. 250).
[5] Chamberlain to Gee, 24 Jan. 1885 (N.L.W., Gee MSS., 8305c, 14).

presented for settlement in a different form'. A polarization of forces seemed to be taking place in rural Wales with an ominous similarity to the troubled situation in rural Ireland. A North Wales Property Defence Association was formed by landowners in December 1885, with the redoubtable J. E. Vincent, barrister and soon Welsh correspondent of *The Times*, as chief publicist.[1] Gee countered in 1886 with the Welsh Land League, which was broadened in 1887 into the 'Welsh Land, Commercial and Labour League', with the establishment of a land court and a 50 per cent. reduction in rental as its programme.[2] In the election of 1886 Trevelyan's Scottish Crofter's Act of 1886 figured on the addresses of several Liberal candidates in Wales. On economic as on other grounds, tension was rising in the country-side.

There was not at this stage a coherent radical attitude towards Welsh land, as there was towards ecclesiastical, temperance, and educational questions. The more cautious element among Welsh Liberals preferred to emphasize the social divisions of the country-side, the subjection of Wales rather than its poverty—'short building leases, excessive game preserving, precarious tenure of chapels and eviction of Nonconformists and Liberals'.[3] Of the new members returned in 1885, Bryn Roberts (Eifion) championed this view. But a rising tide of opinion, of which the vocal 'Young Wales' group was the spearhead, and Thomas Edward Ellis the major spokesman, demanded economic remedies as well as social equality. This element took inspiration from an older, native tradition stemming from 'S. R.' and Michael Daniel Jones. It was the economic exploitation of the tenant that they stressed as much as religious discrimination and political intimidation. In the *Celt*, the Rev. Pan Jones even advocated land nationalization and acted as mentor to rising young radicals such as Herbert Lewis and Lloyd George.[4] This difference of emphasis was to impede the formulation of an economic programme on

---

[1] For Vincent, see the *Dictionary of National Biography* and the *Dictionary of Welsh Biography*. The most useful of his writings are his *Tenancy in Wales* (1889); *The Land Question in North Wales* (1896); and *The Land Question in South Wales* (1897).

[2] *Land Commission, Evidence*, vol. iv (1894), qu. 63,999 ff. (Gee's evidence).

[3] Humphreys-Owen to Rendel, 5 July 1887 (N.L.W., Rendel Papers, xiv. 374).

[4] The Rev. Evan (Pan) Jones (1834-1922), Independent minister at Mostyn, Flint-shire, for over fifty years, was a pugnacious and influential champion of the tenant farmers of Wales. He edited *Y Celt* (1881-4) and *Cwrs y Byd* (1891-1905), both largely concerned with the land question. See his highly individual evidence before the Land Commissioners in 1894 (*Land Commission, Evidence*, vol. iii, qu. 56,200 ff.), in which he stated his opposition to the Liberal policy over land and urged nationalization and state appropriation of the unearned increment on land values. His biography in the *Dictionary of Welsh Biography* exaggerates his ineffectiveness.

a national basis. Even so, the pattern of deserted farmsteads and vacant holdings in Wales was a significant force in the social transformation of late Victorian Britain, where the discontents of the farming community were to shape the course of political debate for thirty years.

(v) *Disestablishment and Democracy, 1880–6*

Against this background of tension, it was disestablishment of the Church which was coming to the fore as the major, as well as the most contentious, issue in Welsh politics. The Commons debate of 1870 had intensified the passions of each side. Bitterness was heightened as a more concerted activity by the Liberation Society during the 1870's was paralleled by increasing revival within the established Church itself. In 1879 the Church Congress met for the first time in Wales, at Swansea, and Dean Edwards of Bangor created a sensation by asserting openly what many had long accepted tacitly, that the Church consisted of only a small minority of the Welsh people.[1] Ravenstein's statistics showed that over a million of the Welsh population habitually spoke in Welsh, and over 800,000 of these, claimed the Dean, were nonconformists. These were no mere paper figures. Welsh nonconformists contributed annually £300,000 in voluntary donations. Other Churchmen were alarmed at the estrangement of the Church from the new currents of public life in Wales. Lord Aberdare complained that Anglicans were showing 'ill-disguised hostility' towards the new undenominational college at Aberystwyth. 'I should be far better pleased', he wrote to a Welsh clergyman, 'if . . . the clergy sometimes joined in promoting objects of general Welsh interest outside the immediate interest of the Church' and he instanced higher education.[2] It should be stated that this was a somewhat harsh judgement, as the Aberdare Committee later found that Churchmen had made a larger share of contributions towards higher education than members of any other denomination.[3]

Reluctantly, traditional attitudes towards the Welsh language were being jettisoned. Archbishop Benson wrote to Gladstone in 1883: 'It seems as if for all practical purposes, Welsh must be regarded

---

[1] *Report of the Nineteenth Annual meeting of the Church Congress at Swansea, 1879* (London, 1880), pp. 354–8.
[2] Lord Aberdare to the Rev. T. Walters, 23 July 1875 (*Letters of Lord Aberdare*, vol. ii, p. 31).
[3] *Report*, p. xvii. The respective proportions were: Churchmen 33 per cent.; Methodists 29 per cent.; Independents 24 per cent.; others 14 per cent.

as a permanent language for not less than a century to come, and that, in the desire to hasten its departure, grave mistakes are made which alienate the people from the clergy.'[1] The attitude of the Blue Books died hard. As we have seen, the first intimation of this was a new attitude towards the Welsh episcopate. In 1874 Disraeli had followed Gladstone's lead by appointing another Welsh-speaking Welshman, Basil Jones, to the see of St. David's, in succession to Connop Thirlwall. This proved to be hardly a concession to national sentiment, since Jones was to do the Church immense harm by his notorious charge to his diocese in 1886, in which he asserted that 'Wales was but a geographical expression', in the same relation to England as were the Highlands to Scotland.[2]

When Bishop Ollivant of Llandaff died in 1882, Gladstone gave much care again towards securing a Welsh successor. As in 1870, the same flood of exhortation and acrimony engulfed the unfortunate Prime Minister. Lord Aberdare was again pessimistic. It was difficult to find a bishop among 'a clergy still, after all their progress, of so low a tone as the majority of the indigenous, home-educated clergy of Wales'.[3] He knew of no suitable candidate. 'All parties . . . give you credit for your desperate efforts to find a true Welshman at St. Asaph —few, very few, would desire to see the experiment repeated.'[4] Others, however, had a different viewpoint. Bishop Hughes of St. Asaph contrasted the position of the Church in the mining valleys of the diocese with the mass of Welsh chapels.[5] On the other hand, the Bishop of Bangor stated that the fundamental difficulty was that the sons of the gentry did not speak Welsh as a rule, 'and we are obliged to choose our clergy from a class where the general tone is far too low'.[6] Some Welshmen advocated the Broad Churchman, Principal Jayne of Lampeter, and more the controversial ritualist Dean of Bangor, popular among nonconformists and an ardent supporter of temperance and educational reform. But these very qualities made him suspect to others. Gladstone reflected: 'perhaps half the letters I receive are about him; all vehement, whether aye or no'.[7] A dozen

---

[1] Archbishop Benson to Gladstone, 23 July 1883 (B.M., Add. MSS., 44109, f. 40).
[2] For Jones, see *Dictionary of Welsh Biography*; Vyrnwy Morgan, *Political and Educational Leaders*, pp. 149–56; H. M. Vaughan, op. cit., p. 115.
[3] Aberdare to Gladstone, 3 July 1882 (B.M., Add. MSS., 44087, f. 124).
[4] Aberdare to Gladstone, 19 Dec. 1882 (ibid., f. 135).
[5] Bishop of St. Asaph to Gladstone, 22 Dec. 1882 (B.M., Add. MSS., 44478, ff. 164–9).
[6] Bishop of Bangor to Gladstone, 2 Jan. 1883 (B.M., Add. MSS., 44479, f. 30).
[7] Gladstone to Bishop of Bangor, 25 Dec. 1882 (B.M., Add. MSS., 44478, f. 196).

candidates were paraded and rejected. In despair, Gladstone lamented: 'A vacancy in a Welsh see costs me more trouble than six English vacancies.' It was important to select a Welshman; 'yet there is special danger, for among the more stirring Welsh clergy there is much wordy and windy preaching as among the Irish'.[1] Eventually the final choice was Archdeacon Lewis of St. David's, 'a pis-aller' and 'an inferior Basil Jones', in the view of Lord Aberdare,[2] and violently attacked by the octogenarian Lady Llanover in what Gladstone termed 'a long rigmarole',[3] but at least possessed of the appropriate national qualifications.

Statistics appeared to show that the revival in the Church was indeed making progress. By 1886 its communicants were enumerated as 81,474, Sunday School pupils as 68,690, and its churches as 1,490.[4] But nonconformity still maintained a clear ascendancy, as the Aberdare Committee recognized in 1881.[5] By 1890, both Methodists and Independents, the two largest sects, gave their totals as over 120,000 members each, while the estimate for the total number of adherents ('hearers' as well as members) for the four major denominations was 815,974.[6] Every major social and cultural movement in Wales derived its impetus from nonconformist leadership.

It was disestablishment which symbolized the nonconformist campaign for social equality, and between 1880 and 1886 the campaign in Wales underwent a fundamental transformation. In 1880 the initiative on the part of the sects lay still essentially with the Liberation Society. The major activity of the Society at this time was directed towards Scotland, where Gladstone's recent speeches had seemed to encourage the demand for Scottish disestablishment.[7] But in Wales it was noted that nine of the members returned in 1880 had supported the Liberation Society either as subscribers or speakers, while a further ten were believed to be sympathetic.[8] The Society noted too that an important principle was enshrined in the Sunday Closing Act and the inquiry into Welsh higher education. The Chairman of the Parliamentary Committee of the Society believed that 'an

[1] Gladstone to the Bishop of Durham, 28 Dec. 1882 (B.M., Add. MSS., 44478, ff. 271–2).
[2] Aberdare to Gladstone, 31 Dec. 1882 (B.M., Add. MSS., 44087, ff. 165–70).
[3] Lady Llanover to Gladstone, 14 Jan. 1883 (B.M., Add. MSS., 44479, ff. 121–4).
[4] *Church Times*, 16 Dec. 1887.
[5] *Report*, p. xlviii.
[6] *Royal Commission on the Church and other Religious Bodies in Wales* (1910), vol. vi (statistics), pp. 8, 23. See Appendix C.
[7] Liberation Society MSS., 12 Apr. 1880.   [8] Ibid.

agitation for the Disest. of the *Church of England in Wales* would be entered on with enthusiasm by Welsh Nonconformists, and the Soc. would thereby be furnished with a leverage in Wales such as it has not hitherto possessed', although it was not suggested that a Welsh Disestablishment Bill was practicable.[1] An early triumph in the new Parliament was the 1880 Burials Act, piloted through the House by Osborne Morgan as Judge-Advocate-General, which remedied a long-standing nonconformist grievance.[2]

The Society was still unwilling to acknowledge the separate status of Wales: the 'Welsh Tracts' which the Society published from October 1877 were merely general theoretical arguments translated into Welsh. A giant Liberationist meeting at Caernarvon in November 1883 was attended by only three Welsh members of Parliament, Rendel and the two veterans, Richard and Dillwyn. Even so, in finance and organization, the Society provided the basic framework for pressure for disestablishment. In December 1883 a completely new constitution for the Society was created in Wales, with regional councils in North and South Wales, and local sub-agents in Llanfyllin, Llanrug, Abergele, Felin-foel, Aberystwyth, and Swansea.[3] The resources of thousands of exile Welshmen in Manchester and London were also harnessed to the cause of religious equality.[4]

The first impression that Welsh disestablishment thus made on the political parties was on the increasingly powerful Liberationist wing of the Liberal Party. Its leading spokesman was Joseph Chamberlain, at the height of his influence as a radical reformer. On Gee's invitation, he visited Wales in October 1884, the first major political figure to do so. At Newtown (18 October) and Denbigh (25 October) his militant pronouncements on behalf of disestablishment and land reform aroused wild enthusiasm. Rendel had written that Wales urgently needed a voice in the cabinet,[5] and for the first time a cabinet minister had committed himself on behalf of Welsh disestablishment.

Chamberlain's campaign reached its climax in the general election

---

[1] Liberation Society MSS., 12 Sept. 1881.

[2] Osborne Morgan had repeatedly introduced a Burials Bill as a private member between 1870 and 1880. Its object was to allow nonconformists to perform burial in parish churchyards with their own forms of service. It was later suggested before the Royal Commission on the Welsh Churches in 1907 that many nonconformists refused to take advantage of the act, lest they antagonize the rector (*Evidence*, vol. iii, qu. 22,147–9). Also see Osborne Morgan, 'Blots in the Burials Act', *Cymru Fydd*, Jan. 1888, pp. 7–13.

[3] Liberation Society MSS., 3 Dec. 1883.

[4] Ibid., 10 Mar., 17 Apr. 1884.

[5] Rendel to Sir Michael Grant-Duff, 7 Oct. 1884 (*Personal Papers*, p. 227).

of November–December 1885: 'disestablishment all round' formed the sixth item of his Unauthorized Programme. It was this that helped those fissures in his party that were fatally widened by the Irish Home Rule Bill. Gladstone, in particular, in spite of his growing sympathy with a variety of Welsh demands, was hesitant to commit himself on the question over which he had committed himself so uncompromisingly in 1870. He told the electors that Scottish disestablishment should be decided according to the wishes of the Scottish people, a view expressed earlier by Hartington, but he would not regard the case of Wales as analogous. To pronounce on the matter before the election would, he told Henry Richard, 'be premature, and would tend to seriously disorganize the action of the Liberal Party in the country generally'.[1]

But events were forcing Gladstone's hands. Scores of Liberal candidates pledged themselves to vote for disestablishment, while the Whig section of the Party organized a counterblast in the form of a letter in *The Times* of 4 November, signed by fourteen Liberal peers, including the Dukes of Westminster, Bedford, and Somerset, warning Liberal churchmen of the danger. On 13 November another letter appeared, this time from the Earl of Selborne stating his reluctance to vote for any 'Liberal' (*sic*) who proposed disestablishment or disendowment of the Church. This sparked off a pained controversy with Gladstone.[2] Gladstone said that he had attempted to avoid determining Liberal votes on the issue of disestablishment, but he doubted whether it could be excluded 'by those of us who have sat in Cabinet with Chamberlain and Dilke'. He believed that the Liberal Party would come to grief in a few years, 'perhaps on this very question'. Selborne, in reply, denied that he would oppose every advocate of disestablishment (he quoted Bright as an example), 'but as between mere party and such a great national interest as I conceive the maintenance of the Established Church to be, the national interest ought to be preferred'.[3] But the final breach between Gladstone and Selborne was not to come over the Church question, about which they were still largely agreed, but over home rule.[4]

Despite the hostility of churchmen, Liberationists made immense

[1] Lord Richard Grosvenor to Richard, 11 Aug. 1885 (N.L.W., Richard MSS., 5505B).

[2] This correspondence ensued from 14 Nov. to 24 Nov. 1885 (B.M., Add. MSS., 44298, ff. 191–200). It is printed *in extenso* in Selborne's *Memorials* (London, 1898), vol. ii, pp. 182–7.

[3] Selborne to Gladstone, 17 Nov. 1885 (B.M., Add. MSS., 44298, f. 193).

[4] Selborne to Gladstone, 28 Jan. 1886 (ibid., f. 203).

gains at the general election of 1885, the nearest point ever attained to the accomplishment of disestablishment in England. Chamberlain's Unauthorized Programme brought Gladstone his majority of 86 in Britain, while 171 Liberals were believed to favour disestablishment.[1] Carvell Williams, secretary of the Liberation Society, was returned for Nottingham.

In Wales, however, the whole controversy was transformed. The Reform and Redistribution Acts of 1884–5 created a political revolution here, more profound even than that of 1868. The Reform Act turned Wales into a political democracy, enfranchising not only the rural vote on a basis of household suffrage, but also thousands of working-class voters, miners, tinplaters, and steelworkers, in the industrial valleys. Glamorgan was changed from a two-member constituency with 12,785 votes in 1880 into five new county divisions, with a combined electorate of 43,449. Monmouthshire, a two-member constituency with 7,609 votes in 1880, became three new constituencies, with a total electorate of 31,541. In rural areas such as Anglesey and Merioneth, the change was equally dramatic. In all, the Welsh county electorate rose from 74,936 to 200,373. While restrictions on the franchise remained—registration requirements and the need for assessment for the poor rate, which disfranchised many working-class voters—political power had clearly been revolutionized. Even more significant was the attendant Redistribution Bill, which transformed the Welsh constituencies into a pattern recognizably modern. Like Ireland, Wales was favoured by the redistribution. While England received approximately one member per 54,000 of the population, for Wales the ratio was one per 45,342. Thus the preponderance the Conservatives demanded to maintain the representation of rural England worked to the advantage of the working-class of Wales. A larger number of distinctively working-class single-member seats was created, elected on a basis of simple majority voting. Five close boroughs, Beaumaris, Cardigan, Haverfordwest, Radnor, and Brecon were disfranchised, and an additional member given to the town division of Swansea. The new system worked to the disadvantage of large urban communities. The great port of Cardiff, with 85,000 inhabitants, returned one member alone, the same as Montgomery District, a network of scattered villages with a popula-

---

[1] Liberation Society MSS., 14 Dec. 1885. For the views of the members returned in 1885 see also W. S. Crawshay and F. W. Read, *The Politics of the Commons* (London, 1886).

tion of only 19,925, or Caernarvon District (population 28,891), the future seat of David Lloyd George, which survived all electoral changes until 1948. But in all this diversity of constituencies, the nation-wide impact of radical nonconformity was the dominant feature. Only in the anglicized border areas, south Monmouthshire (still dominated by the Morgans of Tredegar after 400 years), the Vale of Glamorgan, Radnorshire, Montgomery, and Denbigh Boroughs and the dockyards of Pembrokeshire, did Conservatism survive in any significant strength, although the large and heterogeneous electorate of Swansea and Cardiff made them difficult to organize and therefore uncertain in their allegiance. Elsewhere in Wales Conservatism enjoyed a ghostly existence until after the First World War, with the *plasty* as a beleaguered outpost of traditionalism in an area dominated by radical sentiment.

The debates on the Redistribution Bill in the Commons had been curious. Gladstone, by now the venerated hero of Wales, was obliged to defend the excessive representation of Wales by denying the need for separate treatment. 'The distinction between England and Wales, except in a recital in an Act of Parliament for the purpose of indicating their unity, is totally unknown to our constitution.'[1] He conveniently forgot the Welsh Sunday Closing Act, in which he himself had helped to create this distinction! Conversely, Conservatives were forced to put forward a strange form of Welsh separatism, demanding different treatment for Wales, in order to justify the reduction of her members from thirty-four to twenty-five. Their attempt failed, and thus redistribution, the price demanded by the House of Lords for their acquiesence in parliamentary reform, began a new era in the political history of Wales.

The effects at the election of 1885 were striking. The Conservative Party was swept out almost completely, retaining only four of the thirty-four Welsh seats. Here, indeed, even more than 1868, was the *annus mirabilis* for Welsh Liberalism.[2] Wales, like other parts of the United Kingdom, showed a marked change in the character of its members. Of the thirty-four Welsh members returned, only nine represented the landed gentry, while fourteen came from industry or commerce and a further nine from the legal profession. Over twenty were Welsh-born and about half of these Welsh in speech. Further,

---

[1] *Parl. Deb.*, 3rd ser., ccxciv, p. 378.
[2] A. H. Dodd, *Studies in Stuart Wales* (Cardiff, 1952), p. 215, so describes the 1868 elections in Wales.

fourteen of them were nonconformists. They included some prominent leaders of Welsh dissent, men whose public experience had been
forged in the turbulence of the years since 1868. They included
Alfred Thomas (Glamorgan East), president of the Welsh Baptist
Union, John Roberts (Flint District), chairman of the Methodist
Association of North Wales, and Bryn Roberts (Eifion), another
prominent Welsh Methodist,[1] sober, moderate *bourgeois*, whose politics were dictated by their religion. To a considerable degree contests
in rural areas were fought almost entirely on Welsh questions—
disestablishment, land reform, higher education, temperance. This,
for instance, was the case in Eifion, where Bryn Roberts, a traditionalist follower of the Cobdenite school, defeated Lord Penrhyn's
agent, Ellis Nanney, by nearly 2,000 votes. In a famous victory in
Denbighshire East, Osborne Morgan triumphed over Sir Watkin
Williams Wynn by 393 votes, thus terminating for ever the Wynn
hegemony of 169 years. In all kinds of constituencies, Liberalism
triumphed. Even in the large, sprawling constituency of Cardiff, E. J.
Reed, the naval expert, managed to keep his random coalition of Irish
Catholics and Liberal nonconformists, trade unionists and the Cardiff
Chamber of Commerce in line in this, the largest and, electorally,
the most expensive single-member constituency in the kingdom.[2]
Wealth, rather than Welshness, was the criterion here. In the industrial south, working men preserved a unity of outlook with middle-
class dissenters. Even where a breach did appear, in the Rhondda,
where William Abraham, 'Mabon', agent of the Cambrian Miners'
Association, triumphed over a Liberal employer, it was soon clear
that Abraham, the apostle of industrial peace, was an old-fashioned
Liberal in his political ideas.[3] In Rhondda and in Glamorgan East,
the Liberal Associations were harmoniously reconstituted under the
name of 'The Liberal and Labour Association'. A quarter of a century was to pass before Liberalism itself came under fire.

The effect of these changes in the political structure on the agitation
for disestablishment was profound. The Liberation Society had
created a Leviathan which was rapidly to supersede its authority.
The Society's function had been to create a pressure group in the

[1] For Bryn Roberts, see J. Arthur Price's articles in *Welsh Outlook*, Mar. 1931
and in *Y Ddraig Goch*, June, July 1931. Also see E. Morgan Humphreys in *Y Llenor*,
1943. For Alfred Thomas, see *South Wales Daily News*, 16 Feb. 1898.

[2] Although in the election of 1885, the Irish vote in Cardiff, as in Swansea and
Newport, went to the Conservative candidates, in accordance with Parnell's manifesto
(*Cambria Daily Leader*, 28 Nov. 1885; *South Wales Daily News*, 30 Nov. 1885).

[3] See Eric Wyn Evans, *Mabon* (Cardiff, 1959).

period of inadequate representation for the nonconformist majority of Wales. But democracy had now transferred political power for the first time to the majority of the Welsh people, and their own religious organizations were henceforward to take the initiative with denominational rivalry put aside. If the personnel of leadership was often the same—Gee, Richard, Osborne Morgan—the pressures behind them were very different. Disestablishment was urged less on traditional Liberationalist arguments, based on the unscriptural and unjust nature of any established creed, and more on grounds akin to nationalism. The most damaging criticism launched at the Church now was that of 'the alien Church', *Eglwys Loegr*, the Church of England in Wales.

The significance of this was shortly seen when after much delay Dillwyn, the veteran Liberationist who sat for Swansea, moved a resolution on behalf of Welsh disestablishment in the Commons on 9 March 1886, the first since Watkin Williams's motion sixteen years earlier.[1] Now Dillwyn based his case frankly on Welsh nationality, while Richard, his seconder, gave a long and tedious account of the historical alienation of the Church from the Welsh people. The main opposition speaker, Raikes (Cambridge University), developed arguments that Conservatives were to reiterate monotonously in countless subsequent debates. It was, he maintained, an historical fallacy to describe the Celtic Church as 'alien'. He also denied that any such entity as the Welsh Church existed: it was coterminous with the Church of England. He quoted statistics to illustrate the recent revival of the Church, and denied it was a small minority. He alleged that nonconformists feared the true test, a religious census, and here he struck home. In support, R. A. Cross said that Dillwyn's real aim was English disestablishment.

Not surprisingly the Conservative Party was united against the motion. But the debate failed to give a real indication of Liberal opinion, being complicated by an amendment by two Liberals, Grey and MacInnes, to substitute Church reform for disestablishment in the motion. Dillwyn's motion eventually failed by 229 votes to 241, but the 229 supporters of the motion included five members of the government, among them Harcourt, who explained that they were voting for the motion in order to defeat Grey's amendment.[2]

---

[1] *Parl. Deb.*, 3rd ser., vol. ccciii, pp. 305 ff.
[2] The other four were Childers, Mundella, Herbert Gladstone, and Osborne Morgan (Parliamentary Secretary to the Colonies).

This probably determined some Liberal votes. Nevertheless the total of 229 was impressive, an immense advance on the meagre 45 of 1870, and a great encouragement to Welsh nonconformity. Liberals had voted for the motion by 181 to 23, the latter including Hartington and a Welsh member, H. G. Allen (Pembroke District). Welsh members voted in favour by twenty-seven to three. Most of the cabinet were conspicuously absent, while Gladstone had forbidden Chamberlain from voting.[1]

For the first time, Welsh disestablishment had become a national issue in British politics. Although Chamberlain's failure to vote caused some disappointment, it was clear that a large proportion of the Liberal Party accepted the principle of Welsh disestablishment. Even Gladstone, whose views on disestablishment were still unclear, accepted the right of the Welsh people to determine questions that concerned them, and themselves alone.

(vi) *The Impact of Ireland*

The major force in transforming disestablishment and the other demands of Welsh Liberals into something resembling a nationalist programme, however, was the tumultuous history of Ireland. To most Englishmen and to many Scots, events in Ireland were an ominous warning; to a growing body of younger Welshmen, they were an inspiring example.

Until late in the nineteenth century, Welshmen had shown little sympathy towards the aspirations of their fellow Celts across St. George's Channel.[2] Hatred of Roman Catholicism was an enduring emotion for nearly all Welshmen, and from the days of the Maynooth grant onwards, Welsh Calvinists had resented the activities of popish priests in Irish politics. Further, Welsh hostility had been intensified by the emigration of many thousands of Irishmen (100,000 were estimated resident in South Wales in 1921), fugitives of the Famine, many of them destitute, illiterate, and disease-ridden, into the South Wales and North Wales coalfields and the dock areas of Cardiff, Swansea, and Newport, as well as to some seaside ports such as Fishguard, Bangor, Llandudno, Rhyl, Portmadoc, Holyhead. In the big towns of the South, the Irish of the Greenhill area of Swansea or the Adamsdown district of Cardiff preserved an isolated

---

[1] Garvin, op. cit., vol. ii, p. 292.

[2] There is no adequate account of the relationship between Wales and Ireland in the nineteenth century. C. O'Rahilly, *Ireland and Wales* (London, 1924) is a brief account covering the whole of Irish history.

existence, segregated physically from their Welsh neighbours, and often the centres of drunken violence. In 1882 there had been riots directed against Irishmen in Tredegar, following the murders of Cavendish and Burke in Phoenix Park, Dublin. So numerous were the Irish in mining valleys that the Royal Monmouthshire Militia was popularly designated the 'Pope's Own', owing to its high proportion of papists.[1] The sympathy evinced by Gee, 'S. R.', or 'Hiraethog' towards Kossuth, Garibaldi, and most other nationalist leaders overseas stopped abruptly at St. George's Channel. The sole friend of Irish nationalists in the Welsh press for many years was Robert Ambrose Jones ('Emrys ap Iwan'), in *Y Faner*, himself a man of cosmopolitan background.

In the years after 1880 there came a gradual and significant change in attitudes. On a wide range of issues, the requirements of Wales seemed to find a direct parallel in Ireland. Irish disestablishment had spurred on the cause of religious equality in Wales. The Welsh Sunday Closing Act had followed upon a similar measure for Ireland. Welsh higher education was stimulated by the progress of the university movement in Ireland. Above all, the Irish Land Act of 1881, granting free sale of holdings, fixity of tenure, and arbitration on rents by a land court, encouraged similar demands in Wales. Here, too, there seemed to be a similar social structure, a poor, struggling peasantry largely out of sympathy, in race and religion, with an exploiting landowning class. The success of Parnell's obstruction in the Commons encouraged the Rev. Herber Evans to advocate a national party for Wales also.[2] Even the concept of Welsh home rule was being modestly entertained. Perhaps the main connexion of Wales and Ireland in these years was a cultural one. The young patriots who were associated with the University College at Aberystwyth in the early 1880's were profoundly influenced by the idea of nationalism and more intuitively sympathetic to the ideals of Young Ireland. They were slow to respond to the Parnellite cause: the young Tom Ellis welcomed the Crimes Act of 1884, and it is hard to discover in the period before 1886 the influence of the cultural nationalism of Thomas Davis which Ellis later claimed as a major force in shaping his political philosophy. In practice, however, the young visionaries of *Cymru Fydd* were increasingly to draw upon Irish experience. In particular, Tom Ellis, regarded by many as the potential 'Parnell of

[1] H. M. Vaughan, op. cit., p. 46.
[2] Rev. Herber Evans to Gee, 'Friday', 1883, (N.L.W., Gee MSS., 8310E, 440).

Wales', blended the traditions of Bala and Aberystwyth College with the surge of ideas from Jowett's Oxford, the sensitive appreciation of Celtic culture with the organic folk-state as conceived by T. H. Green and the Idealists, the sense of imperial mission as preached by Ruskin, and the 'constructive' programme of social and political reform as outlined by Toynbee and the Fabians. The result was a comprehensive vision of nationality, more common in central and eastern Europe, part cultural, part political, which transcended the sectarianism of the radicals of the Gee school, even though it implied an equally militant attitude towards practical questions such as disestablishment. Other very young men, such as the barristers Ellis Griffith and Llewelyn Williams, subscribed to the same vision, while the great historian John Edward Lloyd suffused arid academic detail with the passionate glow of patriotic devotion.

It was indicative of the strength of these new ideas that the first approach from Wales to an Irish politician went not to the aloof and aristocratic Parnell, who despised the Welsh, but to the Social Democrat-folk nationalist, Michael Davitt, the very personification of 'widening the area of agitation' beyond Ireland. Despite the bitter opposition of Gee and the older Welsh radical leaders, Davitt spoke at Ffestiniog in February 1886 with Michael Daniel Jones and David Lloyd George on the same platform, the Nestor of the social nationalism of *y werin* with his youthful disciple. Davitt inspired a most enthusiastic response from the quarrymen and subsequently addressed several other meetings elsewhere in North Wales, which he and H. J. Massingham were to find 'the most hopeful and attractive Social Democracy in Europe'.[1] The young militant Tom Ellis drew the moral that race-consciousness should heighten the awareness of nationality and that Welsh and Irish nationalism should be merged with the Social Democrats in a great campaign of social regeneration.[2]

It was clear, nevertheless, that Wales was as deeply divided as the rest of the country when Gladstone's conversion to Irish home rule was inadvertently announced in December 1885. At the general election the powerful Irish vote in Cardiff, Swansea, and Newport had been swung to the support of the Conservative candidates, in accordance with Parnell's manifesto, to the resentment of nonconformists. Many in Wales were still under the spell of Chamber-

[1] Ellis to Daniel, 15 May 1898 (N.L.W., Daniel Papers, 2010). There are some interesting letters from Davitt and Michael Jones at this time in N.L.W., MS. 8823c.
[2] Ellis to Daniel, 17 Feb. 1886 (N.L.W., Daniel MSS., 302). Also see Ellis's article 'Gwleidyddiaeth Genedlaethol', *Y Traethodydd*, Oct. 1886, pp. 186-92.

lain, the apostle of disestablishment, and the 'political idol of the Free Churches'.[1] Many Welshmen followed his directive to Thomas Gee that 'the more the details of the Bill are investigated the less they will recommend themselves to Welshmen'.[2] Among the Methodists in particular there was much heart-searching, where, in addition to Gee, such prominent men as David Davies, M.P., and Richard Davies, M.P., declared against home rule. Gee fulminated against the Home Rule Bill in the *Y Faner*: he objected to making Ireland a 'subordinate and tributary state'[3] and was apprehensive over freedom of conscience for Irish Protestants. But in most parts of Wales Liberals agreed with a Montgomeryshire Liberal who felt that he 'would trust only Gladstone in this doubtful business'.[4] Gladstone's influence swung over Henry Richard and the Rev. John Thomas,[5] *Y Cymro*, *Y Genedl*, and significantly, even the Methodist organ, *Y Goleuad*. While there was general dislike of the land purchase provisions, the farmers of Llanidloes spoke for many in declaring that 'the contest ought not to be fought purely on the Irish question, that we really did not care very much about it, and that we should leave it in the hands of those like Mr. Rendel and Mr. Gladstone who had thoroughly studied it'.[6] Along a very wide spectrum, from traditional apathy to the ardent idealism of the Ellis school, a great many Welshmen could reconcile themselves to home rule, even if it meant 'Rome rule' as well. Plainly, however, Welsh Liberalism was deeply divided. When Hartington, Bright, and others formed the 'Loyal and Patriotic Union' in May 1886, it was joined by such well-known Welsh Liberal members of Parliament as Col. Cornwallis-West, David Davies, Sir J. J. Jenkins, Sir H. H. Vivian, and Sir Robert Cunliffe,[7] all, however, representative of Welsh Whiggery rather than of Welsh radicalism.

When, in the vote on the second Reading on 7 June, the Bill was defeated by 343 votes to 313, twenty-two Welsh Liberals voted for it, seven Liberals and four Welsh Conservatives voted against it, and one Liberal (Richard Davies) abstained. Gladstone at once dissolved Parliament.

[1] Garvin, op. cit., vol. ii, p. 297.
[2] Chamberlain to Gee, 26 Apr. 1886 (N.L.W., Gee MSS., 8305c, 15).
[3] So described by R. W. Dale in a letter to Henry Richard, 20 July 1886 (N.L.W., Richard MSS., 5503B).
[4] Humphreys-Owen to Rendel, 27 Apr. 1886 (N.L.W., Rendel Papers, xiv. 278). Cf. J. Jones to Rendel, 30 Apr. 1886 (N.L.W., Rendel Papers, ix. 337), *Y Goleuad*, 15 May, 19 June 1886.
[5] Owen Thomas and J. M. Rees, op. cit., p. 437.
[6] Humphreys-Owen to Rendel, 6 June 1886 (N.L.W., Rendel Papers, xiv. 187A).
[7] *Baner ac Amserau Cymru*, 5 May 1886; *Y Tyst*, 21 May, 11 June 1886.

The general election of 1886 has been called 'the most decisive ever held in Wales'.[1] It was fought in the country as a whole over the Home Rule Bill, but in Wales local issues were of equal if not of greater importance. Most Liberals, including Stuart Rendel, felt 'we must go to the country on the Gladstone ticket, say as little as we can about Ireland and as much about Church and Land'.[2] Gee, in *Y Faner*, tried to divert attention solely to Welsh affairs. He drew up a comprehensive programme of land reform—security of tenure, inheritance of holdings by tenants, state loans for the purchase of holdings, abolition of the Game Laws and enfranchisement of leaseholders together with disestablishment, intermediate education, standardization of the rates, and payment of members.[3] But Gee, 'Philistine and time-server', in the view of Tom Ellis,[4] was under fire from many quarters and his influence was temporarily on the wane. Liberal candidates, with more or less enthusiasm,[5] put Irish home rule first on their programmes. The other items usually related solely to Wales, with disestablishment and land reform in the forefront. Bryn Roberts (Eifion) asserted that to oppose home rule would mean the delay of all these measures. Tom Ellis, candidate in Merioneth, went farther still: he claimed that Wales, like Ireland, had too long been ignored at Westminster, and the final item on his address was Welsh home rule. Welsh Liberal Unionists generally supported Welsh national claims but laid the main emphasis on the 'betrayal' of Ulster.

There was profound apprehension of 'Welsh disasters' in Liberal circles.[6] Yet, in fact, Liberal control of Wales was strikingly confirmed. While the Gladstonians fared disastrously in Britain as a whole, retaining only 191 seats, in Wales and Monmouthshire twenty-five Liberals, three Liberal Unionists, and six Conservatives were returned. Of the Liberal Unionists, the eighty-three year old C. R. M. Talbot (Mid-Glamorgan) announced his support for Gladstone during the campaign,[7] while Sir Hussey Vivian (Swansea District)

---

[1] By Llewelyn Williams, in Viscountess Rhondda (ed.), *D. A. Thomas, Viscount Rhondda* (London, 1921), p. 58.

[2] Humphreys-Owen to Rendel, 20 June 1886 (N.L.W., Rendel Papers, xiv. 293).

[3] *Baner ac Amserau Cymru*, 9 June 1886.

[4] Ellis to Daniel, 17 Feb. 1886 (N.L.W., Daniel Papers, 302).

[5] Sir Edward Reed (Cardiff) and William Rathbone (Arfon) had many reservations, and both later generally opposed the Bill of 1893.

[6] Carvell Williams to Richard, 7 July 1886 (N.L.W., Richard MSS., 5505B), *Y Goleuad*, 3 July 1886.

[7] *Baner ac Amserau Cymru*, 9 June 1886. *Y Goleuad*, 3 July 1886. Talbot had represented Glamorgan continuously since 1830. He had long been under fire in his constituency for his conservative attitude (cf. *South Wales Daily News*, 14 July 1885).

rejoined the Liberal camp immediately after the contest. This left Gee's protégé Col. Cornwallis-West (West Denbighshire), a wealthy landowner returned unopposed, as the sole Liberal Unionist member in Wales. The Conservatives did capture three marginal borough seats, Pembroke, Monmouth, and also Caernarvon, where the Liberals had an unpopular candidate. Elsewhere, Liberalism remained intact in rural areas and in the big towns alike. Osborne Morgan unexpectedly beat off the Wynn challenge in East Denbighshire by twenty-six votes. An even more remarkable Liberal triumph was in Cardiganshire, where the powerful and philanthropic industrialist, David Davies of Llandinam, with most of his own Methodist denomination behind him and with the backing of leading Cardiganshire Conservatives from Gogerddan, Nanteos, and Trawsgoed, was opposed by Bowen Rowlands, Q.C., a stranger to the constituency and a High Churchman who later became a Roman Catholic. In spite of all opposition, Bowen Rowlands won an astonishing victory by nine votes. In disgust, David Davies renounced his connexion with the University College at Aberystwyth.[1]

Perhaps the victory most closely observed was that of Tom Ellis in Merioneth. It would have been extraordinary if Ellis, a Methodist and the Welsh-speaking son of a tenant farmer, had been defeated, but none spoke more unequivocally the language of the new patriotic fervour coursing through Wales.

The 1886 election had a decisive influence on the political history of Wales. Joseph Chamberlain later declared that by supporting Gladstone Wales had indefinitely postponed disestablishment and other measures on which it had set its heart. Years later, in a discussion with Tom Ellis at the funeral of Thomas Gee, Lloyd George, always lukewarm towards Ireland, repeated this argument.[2] If Wales had declined to vote for home rule in 1886, Gladstone would, he alleged, have yielded and provided a compromise settlement based on 'home rule all round'. Instead, men like Chamberlain, Bright, Spurgeon, and Dale had been lost to Liberalism, and Welsh disestablishment had disappeared for ever. This argument is, however, extremely difficult to sustain. The elections of 1886 greatly advanced

---

[1] David Davies to Lewis Edwards, 19 Oct. 1886, quoted in T. I. Ellis (ed.), *Letters of Thomas Charles Edwards*, pp. 261–2. Davies complained, 'At the last Election I had to be protected by the Police or I should have been kicked perhaps to death', a reference to an incident at Aberystwyth. He also resented the failure of Principal Thomas Charles Edwards to vote for him (J. B. Rogers to T. C. Edwards, 19 Aug. 1886, ibid., p. 259).

[2] Herbert Lewis's diary, 3 Oct. 1898 (Penucha MSS.).

the causes of Liberals in Wales. The Liberal Party was sorely shattered, and only in 1906 would it again have a majority in England. Tory Democracy was gaining rapidly in the big cities. Thus Liberals were far more dependent on their strength in Scotland and Wales, and inevitably far more responsive to their demands. The years between 1886 and 1906 were to form the high noon of Welsh radicalism. Chamberlain had believed that he could persuade his Conservative colleagues to agree to disestablishment, with more generous terms for the Church than Gladstonians could secure, but events were to disprove him. His was virtually a lone voice in the Liberal Unionist ranks, amongst whom the High Churchman Selborne was a more characteristic figure than the Unitarian Chamberlain himself. Neither Conservatives nor Liberal Unionists showed the least disposition to compromise over Welsh disestablishment over the next thirty years. Before the election, many who later were to become Liberal Unionists had advocated disestablishment as an antidote to possible separatist demands in Wales. The Earl of Derby had said that he did not see 'why we should refuse to Welsh loyalty what we have granted to Irish sedition'.[1] But after 1886 the fear of a growing fragmentation and disunion in the Empire came to outweigh all other considerations: the virus of home rule was seen in the mildest of Welsh requests. Chamberlain's continued support of Welsh disestablishment down to 1895 came to be regarded as an individual eccentricity.

Conversely, for the Liberal Party, the election helped to generate a growing sensitivity for Welsh feelings. It is difficult to follow Professor R. T. Jenkins in seeing a mystery in the Welsh adherence to Gladstone in 1886,[2] and more difficult still to agree with him that Gladstone was out of sympathy with Welsh radicalism. Since 1870, as has been seen, Gladstone had shown an increasing awareness of Welsh national characteristics, in the Church, in temperance reform, and in education, more than any other statesman. Even over Welsh disestablishment, his overt hostility of 1870 had been much modified over the years. He had spoken repeatedly in debates on Welsh subjects, and it is not surprising that the professed ally of subject races, Italians, Bulgarians, the Afghan, and the Zulu, should find a warm response in a country which felt itself to be in a not wholly dissimilar

---

[1] *The Times*, 13 Oct. 1885. Also cf. leading article in *South Wales Daily News*, 13 Oct. 1885.

[2] R. T. Jenkins, 'The Development of Nationalism in Wales', *Sociological Review*, Apr. 1935, p. 171. This article is, nevertheless, a valuable analysis of the growth of national consciousness in Wales.

position. Gladstone, in addition, lived in North Wales, had married a Welsh lady, Catherine Glynne, and had attended the *eisteddfod* and other Welsh gatherings. Chamberlain, by comparison, although the apostle of radical reform, had shown little enough willingness to campaign for Welsh issues alone. The magnetism of his Radical Union, which almost drew in the young Lloyd George,[1] lost its attraction when Chamberlain, the Jack Cade of radical circles, appeared in alliance with Stanleys and Cavendishes. Thus after 1886 the attachment of 'gallant little Wales' to Gladstone was proof against all rebuffs.[2]

Perhaps the preference of Wales for Gladstone over Chamberlain is finally symptomatic of the new tenor in Welsh political life that had developed since 1868, a transition from radicalism towards nationalism. A number of factors had produced this transition. Democracy, in granting political authority to the majority of the Welsh people at the national, as subsequently at the local, level had served to reveal the latent nationalism contained in the popular radicalism of 1868, with Ellis and his friends as its spokesmen. The campaign for public education had provided that nationalism with a cultural ideal, and the land depression, with the spur of economic hardship. The Sunday Closing Act afforded a precedent for Welsh legislation, and the formation of a Welsh political party on the lines of the Irish was now an idea widely canvassed. Finally, disestablishment had become a symbol of national recognition. The Irish home rule schism was a fatal blow to the authority of the Liberation Society, and in later years it was the English Church rather than its establishment that was to rouse the passions of nonconformist Welshmen. In all these ways, the 'Welsh question' was becoming a political reality, and aggressive patriots such as Tom Ellis intended to force the needs of their country upon the imperial Parliament and the consciousness of the world beyond.

[1] J. Hugh Edwards, *Life of David Lloyd George*, vol. ii (1913), pp. 142–4.
[2] I have discussed Gladstone's part in Welsh history in two articles: 'Gladstone and Wales', *Welsh History Review*, vol. i, no. 1, 1960, pp. 65–82; 'Liberals, Nationalists and Mr. Gladstone', *Trans. Hon. Soc. Cymm.*, 1960, pp. 36–52.

III

THE WELSH PARLIAMENTARY PARTY
1886–1892

(i) *Disestablishment on the Liberal Programme*

AT Westminster, as in Wales itself, the election of 1886 ushered in
a period of unprecedented activity in the political history of Wales.
Hitherto the political parties had responded to the demands of the
Welsh representatives only in a spasmodic and dilatory manner. The
Welsh member of Parliament, in the words of Stuart Rendel, 'was
almost in an inferior category, a cheaper sort of member',[1] representing a constituency humble in status and meagre in resources. Now,
however, the freedom of manœuvre afforded by opposition and by
the fragmentation of the Liberal Party provided the Welsh, in common with other minorities, with novel opportunities. After a few
weeks in the House, Tom Ellis could report that 'the Welsh members
are gradually waking up. They are getting *uneasy.*'[2] Pressure was
building up for a more decisive effort in impressing the claims of
Welsh radicals than had been provided by the cautious Fabianism
of the ageing Welsh members. Ellis himself personified this growing
impatience, articulate, youthful, militant, 'burning with a peculiar
intensity',[3] and threatening in unspecified terms a 'plan of campaign'
for Wales no less than for Ireland.

Ellis, however, was a lonely voice among the Welsh members in
1886. Two groups among them were overwhelmingly predominant
at Westminster. One was headed by the veteran Henry Richard, who
had for two decades exercised an unofficial leadership over his colleagues. Richard's sympathies, however, lay essentially with bodies
such as the Liberation Society and the National Education League,
and with radicalism in general, rather than with any separate claims
of Wales. He had come back to Wales in middle age, with his political
career well advanced, and was 'the leader, or a prominent leader, of
a section of the House exceedingly English'.[4] He had never been

---

[1] *Personal Papers*, p. 313.
[2] Ellis to Daniel, 4 Sept. 1886 (N.L.W., Daniel Papers, 321).
[3] J. A. Spender, *Sir Robert Hudson: a Memoir* (London, 1930), p. 24.
[4] *Personal Papers of Lord Rendel*, p. 304.

forthright in campaigning for disestablishment in Wales alone, which he believed might well result in the loss of valuable educational endowments. 'Old hands' such as Dillwyn, Vivian, and Fuller-Maitland followed his lead.

The most influential section among the Welsh members, however, inclined neither to rebellion with Ellis nor to cosmopolitan radicalism with Richard. The majority adopted the standpoint of Stuart Rendel in urging pressure within the machinery of the Liberal Party to push forward the claims of Wales. In particular, they maintained that disestablishment, above all other issues, should form the centrepiece of a national programme. It implied, to Rendel, 'a clear and effective issue with all anglicizing influences in Wales, and a practical declaration of the case for Welsh Nationalization outside Wales'.[1] His first objective was to obtain the official support of the Liberal Party, which had so far refused to commit itself. On 28 October 1886 Rendel wrote to John Morley, who was to preside at the forthcoming meeting of the National Liberal Federation at Leeds, and was thus in a powerful position to shape party policy, urging on him that an official pronouncement be made on behalf of Welsh disestablishment. Morley's published reply was most explicit. Wales had too long 'subsisted on general expressions of sympathy', and disestablishment must henceforth be included among 'the active objects of the Liberal Party' on grounds both of abstract justice and of national self-determination. In private, Morley was less enthusiastic: he had 'some misgivings as to whether it is prudent at this moment to rouse a fresh antagonistic interest', and the meeting of the Federation at Leeds proved fruitless.[2] Even so, this forthright public proclamation by a Gladstonian leader presaged the eventual conversion of his colleagues also, and even of their mighty leader.

This initiative by Rendel confirmed the basic change in strategy that had already been indicated in the years after 1880. The disestablishment agitation in Wales was fast cutting adrift from the tutelage of the Liberation Society. The determination of the Society to work for 'disestablishment all round' not only made progress in Wales dependent on a conversion of English opinion, but also alienated nationally minded churchmen in Wales from the Liberal cause. Early in 1887, therefore, Rendel took steps to remove all remaining

---

[1] Ibid., p. 306. Also see Rendel's article on Welsh Disestablishment in the *Contemporary Review*, Dec. 1886.
[2] Morley to Rendel, 30 Oct. 1886 (N.L.W., Glansevern MSS., 271).

control from the Society. He circularized his colleagues, urging that Wales should fight on her own, and cease being 'the catspaw of the Liberation Society'.[1] Since the late election, new machinery had been designed to supersede the organizational framework that the Society alone had provided, for over twenty years. Disunity was the eternal danger to the scattered forces of Welsh Liberalism, and the need to merge together individual Liberal associations into closer union in Wales corresponded with a nation-wide upheaval in the machinery of the Liberal Party. Although the National Liberal Federation had rejected Chamberlain during the home rule crisis, Schnadhorst, its secretary and one of the few prominent Birmingham Liberals remaining in the Gladstonian camp, was anxious to enlarge the representation of local federations and to eliminate the domination of Birmingham. He advised Rendel that 'had you in Wales been not only federated but affiliated, you would have appeared at Leeds and you would probably have . . . got Welsh Disest. accepted as a Party plank'.[2] Schnadhorst was to play a major part in impressing the urgency of the question upon Gladstone.[3] In the next few months Liberal Federations were formed in North and South Wales, at Rhyl and Cardiff respectively, with the great majority of local Associations affiliated to them.[4] These Federations were to enjoy a somewhat ghostly existence over the next twenty years, occasionally flaring into violent energy as during the *Cymru Fydd* controversy. But their existence both as a party and as a co-ordinating machine destroyed the primacy of the Liberation Society in Wales. Liberationist veterans such as Thomas Gee and Dr. John Thomas assented that 'our business is with the great Liberal Party in England'.[5]

In the country as a whole, party opinions on Welsh disestablishment were gradually becoming polarized following the confusion of 1886. Conservatives, naturally, were inflexibly hostile towards disestablishment, and still more towards disendowment. In February 1887 the Leader of the House, W. H. Smith, refused to allow discus-

[1] Rendel to Gee, 18 Mar. 1887 (N.L.W., Gee MSS., 8308C, 258).

[2] Rendel to Humphreys-Owen, 18 Dec. 1886 (N.L.W., Glansevern MSS., 290).

[3] For example, see Schnadhorst to Gladstone, 21 Sept. 1891 (B.M., Add. MSS., 44295, ff. 250–1).

[4] The North Wales Liberal Federation was formed at Rhyl on 14 Dec. 1886, with Rendel as president and W. H. Tilston as secretary; the South Wales Liberal Federation was formed at Cardiff, January 1887, with Dillwyn as president and R. N. Hall as secretary. The executives of the two Federations were represented on a joint body termed the Welsh National Council. The *Annual Reports* of the two Federations form a very valuable source for the structure of Liberalism in Wales in the period 1886–92.

[5] Rev. John Thomas to Gee, 21 Mar. 1887 (N.L.W., Gee MSS., 8311D, 572).

sion of a motion in Dillwyn's name, the new rules of procedure being given precedence on the day allocated.[1] Welsh Tories, such as Arthur Price, not yet the nostalgic nationalist of later years, castigated 'men like Ellis who appeal to the vilest sectarian passions'.[2]

The Liberal Unionists, who held the balance of power in the House, were, however, far less predictable. Their organ, the *Spectator*, regarded Morley's October declaration as a trick designed to divide Chamberlain from his new associates. It conceded the theoretical merits of the case for disestablishment, and admitted that it might prove an antidote to any demand for Welsh home rule.[3] But the ideal of the integrity of the United Kingdom aroused insuperable apprehensions, and the *Spectator* became more and more hostile to Welsh radicalism. The schism over Irish policy made alliance between erstwhile colleagues difficult in any field, and Jacob Bright, Caine, Kenrick, and Richard Chamberlain, all vowed Liberationists, voted against discussion of Dillwyn's motion in February 1887.[4] The most notable amongst them, Joseph Chamberlain, continued to avow his sympathy for religious equality in Wales, and it was his views on this subject that provided the nominal cause for the breakdown of the 'Round Table Conference' and the projected Liberal reunion. His article in the *Baptist*, on 25 February 1887, strongly advocated religious equality in general, and in Wales in particular. He alleged that Welsh disestablishment and other reforms were being indefinitely postponed by Gladstone's obsession with Irish home rule. This was to prove his last open appearance as advocate for Wales although he voted for disestablishment down to 1895. Cornwallis-West and Lord Sudeley were his only supporters among the leading Welsh Liberals. In March 1887 the defection of Chamberlain, followed later on by that of Spurgeon, further enfeebled the Liberation Society.[5]

Many of Chamberlain's Liberal Unionist colleagues, on the other hand, were among the most zealous supporters of the Welsh Church. In particular, the Earl of Selborne and his son, Viscount Wolmer, were earnest advocates of 'Church defence'. Selborne believed that Morley's announcement in October had been made with Gladstone's

---

[1] *Parl. Deb.*, 3rd ser., vol. cccx, pp. 1778 ff.
[2] Arthur Price to J. E. Lloyd, n.d. (Bangor, Lloyd Papers, MSS., 314, no. 416).
[3] *Spectator*, 6 Nov. 1886.
[4] Rendel to Gee, 18 Feb. 1887 (N.L.W., Gee MSS., 8308c, 256). Caine was to become the father-in-law of two future Welsh members, Herbert Lewis and Herbert Roberts.
[5] *British Weekly*, 18 Mar. 1887. Also see the comments of the *Cambrian News*, 4 Mar. 1887.

approval,[1] and, indeed, the statement had an involuntary appearance. On 28 October 1887 Selborne addressed a large gathering at St. David's College, Lampeter, including all four Welsh bishops, and delivered a luminous and comprehensive historical, moral, and philosophical defence of the Welsh Church. He condemned separate legislation of any kind on behalf of the alleged nationality of Wales.[2]

The Liberal Party, however, was rapidly coming to a decision over disestablishment. Morley's declaration stimulated wider response. Harcourt intimated to Rendel that he was 'on our side'[3] and by February Rendel could claim that 'we have now playing on our side the whole of the ex-ministers except Childers'.[4] But the supreme doubt concerned Gladstone, who remained Delphic and remote. In June 1887 he made a memorable visit to Swansea, as the guest of the erstwhile Unionist, Sir Hussey Vivian of Singleton Abbey. But, in spite of the tumultuous enthusiasm of vast crowds of over 20,000, Gladstone had determined to say 'very little—as little as he can—about the Welsh Church question',[5] which he clearly regarded as political dynamite. While he dilated enthusiastically on the reality of Welsh nationality and affirmed that Welsh questions should be determined according to the sentiments of the Welsh people, he made only the briefest reference to disestablishment, and in very guarded terms, though it was enough to cause *The Times* some alarm.[6]

But events were forcing Gladstone's hands, or perhaps it was that, as on so many occasions, he was anxious to give the impression of being swept, reluctantly but helplessly, by an irresistible groundswell of opinion. Harcourt announced that the establishment in Wales was 'an institution which it is impossible to defend on Liberal principles'. The Whig Earl Spencer told the Welsh National Liberal Council at Aberystwyth that the Welsh Church question was 'ripe for settlement'. Most important of all, at the National Liberal Federation at Nottingham on 19 October, Gladstone himself gave his opinion that Welsh and Scottish disestablishment were 'ripe for decision':[7] his labyrinthine equivocations were sufficient for a

---

[1] Selborne to Sir A. Gordon, 4 Nov. 1886 (*Memorials*, vol. ii, p. 250).

[2] *The Times*, 29 Oct. 1887; *Cambrian News*, 4 Nov. 1887. See also Daniel Rowlands, 'Argiwydd Selborne yng Nghymru', *Y Traethodydd*, Jan. 1888, pp. 6 ff.

[3] Rendel to Humphreys-Owen, 18 Feb. 1887 (N.L.W., Glansevern MSS., 307). Cf. A. G. Gardiner, *Life of Sir William Harcourt* (London, 1923), vol. ii, p. 11.

[4] Rendel to Gee, 18 Feb. 1887 (N.L.W., Gee MSS., 8308c, 256).

[5] Lord Aberdare to Lady Aberdare, 3 June 1887 (*Letters of Lord Aberdare*, vol. ii, p. 224).

[6] *The Times*, 6 June 1887.

[7] Ibid., 20 Oct. 1887.

resolution moved by the Welsh Federations, headed by Rendel and Ellis, that disestablishment of the Welsh Church be placed on the Liberal programme, to be carried unanimously. For the next quarter of a century, the issue was to remain in the forefront of political controversy. To Tom Ellis, writing home to his friend, D. R. Daniel, 'Nottingham was memorable'.[1]

Another valuable ally had been found in the renegade Liberal Unionist, George Otto Trevelyan. Rendel, again using his wide connexions with skill and diplomacy, had 'put Trevelyan up to a thing or two about Wales and her national aims',[2] and Trevelyan made a series of stirring speeches in Bangor and Caernarvon at the end of October. There was a suggestion that he might succeed Hanbury-Tracy, the frivolous Whig who sat for Montgomery Boroughs.[3] Later, the Conservatives replied with Welsh speaking tours by Lord Salisbury (in May 1888) and Lord Randolph Churchill (in September 1889). The visit of leading politicians to Wales was quite novel, and underlined the growing prominence of Welsh affairs in political debate.

Thus when Dillwyn's motion came before the Commons again, on 14 May 1889, it had the formal backing of the Liberal Party.[4] The respective arguments were already becoming familiar to both sides. Dillwyn and his colleagues dwelt on the national characteristics of Wales, on the alien nature of the Church, and its association with proselytizing landlords. The defenders of the Church, inevitably Englishmen, Byron Reed (Bradford Central), Raikes (Cambridge University), and Sir Joseph Bailey (Hereford), a border squire and ironmaster who sat on the Brecknockshire County Council, all testified to the recent progress of the Church, especially since the Swansea Church Congress of 1879. The most memorable contribution in support of the motion came from the 'Labour' member for the Rhondda, William Abraham, himself an ardent Methodist, the pathos of his speech being heightened by his apparent unfamiliarity with the English language. The main interest lay in the voting figures. A series of 'whips' had been issued by the Liberal Party, the Irish Party, the Welsh parliamentary group, the Scottish Disestablishment Council, and the Liberation Society. Harcourt, Morley, and Joseph Chamberlain voted for the motion, but the bulk of the Liberal

[1] Ellis to Daniel, 23 Oct. 1887 (N.L.W., Daniel Papers, 344).
[2] Ibid.
[3] Humphreys-Owen, to Rendel, 21 Apr. 1887 (N.L.W., Rendel Papers, xiv. 350).
[4] *Parl. Deb.*, 3rd ser., vol. cccxxxvi, pp. 70 ff.

Unionists, including Hartington and Goschen, were in opposition. The Liberal Unionist *Spectator* considered that the revival of the Welsh Church made disestablishment unnecessary. It believed there was already too much 'local impatience'.[1]

The major feature of the debate was the absence of Gladstone, which caused immense disappointment. Gee and his fellow nonconformists were highly critical. Tom Ellis wrote: 'It was wrong for Gladstone not to vote. I protested to the verge of rebellion.'[2] Robertson Nicoll in the influential *British Weekly* spoke ominously of a reappraisal of the relations of nonconformists with the Liberal leader.[3] These complaints were scarcely allayed by another speech by Gladstone at St. Austell on 12 June, when he made a new declaration. In language of almost wilful obscurity, he affirmed that he had been waiting for a clear intimation of Welsh opinion on disestablishment, and he now considered it to have been given. How it was more or less clear than in previous years, he did not elucidate. But he continued very loath to express himself unequivocally on the 'sore, crying grievance' of the Welsh Church.[4]

Controversy became more acute as the recent progress of the Church was sustained. The personnel of the episcopate was now generally acknowledged to be of vital importance, and thus there was widespread interest in the vacancy caused at St. Asaph by the resignation of Bishop Hughes. *The Times* correspondent had warned that 'controversialists' should be excluded[5] but in fact, in March 1889, there was consecrated A. G. Edwards, the relatively young vicar of Carmarthen.[6] Edwards, never a popular figure, had aroused much antagonism by relaxing the 'Welsh rule' during his headmastership of Llandovery school, but for forty years he was to prove a pugnacious and polemical defender of the privileges of the Church. He had already proved his dialectical calibre in some challenging attacks on nonconformist statistics in *The Times*, and these must have influenced Salisbury in his appointment.

The extent of the Church revival was still a matter for speculation. Nonconformists were inflexibly hostile to a religious census, partly

---

[1] *Spectator*, 18 May 1889.
[2] Ellis to Herbert Lewis, 29 May 1889 (Penucha MSS.).
[3] *British Weekly*, 31 May 1889.
[4] Ellis to Daniel, 12 July 1890 (N.L.W., Daniel Papers, 367). Cf. *Cymru Fydd*, July 1889, pp. 379–81.   [5] *The Times*, 29 Sept. 1888.
[6] For Edwards, see his autobiography, *Memories* (London, 1927); George Lerry, *Alfred George Edwards, Archbishop of Wales* (Oswestry, 1940); and the *Dictionary of Welsh Biography*.

because of general hostility to the principle of state interference, but more fundamentally because it was feared that persons of no religion—nearly half the population of Wales even if all the most ambitious statistics of all denominations were added together—would be persuaded or cajoled into entering their names as churchmen: 'no religion—put him down Church'. In January 1887 Thomas Gee did attempt a census of attendance at all the churches and chapels of Wales, but the Liberal press generally, especially *Y Tyst*, *Y Goleuad*, and the *Cambrian News*, condemned the move as a failure.[1] Humphreys-Owen, no friend of Gee, stated that the census 'has done untold mischief in encouraging the parsons'.[2] After a suspiciously long interval, Gee finally produced figures showing a nonconformist majority of 609,324 in adherents and 263,526 in Sunday school pupils, but clearly he was disappointed with the result and churchmen highly pleased.[3] Some nonconformists admitted the advance of the established Church. The eminent Methodist theologian, Cynddylan Jones, confessed 'The strides it has made in the last fifteen years is [*sic*] amazing and unless it be disestablished soon we shall not be able to urge members against it.' The same writer added that 'If the Church has been a failure in its relation to the education of the masses, the Nonconformity of today is not much of a success.'[4] In October 1889 the Church Congress met for the second time in Wales, at Cardiff, and great satisfaction was expressed at the progress in church building and voluntary contributions, the increasing number of communicants, and the number of funerals, baptisms, and marriages administered by the Church, all indications of the continuing hold of 'the old mother' over her flock.[5]

The most optimistic churchmen, however, could not claim that the Church was predominant. Bishop Edwards of St. Asaph gave figures showing that in 1893 nonconformist communicants totalled 381,795 as against 114,885 for the Church.[6] The adherents of the

---

[1] *Y Tyst*, 14 Jan. 1887 (editorial, 'Rhifo y Bobl'); *Y Goleuad*, 15, 22 Jan. 1887; *Cambrian News*, 14 Jan. 1887. The Methodist *Goleuad* was the most hostile of all.

[2] Humphreys-Owen to Rendel, 7 Apr. 1887 (N.L.W., Rendel Papers, xiv. 340).

[3] *Church Times*, 21 Jan. 1887.

[4] Rev. J. Cynddylan Jones to Gee, 4 Mar. 1887 (N.L.W., Gee MSS., 8306D, 122).

[5] See *Report of the Twenty-Ninth Annual Church Congress at Cardiff, 1889* (London, 1890).

[6] Bishop of St. Asaph, *A Handbook of Church Defence* (London, 1895). The individual denominational totals he gives are as follows:

Methodists	126,509	communicants;	268,415	adherents
Independents	125,578	,,	278,981	,,
Baptists	99,122	,,	215,868	,,
Wesleyans	31,406	,,	69,093	,,

four leading nonconformist bodies he gave as 832,357. But the Church was, nevertheless, apparently advancing at a faster rate, and the realization that it might soon be the largest single religious body in Wales added urgency to the activity of nonconformist leaders.

(ii) *The Tithe Riots*

The question of disestablishment was complicated and embittered during these years by its associations with an older and much disputed controversy, the payment of tithe (*y degwm*). At least since the Tithe Commutation Act of 1836, Welsh nonconformists had objected to tithe payment on religious grounds, as a form of state interference in spiritual affairs. Some, such as 'S. R.' of Llanbryn-mair, had urged that it be devoted to secular purposes; others, more bold, had even advocated total abolition. The chagrin of paying tithe to the Church of an acknowledged minority of the population infused religious protest with national sentiment. Finally, the impact of the agricultural depression from 1879 onwards added to the financial burdens imposed on the distressed farming community. The fact that the annual tithe-rent charge was determined by an individual bargain between landlord and tithe-owner made tithe appear simply as an increment to the already considerable burden of rental. In some counties rates and tithe together absorbed the whole produce of the land. In particular, the distribution of endowments severely handicapped the more thinly populated rural areas. Out of a total of roughly £120,000 per annum from parochial tithe, Glamorgan provided only £16,000, while Anglesey, with only a tenth of its population, contributed as much as £12,000. There was thus a ready audience for nonconformist leaders, Thomas Gee in particular, who attacked the tithe system generally on religious, national, and economic grounds. It was significantly in Gee's own county, in Dyffryn Clwyd in Denbighshire, that the first incidents took place, in August 1886, when three farmers had their goods distrained for a refusal to pay tithe. The Welsh tithe war had begun.

Agitation against the payment of tithe continued intermittently for years to come, and aroused much interest and alarm in England. The violence which rent the Irish countryside, now issuing forth in Davitt's 'plan of campaign' in the autumn of 1886, seemed to be mirrored by a growing resort to violence in Wales also. It was recalled that in Ireland the first agitation in the 1830's had concerned the payment of tithe.[1] Ellis exultantly reported that 'the tithe war is kept up very well, and the farmers of Wales are winning golden opinions in England for sturdiness and backbone. It is a form of the awakening of Wales!'[2] The tithe campaign merged easily into those older social antagonisms aroused by the depression in agriculture. 'Anti-Tithe Leagues' sprang up in almost every county in Wales, and in 1887 amalgamated with Gee's Land League, demanding a reduction of tithes of up to 25 per cent. together with a guarantee of security of tenure.[3] There were several ugly incidents mostly in Denbighshire and Caernarvonshire. The most notable were those in Llangwm in Denbighshire on 25 and 27 May 1887, and at Mochdre on 15 June, when representatives of the Ecclesiastical Commissioners attempted to seize the cattle of some recalcitrant farmers. The disturbance at Mochdre was so great that the county militia was called in and the Riot Act read. In the ensuing scuffle, fifty civilians and thirty-four police were injured.[4] A report on the incident by a magistrate, John Bridge, commented on the difficulties suffered by the parish clergy, particularly in St. Asaph diocese where they were compelled to make reductions or abatements in tithe. The government was so alarmed that when thirty-two men were charged following the disturbances at Llangwm, they were transferred from the local court at Ruthin by a writ of *certiorari* to Queen's Bench. Even so, the tithe troubles continued throughout 1888 and 1889.

The political divisions in Wales, however, were far less clear-cut over the tithe dispute than in previous disputes. On the Liberal side Stuart Rendel, in particular, distrusted the form that the tithe agitation was taking. It would dangerously separate the Liberals of Wales from their English colleagues; the latter favoured the transference of the obligation to pay tithe from occupier to owner, a proposal which the Welsh Anti-Tithe Leagues firmly rejected. It would also tend to revive the connexion between English and Welsh disestablishment, and restore the fatal influence of the Liberation Society.[5] In fact, the Society itself had looked upon the Welsh troubles with

[1] Ellis Griffith to Gee, 11 Oct. 1886 (N.L.W., Gee MSS., 8306D, 94).
[2] Ellis to Daniel, 1 Oct. 1886 (N.L.W., Daniel Papers, 325).
[3] R. E. Prothero, *The Anti-Tithe Agitation in Wales* (London, 1889), p. 9. This account of the tithe disturbances is very useful, provided allowance is made for its obvious bias towards the landlords and the Church. Another analysis, from the nonconformist viewpoint, is given in John Parry, 'Helynt y Degwm', *Y Traethodydd*, Jan. 1887, pp. 47–53.
[4] *Land Commission, Report*, p. 174.
[5] Rendel to Humphreys-Owen, 27 Nov. 1889 (N.L.W., Glansevern MSS., 474).

a jaundiced eye, and had advised against resistance to the legal process of tithe collection.[1] Rendel feared that the tithe campaign would
confuse the basic objective of Welsh disestablishment, and throughout his career discouraged agrarian rebellion in Wales which might
lead to embarrassing and perhaps fatal comparisons with Ireland.
His friend, Humphreys-Owen, was somewhat divided between his
convictions as a Liberal and his interests as a landlord. He feared
that Gee's attack on tithe-rent-charge would menace the rights of
property: 'I know that he advocates the three F's'. . . .'[2] On the other
hand, he saw no harm as a landowner in 'asking the church as
a department of the state to take its share of the burden'.[3] He urged
Rendel that he could not hold aloof from the tithe agitation: 'if we
do not help our friends in every *legal* way we shall encourage them
to look to the violent section as their only trustworthy leaders'.[4]

Rendel and Humphreys-Owen saw that they were fast losing the
initiative to the younger and militant section of Welsh radicalism,
men like the young secretary of the South Caernarvonshire Anti-
Tithe League, David Lloyd George, who asked his friend, Tom Ellis,
unashamedly, 'Do not you think this tithe business is an excellent
lever wherewith to raise the spirit of the people?'[5] Ellis had no qualms
about raising the land question in all its varied forms: where Rendel
suppressed the analogy of Ireland, Ellis flaunted it openly. The Young
Wales spokesmen, young men who had grown to manhood since
1868, and who maintained that a vision of nationality extended to
every aspect of society and not simply to the restricted sphere of
clerical politics, were gradually assuming the leadership of Liberalism in Wales.

Nor were Welsh Conservatives unanimous over the tithe debate.
The formal statement of their official attitude appeared in the letters
written for *The Times* in November 1887 by J. E. Vincent on behalf
of the North Wales Property Defence Association. He avowed simply
that tithe was private property to which the Church had an indefeas-
ible right, a debt which the occupier was legally obliged to fulfil. On
the other hand, many landowners were not unwilling to retain a position in which the odium attached to tithe fell on the Church. Many
felt with Humphreys-Owen that 'the Welsh landlords have no friends.

[1] Liberation Society MSS., 1 Dec. 1886.
[2] Humphreys-Owen to Rendel, 28 Nov. 1886 (N.L.W., Rendel Papers, xiv. 312).
[3] Humphreys-Owen to Rendel, 21 Sept. 1886 (N.L.W., Rendel Papers, xiv. 300).
[4] Humphreys-Owen to Rendel, 10 July 1887 (N.L.W., Rendel Papers, xiv. 376).
[5] Lloyd George to Ellis, 19 May 1887 (N.L.W., Ellis Papers, 679).

The Liberals are our avowed enemies. The Tories have shown that
... they are ready to sacrifice us to secure the English parson's vote.'[1]
A few, it was alleged, feared the growing nationalist feeling among
certain sections of the established Church.[2] These differences of
opinion were to lead directly to the uncertain handling of the tithe
issue by the Salisbury government.

The Welsh tithe troubles made an emphatic impression upon
British politics. Llewelyn Williams exaggerates in saying that they
'brought the question [of disestablishment] within the realm of practical politics'.[3] What they did achieve was a marked hardening of the
political parties towards the general issue of the Welsh Church. For
the first time, Welsh affairs dominated the attention of Parliament.
The Conservative administration was embarrassed by the realization
that on this issue the interests of the Church and of the landed gentry
were not in harmony. On the other hand, the tithe riots confirmed
Liberal Unionists in their fears that Gladstone's 'separatist' policy
was leading to national disintegration. The *Spectator* was roused by
Gee's injunction to Welsh nonconformists to refrain from demonstrations of loyalty to the Queen during her visit to Wales in August
1889, on the grounds that she was the head of the established 'alien
church'. This, the *Spectator* claimed, struck a direct blow at the
supremacy of Parliament.[4] Even the Liberationists of Liberal Unionism showed scant sympathy with the agitation. The Rev. R. W. Dale,
while agreeing that tithe was 'national property', was alarmed lest
Wales might emulate Ireland in its disregard for law. 'It is certain
that your country is passing through a great and perilous change',
he wrote to Gee.[5] Joseph Chamberlain coldly declined to intervene
over the Tithe Bills. Having committed themselves to support of
Gladstone's home rule policy, thus indefinitely postponing disestablishment and land reform, Welsh Liberals must, he wrote, look
to 'their new allies' for aid.[6]

The Liberal Party, as Rendel had hinted, had divergent attitudes
towards the question of tithe. Harcourt, as a staunch Erastian,
showed little concern. He refused to help the Bishop of St. Asaph:
'the Tory Party will always defend the Church as long as only they

[1] Humphreys-Owen to ——, 5 July 1891 (N.L.W., Glansevern MSS., 2178).
[2] Arthur Price to Ellis, 22 Nov. 1891 (N.L.W., Ellis Papers, 1699).
[3] Viscountess Rhondda (ed.), *D. A. Thomas, Viscount Rhondda*, p. 60.
[4] *Spectator*, 17, 24 Aug. 1889.
[5] Dale to Gee, 26 May 1890 (N.L.W., Gee MSS., 8305c, 30, pp. 17–20).
[6] Chamberlain to Gee, 16 Apr. 1890 (N.L.W., Gee MSS., 8305c, 17).

are allowed to rob it'.[1] On the other hand, he took seriously the resentment of the Welsh M.P.s and warned Gladstone against making any arrangement with Hicks-Beach over the Tithe Bill. 'I think you are under some mistake as to the feelings of our Welsh M.P.s on this question. Their hostility is absolute and irreconcilable, and they would greatly resent any such transaction on our part. . . . They are already too suspicious of us and such a proceeding would commit their suspicions with certainty.'[2] Gladstone himself had, as usual, ambivalent emotions. As a resident in St. Asaph diocese, he supported tithe legislation. He promised Archbishop Benson to give the 1889 Bill a 'fair chance' and concurred with the Bishop of St. Asaph in the need to maintain the tithes of the Welsh Church which had 'improved immensely'.[3] The anti-tithe campaign alarmed him, appearing to menace the very structure of society. On the other hand, his sympathy with Welsh ambitions allied to the discreet necessity of political unity prevented him from intervening. His refusal to commit himself over tithe angered Gee and other Welshmen,[4] but Gladstone's silence throughout the debates on the various Tithe Bills in 1889–91 constituted an almost unique act of self-abnegation on an ecclesiastical subject.

The Welsh tithe question soon agitated the House of Commons. Ellis, backed up by Harcourt and R. T. Reid, tried to move the adjournment of the House over the government's handling of the Llangwm trials, but in vain.[5] Hesitantly and uncertainly, the government was forced to act. Their first venture, a Tithe Recovery Bill in 1889, stipulated that tithe could be recovered in the county court in the same way as other debts.[6] This would have had clear advantages in substituting legal machinery for the direct intervention of the clergy, but was obviously inadequate as an overall settlement. Welsh Unionist members attacked it as a piecemeal arrangement, and, although the Bill passed its Second Reading, Harcourt challenged the government so effectively in committee that the unhappy measure was withdrawn on 16 August.

A second bill, wider in scope, was introduced by Hicks-Beach on 27 March 1890.[7] This aimed to make the landowner liable for the pay-

[1] *Memories*, p. 140.
[2] Harcourt to Gladstone, 2 July 1890 (B.M., Add. MSS., 44202, f. 17).
[3] Archbishop Benson to Gladstone, 15 July 1889 (B.M., Add. MSS. ,44109, f. 173).
[4] Gee to Ellis, 31 May 1890 (N.L.W., Ellis Papers, 666).
[5] *Parl. Deb.*, 3rd ser., vol. cccxvii, pp. 1353 ff.
[6] Ibid., vol. cccxxxviii, pp. 741 ff.
[7] Ibid., vol. cccxliii, pp. 39 ff.

ment of tithe and provided facilities for tithe redemption. The two-day debate on the Second Reading was largely consumed by clashes between Welsh Liberals and 'Church defenders', such as Leighton, Raikes, Wolmer, and Reed. The Bill was passed by a majority of 125, but as government business was behindhand, it was withdrawn after only one day in Committee.

A third Tithe Bill was brought in, on 27 November 1890.[1] This consisted of only eight clauses, and concentrated simply on making tithe payable by the owner and not the occupier of land. No less than ten Welsh Liberals spoke in the Second Reading debate, described by Raikes, the Postmaster-General, as 'a preliminary canter to Disestablishment'.[2] While the Bill was passed by 224 to 130, the Welsh members voted against it by twenty-five to five. In Committee, the Bill was further delayed by a long series of amendments, moved mainly by two newly-elected members, Samuel Evans (Mid-Glamorgan) and David Lloyd George (Caernarvon District). Lloyd George wrote to D. R. Daniel with satisfaction: 'We are beginning to obstruct. . . . Bitterness is being imported into the scene. I have stuck 15 amendments down.'[3] Eventually the measure received the Royal Assent on 26 March 1891.

The main significance of the tithe debates, clearly, lies in their preoccupation almost solely with Wales. 'It was a glorious struggle for Wales. Wales practically monopolized the attention of the House for fully three weeks. To my mind, that is the great fact of the Tithe Bill opposition', wrote Lloyd George.[4] Some of the amendments moved by Welsh Liberals were constructive improvements of the procedure of distraint, but Samuel Evans frankly confessed: 'My *private opinion* of the Bill is that it is a good one and will suit us admirably hereafter; and even now it does not terrify me in the least.' It had been, he said, 'acknowledged on all sides of the House that this has been the toughest and best sustained fight ever made by the Welsh Party'.[5] The 1891 Act, by merging tithe-rent-charge with rent, made the payment of tithe easier to enforce, and the unpopularity of the tithe-owner declined so rapidly that the tithe disturbances virtually ceased. In any case, there was not in the Welsh country-side that undercurrent of violent agitation which forms such a recurrent theme in the social history of Ireland from the eighteenth century onwards.

[1] Ibid., vol. cccxlix, pp. 241 ff.   [2] Ibid., p. 323.
[3] Lloyd George to Daniel, 6 Feb. 1891 (N.L.W., Daniel Papers, 2759).
[4] Lloyd George to Ellis, 11 Apr. 1891 (N.L.W., Ellis Papers, 683).
[5] S. T. Evans to Ellis, 'Whit Monday', 1891 (N.L.W., Ellis Papers, 620).

There were no 'Peep-o-day Boys' in Wales: the most recent tradition was that of the Rebecca Riots in South-West Wales, but this area, remote from the influence of Gee, was not the major centre of the tithe agitation.[1] Above all, the tithe question had great influence on the wider question of disestablishment, to which attention again turned, the Liberal Party appreciating, in Lloyd George's words, 'that Welsh questions are very useful—quite as useful as Irish ones —to hurl at the Government'.[2]

The Liberal Party was now formally committed to Welsh disestablishment, as Harcourt made explicit to the North Wales Liberal Federation at Caernarvon on 17 October 1889.[3] But the decisive issue of Gladstone's attitude remained ambiguous. 'We must move him forward on disestablishment', wrote Ellis,[4] and Welshmen waited breathlessly for 'that one word which is wanted to set everything all right.'[5] When Gladstone spoke on behalf of Cameron's motion for Scottish disestablishment, Gee wrote to him, complaining that Wales ought to take precedence. Gladstone's irritating reply refused 'to determine any question of priority'. He considered himself unable to undertake personally any major question other than that of Irish home rule.[6] Morley backed him up in this, and deprecated attacks on him by certain Welshmen.[7] But to Welsh Liberals it was most unsatisfactory. 'I don't think Mr. Gladstone understands or can understand the kind of suspicion and uneasiness that exists in Wales', wrote Rendel,[8] although he loyally maintained that Gladstone's letter to Gee did pledge him to the view that 'the principle [of disestablishment] can be realized without serious difficulty.'[9] Impatience reached its climax at the North Wales Liberal Federation at Rhyl on 30 April 1890, when a resolution was carried that Welsh members should pledge themselves to support a Liberal govern-

---

[1] On the other hand, while Denbighshire and Montgomeryshire were the main centres of unrest in the 1886–9 period, it seems that it was in the former 'Rebecca' territory that the tithe disturbances took longest to die out. There were disorderly scenes at tithe sales in southern Cardiganshire as late as 1894 and 1895, and many questions were asked in the House. For full details of the riotous scenes in west Wales, see the reminiscences of Robert Lewis, tithe agent and collector from 1888 to 1899 (N.L.W., MSS. 15,321–3).

[2] Lloyd George to Gee, 27 Feb. 1891 (N.L.W., Gee MSS., 8310E, 498).

[3] *The Times*, 18 Oct. 1889.

[4] Ellis to Herbert Lewis, 14 June 1890 (Penucha MSS.).

[5] Humphreys-Owen to Rendel, 3 June 1890 (N.L.W., Rendel MSS., xiv. 541).

[6] Gladstone to Gee, 2 July 1890 (N.L.W., Gee MSS., 8306D, 91).

[7] Morley to Gee, 20 Aug. 1890 (N.L.W., Gee MSS., 8307C, 210)

[8] Rendel to Gee, 3 July 1890 (N.L.W., Gee MSS., 8308C, 262).

[9] Rendel to Gee, 7 July 1890 (N.L.W., Gee MSS., 8308C, 263).

ment only if Welsh disestablishment were introduced concurrently with, or immediately after, Home Rule.[1] The 'Rhyl Resolution' became something of a *cause célèbre*, since it adumbrated far more concisely than before the policy of 'independent action' by the Welsh members. One observer claimed that the resolution had been put forward by the disestablishment campaigners in order to forestall the growing influence of Lloyd George, R. A. Griffiths, and those who were advocating 'the chimera' of Welsh home rule.[2] But the great majority of influential Liberal spokesmen, in the press and on the platform, ardently welcomed the resolution, whatever might be its precise significance.

The issue at last seemed to be definitely resolved when Welsh disestablishment came before the Commons for the fourth time on 20 February 1891, on the motion of Pritchard Morgan, the cosmopolitan gold speculator who sat for Merthyr Tydfil.[3] The debate followed the familiar pattern, save that for the first time the Liberal Party formally backed the motion, with the Liberal whips, Arnold Morley and Marjoribanks, as tellers.[4] The Welsh Liberals, with their ally, Trevelyan, again urged the numerical superiority of nonconformity in Wales and the nationhood of Wales. Conservative speakers followed their usual practice in stressing the indivisibility of Wales and England.'Wales has never been a nation', declared Sir Joseph Bailey (Hereford).[5]

The great significance of the debate lay in Gladstone's intervention, immediately following the seconder of the motion. He had told Arnold Morley, the Liberal Whip, three days earlier that he would vote for the motion, but the previous night Rendel had persuaded him to speak also, to the surprise of Harcourt, Morley, and the other Liberal leaders.[6] Gladstone still showed some hesitation. He could

---

[1] *Fourth Annual Report of the North Wales Liberal Federation, 1890*, pp. 5–7. See the enthusiastic comments of *Baner ac Amserau Cymru*, 7 May 1890, and of *Y Genedl*, 7 May 1890.

[2] Humphreys-Owen to Rendel, 4 May 1890 (N.L.W., Rendel Papers, xiv. 536).

[3] *Parl. Deb.*, 3rd ser., vol. cccl, pp. 1242 ff. Pritchard Morgan, the itinerant son of a Wesleyan minister of Usk, had emigrated to Australia *c*. 1864. There he had many political battles with Sir Samuel Griffiths, Premier of Queensland, himself a native of Merthyr. In the Commons, Morgan gained great notoriety through his persistent promotion of his gold-mining ventures in Merioneth: the question of royalties gradually became his major political concern. (*South Wales News*, 12 July 1924: I am also grateful for information here to Mr. W. W. Price, Aberdare.)

[4] Daniel Rowlands, 'Y Ddadl ar Dadgysylltiad i Gymru', *Y Traethodydd*, May 1891, p. 207.

[5] *Parl. Deb.*, loc. cit., p. 1290.

[6] Rendel to Gee, 24 Feb. 1891 (N.L.W., Gee MSS., 8308c, 268).

not assent to some of the allusions made by the mover of the motion. He recalled warmly the great services of the Church in Wales, which he described as 'an advancing Church, a living Church and. . . a rising Church'.[1] On the other hand, as in Ireland it was the Church of the few and the Church of the rich. 'The Nonconformists of Wales were the people of Wales.'[2] As Wales had clearly demonstrated her feelings at successive general elections, the wishes of the Welsh people should be followed. He frankly admitted that his assertion in 1870 that it would be impossible to separate the Welsh and the English churches was an exaggeration. This volte-face was, no doubt, distasteful to Gladstone, and there is some justice in accusations by churchmen that the earlier portion of his speech bore little relation to his peroration. But his attitude contrasted favourably with that of Raikes, the Postmaster-General, whose abusive denigration of Welsh nationality, which he stated to be of interest only to students of folk-lore and archaeology, aroused the anger of Welsh members.[3] At the division, the motion was lost only narrowly, by 235 to 203, the minority including seven Liberal Unionists (among them Joseph Chamberlain), thirty-two Irish Nationalists, and sixteen Parnellites. Including pairs, Welsh members voted in favour by twenty-nine to four.

Gladstone's speech was not convincing to the more doctrinaire advocates of religious equality, but in Wales it aroused immense delight. Gladstone's 'political worshippers', Gee told him, 'were overwhelmed with delight'.[4] In England some churchmen, particularly among the High Church persuasion, warned against the folly of defending the Church by abusing Welsh nationality. 'To condemn national aspirations is to perpetuate the rule of the preacher-journalist', said the *Church Times*, no doubt with Gee in mind.[5] On the other hand, the *Spectator* believed that to give a local majority the right to expropriate ecclesiastical revenues could lead to the abolition of the constitution or the monarchy in the same way.[6]

The growing strength of the disestablishment movement, allied to the uproar of the tithe disturbances, forced churchmen, who could see only a rising tide of materialism, socialism, and atheism already sweeping through Western Europe, into sterner measures of self-

---

[1] *Parl. Deb.*, loc. cit., p. 1264.
[2] Ibid., p. 1265.   [3] Ibid., pp. 1268–9.
[4] Gee to Gladstone, 23 Feb. 1891 (B.M., Add MSS., 44512, f. 121).
[5] *Church Times*, 27 Feb. 1891. On this theme, see also the Rev. D. Howell, *The Welsh Church: the Patriot's Yearning for the Prosperity of Zion* (London, 1890).
[6] *Spectator*, 28 Feb. 1891.

defence. In 1891 the Church Congress met in Wales for the second time in three years, at Rhyl. After a militant 'keynote' speech by the Bishop of St. Asaph again directed against nonconformist statistics of membership, Archbishop Benson delivered a passionate survey of the history of the Welsh Church, which, he eloquently concluded, English churchmen would not permit to be quietly disinherited.[1] However, the statistics provided by churchmen were in curious contrast to the persistency with which Wales appeared to vote for disestablishment.

After the Rhyl Congress, the wealth and power of the Church were fully mobilized. Immediately before the Rhyl meeting, Welsh Liberalism had gained its greatest triumph to date, when the National Liberal Federation at Newcastle had placed Welsh disestablishment second only to Irish home rule on the 'Newcastle Programme'. On 2 October Gladstone himself supported separation of Church and State in Wales and Scotland, and somewhat naïvely urged the two countries to compete in putting forward their claims.[2] In Wales, nonconformists held a counter-demonstration at Rhyl after the Church Congress, where Lloyd George enlivened proceedings by asserting that the Congress had 'floated on barrels of beer'.[3] On 23 February 1892 Welsh disestablishment came before the Commons once again, this time on the motion of Samuel Smith, the austere and humourless Presbyterian cotton-broker who sat for Flintshire.[4] The motion was, somewhat contrarily, supported by Bryce, who stated that the Church of England was in no way threatened, and by Harcourt, who vigorously foretold the doom of established churches all over the world. For the government, Sir Edward Clarke repeated the demand for a religious census. The motion failed by 267 to 227. Harcourt delightedly pointed out how sixty Irishmen in all had supported the motion. Gladstone had been intending to vote but the inclement weather had compelled him to stay at Rendel's residence at Valescure on the Riviera, although he informed Smith of his support.[5]

Thus as the general election of 1892 loomed near, Welsh disestablishment was one of the major issues. In Wales, it was certainly

[1] *The Times*, 7 Oct. 1891.
[2] Ibid., 3 Oct. 1891.
[3] *Church Times*, 13 Nov. 1891.
[4] *Parl. Deb.*, 4th ser., vol. i, pp. 1033 ff. For Smith, see his autobiography, *My Life Story* (London, 1902). In his later years, fear of the infiltration of Roman Catholicism into Britain became his overriding political passion.
[5] Rendel to Samuel Smith, 20 Feb. 1892 (N.L.W., Ellis Papers, 3142); and Harcourt to Gladstone, 24 Feb. 1892 (B.M., Add. MSS., 44202, ff. 131-2).

the dominant theme, with the respective arguments rehearsed end-
lessly from every chapel and memorial hall. 'Disestablishment is
as much a controverted question as any other', Dilke was told, 'because it is the chief plank in the platform of the Tory Party in Wales.
... They will certainly fight it to the bitter end.'[1] On the other hand,
Joseph Chamberlain bid hard for Welsh votes. He told an audience
at Ruabon on 2 January that the Unionists would be far more likely
to achieve disestablishment than the Gladstonians, with their obsession with home rule, and he sponsored a string of six nonconformist
Unionist candidates, of whom four were Methodists.[2] But this eclectic
policy alarmed many churchmen: as a result the Unionists of East
Worcestershire were hesitant in accepting his son, Austen, as a candidate in March.[3] Gladstone's intentions were still somewhat obscure.
His speech at Chester on 27 June was extremely vague on disestablishment, and his election address at Mid-Lothian omitted all reference
to the subject. Nevertheless, Wales seemed certain to vote in overwhelming numbers for the twin (and, it was hoped, connected) causes
of Gladstone and disestablishment.

(iii) *Ellis and the Land Question*

The deepening of the depression in agriculture had provided the
sombre background to the animosity of the tithe campaign. From
1883 the prices of mutton and beef had spiralled sharply downwards,
reducing the stock-raising farmers of Wales to the same desperate
straits as the wheat-growing farmers of the English country-side.[4]
Inevitably, therefore, the land question had become a critical element
amid the tortuous cross-current of Welsh politics: in the northern
counties, agitation against tithe and against excessive rental, against
the alien Church and the English landlord, proceeded side by side.
Thus it was Thomas Gee, the prime mover of the anti-tithe movement, who inspired the large gathering of tenant farmers in North
Wales at Rhyl, on 16 June 1886. Here a formal programme was
drafted, including a land court on the Irish model and a compulsory

[1] J. Jenkins to Dilke, 5 Oct. 1891 (N.L.W., Ellis Papers, 967).
[2] In Anglesey, Cardiganshire, Carmarthenshire (East), Caernarvonshire (Eifion),
Merioneth, Swansea District. The candidates in Anglesey (Morgan Lloyd), Cardiganshire (William Jones), Eifion (William Humphreys), and Merioneth (H. Owen) were
Methodists.
[3] *Church Times*, 11 Mar. 1892. Cf. Garvin, op. cit., vol. ii, p. 537.
[4] W. Ashworth, *Economic History of England, 1870–1939* (London, 1960), pp. 57 ff.
There are useful discussions of the Welsh land question in these years, from the Liberal
and Conservative standpoints respectively, by 'Adfyfr' (T. J. Hughes), 'Landlordiaeth
yng Nghymru', *Y Traethodydd*, July and Sept. 1887, pp. 333–54, 376–99, and by J. E.
Vincent, *Tenancy.in Wales*, 1889.

reduction of rental by 50 per cent. A subsequent meeting at Denbigh, addressed, among others, by Gee, Ellis, and Colonel Cornwallis-West, M.P., the Unionist Lord-Lieutenant for the county, drew up a Land Bill to be introduced into Parliament.[1] This measure was brought before the House of Commons by Bryn Roberts (Eifion) in January 1887. Its objects were compulsory compensation for unexhausted improvements, arbitration to secure fair rents and the restriction of capricious evictions. In many respects this proposal was modelled on Gladstone's Irish Land Act of 1881, save that free sale of holdings was rejected, on the grounds that it would lead to excessively competitive rents for incoming tenants. However, in four sessions before 1887 and 1891 no opportunity was found to debate Roberts's Bill in the House.[2]

Nevertheless, the Welsh land question, with its distinctive characteristics, was gradually emerging from the periphery of political debate. As has been noted, Stuart Rendel and the more experienced of the Welsh members of Parliament were reluctant to introduce the land question as a prominent controversy, and distrusted those who brought it forward. But to Tom Ellis it was a crucial issue. As the son of a Merioneth tenant farmer, he had first-hand experience of the social and economic hardships of the rural community, and was eager to have them debated in the Commons. His intuitive perception of the nature of agricultural distress was buttressed with a Fabian passion for the accumulation of statistical evidence. His friends noted his storing up information even amid the beauty of the Austrian Tyrol.[3] Rendel's allies impugned the motives of the youthful social engineer from Merioneth. Humphreys-Owen complained: 'Even suppose Ellis to be utterly disinterested, what have his clients—the Welsh farmers—to get from either of them? [Dillwyn and Richard]. Of course he is not disinterested, he has his fortune to make and his ambition to gratify and he means to do both by turning Welsh tenant farmers into copyholders on the plan of Ireland. I believe that you will find that he regards that and a Welsh Parliament as of much more importance than our little tinkering business of Disestablishment.'[4] In spite of this overt hostility in some quarters, it was the industrious advocacy of Ellis that conformed more closely to the grievances of rural Wales.

[1] *Baner ac Amserau Cymru*, 3 Nov. 1886. Also see *Y Genedl*, 8 Dec. 1886, where a very direct parallel is drawn between the land questions in Ireland and in Wales.
[2] *Land Commission*, Evidence, vol. i (1894), qu. 13,170 ff. (Bryn Roberts's evidence).
[3] K. Idwal Jones (ed.), *Syr Herbert Lewis, 1858–1933* (Aberystwyth, 1958), p. 26.
[4] Humphreys-Owen to Rendel, 15 June 1888 (N.L.W., Rendel Papers, xiv. 433).

On 29 June Ellis moved a resolution in the Commons on agricultural tenancy in Wales.[1] In a most able speech, he laid equal stress
on the social tensions of the Welsh country-side—the antipathy between landlord and tenant and the subtle political pressures still
exercised—and on economic distress. Basing his argument on Schedule B assessments on the occupier of land, he showed that while rents
had risen by 23·5 per cent. in England between 1842 and 1879, in
Wales they had increased by no less than 34·6 per cent., and he therefore urged the creation of an intermediate authority to regulate
tenure and rental.[2] Ellis was seconded by his close friend and colleague, Arthur Acland (Rotherham), and supported by several other
Welsh members. Inevitably, the reaction from the landowning
interest on the government benches was uniformly hostile. Two
Welsh members, Cornwallis-West (West Denbighshire) and the Hon.
G. T. Kenyon (Denbigh District), pointed out that Ellis's charges
contrasted oddly with the long tradition of hereditary tenancies so
common in many parts of Wales. Stanley Leighton (Oswestry),
Punch's 'Man from Shropshire', indulged in a familiar onslaught
on the Welsh language and on 'professional agitators' in Wales.
The Postmaster-General, Raikes, asserted that Ellis's motion was
a pretext for a general expropriation, and denied the need for
separate Welsh legislation. He drew attention ironically to the absence
of the 'Squire of Hawarden'. Ellis's motion was narrowly lost, by
146 votes to 128, the Welsh members supporting it by twenty-three
to five.

The Welsh land crisis was not allowed to slumber. Ellis himself
sat on the Select Committee on Small Holdings (1888–90) and four
Welsh witnesses were called. In particular, he arranged for Humphreys-
Owen, a reluctant ally but one of the few Gladstonian landlords in
Wales, to expound the need for a peasant proprietorship. Another
Welshman, A. J. Williams (member for South Glamorgan), sat on
the Select Committee on Crown Lands, and urged unsuccessfully
another Liberal proposal, the acquisition of Crown Lands by the newly
formed county councils.[3]

---

[1] *Parl. Deb.*, 3rd ser., vol. cccxxxvii, pp. 1792 ff. For a description of this debate,
see *Baner ac Amserau Cymru*, 4 July 1888, and *Y Genedl*, 11 July 1888.

[2] The comparative reliability of Schedule A and Schedule B assessments for dis-
covering Welsh rental returns is discussed by the Land Commissioners in their *Report*
(1896), pp. 361–2. They conclude that Schedule A, based on the ownership of land,
was the more generally reliable.

[3] *Land Commission, Report*, Appendix A, pp. 68–71. Ellis to Humphreys-Owen,
15 Mar. 1889 (N.L.W., Ellis Papers, 2755).

A further debate, on 16 March 1892, greatly clarified the attitude of the political parties.[1] This was occasioned by the Second Reading of a Tenure of Land Bill for Wales, introduced by Ellis again. To provide security of tenure he proposed not arbitration as previously advocated, but a land court on the Irish pattern. The major importance of this debate lay in an unexpected intervention by Gladstone. Characteristically, he avowed that he must vote against the Bill on practical grounds, but stated also that there was a clear case for 'a thorough, searching, impartial, and dispassionate inquiry' into Welsh agriculture.[2] He acknowledged the social gulf between landlord and tenant in Wales. The detailed information Ellis provided appeared to impress the Liberal leader, and during the next fortnight he was to have several discussions with Ellis over the Schedule B assessment and the need for separating Wales from England in the Inland Revenue returns. A Liberal Unionist, Cornwallis-West, also advocated a royal commission on Welsh land, on the grounds that the 'reckless charges' against Welsh landlords would then be disproved. But the Conservatives were adamant. Landowners such as Gray (Maldon) and Lord Cranborne attacked the implied threat to 'freedom of contract'. Stanley Leighton made his familiar denial of the existence of Wales. Finally, Chaplin, the jovial 'Squire' who presided appropriately over the newly formed Board of Agriculture, warned against the extension of Ulster tenant-right to England and Wales.[3] They wanted no 'moonlighters' and boycotters in Wales. The government would never agree to an inquiry.

The vote was disappointing to Ellis and his friends. Only nineteen of the Welsh Liberals were present at the division, two others walking out and a few (including Rendel) being ostentatiously absent. The Bill was rejected by a large majority. Even so, Ellis was justified in terming it 'the best ever Welsh debate'.[4] The powerful influence of Gladstone had been attracted to the cause, while from both sides of the House had come an articulate call for a royal commission. The discontents of the farmer were thus a dominant question in the forthcoming general election. In passing, it should be noted that the conditions of farm labourers seldom complicated discussion of the 'land

[1] *Parl. Deb.*, 4th ser., vol. ii, pp. 961 ff.
[2] Ibid., p. 985.
[3] Chaplin is amusingly characterized in Hanham, op. cit., pp. 6–7.
[4] Ellis to Ellis Griffith, 21 Mar. 1892 (N.L.W., Ellis Griffith Papers, 383). The two members who walked out were Rathbone (Arfon) and Fuller-Maitland (Brecknockshire). See the comments of *Y Genedl*, 23 Mar. 1892; *Baner ac Amserau Cymru*, 23 Mar. 1892; and *Y Goleuad*, 24 Mar. 1892.

question'. Their wages steadily rose during the depression, and Liberal pamphleteers ignored them.[1] Welsh labourers found no Joseph Arch as their champion, nor have they found an historian since. It was the employing farmer, who owned his tools and stock, who forced the needs of Welsh land into political prominence, forming a Welsh evangelical Populism that found succour from finance and industry, rather than mortal enmity as in the United States, with Tom Ellis as the Welsh Bryan.

(iv) *The Intermediate Education Act*

The most startling practical achievement of the Welsh Liberal members during these years, however, came in the characteristic field of education. In spite of the failure of the last two Gladstone ministries to deal comprehensively with the recommendations of the Aberdare Committee, Welsh higher education continued to be a live political issue. In particular, the proposal for a network of intermediate schools, without which the new University Colleges could scarcely flourish, was not allowed to slumber. In the sessions 1887–8, W. H. Smith made it clear that little action was to be expected from the government in this direction, and thus the initiative passed to the energetic private members from Wales. On their instruction, Mundella, Vice-President of the Council at the time of the introduction of the abortive Bill of 1885, introduced Intermediate Education Bills in 1887 and 1888, but neither was discussed. On the Conservative side, a similar measure was brought forward by the Hon. G. T. Kenyon (Denbigh District). This would have created separate boards for North and for South Wales, and was criticized for affording an excessively strong representation to voluntary and endowed schools,[2] but this measure also failed to proceed beyond the formal First Reading.

In the 1889 session, however, a far more determined effort was made. In the sphere of education, the two most influential of the Welsh representatives, Stuart Rendel and Tom Ellis, worked in complete harmony. Rendel, newly appointed as chairman of the 'Welsh Party', had determined on intermediate education as the major objective of the session, and had skilfully elicited the backing of several Welsh Conservative members. To Ellis, education and a reform of local government were essential features of the Fabian programme of

[1] This point is stressed by David Williams, 'Rural Wales in the Nineteenth Century', *Journal of the Agricultural Society*, 1953. He points out that the massive migration from rural Wales in the later nineteenth century was largely a migration of farm labourers.
[2] *Cambrian News*, 6 May 1887.

social reconstruction. On the suggestion of Bryn Roberts (Eifion), the Welsh members balloted jointly, the member fortunate in the draw introducing the Welsh measure agreed upon. Roberts's own favoured project was his own Land Bill, but, on negotiation with his colleagues he agreed to waive it in favour of Mundella's Education Bill.[1] Rendel himself was successful in the draw, being placed fourth on the list of private members, and it was thus Rendel who conducted through the House that legislation which laid the foundations of Welsh higher education.

The Bill came up for its Second Reading on 15 May 1889.[2] It differed from its predecessors in some important respects. Since the Local Government Act of 1888 had now been implemented, Rendel's measure proposed to make the new county councils the local educational authority. The councils would forward schemes for intermediate schools to the Charity Commissioners; the schemes would then go before the Education Department, and finally would be laid before Parliament. A half-penny rate would be levied, backed by an equivalent treasury grant. The new schools would be strictly undenominational. Finally, a national Welsh council of education was to be constituted.[3]

The prospects were not auspicious for Rendel when he rose on 15 May: only the previous night there had been a rancorous debate on Dillwyn's disestablishment motion. But Rendel received influential support. Once again, Gladstone intervened effectively, and emphasized the 'unquestioned neglect' of Welsh education.[4] Mundella pointed out that adequate educational machinery was already in existence. Ellis showed how several endowments, the Howell and Ashford trusts, and the Meyricke funds, had been alienated from Welsh uses. Most important of all, Sir William Hart-Dyke, for the government, who had previously intimated privately to Rendel his sympathy for the measure,[5] promised that government assistance would be given. He did imply reservations over some clauses, particularly that to make county councils the sole local authority, but

---

[1] Letter by Bryn Roberts to *Liverpool Daily Post*, n.d. (MS. copy in Bryn Roberts Papers, N.L.W.).

[2] *Parl. Deb.*, 3rd ser., vol. cccxxxvi, op. 121 ff.

[3] Its details are very clearly summarized by David Evans, 'Y Ddeddf Addysg Ganolraddol Gymreig', *Y Traethodydd*, Jan. 1890, pp. 5–21. See also A. C. Humphreys-Owen, 'Welsh Intermediate Education', *Cymru Fydd*, Mar. 1888, pp. 140–51, and J. R. Webster, op. cit., ch. vii.

[4] *Parl. Deb.*, loc. cit., p. 135.

[5] *Personal Papers of Lord Rendel*, p. 308.

was generally encouraging. The sole dissentient was the incorrigible Marcher squire, Stanley Leighton (Oswestry) who condemned equally the new powers given to nonconformist county councils, the burden of rates imposed on Welsh farmers, and the undenominational nature of the new schools. But the Leader of the House, W. H. Smith, ignored him, and the Bill received a Second Reading without a division.

In committee, however, there were many anxious moments. The Bill had now been formally taken over by the government, and Hart-Dyke, 'with large-hearted Liberalism',[1] had offered the services of the government draftsmen. This offer caused much heart-searching among Welsh members, but Ellis, after a long conversation with Acland at the National Liberal Club, prevailed upon them to accept it.[2] But then a series of drastic amendments were put forward by the government. The proposed Board of Education was struck out and instead the powers of the Charity Commissioners were to be perpetuated. More important, the county councils were to be replaced as the local authority by local county committees, consisting of five members, three being nominated by the councils, two by the Privy Council. Indeed, it was only after much pressure that Hart-Dyke agreed even to leave the county council representatives in a majority at all. Finally, Monmouthshire was to be excluded, in contrast to all previous enactments on Welsh education.[3]

After these alterations, Gee, with his habitual simplification of political strategy, urged Rendel to drop the Bill. Equally characteristically, this was also the view of the Liberation Society.[4] But Rendel saw the need for intelligent compromise. 'Finding I will not drop the measure *forthwith* they [the government] wish to create some crucial, but less offensive, amendment on which to force us to drop it.'[5] A vital test came on the amendment to exclude Monmouthshire from the Bill.[6] Rendel insisted on debating the matter fully. Three of the four Monmouthshire members condemned the amendment, as did three Conservatives, Kenyon, Swetenham (Caernarvon), and Puleston (Devonport). It was pointed out that Monmouthshire was invariably included in Wales for educational purposes.[7] The govern-

[1] *Personal Papers of Lord Rendel*, p. 309.
[2] A. H. D. Acland to Mrs. T. E. Ellis, n.d. (N.L.W., Daniel Papers, 30).
[3] Liberation Society MSS., 24 June 1889.
[4] Ibid.
[5] Rendel to Gee, 6 July 1889 (N.L.W., Gee MSS., 8308c, 261).
[6] *Parl. Deb.*, 3rd ser., vol. cccxxxvii, pp. 1388 ff.
[7] For example, in the Commission of 1846, the Schools Inquiry Committee of 1864,

ment gave way, and withdrew the amendment on 10 July. Welsh Liberals were still resentful at the changes made in the Bill, but, with Rendel and Ellis both on the side of compromise, they agreed at a meeting with Hart-Dyke to accept it, as amended.

It was a wise decision. In spite of the gloomy forecasts of some Liberals in Wales, the Bill passed through the Lords 'with the most astonishing ease and rapidity',[1] passing unscathed through a few condemnations of the principle of State support for secondary education by a few die-hard peers. The Bill received the Royal Assent on 12 August. Ellis artfully obtained a Welsh printed version by boosting the sales of the Local Government Act, also printed in Welsh.[2]

The Welsh Intermediate Education Act of 1889 is a remarkable exception to the usual story of party rancour over Welsh affairs. The Conservative government revealed an unprecedented sympathy towards Welsh aspirations. Smith and Hart-Dyke were of inestimable assistance to the Welsh members. Later on, there was an unseemly dispute over who should claim the credit: in the 1895 election, Hart-Dyke told his constituents in Kent that the Bill was the work of the government and had been only reluctantly supported by the Welsh Liberals, lest they should lose popularity.[3] This is plainly a distortion. The major credit lies with Rendel, whose sureness of touch made the measure acceptable in principle to the government. Even so, this episode in 1889 is a pleasant exception to the usual pattern of party warfare. Liberals and Conservatives co-operated, and even Charles Bradlaugh,[4] the isolated and persecuted atheist, assisted in giving the measure priority in committee. It was supported in Wales on a very wide front ranging from Thomas Gee to Dean John Owen of St. Asaph. The Bishop of Chester helped convince Lord Salisbury of its necessity. The Act did not exactly anticipate Balfour's wider measure in 1902: the local government elections of 1889 made it inevitable that county councils would not be allowed to remain as the local authority in Wales. But, in organization and direction, Welsh intermediate education now formed a coherent system far in advance of

the Oxford and Cambridge Act of 1877, and the University College of South Wales and Monmouthshire of 1883.

[1] *Personal Papers*, p. 311.

[2] Ellis to Herbert Lewis, 24 July 1889 (Penucha MSS.; copy in N.L.W., Ellis Papers, 2883).

[3] *The Times*, 5 Aug. 1895. See also issues of 8 Aug. (letter by Humphreys-Owen), 9 Aug. (letter by Hart-Dyke), and 10 Aug. (letters by Rendel and the Hon. George Kenyon). Also see A. J. Mundella to Gladstone, 28 Oct. 1889 (B.M., Add. MSS., 44258, ff. 264–5).

[4] *Personal Papers*, p. 309.

that in England. Its financial support was to be strengthened by the Technical Instruction Act of 1889 and the Local Taxation Act of 1890.[1] In 1896 the Central Welsh Board was set up, with Humphreys-Owen as Chairman, to co-ordinate the whole system. Finally, of course, the Welsh Intermediate Education Act afforded another valuable precedent for separate legislation for Wales, on this occasion with the inclusion of Monmouthshire. Educationally, socially, and administratively, it was one of the most impressive memorials of the political awakening of Wales.

Brief reference should be made to some other important developments in Welsh education in this period, with which the political parties were only marginally concerned. The Education Commission in 1886–8, which inquired into the elementary education system, with Lord Cross as chairman, excited much interest in Wales, since its members included such staunch nonconformists as the veteran Henry Richard and the Rev. R. W. Dale. Its evidence showed how thoroughly the Board School system had penetrated throughout Wales. Its major significance for Wales, however, lay in the pressure from a new body of scholars and educationalists formed in 1885, Cymdeithas yr Iaith Gymraeg, 'The Society for the Utilization of the Welsh Language'.[2] Its vigorous secretary, the journalist, Beriah Gwynfe Evans, gave evidence before the Commission.[3] Richard found the pressure from this body to be so intense as to be 'rather embarrassing',[4] but it succeeded in its major ambition of securing the recognition of Welsh as a grant-earning subject under the elementary education code, on an equal footing with other languages.[5] No longer would there be absurd anomalies such as the appointment of a brilliant scholar, John Morris Jones, to a lectureship at Bangor, only to find he had no students to teach.[6]

In the field of university education, the campaign for a degree-conferring University of Wales gathered momentum. An important

[1] The Local Taxation Act assigned the 'whisky money' to education.
[2] See Baner ac Amserau Cymru, 27 Jan. 1886, and Y Goleuad, 26 June 1886, for a discussion of the Society's composition and function.
[3] Third Report of the Commissioners appointed to inquire into the Elementary Education Acts, 1887 (C. 5158), vol. iii, qu. 42,563 ff. Evans was a prominent figure in Welsh public life for over thirty years. At various times, he was Welsh editor of the South Wales Daily News, editor and proprietor of the Genedl and editor of Y Tyst. He was the author of the satirical surveys of Welsh politics written under the pseudonym of 'Dafydd Dafis'. See E. Morgan Humphreys, Gwŷr Enwog Gynt: yr ail Gyfres (Aberystwyth, 1953), pp. 120–31.
[4] Richard to Gee, 1 Nov. 1886 (N.L.W., Gee MSS., 8308c, 304).
[5] Final Report of the Commissioners, 1888 (C. 5485), pp. 144–5.
[6] D. Emrys Evans, op. cit., p. 54; Lloyd (ed.), Sir Harry Reichel, p. 82.

conference of Welsh educationalists was convened by the Cymmrodorion Society at Shrewsbury in January 1888, under the chairmanship of Professor John Rhŷs, the Professor of Celtic at Oxford
University. After some dispute, proposals were put forward to the
Lord President of the Council for a university charter. A further
meeting in November 1891, also at Shrewsbury, decided in favour of
a teaching university rather than simply an examining university,
conferring degrees only on its own students.[1] 'The educational fervour in Wales has evidently impressed the government', wrote Lord
Aberdare.[2] In every department, discussion on education in Wales
was intense and fruitful, transcending denominational barriers.
The old controversy over the Meyricke Funds of Jesus College,
Oxford, was resumed, when Dean Owen of St. Asaph proposed
extending them to other colleges in Oxford.[3] This was a matter of
much substance, since the new intermediate schools promised an
overwhelming increase in the number of young Welsh university
undergraduates.

The abiding impression which must remain is of the remarkable
zeal for education in Wales. Viriamu Jones could reflect, with understandable exaggeration, in 1896 that 'the history of Wales during the
last twenty-five years has been little else than the history of its educational progress'.[4] To H. A. L. Fisher thirty years on, the national
enthusiasm for education was still a cause for wonder.[5] It was as
pronounced in the massive voluntary contributions made to the new
University Colleges and to projects such as Morris Jones's Welsh
Grammar by the working men of Wales, miners, farmers, and quarrymen, as in the formal structure of primary, intermediate, and university education. To some extent, the religious acerbity of Welsh
social life was put aside. 'There is no reason why bones of contention
should prevent a Dean who is supposed to be feasting on a "fatted
calf" . . . from co-operating for Welsh Education with an earnest
Liberationist leader', wrote Dean John Owen to Tom Ellis.[6] On both
sides of the House of Commons, Welsh members emphasized the
urgent need of expanding the resources of Welsh national education.

[1] D. Emrys Evans, op. cit., pp. 37 ff. Cf. W. Lewis Jones, 'Y Brifysgol i Gymru'
Y Traethodydd, July 1892, pp. 273–80.
[2] Lord Aberdare to the Rev. J. Wynne Jones, 7 Nov. 1891 (Letters of Lord Aberdare,
vol. ii, p. 287).
[3] Dean Owen to Ellis, 4, 12 June 1890 (N.L.W., Ellis Papers, 1595, 1596).
[4] J. Viriamu Jones, 'The University of Wales', Wales, Jan. 1896, p. 6.
[5] H. A. L. Fisher, An Unfinished Autobiography (London, 1940), p. 102.
[6] Dean Owen to Ellis, 4 June 1890 (N.L.W., Ellis Papers, 1595).

The Welsh Intermediate Education Act of 1889 is the major land-mark in this movement. It has received scant notice from English historians. The *Annual Register* dismissed it in a brief paragraph.[1] But it ushered in the educational revolution of 1902, together with a wider social revolution through increased mobility and opportunity, and over no other issue was national pride in Wales more genuinely manifested.

(v) *Home Rule for Wales*

It was during these years that the cry, faint but seductive, of 'Welsh home rule' first began to disturb the political scene. But, whereas Irish nationalism sought the maximum degree of exclusion from the political structure of Britain and merged all its varied protests into the demand for political separation, in Wales national feeling evolved only very hesitantly and gradually towards a separatist posi-tion. Thomas Gee and the Rev. John Thomas avowed openly what the Irish Nationalists themselves had been compelled tacitly to recog-nize since 1886, that 'our business is with the great Liberal Party in England'.[2] In Wales there was a profusion of Isaac Butts, but very few Parnells. The aged Michael Daniel Jones, with his bitter hostility to all things English, remained an isolated figure. Even when Chamber-lain proposed a solution of the Irish question in 1886 upon a basis of 'home rule all round', he found little support in Wales, although this idea intrigued the young David Lloyd George and coloured his thinking throughout his political career.[3]

However, after 1886 a new spirit began to emerge in Wales, stimu-lated by the intense awareness of nationality shown by the early students at the University College of Wales at Aberystwyth and their contemporaries, to find practical expression in the movement known as *Cymru Fydd* ('Young Wales'). Its very name suggested the forward-looking optimism of a new, rebellious generation; like Young Ireland and Young Italy, its programme appeared 'a mani-festo against old age'.[4] As in so many nationalist revivals of the later nineteenth century in central and eastern Europe and in Scandinavia, *Cymru Fydd* conceived its national mission in terms of a native cultural

[1] *Annual Register, 1889*, p. 6.
[2] Rev. John Thomas to Gee, 21 Mar. 1887 (N.L.W., Gee MSS., 8311D, 572). Cf. Owen Thomas and J. Machreth Rees, op. cit., p. 407.
[3] Garvin, op. cit., vol. ii, p. 217 n.
[4] Elie Kedourie, *Nationalism* (London, 1960), p. 101.

and linguistic tradition. To Llewelyn Williams, one of its most ardent and eloquent members, it was concerned with 'True politics'—with education, literature, music, and art, with debating societies and reading rooms as much as with electioneering.[1] It resembled continental cultural nationalism also in being based to a considerable degree on the intelligentsia, on historians such as John Edward Lloyd and *litterateurs* such as O. M. Edwards. Again, as in similar nationalist movements, its initial impetus came from emigré Welshmen, the first *Cymru Fydd* society being formed in London in 1886, and the second in Liverpool. In Wales, however, the movement for long made little headway. Not until the founding of a society at Barry in 1891 was a bridgehead established in South Wales. The movement then spread rapidly throughout Wales, but there was a strange unreality about this progress, since in many parts of the country *Cymru Fydd* and the traditional organization and personnel of nonconformist Liberalism were barely distinguishable.

Even so, the new quality of nationalism in Wales was unmistakable, and was widely debated. *Cymru Fydd* found widespread support in the popular press, from the veteran Gee in *Y Faner*, where the term *Ymreolaeth* (home rule) was coined,[2] to the young Lloyd George, whose latest publication he himself described significantly as 'thorough Nationalist and Socialist—a "Regenerator" in every way'.[3] He advised D. R. Daniel to limit liability on capital to £100 to avoid the consequences of libel suits! In January 1888 *Cymru Fydd* issued its own journal, a monthly under the editorship of T. J. Hughes ('Adfyfr'), and subsequently of R. H. Morgan and Owen M. Edwards. The success of young Welsh home rulers in by-elections—S. T. Evans and Lloyd George in particular—strengthened the hand of Ellis at the House of Commons in evolving a comprehensive nationalist programme that would transform the quality of daily life. Initially, *Cymru Fydd* remained almost entirely a cultural and educative movement: Llewelyn Williams warned against emulating the Irish Nationalist Party. 'What a sordid party it is compared with the Young Ireland party of the forties! That is not the sort of "Nationalism" I should like to see in Wales—a Nationalism divorced from

[1] Llewelyn Williams to J. E. Lloyd, 21 Sept. 1894 (Bangor, Lloyd Papers, MSS. 314, no. 592).

[2] By 'Emrys ap Iwan' (Robert Ambrose Jones). See T. Gwynn Jones, *Cofiant Emrys ap Iwan* (Caernarvon, 1912).

[3] Lloyd George to Daniel, 12 Dec. 1887 (N.L.W., Daniel Papers, 2744). The reference was to the Caernarvon journal, *Udgorn Rhyddid*, with which Lloyd George later severed his connexion.

everything except politics'.[1] However, Ellis insisted on extending this programme into the political field also and emphasized 'the necessity of declaring for self-government, if we are to have a *national* programme and a real working *national* party'.[2] The demand for a national legislature in Wales grew more articulate. The press noted that Gladstone's speech at Singleton Abbey in Swansea in 1887 was punctuated by cries of 'Home Rule for Wales'.

But the efforts to translate this sentiment into practical organization showed little clear direction. The first important initiative came at a significant meeting of the Welsh National Council at Newtown on 9 and 10 October 1888, at which John Morley was present.[3] It followed a prolonged agitation by the South Wales Liberal Federation to enlarge the composition of the Council to include representatives of the Welsh Land League, *Cymru Fydd* and kindred organizations, and to create an independent Welsh Party in the Commons on the lines of the Irish Nationalists. Both these proposals met with opposition from the North Wales Liberal Federation, and from Osborne Morgan in particular. The views of the Liberals of North and of South Wales were thus the exact reverse of those they were to adopt during the *Cymru Fydd* crisis seven years later. In the event, a compromise formula was arrived at in the Newtown meeting: the predominance of official Liberalism on the Council was stringently maintained, while a vague resolution 'called the attention of the Welsh members to the necessity of more effectual organization' on behalf of Welsh interests. A parliamentary sub-committee was also set up to watch over Welsh parliamentary business. The presence of Morley suggested that this was nationalism in only its most diluted form, and the character of the National Council showed little change in subsequent years. Its function, wrote Ellis, 'was to help secure the unity of Wales and help it to claim its right when the day of settlement comes'.[4]

A different, but highly significant, approach to local self-government came with the Local Government Act of 1888, which created county councils. Ellis was quick to appreciate the value of this

---

[1] Llewelyn Williams to J. E. Lloyd, 21 Sept. 1894 (Bangor, Lloyd Papers, MSS. 314, no. 592).   [2] Ellis to Herbert Lewis, 28 Sept. 1888 (N.L.W., Ellis Papers, 2877).
[3] This important meeting was given extensive coverage in the Welsh press. See *South Wales Daily News*, 9 and 10 Oct. 1888; *Baner ac Amserau Cymru*, 13 and 17 Oct. 1888; and *Y Genedl*, 24 Oct. 1888, for full accounts and comment. There is further discussion in *Y Tyst*, 14 Oct. 1888; *Y Goleuad*, 15 Oct. 1888; and the *Cambrian News*, 12 Oct. 1888. All were disposed to be optimistic at the degree of unity attained at Newtown, save for the *Cambrian News*.
[4] Ellis to Herbert Lewis, 21 June 1889 (Penucha MSS.).

measure. He moved an amendment ineffectually in the Commons to set up a general advisory council for Wales.[1] Although this was withdrawn, section 81 of the Act, allowing county councils to form joint committees over matters of common concern, was to be effectively exploited by Lloyd George and other home rulers in the future.[2] The first elections to the new councils in January 1889 created a profound social and political revolution throughout Wales. Acland noted that 'the Welsh national feeling is very strongly brought out by these county council elections'.[3] In the event, the Liberals won control of every county save Brecknockshire, most by a wide margin. In North Wales, 175 out of 260 councillors were Liberal; in South Wales and Monmouthshire they numbered 215 out of 330.[4] Ellis observed: 'The Monmouthshire victory is of *immense* importance for it means that it will cast its lot with Wales.'[5]

The county council election results, which the events of the next thirty years largely confirmed, created a social transformation more striking even than the extension of democracy at the national level. The age-long ascendancy of landowners on the magistrates bench, self-perpetuating governors of the country-side, was abruptly terminated.[6] Nowhere was the change more dramatically illustrated than in Denbighshire, where the redoubtable Gee became the first chairman of the new county council, while in Montgomeryshire Humphreys-Owen gained preference over the Earl of Powis. From this time onwards, the traditional supremacy of the gentry over local life was rapidly undermined. On the other hand, it is arguable that the very effectiveness of this transfer of power on a local basis eventually blunted the appeal of the wider objective of Welsh home rule. In this sense, the very success of Welsh radicals in furthering social and political democracy heralded their own decline.

[1] *Parl. Deb.*, 3rd ser., vol. cccxxiv, pp. 1243 ff. For Ellis's views on the possibilities of the Local Government Act, see *Cymru Fydd*, June 1888, pp. 355–6, and 'Wales and the Local Government Act, 1894', *Addresses and Speeches* (1912), pp. 165 ff.

[2] Notably in the draft joint council agreed to at a meeting of thirteen Welsh county councils at Shrewsbury in Dec. 1891. It was also to be exploited by Lloyd George in the controversy over a national council to administer Church temporalities in June 1895 (see Chapter IV below).

[3] Acland to Robert Hudson, 26 Jan. 1889 (quoted in J. A. Spender, op. cit., p. 22).

[4] *South Wales Daily News*, 29 Jan. 1889. In the 1892 elections the Liberals made further gains, winning 400 seats to the Unionists' 194; however, the Liberals lost control of Radnorshire.

[5] Ellis to Ellis Griffith, 21 Jan. 1889 (N.L.W., Ellis Griffith Papers, 342).

[6] Although in Wales, as in England, a remarkable feature of the election returns was the success at the polls of many leading landed proprietors. For example, Llanystumdwy, Lloyd George's home village, returned Ellis Nanney, his opponent in the 1890 by-election (*Y Genedl*, 30 Jan. 1889).

In Parliament, the various efforts made by Welsh members to sponsor schemes tending towards local devolution presented a confused and erratic appearance. The impressive unanimity shown over disestablishment or intermediate education was significantly absent. Even so, the proposals in themselves are of more than academic interest. An interesting measure proposed in 1888 was that of a Standing Committee to consider all bills relating to Wales.[1] The initiative had come originally from the Scottish members. W. H. Smith, the leader of the House, had moved that the four Standing Committees (on Law, Trade, Shipping, and Agriculture), originally created in 1882, be revived. The Scots members, backed up by Gladstone, then urged unsuccessfully that a Scottish Committee be established also. The Welsh members, led by William Rathbone, a Liverpool merchant who sat for Arfon, then followed suit with an identical demand for Wales. Osborne Morgan pointed out how Scotland was treated far more favourably than was Wales, with a Secretary of State, a Lord Advocate and Solicitor-General, while six members of the 1886 cabinet were Scottish representatives. On this occasion, more interest attaches to the speeches against the motion, particularly as they illustrate the concern felt by Conservative members for constituencies in the English marches at the new temper in Wales. Raikes, the Postmaster-General and a habitual antagonist of the Welsh Liberals, asserted that English Acts of Parliament naturally applied to Wales. Again he ridiculed Welsh culture, stigmatizing Welsh literature as 'bardic fragments', and alleged that the motion was a mere pretext for Welsh home rule.[2] What would follow? *Proximus ardet Ucalegon.* He concluded by quoting the medieval precept, *Nolumus fines Angliae mutari.* Sir Joseph Bailey (Hereford) asserted that Wales did not require separate educational legislation, an extraordinary assertion in the light of recent debates. S. Gedge (Stockport) asserted that Wales differed from Cheshire and Shropshire only in its possession of a language that only an insignificant and illiterate minority understood. Finally, W. H. Smith prophesied that this modest motion would lead in fact to imperial disintegration. In a small House, the motion failed by 135 to 113, only eleven Welshmen troubling to vote for it, as against forty-one Irish. Even so, it foreshadowed the later creation of a Welsh Standing Committee in 1907 and subsequently the Grand Committee established by the Macmillan government in 1960.

[1] *Parl. Deb.,* 3rd ser., vol. cccxxiii, pp. 469 ff.
[2] Ibid., p. 482.

A different initiative came in 1890 when Alfred Thomas, the worthy though unimaginative Baptist who represented East Glamorgan, moved the creation of a Welsh Secretary of State, but the government was inevitably hostile.[1] A far more ambitious scheme was an extraordinary National Institutions (Wales) Bill which Thomas brought up in February 1892.[2] This omnibus measure would set up a Welsh Secretary of State, together with a national council with a variety of functions, a Welsh education department, local government board, and museum. It was backed up by seventeen Welsh members. The national council would consist of the thirty-four Welsh members, with a further sixteen selected by county and county borough councils, and it would take over the powers of the Local Government Board, the Board of Guardians, the Commissioners for Works, and the Charity Commissioners in Wales. It was an entirely academic proposal, which bore the stamp of Ellis's administrative acumen. Two Welsh members openly opposed it, Bryn Roberts (Eifion) because he held that any form of home rule would weaken the Liberal Party,[3] and D. A. Thomas (Merthyr Tydfil) because it would provide little real power of self-government and would give the smaller counties too much influence.[4] Other influential members, including Rendel, Vivian, and Osborne Morgan, refused to back the Bill and it was quietly dropped. The total impression of these various devolutionary proposals is one of confusion and disunity. Ellis, writing amid the archaeological splendour of Luxor in Egypt, maintained that 'the policy for Wales is to get her case "*conferred upon*", everywhere and at all times possible'.[5] But the events of the years after 1886 show a great deal of uncertainty as to what that case was.

It would give a totally false impression to lay undue stress on the movement for self-government, in all its ramifications. In North Wales, the movement was still feeble. Ellis admitted that the North Wales Liberal Federation, unlike its counterpart in the South, was hesitant over home rule, while Lloyd George's identification with the movement was plausibly believed to have reduced his majority in the Caernarvon by-election of 1890.[6] The enthusiasm of Ellis and his intellectual friends for national communities, fortified in Ellis's

[1] Ibid., vol. cccxli, pp. 1069 ff.
[2] The text of the bill is printed in the *South Wales Daily News*, 11 Jan. 1892. There is a discussion of the measure in Edgar L. Chappell, *Wake up! Wales* (London, 1943), pp. 20–30.
[3] *South Wales Daily News*, 14 Mar. 1892.   [4] Ibid., 30 Mar. 1892.
[5] Ellis to Ellis Griffith, 6 Mar. 1890 (N.L.W., Ellis Griffith Papers, 356).
[6] Ellis to W. J. Parry, 28 May 1890 (Bangor, Coetmor MSS., 1B).

case by a dramatic visit to Africa in 1890 during which he discussed the possibilities of imperial federation with Cecil Rhodes, was all too often remote from the sectarian and agrarian disputes which formed the reality of Welsh radicalism. Ellis's great speech at Bala, in September 1890, in which he openly urged a Welsh legislature, fell upon stony ground, and gradually Ellis and *Cymru Fydd* parted company.[1] The magazine *Cymru Fydd* ceased publication in 1891, and Owen Edwards turned more profitably to the literary journal, *Cymru*.[2]

Equally fundamental was a growing divergence of opinion in Wales between the industrial coalfield and the rural hinterland. The discussions over Alfred Thomas's National Institutions Bill at Llandrindod Wells in the autumn of 1891 showed these fissures clearly. South Wales Liberals were critical of the preponderance afforded to the smaller counties on the National Council, and Glamorgan threatened to secede. Equally, wrote Herbert Lewis, 'the smaller counties absolutely decline to allow themselves to be swamped by Glamorganshire and Monmouthshire'.[3] The two extremes were represented by Glamorgan, who advocated one member per 50,000 population, and Radnor, who wanted one per county on the lines of the American Senate.[4] The large towns of the South were disillusioning to ardent young patriots. Llewelyn Williams's editorial efforts to run first the Barry *Star* and later the Swansea *Daily Post* on Welsh nationalist lines were doomed to futility. He was depressed by 'the howling wilderness of Swansea Philistinism' and by Barry, 'a large rapidly-growing town. . . intent on nothing but money-making'. Above all, Cardiff was 'lost to Welsh nationalism'.[5] Its member, Sir Edward Reed, affirmed that 'the great commercial and cosmopolitan town of Cardiff', with a population of 150,000, could not be severed from its economic relations with the industrial areas of England.[6] On the Cardiff Liberal Association, which claimed in its Annual Reports to be the largest in the country, ardent Welshmen such as Edward

---

[1] There is a full discussion of the Bala meeting in *Baner ac Amserau Cymru*, 24 Sept. 1890, and *Y Genedl*, 24 Sept. 1890.

[2] It had been noticeable that when the editorship of *Cymru Fydd* changed hands in June 1889, it was far more literary and cultural and much less political under R. H. Morgan and Edwards than it had been under 'Adfyfr'. R. H. Morgan frankly criticized the previous editorial policy as being 'too narrow in scope' and too rancorous and censorious (editorial in *Cymru Fydd*, June 1889, p. 273).

[3] Herbert Lewis to Ellis, 7 Mar. 1892 (N.L.W., Ellis Papers, 1397).

[4] Herbert Lewis to Ellis, 9 Mar. 1892 (N.L.W., Ellis Papers, 1398).

[5] Llewelyn Williams to Ellis, 19 Feb. 1892 (N.L.W., Ellis Papers, 2134). Llewelyn Williams to Edward Thomas, 6 Apr. 1893 (Cardiff, Cochfarf Papers).

[6] Letter by Reed in *South Wales Daily News*, 17 Mar. 1891.

Thomas (*Cochfarf*), with his passionate concern for Welsh literature, music, and antiquities, were swamped by the mass of professional Liberals.[1] In England, Welsh home rule found few friends. It was mainly of interest to intellectuals such as Matthew Arnold and Andrew Reid of the *Westminster Review*.[2] A few statesmen such as Lord Rosebery toyed with the idea of 'home rule all round', but even such friendly journals as the *British Weekly* thought that Welsh issues could be determined at Westminster alone, particularly the great question of disestablishment.[3]

This, however, is not the whole story. The ferment within Wales was increasing in pace and intensity. Dilke was told that 'the Welsh national question . . . should not be made a party question. . . . It should be the means of cementing together all sections of the community, and . . . but for the Church Establishment it would be looked upon in that light by Welshmen generally irrespective of party or creed.'[4] Among some Welsh High Churchmen, men such as Arthur Price and the Rev. Edwin Jones, reverence for the old British Church led to sympathy for Welsh home rule. 'The very same selfish reasons that make these men stick up for tithes will make them nationalists.'[5] Ritualism, wrote one correspondent to Ellis, would lead in time to a Welsh Parliament.[6] *Cymru Fydd* was rapidly extending to all parts of Wales. Ellis was devoting himself to the education of his Liberal colleagues in the realities of the Welsh national question. 'The *cause*', he informed a Caernarvonshire friend, 'is making wonderful progress.'[7]

(vi) *The Welsh Parliamentary Party*

This multitude of proposals, disestablishment, intermediate education, land reform, governmental devolution, came to resemble a national programme, and not simply a series of individual initiatives by particular members, because of a new cohesion and unity among the Welsh members of Parliament. It was this that gave form and

---

[1] For 'Cochfarf', see the *Dictionary of Welsh Biography*.

[2] Andrew Reid to Gee, 8 July 1892 (N.L.W., Gee MSS., 8308c, 250). For Matthew Arnold's views, see his article on 'Welsh Disestablishment', *National Review*, Mar. 1888, pp. 1–13.

[3] *British Weekly*, 14 Feb. 1892.

[4] J. Jenkins to Dilke, 5 Oct. 1891 (N.L.W., Ellis Papers, 967).

[5] Arthur Price to Ellis, 22 Nov. 1891 (N.L.W., Ellis Papers, 1699). For the interesting personality of Price, see E. Morgan Humphreys, *Gwŷr Enwog Gynt* (Aberystwyth, 1950), pp. 75 ff.

[6] Arthur Price to Ellis, 21 Oct. 1891 (N.L.W., Ellis Papers, 1698).

[7] Ellis to W. J. Parry, 28 May 1890 (Bangor, Coetmor MSS., 1B).

direction to the complex issues convulsing Welsh political life between 1886 and 1892. Hitherto Welsh members had been notoriously unobtrusive and inarticulate. One keen observer noted how in fifty years they had never made a mark. 'The limit of their ambition seems to be County Court Judgeships.'[1] But after 1886 the position was very different. After 1886 the Welsh members of Parliament were transformed both in composition and in organization. For the first time, they were to resemble a coherent and distinct party.

The ultimate transformation in the personnel of the Welsh representation came in a series of by-elections. In seven vacancies, seven Liberals were returned, all comparatively young, all Welsh-born and nonconformist, and all in some sense representative of the nationalist fervour coursing through Wales. Some were to dominate Welsh public life for many years to come. In one constituency after another, a stern contest was waged in the local Liberal Association between traditional influences and the nationalist sympathizers of *Cymru Fydd*. Elderly members such as David Pugh and C. R. M. Talbot were being harassed by their local constituency parties. Humphreys-Owen, a sound Liberal but an Anglican in religion and a landowner by occupation, had the humiliation of being rejected as candidate by four successive North Wales constituencies in favour of nonconformist Welshmen between 1888 and 1891.[2] Arthur Price, still in an indeterminate no-man's land between romantic Toryism and ritualistic nationalism, spoke ominously of the 'ultra-democratic movement' sweeping through Wales.[3] At Merthyr in 1888 came the first trial of strength, when two successive by-elections were fought. The first returned David Alfred Thomas, a young colliery-owner of independent mind, but at this time ardent for the national causes, at the expense of the Liberal churchman, G. W. E. Russell. Thomas was to play an unhappy, isolated role in political life, but for twenty years he remained an original and influential mind among the Welsh Liberals.[4] As his fellow-member, there was returned Pritchard Morgan,

[1] Henry W. Lucy, *A Diary of the Salisbury Parliament, 1886–1892* (London, 1892), p. 83. Lucy (1843–1924) was parliamentary correspondent of the *Daily News*, and for many years wrote the 'Essence of Parliament' feature in *Punch*. See his autobiography, *Sixty Years in the Wilderness* (London, 1909).
[2] In Caernarvon Boroughs, Denbigh Boroughs, West Denbighshire, and Flint Boroughs.
[3] Arthur Price to J. E. Lloyd, 12 May 1891 (Bangor, Lloyd Papers, MSS. 314, no. 439).
[4] For Thomas, see Viscountess Rhondda (ed.), *D. A. Thomas, Viscount Rhondda*, which contains interesting chapters on Thomas's industrial and political careers by David Evans and Llewelyn Williams respectively. J. Vyrnwy Morgan, *Life of Viscount*

a gold speculator whose search for El Dorado took him as far afield as Australia and Korea: to *Tarian y Gweithiwr*, the miners' journal, he was *Yr Aelod dros China* (the member for China). Morgan was a political free-lance unpopular with his colleagues. His return was a rebuff both for the Merthyr Liberal Association and for the *Cymru Fydd* element who had favoured the Baptist barrister, Ffoulkes Griffiths, which suggested that the local influences controlling Merthyr politics were still immune from long-range pressure as they had been in 1868.[1] In 1889 and 1890 the two aged squires who represented East and West Carmarthenshire died, and were succeeded by Abel Thomas and J. Lloyd Morgan, two nonconformist barristers of similar background. A solicitor of nationalist outlook, David Randell, filled the vacancy at Gower in 1888, his Methodist religion and his activity in tinplate union litigation securing a safe return over the powerful Conservative, Sir John Dillwyn-Llewelyn of Penlle'r-gaer. Another important acquisition was Samuel Evans, an Independent and the son of a Skewen grocer, who was to rise to the presidency of the Court of Admiralty. Evans in time was to devote himself largely to his legal practice—'a lawyer on the make' was Rendel's description[2]—but in 1890 his return for Mid-Glamorgan was regarded as a notable triumph for nonconformity and Welsh home rule.

Finally, there was the return at Caernarvon in April 1890 of the twenty-seven-year-old solicitor, David Lloyd George, whose fame had rung throughout Wales in the Llanfrothen burial case as a new tribune of the people.[3] Already, Lloyd George's uncompromising yet

Rhondda (London, 1918) is prolix and almost useless. Vitriolic but occasionally illuminating comments on the Welsh members are provided by T. Marchant Williams, *The Welsh Members of Parliament* (Cardiff, 1894).

[1] This fascinating by-election is fully covered in the *Merthyr Express* and the *South Wales Daily News*, Aug.–Oct. 1888. Morgan had virtually the field to himself from 25 Aug. to 2 Oct., when the Merthyr Liberal Association belatedly nominated Ffoulkes Griffiths. Thereafter, in spite of the aid of a galaxy of outside speakers, including Tom Ellis, D. A. Thomas, and 'Mabon', Griffiths quite failed to make up lost ground, and polled only 4,956 to Morgan's 7,149. Morgan received the support of local Unionists, as well as of the Licensed Victuallers, but he also seems to have received much working-class backing, especially in Aberdare. This election deeply divided the frail Merthyr Liberal Association, and it disappeared from view until 1909. For Morgan see p. 91, n. 3 above.

[2] Rendel to Humphreys-Owen, 10 Dec. 1895 (N.L.W., Glansevern MSS., 672). For Evans, see the *Dictionary of National Biography*, supplement 1912–21, and the *Dictionary of Welsh Biography*.

[3] None of the innumerable biographies, memoirs, and sketches of Lloyd George can be considered satisfactory. Much the most useful for his activities in Welsh politics remains Watkin Davies, *Lloyd George, 1863–1914* (London, 1939). There is useful information in the multi-volume studies by H. du Parcq (4 vols., 1913) and J. Hugh

mercurial tactics had made him suspect in some quarters. The cautious Rathbone, member for Arfon and a strong opponent of Welsh home rule, agreed with his Liberal agent that Lloyd George's nomination would cause the loss of the seat.[1] Arthur Price, with his *penchant* for vituperation, found Lloyd George 'irreconcilable and unpractical', though 'very able'.[2] Humphreys-Owen, defeated for the Caernarvon nomination by local Welsh sentiment, considered Lloyd George no more than 'a second-rate county attorney',[3] a memorable misjudgement indeed. He looked forward with grim pleasure to Lloyd George's defeat. Indeed, Lloyd George's return was highly problematical: the seat had returned a Conservative, Swetenham, in 1886. The safe Liberalism of small towns like Criccieth, Pwllheli, and Nevin was counterbalanced by the Tory influence of Bangor, a cathedral city. Caernarvon and Conway were uncertain in their allegiance with Tory strength shown in municipal elections.[4] Lloyd George had preferred to campaign by remote control here, leaving the active intervention to his friends, D. R. Daniel and Beriah Evans. In view also of the harassing tactics of men like the powerful Rev. Evan Jones, Caernarvon, who attempted to gain a clear declaration from the Liberal candidate in favour of 'independent action' if the Welsh demands were not sponsored by the Liberal leaders, Lloyd George's eventual victory by the narrow margin of eighteen votes was no mean accomplishment. The new member's maiden speech on 3 June showed that 'Young Wales' had gained a most valuable recruit, and for thirty years the career of Lloyd George was to provide the decisive catalyst in Welsh politics.

In addition to these changes in composition, the organization of the Welsh members was also completely overhauled. Previously there had been only a loose association under the nominal leadership of Henry Richard, but now, on Richard's death in 1888, Rendel took

Edwards (5 vols., 1913–24), but both are highly uncritical. Frank Owen, *Tempestuous Journey* (London, 1954), the only study yet based on the Lloyd George papers (in the possession of the Beaverbrook foundation) is sensationalist and disappointing.
[1] W. Rathbone to R. D. Williams, 21 Mar. 1890 (Bangor, MS. 1125, no. 158). For Rathbone, see Eleanor Rathbone, *William Rathbone, a Memoir* (London, 1905); Sheila Marriner, *Rathbones of Liverpool* (Liverpool, 1961).
[2] Arthur Price to Lloyd, 14 Oct. 1892 (Bangor, Lloyd Papers, MS. 314, no. 449).
[3] Humphreys-Owen to Rendel, 19 Aug. 1888 (N.L.W., Rendel Papers, xiv. 496).
[4] The Caernarvon election is fully covered in *Y Genedl*, 26 Mar.–16 Apr. 1890. See particularly the letter of the Rev. Evan Jones in the issue of 16 Apr. While the *Genedl* strongly supported Lloyd George, the other Caernarvon Liberal journal, *Yr Herald Cymraeg*, was very lukewarm, and was attacked by the *Genedl* for giving prominence to a letter which suggested that the return of the Conservative candidate, Ellis Nanney, would bring greater economic benefits to the Caernarvon Boroughs.

steps to provide a more organized group. Rendel later claimed in his memoirs that a Welsh Party on the lines of the Irish had been his ambition since entry into politics, but the evidence is strong that the initiative he took in 1888 was designed in part to placate, in part to forestall, the rising nationalism of *Cymru Fydd* and of the South Wales Liberal Federation.[1] On Richard's death, Rendel was almost casually elected chairman of 'the Welsh Parliamentary Party', while in place of two secretaries, two whips were appointed, in this case, D. A. Thomas and A. J. Williams (South Glamorgan). Proposals were agreed to concerning the organization of a definite plan of campaign for each session, with joint balloting for Welsh members and pressure being put on the major parties.[2] To many contemporaries, all this was an alarming duplicate of the separatism of Ireland. The *North Eastern Daily Gazette*, condemning it, commented that 'The quondam barbarian has ever been quick to ape the lighter graces of civilization when emerging from barbarism'.[3]

The degree of independence involved in this new party organization, however, proved most illusory. When the South Wales Liberal Federation drafted its series of proposals for the consideration of Welsh members late in 1888, the third clause, which recommended an independent Welsh party on the lines of the Irish, caused much hesitation. Few were overtly enthusiastic. Even Tom Ellis was somewhat equivocal.[4] There was little fear over the next thirty years that the Welsh Liberals would cease to respond to the Liberal leadership. Coupland's statement that as long as Gladstone hesitated over disestablishment, 'the Welsh Liberals were not fully integrated into the Liberal Party', has no foundation in fact.[5] Rendel was the last man to move a separatist movement, while Tom Ellis, the close friend of Grey, Buxton, Fowler, Haldane, and Asquith, was intimately aware of the possibilities of influence within the charmed circle of the

[1] Rendel to Gee, 28 Dec. 1890 (N.L.W., Gee MSS., 8308c, 265). Rendel to the Rev. Josiah Jones, 17 Apr. 1893 (N.L.W., MS. 6411b). As recently as Jan. 1888 Rendel had argued in *Cymru Fydd* (Jan. 1888, pp. 20–28) that the acceptance of Welsh disestablishment as part of the Liberal programme made further independent Welsh action ('mere Welsh agitation in Wales') unnecessary. This view was strongly criticized by the executive of the South Wales Liberal Federation, and led to a frank correspondence between Rendel and 'Adfyfr', the editor of *Cymru Fydd* (N.L.W., Glansevern MSS., 8433–5).

[2] *South Wales Daily News*, 13 Dec. 1888. This important move was announced only very casually in the Welsh press: in fact only about fifteen or sixteen members seem to have attended the meeting which replaced the 'secretaries' with Whips. Bryn Roberts and Rathbone, however, were the only two dissentients.

[3] *North Eastern Daily Gazette*, 26 Aug. 1886. For a sympathetic view of the Welsh Party, see the *British Weekly*, 26 Mar. 1891.

[4] *Cymru Fydd*, Oct.–Nov. 1888.

[5] R. Coupland, *Welsh and Scottish Nationalism* (London, 1954), p. 220.

patrician leadership of the Liberal Party, and the futility of working outside it. The Welsh members were totally dependent on the good offices of the Liberal front bench, as were the Irish Nationalists in fact since the home rule split of 1886. Consequently, there was scarcely any support for an overt breach with the Liberal Party in later years. Almost the only occasion it was seriously considered by the Welsh members was on Ellis's death in 1899, when two members alone favoured 'independence', Herbert Lewis and Lloyd George. As a result the degree of unity attained by the Welsh members was never very pronounced. Sir Edward Reed (Cardiff) remained aloof on the front bench: his interest, Rendel complained, was almost wholly confined to dockyards.[1] Bryn Roberts was another constant opponent of rebellion. There were constant disputes, intrigues, and accusations; the correspondence of the Welsh members reveals an extraordinary picture of malice, pettiness, and mutual hostility. Partly explicable on personal grounds, this was primarily due to the amorphous nature of the Welsh Party. It never possessed the rigid discipline, backed up by stringent financial control, that characterized the Irish Party. The Welsh Party never, for example, agreed that party decisions were binding on members, or that the authority of the Welsh whips was mandatory. It was never independently financed. It was rather a loose association on the lines of the radical groups of the 1850's and 1860's, unified in general principle but incoherent in empirical action.

Nevertheless, enough was achieved during these years to make the Welsh Party a significant and controversial force in political affairs. Over questions such as disestablishment, tithe payment, education, agricultural and temperance reform, it succeeded in welding the disparate aspirations of Welsh members into organized action and in co-ordinating the activities of constituency associations. Following upon Welsh laws and Welsh committees, a Welsh Party seemed to many a portentous advance towards national status. A considerable triumph was gained in 1891 over local option, another distinctively Welsh and nonconformist issue.[2] Against the opposition of the government, Bowen Rowlands (Cardiganshire) carried the Second Reading of a Welsh Liquor Traffic Local Veto Bill by six votes. It was, wrote Lloyd George, 'a splendid victory' and 'quite unexpected'.[3] The government were given more trouble in February 1892, when,

---

[1] Rendel to Gee, 10 Oct. 1892 (N.L.W., Gee MSS., 8308c, 272).
[2] *Parl. Deb.*, 3rd ser., vol. cccli, pp. 590 ff.
[3] Lloyd George to Ellis, 11 Apr. 1891 (N.L.W., Ellis Papers, 683).

on Lloyd George's censure motion against the old grievance of English judges, they escaped by twenty votes.[1]

The Irish members provided much instructive guidance in the arts
of obstruction, and the Welsh proved apt and enthusiastic pupils.
Over the Clergy Discipline Bill of 1892, the Welsh members introduced several new refinements, as Archbishop Benson had ominously
anticipated.[2] Against the combined opposition of both front benches,
of Balfour and Gladstone, a small group of Welshmen, Ellis, Evans,
Lloyd George, and Wynford Philipps, a Pembrokeshire landowner
who had recently defeated Keir Hardie at Mid-Lanark, forced five
divisions on the Second Reading, on the grounds that the state should
not attend to spiritual discipline. In the Standing Committee on Law,
amendment after amendment was moved by the Welsh quartet,
despite Gladstone's earnest opposition. On the report stage, on
2 June, they forced no less than twenty-one divisions, and not until
27 June did the Bill, in itself innocuous and perfunctory enough,
become law. *The Times* censured this 'shameless obstruction'; the
Spectator castigated 'these Parliamentary pests'.[3] Rendel was driven
to despair by 'the madness of Wales in slapping John Morley and Mr.
Gladstone in the face',[4] and exhibiting hostility to the Church as
a Church and not simply as an establishment. Rendel felt his life
work was ruined. When he suggested to Morley that 'we must stand by
Lloyd George for the sake of his seat, he very warmly replies, "Let him
lose his seat, I hope he will" '. But from Welsh Liberal Federations
came a torrent of congratulations to Lloyd George and his friends.[5]

The general election of 1892 triumphantly vindicated this policy
at the polls. The temper of Wales tended to endorse militancy. 'Rathbone and Smith won't do for Wales.'[6] The Welsh Party should, it was
urged, sit in a 'solid phalanx' in the House to demonstrate its solid-
arity on behalf of Welsh nationalism.[7]

[1] H. W. Lucy, op. cit., pp. 490–2. Cf. *Baner ac Amserau Cymru*, 24 Feb. 1892 and
Y Genedl, 24 Feb. 1892.
[2] Archbishop Benson to Gladstone, 8, 10 July 1891 (B.M., Add. MSS., 44109,
ff. 197–202).
[3] *The Times*, 24 May 1892; *Spectator*, 4 June 1892.
[4] Rendel to Humphreys-Owen, 29 May 1892 (N.L.W., Glansevern MSS., 597).
[5] Rendel to Humphreys-Owen, 28 May 1892 (N.L.W., Glansevern MSS., 596). See
the comments of *Baner ac Amserau Cymru*, 1 June 1892; *Y Genedl*, 25 May 1892; and
the *Cambrian News*, 27 May 1892.
[6] William Rowlands to Ellis, 28 July 1888 (N.L.W., Ellis Papers, 1903). It was noted
that Rathbone walked out without voting during the Welsh Local Option debate of
1891 and the Welsh Land debate of Mar. 1892 (*Y Genedl*, 23 Mar. 1892).
[7] Herbert Lewis to Gee, 16 Nov. 1891 (N.L.W., Gee MSS., 8307c. 155). This was
also strongly advocated by the *Genedl*.

In particular, the 1892 election was a rout for Joseph Chamberlain in Wales. No less than eight Unionist candidates, mostly under his sponsorship, advocated disestablishment.[1] The addresses of the Unionist candidates for Swansea District (Herbert Monger) and for Anglesey (Morgan Lloyd) are almost indistinguishable from those of their Liberal opponents. The addresses of ten other Unionist candidates omitted all reference to disestablishment. Generally, Unionist candidates were silent on 'the claims of Wales' and their most obvious feature is an attempt to appeal frankly to Welsh Protestant prejudice against the Roman Catholic Church on behalf of the nonconformists of Ulster.[2] On the Liberal side, disestablishment appeared on every address, usually second on the list to Irish home rule, but actually first in six addresses.[3] Land reform, devolution, temperance reform, and education also gained wide mention, and indeed eleven Welsh Liberal candidates dealt only with Welsh issues.[4] In the country as a whole, Welsh disestablishment figured on the addresses of large numbers of Liberal and Unionist candidates, especially those of the Liberal candidates for Liverpool, with its large Welsh population.[5]

Liberalism and especially 'Young Wales' gained a massive triumph, with the circumstances almost wholly in their favour. Radnor, Monmouth District, and Pembroke District were regained, and Conservative representation cut down to three border seats. Chamberlain's stratagem failed utterly. In Cardiganshire, William Jones, a Birmingham draper who had appealed to the large Methodist vote, lost to the High Churchman, Bowen Rowlands, by over 2,000 votes.[6] In Caernarvon, Lloyd George increased his majority against Sir John Puleston, constable of Caernarvon Castle and a popular opponent. Other supporters of *Cymru Fydd* returned were Herbert Lewis (Flint) and Frank Edwards (Radnorshire), both lawyers, and the latter actually a cousin of the belligerent Bishop of St. Asaph. The Liberal

---

[1] Cf. speech by S. T. Evans, *Parl. Deb.*, 4th ser., vol. xxxi, p. 1717.

[2] A particularly glaring case is the address of Col. Cornwallis-West in West Denbighshire.

[3] Those of Lloyd George, Herbert Lewis, Lloyd Morgan, Herbert Roberts, A. J. Williams, Alfred Thomas.

[4] Those of Lloyd George, Herbert Lewis, Lloyd Morgan, Herbert Roberts, A. J. Williams, D. A. Thomas, Tom Ellis, T. P. Lewis, Rendel, W. Fuller-Maitland, T. H. Williams (defeated at Denbigh District).

[5] Ellis Griffith was candidate for the Toxteth Division.

[6] Letter by C. Marshall Griffith, *The Times*, 26 Apr. 1892. See the comments of the Methodist *Goleuad*, 30 June, 21 July 1892, and of the *Cambrian News*, 15, 22 Apr. 1892 and subsequent issues.

Unionists disappeared from Welsh history. A Methodist timber merchant, Herbert Roberts, ousted Cornwallis-West in West Denbigh by
over 2,000 votes, while Carmarthen District, whose member Cowell-
Stepney had turned Liberal Unionist in 1891, returned to its old
allegiance in the form of the emigré American consul at Cardiff,
Major Rowland Jones, born at Tregaron but now a hero of Gettys-
burg. Some of the Liberal majorities were astronomically large. Nine
were over 2,000, while at Merthyr Tydfil the bizarre combination of
D. A. Thomas and Pritchard Morgan swamped B. F. Williams, the
Recorder of Cardiff, by over 9,500, the largest majority in the British
Isles.

In the country generally, Gladstone's expectations were not fulfilled. The 'flowing tide' seemed to have been sadly checked by the
O'Shea divorce scandal, and his majority was only forty, 355 Liberals
and supporters being returned against 315 Unionists. This meant
that the Welsh members were afforded an unparalleled measure of
power, since, numbering thirty-one, they could hold the balance as
the Irish had done in 1885. These Welshmen seemed a compact and
determined band. Over two-thirds were Welsh-born, many of humble
origins. Six had received their basic education at the local village
elementary school. They derived mainly from two groups, fourteen
from the legal profession, a further fourteen from business or industry.
Finally, twenty-two out of the thirty-one were nonconformists.[1] Never
had Wales possessed such decisive influence in determining the course
of political events, and contemporaries looked forward, eagerly or
anxiously, to see how they seized their new opportunities.

[1] Their denominations were Calvinistic Methodists, 8; Independents, 6; Baptists, 4;
Unitarians, 2; Presbyterians, 1; uncertain (D. A. Thomas), 1. For D. A. Thomas's
religious beliefs, or lack of them, see Viscountess Rhondda, *This was My World*
(London, 1933), p. 7. The other nine were all Anglicans, viz. Fuller-Maitland, Osborne
Morgan, T. P. Price, Frank Edwards, Sir Hussey Vivian, Sir Edward Reed, W. Bowen
Rowlands, Stuart Rendel, C. F. Egerton Allen. Bowen Rowlands later became a
Roman Catholic.

IV

THE TURNING-POINT
1892–1896

(i) *Gladstone and the Land Commission*

In 1892 Welsh radicalism had reached the parting of the ways. For over a quarter of a century liberalism and nationalism had seemed to advance together, with the extension of political democracy fore-shadowing a unified vision of nationality. The whole course of Welsh history since 1868 had seemed to point inexorably to a complete recognition of the national status of Wales. But the experience of the years from 1892 to 1896 was to reduce these dreams to sober and harsh reality. At Westminster the realities of total dependence on the Liberal leadership served to show the disunity, even the futility, of the Welsh Party when presented with a real opportunity. In Wales itself, the bitter aftermath of the disintegration of the *Cymru Fydd* movement cruelly emphasized how shallow was the Welsh demand for separatism. After 1892, therefore, the character of Welsh radical-ism came to be transformed. It gradually came to shed its nationalist colouring, leaving only a bitter memory to poison the future course of the Welsh national movement.

Yet in August 1892, when Gladstone formed his fourth and final ministry, the future seemed propitious. Although Irish home rule was the overriding issue, Gladstone's 'only public pledge and tie in honour in public life',[1] he could survive only by pacifying the varied groups which made up his precarious majority. He had to satisfy those of his followers whose interest lay elsewhere in the Newcastle Programme. Prominent among these were the Welsh members, who had shown increasing signs of independence since 1886. A member of Gladstone's family wrote: 'Unless the Welshmen are kept within reasonable bounds, the Government must fall.'[2]

The first task was to ensure Welsh representation in the new ministry. Osborne Morgan was offered his old post of Judge-Advocate-General, but declined. Sir Edward Reed (Cardiff) was

---

[1] Gladstone to Harcourt, 14 July 1892 (B.M., Add. MSS., 44202, f. 157), 'Secret'.
[2] *Personal Papers of Lord Rendel*, p. 197.

invited to sit on the Commission of the Treasury, but after some vacillation, he refused on the grounds that this office was too unimportant for the member for 'the largest constituency in the Kingdom with a single member'.[1]

One Welsh appointment was made, however, and aroused the greatest interest. This was the appointment of Tom Ellis as Junior Lord of the Treasury and Deputy Whip. Rendel had suggested his nomination for office on the avowed grounds that 'Wales should have a man in Welsh ranks trained from early life to administrative work and ministerial responsibility'.[2] It would also, of course, firmly restrain with the reins of office the erstwhile rebel against the Clerical Discipline Bill. Hitherto, Wales had virtually no one experienced in office or departmental business: Osborne Morgan had been its sole Privy Counsellor. Ellis had been approached some months before, and the offer caused him much anxious concern. He sought the advice of his friends as to how far his independence in pressing Welsh claims would be restricted if he accepted. Lloyd George advised acceptance on the grounds that the ministry should contain some new radical blood, which suggests that even he put severe qualifications to the idea of 'independent action'.[3] Eventually, after much pressure from Morley, Ellis consented to serve. It would leave him free to work for Wales in the autumn, and would allow for effective influence to be 'quietly and unostentatiously wielded in the service of Wales'. Many Welshmen, however, hotly contested this view, among them John Gibson, the belligerent editor of the *Cambrian News*, who maintained that the 'Parnell of Wales' had been permanently gagged.[4] In the view of Arthur Price two months later, 'all hope of Welsh Nationalism doing anything for some time ended when Ellis grasped the Saxon gold'.[5] The issue remains highly contentious down to the present time.

[1] Reed to Gladstone, 16 Aug. 1892 (B.M., Add. MSS., 44515, f. 176. Also see ff. 201, 202, 219).

[2] Rendel to the Rev. Josiah Jones, 17 Nov. 1892 (N.L.W., MSS., 6411B).

[3] Ellis to Ellis Griffith, 25 Aug. 1892 (N.L.W., Ellis Griffith Papers, 385).

[4] In the *Cambrian News*, 26 Aug. 1892, Gibson discussed these criticisms of Ellis's acceptance of office, but decided to reject them; but by 28 Oct. he had concluded that Ellis was 'lost to Liberal Wales'. Throughout 1893 and 1894 he was persistently critical of Ellis as 'an official hack'. Gibson, editor of the *Cambrian News* from 1873 to 1915, was one of the most formidable figures in Welsh journalism.

On the other hand, *Y Tyst*, 26 Aug. 1892, was non-committal about Ellis's appointment, while Gee in *Baner ac Amserau Cymru*, 24 Aug. 1892 and subsequent issues, was positively enthusiastic, regarding it as an indication that disestablishment would be guaranteed a high place in the Liberal programme.

[5] Price to J. E. Lloyd, 14 Oct. 1892 (Bangor, Lloyd Papers, MSS. 314, no. 449).

Another appointment of particular interest to Wales was that of Arthur Acland, who now sat on Caernarvonshire County Council, to administer education. An 'arrangement' to have him as Chief Whip had broken down when Gladstone insisted on Marjoribanks, but as Vice-President of the Council Acland could wield great influence.[1] He had long been active in promoting the Welsh education movement, and could be expected to be sympathetic to intermediate education schemes, to the demand for a national university and for the teaching of Welsh in schools. Welshmen also applauded the choice of H. H. Asquith as Home Secretary. As a frequent speaker for the Liberation Society, he was known to favour Welsh disestablishment.

Pressure was rapidly brought to bear on the government. On 8 August, at a meeting in Committee Room 7 in the Commons, the Welsh members unanimously passed a resolution urging that Welsh disestablishment be given second place in the Liberal programme. Rendel was re-elected as chairman, with D. A. Thomas and Herbert Lewis as whips.[2] Gladstone soon showed impatience at their demands. On 3 September he complained to Rendel of Ellis's impossible request that Welsh disestablishment be placed immediately after Irish home rule in the Queen's Speech.[3] But it could scarcely be denied that the dilemma was largely of his own making. Since the passage of the Sunday Closing Act of 1881, Gladstone had supported a variety of Welsh measures with such warmth that he had himself stimulated national feeling. Towards the Welsh members, says the Archbishop of Wales, Gladstone had looked 'with a fatherly sympathy . . . and an almost stooping condescension'.[4] Further, Gladstone had been staying with Rendel at No. 2 Carlton Gardens while forming his new ministry, and had agreed to Rendel's three major requests, namely a Church Suspensory Bill, an inquiry into Welsh land, and a university charter.[5]

Gladstone committed himself further in a speech at Cwm-llan, near Snowdon, on 13 September. This picturesque occasion created a vivid impression throughout Wales. Lloyd George, Tom Ellis, and Bryn Roberts gave patriotic addresses in Welsh, and then Gladstone himself spoke, the craggy face of Snowdonia lending a transcendent majesty to his words. The specific contents of his speech, the usual cautious references to the importance of a settlement of the Church

[1] Ellis to Daniel, 10 Aug. 1892 (N.L.W., Daniel Papers, 394).
[2] *South Wales Daily News*, 9 Aug. 1892.
[3] Gladstone to Rendel, 3 Sept. 1892 (B.M., Add. MSS., 44549, f. 6).
[4] *Memories*, p. 145.   [5] *Personal Papers*, p. 311.

and the land questions, were less important than the apparent tone
of Gladstone's remarks. He referred to Welsh nationhood with great
warmth, and deplored the way in which successive governments had
ignored it.[1] It is not surprising that Welsh Liberals interpreted this as
implying that the new ministry intended to make full amends.

With these expectations aroused, Rendel used his personal friendship with Gladstone to spur him on. He refused office himself, direct-
ing his efforts solely to 'getting Mr. Gladstone and the Cabinet to
give official priority to Wales'.[2] He deplored the suspicion shown
towards the Premier's intentions by the Welsh Liberal Federations.
Acland was another diligent advocate of Welsh interests. Gladstone
wrote to him, somewhat wearily, on 23 October, 'Disestablishment
evidently stands No. 1; and I suppose Land stands No. 2? . . . If anything serious is to be done on these two matters, Wales will hardly
be able to get any further time.'[3] Clearly, his thoughts were mainly
on Ireland. But even Harcourt urged the need to 'satisfy the *genus
irritabile* of Wales'.[4]

The younger section among the Welsh members was anxious for
guarantees. The initiative now lay increasingly with Lloyd George,
Herbert Lewis, D. A. Thomas, and their associates, who regarded
the Fabian methods of 'Rendelism' as too cautious and ineffective.
A new convert to this view was Sir Edward Reed (Cardiff), previously
an inactive member in Welsh interests, but now an advocate of secession from the Liberal Party. Rendel angrily denounced 'the brazen
impudence of that self-seeking bully and impostor', but several other
South Wales members, Alfred Thomas, Major Jones, and David
Randell, followed Reed's example.[5] This was a most dangerous move,
in the light of the fissiparous tendencies of the Liberal Party and the
precarious majority of the government. In these circumstances, Gladstone had no alternative but to listen.

The first Welsh issue with which Gladstone had to deal was the
demand for an inquiry into the condition of Welsh agriculture. In the
debates of 1888 and 1892 several Liberal members had called for
a royal commission. In May 1892 the Welsh landowners, led by
Cornwallis-West, had made a similar request, but the government

[1] *The Times*, 14 Sept. 1892.
[2] Rendel to Gee, 30 Oct. 1892 (N.L.W., Gee MSS., 8308c, 274).
[3] Gladstone to Acland, 23 Oct. 1892 (B.M., Add. MSS., 44549, f. 30).
[4] Harcourt to Gladstone, 30 Oct. 1892 (B.M., Add. MSS., 44202, f. 274).
[5] Rendel to Humphreys-Owen, 11 Oct. 1892 (N.L.W., Glansevern MSS., 612).
Cf. *Cambrian News*, 23 Dec. 1892.

failed to respond. Gladstone himself had seemed to countenance the demand. In the debate in March he had stated the necessity for a full inquiry so that the question might be 'probed to the bottom'. He had reiterated this in his Snowdon speech in September, and yet again in a recent correspondence in *The Times* with Lord Sudeley and the secretary of the North Wales Property Defence Association, over rents in Wales.[1] In addition, Ellis was anxious to disprove his own critics, and show that he could 'push on Welsh questions substantially' while in his new office. Thus he sent an early memorandum to Asquith, outlining the scope and purpose of a royal commission on Welsh land. Asquith's pencilled comment was, 'Accepted. Will bring terms of reference before Mr. G.'[2]

Gladstone, however, now proved unexpectedly hostile. In his memoirs, Rendel states that he himself warmly advocated a land commission and was the first to protest when Gladstone appeared unfavourable.[3] But the evidence makes it abundantly clear that this was not so, and that the suspicions of 'Young Wales' regarding Rendel's attitude were, on this occasion at least, fully justified. For while it had been generally assumed that the government would institute a royal commission, Rendel himself favoured the more restricted mechanism of a select committee. He had never been enthusiastic about pushing the land question to the fore: disestablishment, he believed, should be the major objective. He was also averse from an inquiry on the sole grounds of economic hardship in Wales, and considered Gladstone's Snowdon speech to have been 'a somewhat unlucky impromptu'.[4] Later, he gave his reasons in detail for objecting to a royal commission; it would shelve the problem rather than solve it, its membership would be too small and the terms of reference too narrow. Further, there were already numerous royal commissions in existence (on Scottish Crofters, Evicted Tenants and the Poor Laws) and the endless multiplications of commissions would discredit the mechanism.[5]

Gladstone required much pressure before he took any action. Rendel conducted very confidential negotiations with him, and at the cabinet meeting of 11 November the issue of a commission or a committee on Welsh land was the first item on the agenda.[6] At this meet-

---

[1] *The Times*, 12, 26 Oct. 1892.
[2] Ellis to Asquith, 21 Oct. 1892 (Bodleian, Asquith Papers, box 19).
[3] *Personal Papers*, p. 312.
[4] Rendel to Gee, 30 Oct. 1892 (N.L.W., Gee MSS., 8308c, 274).
[5] Rendel to Gee, 17 Nov. 1892 (N.L.W., Gee MSS., 8308c, 276).
[6] Cabinet Minutes (B.M., Add. MSS., 44648, f. 28).

ing, the cabinet agreed on an inquiry, and Gladstone then informed Rendel that a committee was 'viewing the nature of the case, the better and the safer instrument. It is not the Irish case over again; a Commission might look as if it was.'[1] He also favoured a committee on technical grounds.

Whatever the practical advantages of a committee might be, it was quite unsatisfactory to most Welsh Liberals. Ellis wrote angrily: 'The offer of a Select Committee is a wretched one, and we will not have it. It would be worse than nothing.'[2] Only a royal commission would be able to take evidence on the spot throughout Wales: for poor Welsh farmers to travel to a committee in London would be extremely difficult. Furthermore, Wales expected nothing less than a commission, in view of the commissions appointed to further Irish and Scottish interests.[3] Ellis then approached Asquith: 'Anything short of a Royal Commission . . . would be a bitter disappointment.' 'To appoint a Departmental Committee after all the declarations made would be . . . a grudging and unhandsome policy towards the portion of the United Kingdom which has most loyally stuck to the Liberal Party. . . . I *have left* and leave the matter entirely in your hands.'[4] Apart from a doubt as to the number of commissions already existing, Asquith fully agreed with Ellis, and thought his list of proposed commissioners 'very representative and fair'.[5] Morley was also sympathetic. Finally, Ellis saw Harcourt on 23 November, and that genial cynic proceeded to tell Gladstone that 'it would give great satisfaction to the Welsh generally, and tend to keep them quiet if their hopes are not entirely fulfilled on the Church question'.[6]

Ellis also elicited the support of his colleagues, particularly Herbert Lewis and Lloyd George, and they combined to put pressure on Rendel. Lewis wrote to Rendel in the strongest terms, demanding a commission on the lines of the 1889 Sunday Closing Commission.[7] He pointed out that Gee and others were already accumulating evidence. Lewis also attempted to summon the special committee of Welsh M.P.'s appointed to keep a watch on the progress of Welsh

---

[1] Gladstone to Rendel, 12 Nov. 1892 (B.M., Add. MSS., 44549, f. 39), 'Confidential'.

[2] Ellis to Herbert Lewis, 7 Nov. 1892 (Penucha MSS.; copy in N.L.W., Ellis Papers, 2896).

[3] Ellis to Herbert Lewis, 18 Nov. 1892 (Penucha MSS.; copy in N.L.W., Ellis Papers, 2899), 'Private'.

[4] Ellis to Asquith, 22 Nov. 1892 (Bodleian, Asquith Papers, box 19).

[5] Ellis to Herbert Lewis, 19 Nov. 1892 (Penucha MSS.), 'Private'.

[6] Harcourt to Gladstone, 23 Nov. 1892 (B.M., Add. MSS., 44202, f. 287), 'Secret'.

[7] Lewis to Rendel, 12 Nov. 1892 (Penucha MSS., copy).

affairs. He wrote to Ellis: 'I am delighted that you have seen Asquith and made such an impression on him. Weakness on Rendel's part at this juncture would be deplorable.'[1]

Gradually Rendel gave way. On 14 November he thought a commission 'very doubtful'. He added, ' You will remember we have *forced* an assent to our demand in respect of Disestnt. and there is a limit to the use of force.'[2] But the next day he claimed to have an open mind: 'I was not sufficiently alive to the strength of Mr. G.'s language.'[3] On Ellis's initiative, the question was again before the cabinet on 23 November. Gladstone was still reluctant, but finally gave way on 14 December.[4] Lewis told Ellis: 'We would have been in a sad plight but for your remonstrances.'[5]

The struggle for a Land Commission contains many interesting features. The main credit unquestionably lies with Ellis, and no episode demonstrates more the wisdom of his decision to assume office. The affair reveals the fatal weakness that was beginning to be shown among the members of the Welsh Party, that lack of cohesion which was preventing them from using their opportunities in a manner comparable to the Irish. When the testing time came, they split in all directions. Ellis and Lewis had to coerce even such a stalwart of *Cymru Fydd* as Sam Evans. Rendel, as has been seen, was averse from an extreme policy. D. A. Thomas was frankly hostile,[6] as was Bryn Roberts, a constant opponent of separatism. Roberts wrote later: 'I have all along considered it a mistaken step to have a Commission, especially when it was got on the obligation that the Welsh landlords have been more extortionate than the English. I am of the opinion that the allegation will be disproved. . . .'[7] The episode also reveals the attitude of the government—Ellis, Acland, to a lesser extent, Asquith, the promoters of the Welsh cause, the rest indifferent, with Gladstone himself, though showing much sympathy, impatient with any diversion from Irish affairs. In these circumstances, the successful fight for a Land Commission was a remarkable achievement by the Liberals of Wales.

By May 1893 the Commission was appointed, and it held its first

---

[1] Lewis to Ellis, 21 Nov. 1892 (N.L.W., Ellis Papers, 1404).
[2] Rendel to Lewis, 14 Nov. 1892 (Penucha MSS.).
[3] Rendel to Lewis, 15 Nov. 1892 (Penucha MSS.). Ellis to R. A. Hudson, 22 Nov. 1892 (N.L.W., Ellis Papers, 2813).
[4] Rendel to Gee, 14 Dec. 1892 (N.L.W., Gee MSS., 8308c, 277).
[5] Lewis to Ellis, 19 Dec. 1892 (N.L.W., Ellis Papers, 1407).
[6] D. A. Thomas to Lewis, 25 Nov. 1892 (Penucha MSS.).
[7] Bryn Roberts to Vincent Evans, 18 Mar. 1893 (N.L.W., Vincent Evans Papers).

session on 25 May. It consisted of nine members. The chairman was Lord Carrington, a young Liberal peer. Two represented the tenant farmers, Richard Jones and J. M. Griffiths. There were also Edwin Grove (chairman of Monmouthshire County Council), Professor John Rhŷs (principal of Jesus College, Oxford in 1895), and David Brynmor Jones, Q.C., M.P., brother of Viriamu Jones. These six may be classified as broadly Liberal and eventually signed the Majority Report. The landlords were represented by Lord Kenyon and Sir J. T. Dillwyn-Llewellyn, while Frederic Seebohm, a Liberal Unionist, was an authority on Celtic tribal tenures. The last three signed the Minority Report. Thus the Commission had a strong Liberal bias. It sat until 5 December 1895, and its Report came out in 1896 when the Liberals had fallen from power.

It is impossible to do more than summarize the main features of the Royal Commission. Its findings, drafted by its able secretary, Lleufer Thomas, present a priceless abundance of source materials for historians of the social development of Wales, the seven bulky volumes of evidence, conclusions, and appendices ranging widely over many aspects of the rural scene.[1] The presence of several Welsh-speaking members on the Commission gave it a far wider scope than any previous inquiry, as it travelled around Wales. Its 1,086 witnesses included 106 landowners, 110 land agents, 516 tenant farmers, and 82 freeholders.[2] Only twenty-one labourers, however, gave evidence, Gladstone stating in the Commons that the conditions of farm labourers were not the primary concern of the Commission.[3] At first, progress was slow, the Commissioners unanimously agreeing that many farmers were deterred from coming forward through fear of eviction. There is evidence to show that the landowners, with the able legal assistance of their counsel, J. E. Vincent, were better armed than their radical opponents in the marshalling and presentation of evidence. Rhŷs viewed with apprehension the temporary loss of the legal acumen of Brynmor Jones in 1893. 'We shall be helpless without him—we shall have no lawyer to tackle these twisty agents.'[4] As a substitute, he tried unsuccessfully to obtain Lloyd George, 'if he is not too objectionable to the Tories'. Later Brynmor Jones complained how in Pembrokeshire, 'no-one attends on the Liberal side to give confi-

---

[1] *Evidence*, vols. 1 and 2 (1894); vols. 3 and 4 (1895); vol. 5, *Report and Appendices*, *Index* (1896).
[2] *Report*, p. 7.
[3] *Parl. Deb.*, 4th ser., vol. x, p. 506.
[4] Rhŷs to Ellis, 17 Sept. 1893 (N.L.W., Ellis Papers, 1750).

dence and cross examine, while Vincent. . . is as vigilant as ever'.[1]
He confided that Liberal members of the Commission were lax in
attendance. In short, the view entertained by both sides beforehand
that the cause of the tenant farmers would be the more effectively
presented of the two, with the large numbers of legal members of
Parliament and the organizing skill of Gee and his colleagues, seems
to have been disproved. Despite their initial hostility to the Commissioners, the Welsh landowners put up a far more impressive showing
than many among their ranks had anticipated.

Nevertheless, the Commission brought much satisfaction to Welsh
Liberals. By September 1893 even Bryn Roberts had lost his earlier
pessimism and believed that the inquiry was 'turning out pretty well'.[2]
Professor Rhŷs thought that the longer it went on, the more favourable it would be to the Liberal cause.[3]

Testimonies before the Commission illustrated in the clearest way
the complete cleavage between the two main sections of opinion in
Wales. On the Liberal side, witnesses were almost unanimous in demanding security of tenure, compensation for unexhausted improvements, and compulsory fixing of rents through a land court. They
laid stress on the tension caused by the difference in race, religion,
language, and political outlook existing between the great majority
of landlords and their tenants. Tom Ellis dwelt on the excessive
rental in Wales, and Thomas Gee on the discrimination employed
against nonconformist tenants.[4] Llewelyn Williams alleged that
Welsh landowners had discouraged their tenants from coming forward to testify.[5] A. J. Williams demanded that rents be fixed for
seven years by a land court.[6] Bryn Roberts condemned the various
Agricultural Holdings Acts as failures, although he preferred arbi-
trators, chosen by mutual agreement, to a tribunal.[7] All agreed that
the main evils were insecurity caused by capricious landlords and the
excessive land hunger among applicants for holdings.

The evidence of the landowners and their agents seems to depict
a different world, a world of long tenancies and harmonious relationships. The case here was equally clear. While usually agreeing that
there were some unsatisfactory features of Welsh agriculture, they all

---

[1] Brynmor Jones to Ellis, 7 Mar. 1894 (N.L.W., Ellis Papers, 1011).
[2] Bryn Roberts to Ellis, 26 Sept. 1893 (N.L.W., Ellis Papers, 2268).
[3] Rhŷs to Ellis, 17 Sept. 1893 (N.L.W., Ellis Papers, 1750).
[4] *Evidence*, vol. i, qu. 16,910 ff. (Ellis's evidence), and vol. iv, qu. 63,999 ff. (Gee's evidence).
[5] Ibid., vol. iii, qu. 37,825 ff.   [6] Ibid., vol. v, qu. 77,619 ff.
[7] Ibid., vol. i, qu. 13,170 ff.

condemned the idea of a land court as an intolerable interference with freedom of contract. It would turn them into mere rent chargers and would disrupt the intimate relations between owner and occupier. They denied that conditions were as serious as depicted by Liberal 'agitators'; rents were moderate and estates well managed. They pointed out the long hereditary tenancies of many Welsh families. The institution of an arbitrary tenant-right would make landlords far less willing to undertake improvements. Cornwallis-West,[1] Lord Penrhyn, Lord Stanley of Alderley, Sir Joseph Bailey, and J. E. Vincent were their leading spokesmen. All denied any discrimination against any Liberal or nonconformist tenant. They considered the most feasible solution to agricultural distress to be state relief for landowners, for instance through rating reform. No government should restrict their right to charge an economic rent and to allow tenancies to be governed by the laws of supply and demand.

This absolute divergence was eventually reflected in the Majority and Minority Reports, but these did not appear until 1896. When the Liberals fell from power, in June 1895, the Commission was still in session. During this period it excited little interest from political parties. The Unionist Party agreed with the view of Welsh landlords in the House of Lords, Lords Penrhyn, Harlech, and Stanley of Alderley, expressed at the time of the appointment of the Commission, that the whole inquiry was unfairly contrived and 'a harvest for Radical barristers'.[2] It was clear that the political effectiveness of the Commission depended on the result of the election. Thus the return of the Unionists again lent an air of unreality to its later sessions. Its findings were made to appear academic by ten years of Unionist government.

(ii) *The University of Wales*

The second request presented by Rendel to Gladstone on the formation of his ministry was for a charter to create a federal Welsh university. This commanded very wide and enthusiastic support among all parties and denominations, and Gladstone's frequently expressed sympathy for Welsh education led to high expectations. Acland's appointment as Vice-President of the Council seemed to be a favourable omen. His three years in office were to be distinguished

---

[1] Ibid., vol. iv, qu. 60,237 ff. (Cornwallis-West's evidence).
[2] *Parl. Deb.*, 4th ser., vol. x, pp. 849 ff.; H. M. Vaughan, op. cit., p. 185.

by many progressive educational achievements, but nowhere were his efforts more completely successful than in Wales.

Acland wasted no time in bringing the question to Gladstone's attention. On 20 October 1892 he wrote suggesting an inquiry into the university problem by a capable commissioner and recommending Owen M. Edwards for the task.[1] Gladstone at first seems to have misunderstood this as a demand for legislation,[2] but on 7 November he agreed that Edwards be appointed to lay information before the government.[3] Acland announced this decision to a representative educational gathering at Shrewsbury. Edwards rapidly completed his work, and reported to the Privy Council early in the new year.

There were, however, several difficult questions to be resolved, in particular the position of the Anglican college at Lampeter and the relation of the University to the new intermediate schools. Main controversy at this stage, however, centred on the nature of the University itself. Some educationalists, notably Dr. R. D. Roberts, wanted simply an examining body, on the lines of London University, which could confer degrees on any student of sufficient academic standing. This would enable pupils of theological and other smaller colleges to present themselves for degrees. But the majority, headed by Principal Viriamu Jones, demanded a teaching university: no candidate should be admitted to its degrees unless he or she had pursued a course of study at one of the three constituent Welsh University Colleges. This view carried the day. The Shrewsbury conference had appointed three representatives, Dr. Isambard Owen, Brynmor Jones, and Cadwaladr Davies, to draft a charter, and it was duly submitted to conference on 6 January 1893. It specifically prescribed a teaching university, and also excluded St. David's College, Lampeter, the inclusion of which had been recommended by the Aberdare Committee of 1881. It was approved by the Privy Council and then laid before Parliament.

Acland had told Gladstone that 'he did not urge it [the University] *politically* but *educationally*'.[4] Now, however, politics briefly intruded. Two Welsh members, Bryn Roberts and D. A. Thomas, who both throughout their careers followed independent courses, attempted to amend the charter in favour of an examining body.[5]

[1] Acland to Gladstone, 20 Oct. 1892 (B.M., Add. MSS., 44516, ff. 192–5).
[2] Acland to Gladstone, 6 Nov. 1892 (B.M., Add. MSS., 44516, ff. 250–1).
[3] Gladstone to Acland, 7 Nov. 1892 (B.M., Add. MSS., 44549, f. 73).
[4] Acland to Gladstone, 6 Nov. 1892 (B.M., Add. MSS., 44516, f. 250).
[5] *Parl. Deb.*, 4th ser., vol. xvi, pp. 1442–56.

They wanted, they claimed, a truly national charter. In a brief and confused debate, they were inevitably supported by Stanley Leighton, who criticized the exclusion of Lampeter. But their view found little support in the House as a whole. Two other Welsh members, Brynmor Jones (Stroud) and Samuel Evans, strongly advocated a teaching body, Evans quoting figures to show that of the 2,718 students to pass through the three Welsh colleges since 1872, 1,857 came from the poorer classes. The Hon. G. T. Kenyon (Denbigh), a Unionist who proved himself a good friend to Welsh education, also defended the charter, while Acland stated that it was essentially a further development of the Act of 1889. The motion was negatived without a division.

The same day, 29 August 1893, Bishop Jayne of Chester, himself half-Welsh and a former principal of St. David's College, Lampeter, moved that the Royal Assent be withheld until Lampeter was included.[1] He attacked the 'godless' nature of Welsh Board Schools and claimed that Lampeter was being victimized by 'aggressive and intolerant denominationalism in Wales'. Jayne found ready support from the Bishops of St. David's, St. Asaph, London, and Salisbury. For the Liberals, Lord Aberdare explained his change of front since 1881. He said that Lampeter had shown little willingness to join the University. The Lord Chancellor, Herschell, more tersely, remarked that the issue was not whether Lampeter should be permanently excluded, but whether the university charter should be permanently delayed until Lampeter made up its mind. In fact, the motion was carried by forty-one votes to thirty-two, but, as Gladstone had already intimated to Dean John Owen, the government decided to ignore it. Lampeter College had undoubtedly shown considerable reluctance towards the University movement. The charter did contain a reservation clause which would have enabled Lampeter to enter it by a supplementary charter, but for sixty years Lampeter made no attempt to do so. One of its later students was to describe it 'as not a Welsh college at all, but merely a college in Wales'.[2] The Dean of St. Asaph defended Bishop Jayne's action: 'according to our lights we only did the task our duty to the College as well as to Wales required'.[3] But the episode merely aroused further sectarian feeling over education

[1] Ibid., pp. 1316–35.
[2] D. Parry-Jones, *Welsh Country Upbringing* (London, 1948), p. 117.
[3] John Owen to Ellis, 6 Mar. 1894 (N.L.W., Ellis Papers, 1591). Owen's attitude is further discussed in Eluned E. Owen, *The Early Life of Bishop Owen* (Llandysul, 1958), pp. 159 ff.

and isolated the Established Church to an increasing degree from the flourishing University of Wales.

Events now moved rapidly. On 30 November 1893 the charter received the Royal Assent, and the constituent bodies of the University, the Court, the Senate, and the Guild of Graduates were subsequently created. The first Chancellor was Lord Aberdare; when he died almost immediately after his appointment he was succeeded by the Prince of Wales, Gladstone declining the offer.[1] Henceforth, the University of Wales moves out of the British political scene. Financially, its basis was now secure. Although Harcourt was at first unsympathetic to an initial request by Viriamu Jones for a grant of £100,000, he eventually was persuaded to allow £20,000, while a further £50,000 were raised by voluntary effort.[2] Under the guiding genius of Principal Viriamu Jones, the University made rapid progress. It was an outstanding instance of national achievement, and placed Wales in this respect fully on an equality with Scotland and Ireland.

But the denominational bitterness, which vitiated Welsh educational development, could not be permanently concealed. During these years Welsh local authorities put forward their schemes, one by one, for intermediate education in their respective counties, and laid them before Parliament. No complaint was lodged in the Commons, but in the Lords repeated attacks were made on these schemes for their alleged discrimination against Church schools. Motions were carried against the Caernarvonshire and Merioneth schemes in 1893,[3] and the Flintshire and Denbighshire schemes in 1894,[4] the Welsh bishops in the van of the attack. The Royal Assent was given to these motions, and the schemes were thus delayed. By way of retaliation, Herbert Lewis and Lloyd George tried unsuccessfully in the Committee of Ways and Means to reduce the vote from the consolidated fund to the Lords by £10,000 by way of protest.[5] Harcourt angrily condemned their behaviour to Gladstone.[6] The impressive national unity which largely characterized the university and intermediate education movements was genuine enough, but it could not wholly subdue the legacy of bitter political sectarianism which lay beneath

---

[1] W. Rathbone to Gladstone, 2 Apr. 1895 (B.M., Add. MSS., 44520, f. 113).
[2] Viriamu Jones to Ellis, 7 Apr. 1895 (N.L.W., Ellis Papers, 1139).
[3] *Parl. Deb.*, 4th ser., vol. x, pp. 1004 ff.; ibid., vol. xvi, pp. 1841 ff.
[4] Ibid., vol. xxiii, pp. 598 ff.; ibid., vol. xxv, pp. 1437 ff.
[5] Ibid., vol. xxix, pp. 137–9.
[6] Morley to Gladstone, 23 Aug. 1894 (B.M., Add. MSS., 44257, f. 171).

the surface, and was soon to make the question of Welsh education one of the great political controversies of the day.

(iii) *Gladstone and Disestablishment*

Important though they were to Welshmen, the questions of land and education were secondary to the vital and far-reaching issue of the 'alien Church'. John Morley had written that 'Home Rule is not more essentially the Irish national question than disestablishment and disendowment are essentially the Welsh national question'.[1] This was the measure demanded of the government, not merely by the thirty-one Welsh Liberal members, but by British nonconformity in general. This was the third, and by far the most difficult, branch of the Welsh upas tree which Rendel had asked Gladstone to sever on that night in No. 2 Carlton Gardens in August 1892. From the United States, the great steel magnate, Andrew Carnegie, urged the Premier that he grant Wales 'justice in religious matters'.[2]

The attitude of Gladstone towards Welsh disestablishment during these years forms a difficult problem. Most Welsh historians and publicists, both churchmen and nonconformists, have generally assumed that there was a fundamental antipathy between the ageing High Churchman and the rebellious young spokesmen of nonconformist Wales, and that he used every artifice to obstruct a measure which he regarded as anathema.[3] However, the record of Gladstone's turns of policy reveals a different and more complex picture of his views, in which he emerges as a subtle politician no less than an idealistic visionary.

From the first, great pressure was imposed on him to fulfil the expectations aroused by the Newcastle Programme, and by his own previous declarations. He had been in close touch with Rendel on the formation of his administration, and Rendel had proposed the introduction of a Welsh Church Suspensory Bill. This measure, by making the emoluments of any office in the four Welsh dioceses held under public patronage subject to the pleasure of Parliament, would put ecclesiastical revenues in the hands of the sovereign, and so commit Gladstone to a practical measure entailing the principle of disestablishment. A Suspensory Bill would also prevent a recurrence of the situation that had arisen in Ireland between 1869 and 1871,

[1] Morley to Gee, 20 Aug. 1890 (N.L.W., Gee MSS., 8307c, 210).
[2] Carnegie to Gladstone, 17 Aug. 1892 (B.M., Add. MSS., 44515, f. 187).
[3] See, for example, David Williams, *Modern Wales*, p. 266; T. I. Ellis, *Cofiant Thomas Edward Ellis*, vol. ii, p. 208; T. Gwynn Jones, op. cit., p. 573.

when the Disestablishment Act came into force: in these two years, the number of curates had risen from 563 to 921, and nearly £1,800,000 had been paid to them in compensation. Although reluctant to give this measure a high priority on the Liberal programme, Gladstone seems to have accepted it without demur. There are no grounds for believing that he had misgivings about the principle involved. He wrote to a Welsh clergyman in September that, while he welcomed the 'increased ability and life of the Welsh Church', he considered disendowment inseparable from disestablishment.[1] The following February he wrote to Dean John Owen that, while disestablishment was 'at present impossible', a Suspensory Bill was an essential preliminary. 'I do not in the least apprehend that the actions of the Church would be paralysed by the adoption of such a measure.'[2]

Again, Gladstone was fully aware of the change in the composition of his Party since the Irish home rule schism of 1886. Historians, perhaps, have under-estimated the extent of Gladstone's radicalism in his old age. He had agreed with Harcourt on the eve of the late election on the need for a 'good bill of fare', including temperance reform, parish councils, 'one man one vote', and Welsh disestablishment, a programme which would not only conciliate the various sections among his followers but would also prepare a comprehensive challenge in preparation for the coming clash with the House of Lords.[3]

Thus, in the autumn of 1892, the Welsh Suspensory Bill was drafted by Gladstone and Asquith. It was discussed by the cabinet on 30 October, Gladstone noting, 'To be taken up by the *Govt*. But this may be reconsidered.'[4] By the turn of the year, the Suspensory Bill was placed on the projected list of Liberal measures.[5] Gladstone's main concern was to make it quite certain that the Church of England was in no way affected. He wrote to Rendel on 16 November suggesting that the Bill should apply simply to the twelve Welsh counties, and not the four dioceses (which included not only Monmouthshire, but also several English border parishes). 'I think it a great object to keep clear of all English entanglements', he wrote.[6]

[1] Gladstone to the Rev. W. Morgan Jones, 17 Sept. 1892 (B.M., Add. MSS., 44549, f. 10).
[2] Gladstone to John Owen, 15 Feb. 1893 (B.M., Add. MSS., 44549, f. 63).
[3] Gladstone to Harcourt, 18 July 1892 (B.M., Add. MSS., 44202, f. 166), 'Secret'.
[4] Cabinet Minutes (B.M., Add. MSS., 44648, f. 12).
[5] Ibid., f. 83. The order of legislation was: 1. Irish Home Rule; 2. Local Government; 3. L.C.C.; 4. Registration; 5. Conspiracy; 6. Welsh Church.
[6] Gladstone to Rendel, 16 Nov. 1892 (B.M., Add. MSS., 44549, f. 40). Also cf. Rendel to Humphreys-Owen, 18 Nov. 1892 (N.L.W., Glansevern MSS., 621), 'Secret'.

Rendel, however, persuaded him to revise this obviously impractical suggestion. The same question arose during the drafting of the Bill. Gladstone asked whether it was judicious to employ the term, 'Church of England' in the Bill. 'Our friends will like the assertion implied in "Ch. of England", but will not our opponents make much of it as showing that the Bill is part of a latent design against the Ch. of England, and will not this tell?'[1] He also sought an assurance that the Bill did not extend beyond Wales and Monmouthshire and was confined solely to public and not to private patronage. Asquith robustly defended the use of the title 'Church of England'. 'We cannot conceal the fact that, *pro tanto* that church is to be affected.'[2]

The Bill also caused a characteristic *contre-temps* between Gladstone and Queen Victoria, who protested against the measure, saying that she had 'always supposed Mr. Gladstone to be the loyal friend of the Church of England of which she was the head'.[3] Gladstone sarcastically told Asquith, 'H.M.'s studies have not yet carried her out of the delusive belief that she is still by law the "Head" of the Church of England'.[4] Asquith replied that 'it was difficult to follow the processes of the Royal mind'.[5] The Bill was clearly a preliminary to disestablishment, and it was the government's view that the four Welsh dioceses could be treated separately.

The approach of legislation on the Welsh Church, by far the nearest approach yet towards a general disestablishment, aroused national interest. The Church Defence Institution began to mobilize its forces, while Bishop Edwards inveighed at the St. Asaph Diocesan Conference against 'hacking to pieces' the ancient British Church.[6] Tom Ellis believed that 'the Tories will fight Welsh Disestablishment far more fiercely than they have ever fought Home Rule'.[7] On the Liberal side, the Liberal Churchmen's Union, led by G. W. E. Russell, gave the Welsh Church Bill a cautious blessing. But the more ardent Liberationists were afraid that it would merely shelve the problem. Carvell Williams, the secretary of the Liberation Society, wrote to Rendel, protesting that Welsh and Scottish disestablishment were not being taken up by the government. Rendel termed

[1] Gladstone to Asquith, 23 Feb. 1893 (B.M., Add. MSS., 44549, f. 67).
[2] Asquith to Gladstone, 23 Feb. 1893 (B.M., Add. MSS., 44517, f. 50).
[3] *Personal Papers of Lord Rendel*, p. 101.
[4] Gladstone to Asquith, 26 Feb. 1893 (B.M., Add. MSS., 44549, f. 68).
[5] Asquith to Gladstone, 26 Feb. 1893 (B.M., Add. MSS., 44517, f. 54).
[6] *Church Times*, 16 Sept. 1892.
[7] Ellis to the Rev. Gwynoro Davies, ? February 1893, quoted in J. Hugh Edwards, *Life of David Lloyd George*, vol. iii (London, 1913), p. 101.

this letter 'unhelpful' and did not reply immediately.[1] He failed to satisfy Williams, who sought the aid of Ellis instead. Rendel's main fear was lest Welsh disestablishment be permanently blocked by association with Scottish disestablishment, which was, he maintained, not so clear a national demand. He found Gladstone 'playfully perverse' on this point, and regarded his support for the Suspensory Bill as the limit of his assistance.[2] He strove to have the Welsh Bill prominent in the Queen's Speech: it would commit the government and would gain Wales precedence over Scotland. Harcourt, Asquith, and Ellis were useful allies here, and he largely succeeded.

Thus the Welsh Church Suspensory Bill appeared in the Queen's Speech, and was introduced by Asquith on 23 February.[3] He had been doubtful whether the debate would be completed on the same day,[4] but in fact the result was very satisfactory for the government. Ellis, who once again showed his usefulness in office, had primed Asquith with statistical evidence demonstrating the condemnation of the establishment at successive elections,[5] and Asquith made great play with quotations Ellis had supplied from Lord Salisbury and Matthew Arnold showing the strength of nonconformity in Wales. His speech was admirably lucid in outlining the necessity for paying attentive respect to Welsh national feeling. The Unionists were very badly served by their main speaker, Sir John Gorst: his speech, Gladstone said later, might have been composed in an ice-chamber. Sterner opposition came from the Church Parliamentary Committee (the 'Black Brigade' to its opponents),[6] mainly young men, including Viccary Gibbs (St. Albans), Arthur Griffith-Boscawen (Tonbridge), and Sir Frank Powell (Wigan), who all stressed the recent progress of the Welsh Church and its services to Wales in the past. A most remarkable contribution came from Lord Randolph Churchill, in almost his last major speech. He spoke at great length and with considerable violence on the spoliation of the national Church. With that nervous iteration that was to herald his fatal decline, he alleged that the government's real aim was 'Votes! Votes! Votes! Votes! Votes!'[7] Churchill, in fact, aided the Liberal cause by provoking

---

[1] Carvell Williams to Ellis, 3 Dec. 1892 (N.L.W., Ellis Papers, 2096).
[2] Rendel to Gee, 30 Oct. 1892 (N.L.W., Gee MSS., 8308c, 274).
[3] *Parl. Deb.*, 4th ser., vol. ix, pp. 204 ff.
[4] Asquith to Gladstone, 21 Feb. 1893 (B.M., Add. MSS., 44517, ff. 45–46).
[5] Notes by Ellis and Asquith on the Suspensory Bill (Bodleian, Asquith Papers, Box 14).
[6] A. Griffith-Boscawen, *Fourteen Years in Parliament* (London, 1907), p. 41.
[7] *Parl. Deb.*, loc. cit., p. 276. Cf. 'Pigott! Pigott!! Pigott!!! Pigott!!!! Pigott!!!!!'

Gladstone with his personal attacks to speak far more vigorously than had been expected.[1] Gladstone illustrated how the principle of separate legislation for Wales was now firmly established. The Church would not suffer, but on the contrary would flourish when dependent on voluntary effort and enthusiasm. Existing vested interests would not be affected. 'There is a strong presumptive argument for disestablishment wherever the adherents of the Establishment are in a minority.' In a peroration which set the House ablaze, he rebutted Churchill's bitter attack—'Vote! Vote! Vote! for Irish Home Rule and Welsh Disestablishment'.[2]

The Opposition took the unusual course of dividing the House on the First Reading, but, with the Irish vote solidly behind it, the Bill passed by the surprisingly large majority of fifty-six (301 votes to 245). Ellis had the honour of telling in this fateful debate. A friend wrote to him shortly afterwards that Churchill had helped the cause by provoking Gladstone. 'He lashed the old lion into fury which made him speak far more strongly for us than . . . was his original intention; he is pledged irretrievably now.'[3]

The Suspensory Bill stirred up deep feelings throughout the land, for it aroused the hostility of one of the great institutions and vested interests, whose maintenance was a basic tenet of the Conservative creed. At the English Church Union, the platform for the High Churchmen, Lord Halifax described the Bill as 'robbery'.[4] Headed by Archbishop Benson, the English episcopate thundered against the Bill from a hundred platforms, Bishop Thorold of Winchester condemning it with especial vehemence. Diocesan conferences reverberated with attacks on the government, while Sir Michael Hicks-Beach even ventured to hold a meeting in the heart of enemy territory at Caernarvon. The climax of the campaign came with a large assembly at the Albert Hall on 15 May, when the Archbishops of Canterbury and York, the Earl of Selborne, four bishops, Professor Jebb, M.P., Colonel Cornwallis-West, and others exercised their combined eloquence against the Bill.[5] The speeches reveal some variation. The majority condemned the threat to endowments, but Archbishop Benson himself thought disestablishment the greater evil. A nation, he said, must have 'a spiritual personality', and he would sooner live

---

[1] H. W. Lucy, *A Diary of the Home Rule Parliament, 1892–5* (London, 1895), pp. 67–68.
[2] *Parl. Deb.*, loc. cit., p. 277.
[3] Osmond Williams to Ellis, 1 Mar. 1893 (N.L.W., Ellis Papers, 2060).
[4] *Church Times*, 10 Mar. 1893.   [5] *The Times*, 16 May 1893.

under a nonconformist establishment than none at all. The aged Selborne considered the meeting a great success.[1]

This attitude of implacable hostility gained general support among Unionists and Anglicans. There was some substance on these occasions in the jibe that the Church was the 'Tory Party at prayer'. But this critical view towards the Bill was not universal even here. The Church campaign aroused doubts, in particular, among Liberal Unionists. Some were leading opponents of the measure—Wolmer, Goschen, and Hartington, for example—but others could not wholly reject their Liberal antecedents. To the *Spectator*, the Bill was not so much objectionable in principle as in its practical implications. Its flaw lay not in attacking endowments as such, but rather in paying heed to localized opinion and encouraging piecemeal legislation. The *Spectator*'s editors, Hutton and Townsend, did not oppose the secularization of tithe, but suggested that it might be fulfilled more equitably in a general concurrent endowment of all sects. They disapproved of some of the statements made at the Albert Hall meeting: the state did have the right to re-allocate ecclesiastical property on occasions.[2] Some prominent members of the clergy also publicly supported the principle of the Bill, including Canon Scott Holland, a founder of the Christian Social Union, and Dr. Percival, headmaster of Rugby School.

On the Liberal side, the Bill was received with varying degrees of enthusiasm. It was warmly welcomed by the Liberation Society, which began an inquiry into petitions against the Bill.[3] The Welsh members generally regarded the Bill as an overdue indication of action by the government. The original intention of the ministry seems to have been to take the Bill after Easter, but the Welsh members, led by Lloyd George and Herbert Lewis, forced Rendel to persuade Gladstone to introduce it earlier.[4] But irritation grew in Wales when it became clear that until the Irish home rule question was solved, the Welsh Church issue could not be settled. The second Home Rule Bill, introduced in February, consumed nearly all the session, and did not receive its Third Reading in the Commons until 1 September, to be rejected by the Lords a few days later. The Second Reading of the Suspensory Bill was more and more delayed, and it

[1] *Memorials*, vol. ii, p. 300.
[2] *Spectator*, 25 Feb., 15 Apr., 20 May 1893.
[3] Liberation Society MSS., 20 Mar. 1893.
[4] *Y Genedl*, 28 Feb. 1893; cf. article by Lloyd George in *British Weekly*, 2 Mar. 1893.

was obviously a dead letter long before its formal withdrawal on 18 September.

The government, however, could ignore the Welsh Party only at its peril. Many of them were incensed that Ireland monopolized the attention of the House, and felt a sense of betrayal. Already the younger Welsh members had gravely embarrassed the government by introducing a Local Option Bill for Wales in March, side by side with Harcourt's more general measure. This measure, sponsored by the Welsh-American Major Jones (Carmarthen), was an extreme temperance proposal, granting virtually complete rights of prohibition to a local two-thirds majority, without compensation. Harcourt was compelled to speak in its support, and it passed its Second Reading by 281 votes to 245.[1] There was a threat of similar independent action in other spheres to harass further the unhappy ministry.

As the Home Rule Bill dragged out its long and stormy course, the Welsh members sought firmer guarantees over an overall disestablishment measure. They were backed up by powerful nonconformist journals such as the *British Weekly* and the *Methodist Times*, and by the Welsh press without exception, as well as the new Welsh edition of Scott's *Manchester Guardian*. A motion by Lloyd George at a meeting of the Welsh members that a letter be sent to Gladstone was carried by thirty votes to one, the dissentient being Bryn Roberts, and Rendel wrote on their behalf on 26 June. On 5 July Gladstone replied that the Home Rule Bill blocked the way. He denied that 'the declarations at Newcastle' announced any order of business, but assured Rendel that Welsh disestablishment remained 'an essential part of the Liberal policy and plans'. Rendel wrote a second time on 28 July, demanding that Welsh disestablishment be placed in the forefront of the next session, but Gladstone's reply on 8 August, while promising a disestablishment measure in the future, declined to give any assurance of priority.[2] This was very unsatisfactory to most Welsh Liberals. At the South Wales Liberal Federation at Aberdare on 14 August a resolution was carried that the Welsh members form an independent party unless disestablishment were taken as the first government measure in 1894.[3]

There was strong backing for this move. D. A. Thomas threatened that the Welsh Party might withdraw its support for Irish home

[1] *Parl. Deb.*, 4th ser., vol. x, pp. 93 ff.
[2] These letters are published *in extenso* in the *South Wales Daily News*, 16 Aug. 1893. Cf. Liberation Society MSS., 9 Aug. 1893; Archbishop of Wales, op. cit., p. 155.
[3] *South Wales Daily News*, 15 Aug. 1893.

rule,[1] while pressure was put on Ellis from his constituency to insist on an autumn session in which disestablishment could be passed.[2] The only dissident voice in Wales was that of Bryn Roberts, who issued a statement which condemned internecine attacks on the Liberal Party.[3] He wrote to Gladstone to this effect, receiving a reply congratulating him for his 'political insight' and 'temperance'.[4] For this attitude, Roberts was bitterly, even viciously attacked by a leading .Methodist, the Rev. Evan Jones, Caernarvon, and criticized by his own constituency party in Eifion.[5] Apart from him, Wales seemed to present a solid front. It had it in its power to bring the government to heel, and a decisive meeting of the Welsh party on 1 September seemed to present an opportunity.

The meeting proved to be an anticlimax. At the critical moment, as on so many occasions before and since, brave threats of independent action dissolved when brought up against the realities of political power. Three motions were moved. The first, moved by David Randell (Gower), would have formed an independent party forthwith but this was lost by fourteen to seven, the minority consisting only of South Wales members, including Major Jones, D. A. Thomas, and Sir Edward Reed, the last an incongruous figure in such company. The second was moved by D. A. Thomas and proposed an independent party if the government gave no definite assurance about the next session, but, in spite of being supported by Lloyd George and Ellis, this failed by nineteen to six. The third, moved by Lloyd George and seconded by Ellis, proposed that the Welsh members reconsider their position if the Welsh Disestablishment Bill were not 'in such a place in the ministerial programme for the next session as will enable the House of Commons to carry it through all its stages, and send it to the Lords before the session is over'. This moderate motion was still opposed by Bryn Roberts and four others, but was carried, by fifteen to five.[6]

Ellis wrote triumphantly how he and Lloyd George had conquered both the 'ambitious little group' of southern members, led by D. A.

[1] *British Weekly*, 24 Aug. 1893.
[2] Haydn Jones to Ellis, 4 Aug. 1893 (N.L.W., Ellis Papers, 1098).
[3] *Baner ac Amserau Cymru*, 31 Aug. 1893.
[4] Gladstone to Bryn Roberts, 23 Aug. 1893 (N.L.W., Bryn Roberts Papers, 69).
[5] For the Evan Jones–Bryn Roberts correspondence, see the Bryn Roberts Papers, 102–5 (N.L.W.).
[6] There are full accounts of this meeting in the *South Wales Daily News*, 2 Sept. 1893 (by Vincent Evans), and *Baner ac Amserau Cymru*, 6 Sept. 1893. There are also full notes in Herbert Lewis's handwriting in the Penucha MSS.

Thomas and Major Jones, and the 'stick-in-the-muds' led by Bryn
Roberts. 'Welsh disestablishment next session is certain.'[1] This meeting saw the pinnacle reached in harmonious co-operation between
Ellis and Lloyd George before their later estrangement. But the divisions revealed at this meeting had a lasting duration, and from this
point dates that disillusionment with political radicalism which was
increasingly to permeate among many Welsh Liberals, and to convince them of the ultimate impotence of the vaunted 'Welsh Party'.
The suspicion grew that the uncertainty of the Party faithfully
reflected the temper of Wales itself. Some politicians retained a san-
guine belief that 'things will soon be right again',[2] but it was clear
that a concerted Welsh effort to force through Welsh disestablishment, by persuasion or blackmail, was unlikely.

In the autumn of 1893, as in most autumns, therefore, there came
a period of calm. The Church Defenders called off their campaign,
and Lord Salisbury could discuss the political situation at Cardiff
on 29 October without once discussing disestablishment. On the
Liberal side, the veteran Gee had produced a measure of his own
which included the abolition of compensation on the 1869 model,
the secularization of cathedrals, and the transfer of tithes, burial-
grounds, and the proceeds of palaces, parsonages, and glebes to the
Welsh tithe fund—a highly radical proposal, although some considered its pension scheme too generous to the clergy.[3] It was too
dangerous for most of the Welsh members. Sam Evans thought it
might frighten the 'timid disestablishers', Albert Spicer (Monmouth)
urged Gee to be 'a little more generous', while D. A. Thomas
thought that the details should be discussed with the government.
'I am afraid the prospects of Welsh Disestablishment are not very
bright at the moment', he wrote.[4]

In fact, although there was widespread criticism by nonconformists of Gladstone's alleged hostility, the government was already
preparing a fully fledged Welsh Disestablishment and Disendowment
Bill. Asquith was in consultation with Gladstone on the subject in
November,[5] and Gladstone now expressed his full agreement with

[1] Ellis to Daniel, 3 Sept. 1893 (N.L.W., Daniel MSS., 416).
[2] W. M. Griffiths to Bryn Roberts, 16 Sept. 1893 (N.L.W., Bryn Roberts Papers, 73).
[3] Draft in N.L.W., Ellis Papers, 668. Gee to Ellis, 30 Aug. 1893 (N.L.W., Ellis
Papers, 669). The tithe fund would assist farmers in purchasing allotments.
[4] Evans to Gee, 8 Dec. 1893 (N.L.W., Gee MSS., 8305c, 62). Spicer to Gee, 8 Jan.
1894 (N.L.W., Gee MSS., 8308c, 344). D. A. Thomas to Gee, 18 Dec. 1893 (N.L.W.,
Gee MSS., 8309c, 354).
[5] Asquith to Gladstone, 7 Nov. 1893 (B.M., Add. MSS., 44517, f. 299).

the treating of small English diocesan parishes within the Welsh geographical borders as a part of Wales. 'The treatment of Monmouthshire in Wales, is, I apprehend, quite modern, though it may be very proper.'[1] The first draft was complete by 30 November,[2] and on 19 January 1894 a memorandum was prepared for the cabinet by Ellis. Asquith noted that this 'may be regarded as an authentic summary of the views or desires of the Welsh Party'.[3] Rendel recalled later, 'You will of course understand that the Bill was practically settled before I retired'.[4] A speech by Ellis at Newtown on 8 February 1894 gave a strong hint that disestablishment would figure prominently on the ministerial programme.[5]

It was at this moment that Gladstone retired on 3 March, largely over disagreement about the naval estimates and whether to hold a general election, and certainly not over disestablishment.[6] There were some important consequences for Wales. Rendel regarded the time appropriate for his retirement to the Lords, after a career of remarkable self-effacement. He issued public statements expressing satisfaction at the esteem gained by the Welsh Party, than whom no body was 'more united, more capable and, for their numbers, more influential', a judgement many found hard to sustain.[7] But in private, he told Humphreys-Owen of his bitter disillusionment at the ungenerosity shown towards him by younger men like Lloyd George. 'In Welsh affairs, there seems a conscious preference for unrealities.'[8] With the retirement of Gladstone, his usefulness to Wales was ended. In addition, Marjoribanks also went to the Lords, and Tom Ellis now succeeded him as Chief Whip, amid further execrations from certain sections of the Welsh press which saw this as a final sacrifice of his independence.[9] But the main change concerned the leadership. Nonconformists widely assumed that Gladstone's departure meant a great improvement in the position of Welsh disestablishment, but

[1] Gladstone to Asquith, 10 Nov. 1893 (B.M., Add. MSS., 44549, f. 154).
[2] Draft in Asquith Papers, box 14 (Bodleian).   [3] Ibid.
[4] Rendel to the Rev. Josiah Jones, 1 May 1894 (N.L.W., MS. 6411B).
[5] *Baner ac Amserau Cymru*, 14 Feb. 1894. The occasion was the annual meeting of the North Wales Liberal Federation.
[6] As suggested by Griffith Boscawen, op. cit., p. 47.
[7] Rendel to Gee, 22 Mar. 1894 (N.L.W., Gee MSS., 8308c, 282). Rendel and Gee were never intimate.
[8] Rendel to Humphreys-Owen, 4 Mar. 1894 (N.L.W., Glansevern MSS., 649), 'Confidential'.
[9] For example, *Cambrian News*, 9, 16 Mar. 1894. But Ellis's elevation was welcomed in the *South Wales Daily News*, 7 Mar. 1894; *Y Tyst*, 16 Mar. 1894; *Y Goleuad*, 16 Mar. 1894; and in more measured fashion in *Baner ac Amserau Cymru*, 7 Mar. 1894.

injustice was done to him on this score. It was undeniable that Irish home rule delayed the advent of a Welsh Disestablishment Bill, but it was hard to dispute that Ireland was a unique case, a cancer that menaced the political integrity of the United Kingdom. Equally, Gladstone showed a consistent sympathy with the principle of disestablishment since he 'crossed the Rubicon' (in Robertson Nicoll's words) in 1891. Here, above all, the sacred cause of nationality was involved. Gladstone was compelled to approach the issue cautiously in the years 1892–4 if only because so much rested on a conversion of English opinion. Nevertheless, with the assistance of Asquith and Ellis, Gladstone brought Welsh disestablishment steadily nearer and made it a practical possibility. To see him simply as an obstacle, as a 'drag on the wheel',[1] is to misread his later career.

(iv) The Disestablishment Bills of 1894–5

To succeed Gladstone, the Queen sent for Lord Rosebery, instead of Harcourt as had been generally assumed, or Lord Spencer as Gladstone himself proposed. A dozen Welsh radicals were rumoured to be contemplating resignation over the choice of a peer, including Ellis,[2] but in fact Rosebery's advent to power was relatively tranquil. Ensor states that nonconformists were hostile to Rosebery, owing to his links with horse-racing and the aristocracy.[3] In fact, his succession received wide nonconformist acclamation, especially as he was known to dislike an exclusive preoccupation with Irish home rule. His first speech as Premier included a warm advocacy of Welsh disestablishment ('the case of Wales is the judgement of a nation') and Robertson Nicoll termed it a 'splendid beginning'[4]. Meanwhile, the Welsh members were quick to show their nuisance value. A mischievous motion to the Address by Labouchere on 13 March to abolish the House of Lords was supported by eleven Welsh radicals, together with Scottish, Irish, and Labour members, and carried against both front benches by two votes. It was an unfortunate baptism for Ellis, and Gladstone was told that Marjoribanks was 'sadly missed in the whipping department'.[5]

---

[1] So described in William George, My Brother and I (London, 1958), p. 176.
[2] Western Mail, 3 Mar. 1894; South Wales Daily News, 5 Mar. 1894.
[3] R. C. K. Ensor, England 1870–1914 (Oxford, 1936), pp. 215–16.
[4] British Weekly, 15 Mar. 1894. Also cf. the generally enthusiastic response of Baner ac Amserau Cymru, 7 Mar. 1894. Rosebery's imperialism attracted many nonconformists in Wales as elsewhere, notably Tom Ellis. More remarkably, Lloyd George welcomed Rosebery's advent and claimed that his imperialist views would prove a source of strength to the government (South Wales Daily News, 5 Mar. 1894).
[5] George H. Murray to Gladstone, 4 Apr. 1894 (B.M., Add. MSS., 44518, f. 151). For

When the ministerial programme was announced, however, the Welsh Disestablishment Bill was placed not merely after the budget but also after Bills dealing with Registration and Evicted Tenants. There was considerable disappointment in Wales. The Montgomery-shire by-election in April seemed to be a portent, Humphreys-Owen, Rendel's successor, getting home by only 225 votes, a drop of 600. This was attributed by a leading Montgomeryshire Liberal to the protectionism of Wynn, the Unionist, which won over many farmers, and to the delay over disestablishment.[1] Finally, in April, three Welsh members, Lloyd George, D. A. Thomas, and Frank Edwards (Radnorshire), joined shortly afterwards by Herbert Lewis, informed Ellis that they would no longer receive the Liberal Whip. At a great meeting at Caernarvon they declared themselves to be independent members, as the government had failed to give the pledges demanded the previous autumn.[2]

At last, therefore, the oft-threatened 'Welsh Revolt' had come into being. But it was after all a diminutive affair, in the light of past declarations, many of the South Wales rebels of the meeting on 1 September, Randell and Major Jones for instance, refusing to join.[3] However, the movement was sufficiently ominous while the 'Four', as they were called, toured North Wales from Caernarvon to Holy-well. Lloyd George exulted, 'Even cautious North Wales is with us. Ellis was roundly condemned by several speakers.'[4] Herbert Lewis explained their attitude. 'My recent talks with Ministers and Mem-bers have convinced me that Wales is simply being led on from step to step without any definite goal in view, that we have nothing to gain by subservience to the Liberal Party, and that we shall never get the English to do us justice until we show our independence of them.'[5] He appealed to Ellis to 'come and lead us', but in vain. Lloyd George, inevitably, expressed himself more violently. '[He said], we

further criticisms of Ellis's performance as Chief Whip see R. Farquharson, *In and Out of Parliament* (London, 1911), pp. 222–4.

[1] Richard Jones to Ellis, 9 Apr. 1894 (N.L.W., Ellis Papers, 1222). Cf. *Liverpool Daily Post*, 27 Mar. 1894.

[2] *South Wales Daily News*, 14 Apr. 1894.

[3] Cf. Lloyd George to Alfred Thomas, n.d. (Cardiff, Pontypridd Papers). Major Jones, a leader of the 'forward party' six months earlier, was particularly scathing towards the revolt, which he termed, in a published letter to the Rev. Towyn Jones, 'the disaffection of cranks'. He maintained that the guarantees asked of the govern-ment in September had now been given (*South Wales Daily News*, 23 May 1894).

[4] Lloyd George to Alfred Thomas, n.d. (Cardiff, Pontypridd Papers). For an ac-count of the meetings held by the 'Four', see the *South Wales Daily News*, 15–23 May 1894, and *Baner ac Amserau Cymru*, 23 May 1894.

[5] Lewis to Ellis, 'Sunday Evening' (N.L.W., Ellis Papers, 1411).

should be just as well off with a Tory as a Liberal administration and said he was completely indifferent so long as he got money from his constituents whether it was paid as blackmail or not.' He explained that they would vote for measures recognized as having a prior claim, such as the budget, but would abstain over Bills which would destroy the chances of disestablishment.[1]

Welsh opinion was greatly exercised over the 'Revolt'. Relations between the Welsh members were deeply embittered, the miners' leader, William Abraham, describing Lloyd George and D. A. Thomas as 'those conceited, ill-humoured, envious twins'.[2] Another dangerous enemy roused by the rebellion was Sam Evans. Ellis was severely pained by the breach and believed that a permanent barrier had been erected between the 'Four' and their colleagues, despite outward cordiality. The 'hop, skip and jump policy' had gravely impaired the Welsh cause. Towards Lloyd George, his attitude became increasingly hostile, even contemptuous in his disparagement of his historical ignorance.[3] Some Welsh Liberals intimated that they would withdraw their support from the rebels.[4] But the majority of the Welsh press was solidly behind the 'Four', notable among them Gee, the editors of the *Genedl* and of the *Herald Cymraeg*, 'the latter my inveterate foe', said Lloyd George.[5] The London correspondent of the staid *South Wales Daily News*, Vincent Evans, was reprimanded by his editor for biased reporting in favour of the rebels.[6] The denominational journals were enthusiastic.

In any event, the first exasperation had died down when Asquith introduced the first ever Welsh Disestablishment Bill on 26 April.[7] He outlined its complex technicalities with his accustomed lucidity. Its main features were that on 1 January 1896, the Church in the thir-

[1] Humphreys-Owen to Rendel, 25 May 1894 (N.L.W., Glansevern MSS., 663). Lloyd George to Ellis, n.d. 1894 (B.M., Herbert Gladstone Papers, Add. MSS., 46022, ff. 94–97). Also see the interview with Lloyd George in the *British Weekly*, 27 Apr. 1894.

[2] Abraham to Ellis, 16 Oct. 1894 (N.L.W., Ellis Papers, 12–13).

[3] Ellis to Daniel, 12 July, 26 Sept. 1894 (N.L.W., Daniel Papers, 430, 436).

[4] Walter Owen to Ellis, 22 May 1894 (N.L.W., Ellis Papers, 1621). There was also opposition to the 'Revolt' expressed in the South Wales Liberal Federation, whose president was D. A. Thomas (*South Wales Daily News*, 30 May 1894).

[5] Lloyd George to Herbert Lewis, ? Apr. 1894 (Penucha MSS.). The respective editors were E. Lloyd Williams and D. Rees. Apart from the *Faner*, the enthusiasm of the Welsh language press is shown in *Y Genedl*, 24, 31 Apr. 1894; *Y Tyst*, 27 Apr. 1894; and, much more guardedly, in *Y Goleuad*, 27 Apr. 1894. The Baptist organ, *Seren Cymru*, also favoured the 'Revolt', as did the *Cambrian News*.

[6] John Duncan to Vincent Evans, 26 Apr. 1894 (N.L.W., Vincent Evans Papers). This criticism is fully justified by Evans's daily columns in the newspaper in March and April 1894.　　　　　　　　　[7] *Parl. Deb.*, 4th ser., vol. xxiii, pp. 1455 ff.

teen Welsh counties would be disestablished, ecclesiastical law would cease to apply in Wales, the bishops and clergy would no longer sit in the Lords and in Convocation, and a synod and a representative body would deal respectively with the new constitution and the landed property of the new Church. Among the sweeping disendowment provisions was the establishment of a three-member commission to maintain cathedrals, parsonages, and other fabrics. Private benefactions made since 1703 would be retained by the Church, but tithe would be vested in the county councils, and burial-grounds and glebe in the new parish councils. The proceeds would be devoted to charitable works, hospitals, schools, parish halls, libraries, and art galleries. A pension scheme would compensate incumbents for existing interests, but no compensation would be extended to curates or to public patrons. The result would be that, of a revenue of £279,000 per annum, £45,000 from capitular and episcopal endowments, with grants from the ecclesiastical commissioners and Queen Anne's Bounty, would be diverted to the use of the new Welsh Church, but otherwise it would be entirely a voluntary body. A total of £233,000 from the endowments of benefices would be secularized.

By contemporary standards, it was a most radical measure. Sir Michael Hicks-Beach described it as 'plunder and sacrilege'.[1] He turned to the familiar Unionist view that Wales had 'no separate national existence' and could not therefore receive separate legislation. The proposals for disestablishment and disendowment alike seemed to him thoroughly inequitable. The debate then proceeded on stormy but familiar lines, Welsh members and Church spokesmen repeating arguments already well-worn. On the second day Lloyd George, while generally welcoming the Bill, claimed that the compensation provisions were too generous. For the Opposition, Balfour shrewdly pointed out that the reallocation of tithe would be unfair to the more populous Welsh counties—a point not lost on some South Wales members.[2] Professor Jebb attacked the 'alien church' argument on historical grounds, while Sir Richard Temple (Kingston) and Lord Wolmer (W. Edinburgh), two stalwarts of the 'Church Brigade', claimed that Welsh opinion was not in favour of the Bill. Bryce wound up for the government, and the measure was read a first time without a division.

[1] *Parl. Deb.*, 4th ser., vol. xxiii, p. 1487. For Hicks-Beach's views, see Lady Victoria Hicks-Beach, *Life of Sir Michael Hicks-Beach* (London, 1932), vol. ii, p. 6. Also see the Bishop of St.Asaph, 'The Church in Wales', *Nineteenth Century*, July 1895.
[2] See the speech of D. A. Thomas, later in the debate.

The position of the ministry made it inconceivable that the Bill would pass into law, but Welsh members hoped that it would at least pass through all its stages in the Commons, so that the country could be presented with a clear-cut issue. Much satisfaction, therefore, was shown at Rosebery's declaration at Birmingham on 23 May that the government would not go to the country until Welsh disestablishment was passed by the Commons. A meeting of the Welsh party on 25 May, under their new chairman, Osborne Morgan, rejected a resolution by the 'Four' which demanded firmer guarantees, and carried Alfred Thomas's motion congratulating the government on their decision.[1]

As in 1893, the Bill aroused much feeling throughout the country. The Church now felt more secure as the delayed nature of government business and the safeguard of the Lords' veto made the passage of the Bill most improbable. After a series of unfavourable by-elections, the government's precarious majority was now barely twenty. Nevertheless, there were vigorous protests, particularly as Fowler's Parish Councils Act was already felt to be in some sense a measure of disestablishment on a local scale. On 15 May a manifesto signed by the entire episcopate, save for the Bishop of Worcester, was issued denouncing the Bill.[2] Since the Rhyl Congress in 1891 the Church had been fully mobilized, and now a 'Central Church Committee' was formed, its executive consisting of the Bishop of St. Asaph, Viscount Wolmer, M.P., Lord Cranborne, M.P., and Arthur Griffith-Boscawen, M.P.[3] Under the chairmanship of the Duke of Westminster, it organized scores of meetings up and down the country, its strong links with the squirearchy affording ready ammunition for Lloyd George and his friends.

Inevitably, however, there were some prominent Anglican dissentients. G. W. E. Russell of the Liberal Churchmen's Union defended the Bill before the Liberation Society. Other churchmen claimed that the Welsh Church would be healthier without the incubus of the state connexion. This was the burden of an able pamphlet by the Rev. J. Frome Wilkinson, sponsored by Gladstone's son, the Rev. Stephen Gladstone.[4] Similarly, a letter in *The Times* on 4 May by Dr. Percival, the headmaster of Rugby, strongly condemned the tactics of the

---

[1] *South Wales Daily News*, 26 May 1894.
[2] *Church Times*, 18 May 1894.
[3] Griffith-Boscawen, op. cit., p. 57.
[4] J. Frome Wilkinson, *Disestablishment* (*Welsh and English*) (London, 1894). Cf. Rev. Stephen Gladstone to Wilkinson, 29 Feb. 1894 (N.L.W., Ellis Papers, 3149).

bishops. This letter, which caused a great stir, was given added significance when in the following February, to the horror of High Churchmen, Percival was appointed to the see of Hereford.[1] Perhaps most interesting of all was the so-called 'Bangor scheme' of January 1895, issued by five Welsh churchmen, namely Arthur Price, the Rev. R. Edmonds Jones (Warden of Bangor Divinity School) and the vicars of Bangor, Welshpool, and Llanidloes.[2] There is a suggestion that the ubiquitous hand of Lloyd George was, even here, as ready in conciliation as in extremism, in unexpected and temporary collusion with the Bishop of Bangor.[3] Price wrote to Ellis optimistically that he thought most Welsh clergymen would support it. If Ellis was willing to compromise over tithe, 'if you can put patriotism before sect and party, the sole difficulty in the way of Welsh unity and Welsh self-government is removed, as . . . a large section of the Welsh clergy will give to Welsh Home Rule their enthusiastic support'. Even the editor of the *Western Mail* thought compromise over endowments inevitable.[4] This scheme, however, like most compromises, failed to satisfy either side.

There was also some Liberal Unionist support for the Bill. Joseph Chamberlain criticized some of its provisions, but stated in a letter in *The Times* that he would vote for the Second Reading. At Birmingham on 16 October he reaffirmed his support for the principle of disestablishment, but stated that the Welsh Church was deserving of far more generous treatment than the Irish, against which much more was to be said on national grounds. He further embarrassed his allies by his letter to John Morgan, the editor of the *Aberystwyth Observer*, on 31 January, stating that Welsh disestablishment was inevitable, and that a Unionist government alone could provide generous treatment in dealing with Church funds. The unfortunate Morgan was soon expelled from the local Conservative Club, for maintaining what was clearly true, that many prominent Welsh churchmen supported disestablishment.[5]

Long before this, however, the Welsh Disestablishment Bill was

---

[1] William Temple, *Life of Bishop Percival* (London, 1921), pp. 130–1. Cf. *Church Times*, 8, 15 Feb. 1895; *Spectator*, 19 May 1894, 8 Feb. 1895.

[2] Draft in Ellis Papers (N.L.W.), 1701. Cf. *National Church*, Feb. 1895, p. 35, and Mar. 1895, p. 71. (I am grateful to Miss Eluned E. Owen for these references.)

[3] Eluned E. Owen, op. cit., pp. 179–81. Cf. Hartwell-Jones, op. cit., p. 59. Bishop of St. Asaph to Principal Owen, 16 Feb. 1895 (Bishop Owen MSS.).

[4] Price to Ellis, 21 Jan. 1895 (N.L.W., Ellis Papers, 1701), 'Confidential'. William Davies (acting editor, *Western Mail*) to Principal Owen, 26 Nov. 1894 (Bishop Owen MSS.).

[5] Letter by Morgan in *The Times*, 1 Mar. 1895. Cf. *Liberal Magazine*, Mar. 1895.

defunct. Speeches by Asquith and Fowler had indicated that a Second Reading was most unlikely. The 'Whips' of the rebel 'Four', Frank Edwards and Herbert Lewis, wrote unofficially to Ellis about the position on 1 June, and Ellis confirmed, in scathing terms, that the Bill would either be passed in 1894 or, if the progress of government business made that impossible, as a first measure in 1895.[1] A more official communication came from Osborne Morgan, as leader of the Welsh Party, to Harcourt. Harcourt showed little sympathy, and bluntly informed Morgan that he was one of the biggest bores in the House.[2] It was no surprise when Harcourt announced the withdrawal of the Bill on 18 July. Rosebery promised that it would have first place on the ministerial programme in 1895. Lloyd George, in an aggressive address before the South Wales Liberal Federation in August, said that Wales would hold Rosebery to his word.

In 1895 the Liberal ministry was in a feeble condition. Ellis had an anxious task as Whip, and the prospect of legislation was slight. The most that could be hoped for was that, in challenging the Lords by 'filling up the cup', disestablishment might somehow be scrambled through the Commons. Hopes were raised by Rosebery's address to the National Liberal Federation at Cardiff on 18 January. He dealt with disestablishment in philosophical vein. The essence of the Church was spiritual, and there should be a right of 'national option' to create equality between the churches. He also revived the idea of 'home rule all round'.[3]

Thus, on 25 February 1895, Asquith introduced a Welsh Disestablishment Bill for the second time. He had been under pressure from Wales to alter some provisions. D. A. Thomas urged that tithe be paid into a central fund and allocated nationally on a population basis, but this was opposed by almost all the Welsh members. Carvell Williams, for the Liberation Society, had urged more severe measures, the opening of cathedrals to all religious bodies, payment of tithe into a central fund, the vesting of churches in the Commissioners, and the appropriation of burial fees; but the government draftsmen dismissed these as 'largely sentimental grievances'.[4] Ellis urged Asquith: 'Change the Bill as little as possible.'[5] Asquith's measure was thus largely identical with that of 1894.[6] The parochial

---

[1] Ellis to Lewis, 11 June 1894 (Penucha MSS.).
[2] Archbishop of Wales, op. cit., p. 162.   [3] *The Times*, 19 Jan. 1895.
[4] Memo. by J. Dryhurst, 11 Dec. 1894 (Bodleian, Asquith Papers, box 14).
[5] Ellis to Asquith, 15 Jan. 1895 (Bodleian, Asquith Papers, box 14).
[6] *Parl. Deb.*, 4th ser., vol. xxx, pp. 1487 ff.

revenue of £233,000 per annum would again be secularized. The debate lasted for two days, the 'Church Brigade' and the Welsh members virtually monopolizing the proceedings. A notable criticism of the Bill came from a nonconformist Unionist, J. Rentoul (East Down), who attacked the belief that the Irish Church had flourished since its disestablishment in 1869. The Bill was read a first time on 28 February.

Amid increasingly obvious signs of ministerial collapse, Asquith brought forward the Bill for a Second Reading on 21 March. In the interim, the Unionists had been concentrating fire on the Bill in by-elections,[1] while the Oxford Union carried a motion against it for the third time by 121 votes to 43.

Asquith's speech on the Second Reading must rank as among the finest of his career.[2] Hicks-Beach, who followed him, termed it 'an intellectual treat'. He upheld the right of the state to disestablish, as it had done in Ireland. The history of the Welsh Church showed that, while it was national in its inception, its incorporation into the Church of England had led to its being denationalized. He emphasized the strength of Welsh nonconformity: 4,000 chapels and not one without a Sunday service. He asked if the state needed a Church as 'a standing witness' to religion, particularly if that Church were empty.[3] In reply, Hicks-Beach said 'the Church was the state in its spiritual aspect'.[4] The state had no right to touch Church property, while the Bill would sorely impoverish the clergy. The debate lasted five days, and tended to be highly repetitive. Liberal speakers included ten Welshmen, of whom Sam Evans made perhaps the ablest contribution, together with Trevelyan, Bryce, Lockwood, Birrell, and G. W. E. Russell, whose interesting speech quoted Shakespeare's *Henry V* to justify disendowment.[5] Harcourt wound up for the government. The Opposition speakers included no Welshmen. Among them were Henry Matthews (a Roman Catholic, who embarrassingly justified the principle of disendowment), Sir Edward Clarke, Gorst, Goschen, Balfour, and the 'Church Brigade'. Balfour concluded by claiming that the government intended to destroy the Church.

Much interest attached to the division, and Welsh Liberals could

[1] Ellis to Lewis, 5 Feb. 1895 (Penucha MSS.).
[2] *Parl. Deb.*, 4th ser., vol. xxxi, pp. 1574 ff.; cf. John Owen, 'Araeth Mr. Asquith', *Y Geninen*, Apr. 1895.
[3] *Parl. Deb.*, loc. cit., p. 1594.
[4] Ibid., p. 1597. [5] Ibid., vol. xxxii, pp. 201-2.

be well pleased with the result. On 1 April the Bill passed by 304 votes to 260. Its supporters included twenty-nine Liberal churchmen, two Liberal Unionists (Joseph Chamberlain and A. C. Corbett), and nearly all the Parnellites. Sixteen Liberal Unionists were absent unpaired as were two Liberals (Macfarlane and Coldwells) and one anti-Parnellite (O'Driscoll). Gladstone was paired with C. P. Villiers in favour of the Bill. There seemed to be a real prospect of a Welsh Disestablishment Bill passing through the House of Commons.

Different pressures were now brought to bear on the Bill, to the further embarrassment of the tottering government. The Liberal Churchmen's Union now showed alarm at some of its more stringent provisions, and G. W. E. Russell, Asquith's Under-Secretary at the Home Office, conveyed their disapproval of the proposal to secularize cathedrals, of the non-payment of compensation to curates, and of some of the objects to which the secularized endowments would be devoted.[1] More powerful and decisive was the pressure being exerted by the *Cymru Fydd* movement which now threatened to submerge all Welsh Liberalism beneath the call for Welsh home rule. *Cymru Fydd* saw in the Disestablishment Bill a unique opportunity for advancing the principles of separatism, and, as will be seen, this was to play an important part in bringing down the government.

The Committee Stage on the Bill began on 6 May. The government would obviously be in difficulties. As early as 3 April, 250 amendments or instructions had been handed in, 148 by four Unionist members alone.[2] The Church Parliamentary Committee, with Sir Richard Webster as chairman and Griffith-Boscawen as secretary, had carefully organized obstruction, and the Opposition front bench, Balfour and Hicks-Beach prominent among them, often lent support.[3] The government had little enthusiasm for Welsh Disestablishment or any other Bill, by this time, and Asquith had inadequate support. Sir Frank Lockwood, the Solicitor-General, fresh from harrying Oscar Wilde in the witness-box, was considerably less impressive when himself placed on the defensive, while Russell, the Under-Secretary, was also ineffective. Asquith's other lieutenant, Bryce, was often embarrassed by the barrage of ecclesiastical technicalities, in spite of his great legal knowledge, and Asquith had thus to bear the

[1] Russell to Asquith, 25 Mar. 1895 (Bodleian, Asquith Papers, box 14).
[2] *The Times*, 3 Apr. 1895.
[3] Griffith-Boscawen, op. cit., pp. 69 ff. Sir Richard Temple, *The Story of My Life* (London, 1896), vol. ii, pp. 294 ff.

great burden of defence almost alone.[1] In addition, some of his Welsh supporters behind him soon produced some troublesome crossfire. A national convention, called by the *Cymru Fydd* movement at Aberystwyth on 18 April, had demanded that tithes be paid into a national fund and distributed on a national basis, and that a national council, to replace the three commissioners, be set up to administer Church temporalities.[2] D. A. Thomas and Lloyd George, still playing the role of mutually independent free-lances, undertook to sponsor these two proposals.

On the first day of Committee, during an instruction by Boscawen to divide the Bill into two parts, treating disestablishment separately from disendowment (an instruction aimed at the Liberal Churchmen's vote), D. A. Thomas moved to obtain a national allocation of tithes. However, no Welshman supported him, and Boscawen's move failed by thirty-five.[3] The Opposition then concentrated on eliminating various border and other areas from the operation of the Bill— South Pembrokeshire, parts of Montgomeryshire, Radnorshire, Flintshire, and Monmouthshire were all solemnly discussed. The Monmouthshire amendment afforded the Hon. Frederick Courtenay Morgan (Unionist, South Monmouthshire), the last of a dynasty which had sat intermittently for the county since 1547, the opportunity to make one of his very rare speeches in thirty-two years in the House.[4] The government won through by the narrow margin of twenty-five.

It was on the fifth day of Committee, 20 May, that the first major crisis arose. Lloyd George rose to move that a national council be set up, as under Clause 81 of the Local Government Act of 1888, to administer the national fund in place of the Commissioners.[5] Asquith had been forewarned of this move. Bryn Roberts wrote to him confidentially: 'I think you ought to be acquainted with the fact that the Welsh members are by no means unanimous on the question. I was present at the first meeting of the Welsh members at which the amendment was discussed and strenuously opposed it. The sense of

---

[1] Asquith, *Fifty Years in Parliament* (London, 1926), p. 229. Augustine Birrell, *Sir Frank Lockwood* (London, 1898), pp. 157–8. Lockwood was censured by opposing counsel for his tactics in the case of *Regina* v. *Wilde* at the Old Bailey (H. Montgomery Hyde, *The Trial of Oscar Wilde*, London, 1948, pp. 88–90).

[2] *South Wales Daily News*, 19 Apr. 1895.

[3] *Parl. Deb.*, 4th ser., vol. xxxiii, pp. 537 ff.

[4] In 1905 D. A. Thomas calculated the duration of his speeches in the Commons as five seconds a year.

[5] *Parl. Deb.*, 4th ser., vol. xxxiii, pp. 1615 ff.

the meeting was so evidently against it that Mr. Lloyd George proposed to adjourn the discussion . . . and this was agreed to. I was not present at the next meeting and I think if you will enquire of the deputation you will find that there was only a small minority of the members present and so Mr. George got his way.'[1] This is confirmed by the minute in Herbert Lewis's diary which notes that this meeting on 9 May was attended by eleven Welsh members only, including the 'Four' but none of their major adversaries.[2] Roberts went on: 'The object is to help on the question of Welsh Home Rule, a movement that has no hold whatever on the Welsh people at large. . . . I hope the government will stick to the Bill on this point and if that is done, the support of the amendment will collapse. I know that Mr. S. T. Evans agrees with this view and he pressed me to communicate with you.' Roberts concluded that a council would not be competent to deal with the judicial and administrative functions of the Commissioners.

Therefore, in the House on 20 May, Asquith opposed the amendment on the grounds that the Commissioners would be more likely to provide impartial administration. In reply, Lloyd George (to whom Asquith had acidly referred as 'the honourable member' rather than the customary 'my honourable friend') frankly stated that the issue was one of home rule. If Asquith could not entrust a body elected by Welsh councils with £200,000, how could he trust a national Parliament?[3] Hicks-Beach, scenting trouble, eagerly supported the amendment. In alarm, Osborne Morgan, who had presided over the meeting that had accepted Lloyd George's amendment, now appealed to him to drop it. Lloyd George appealed to the government again, supported by his fellow-rebel, Herbert Lewis. Asquith yielded to the extent that he promised that the matter could be discussed again later on, on the ninth clause. Lloyd George then tried to withdraw his amendment, but the Opposition refused to allow this.[4] So Lloyd George was placed in the ignominious position of having to vote against his own amendment. Nineteen Welsh members supported the government, and the amendment was narrowly defeated by 198 votes to 188. Lloyd George, however, continued his intrigues on behalf of his scheme, and the standing of the govern-

---

[1] Bryn Roberts to Asquith, 18 May 1895 (Bodleian, Asquith Papers, box 14).
[2] Herbert Lewis's Diary (Penucha MSS.).
[3] Parl. Deb., loc. cit., p. 1637.
[4] The Times parliamentary correspondent had stated that the Church Party had 'agreed to co-operate' with Lloyd George (The Times, 18 May 1895).

ment was gravely weakened by the entire episode. The third clause was scrambled through later in the day by eighteen votes.

Asquith struggled on with what he later termed his 'thankless task'.[1] Concessions were made in abundance. On 17 June the Church was allowed endowments which had come into its possession from 1662 to 1703. Later, on Jebb's amendment, came the cession of cathedrals, burial-grounds, and chapels of ease. This was greeted with Welsh protests, and even the loyalist Bryn Roberts stated Asquith had gone too far. 'The Welsh Members had taken but little part in the discussion . . . because they were anxious not to impede the progress of the Bill, but the Rt. Hon. Gentleman the Home Secretary must not assume their silence was due to apathy or want of interest.'[2]

A further blow to the government came on 19 June, when it was revealed that Gladstone had cancelled his pair with Villiers in support of the Bill, as there were some 'points of detail' over which he wished 'liberty of action'.[3] This re-emergence of the retired statesman has lent further fuel to those who have seen in Gladstone only unrelenting hostility to Welsh disestablishment. He had conveyed his disapproval of some provisions in the Bill to Chamberlain at Cannes in January, and on 28 March Chamberlain met the Bishop of St. Asaph in London to discuss the subject.[4] The next day the bishop interviewed Gladstone and told him of the concern felt that the cathedrals and churchyards would be seized. Gladstone was sympathetic, and it was almost certainly on these two points that he disapproved of the Bill.[5] In May Gladstone told G. H. F. Nye that he hoped the Bill would be as generous as that of 1869.[6] It is impossible to say when Gladstone informed Ellis, as Chief Whip, of his decision, but as Gladstone had been away at Kiel for some time before 19 June, the presumption is strong that the unwelcome information was concealed for several weeks, in the hope that Gladstone would change his decision. It is, however, very doubtful whether this move indicated any fundamental change of mind on Gladstone's part. He had always opposed the secularization of cathedrals, as at Glenalmond in October 1891, at the time of the Newcastle Federation.[7] A Welsh member wrote later to him to get his assurance that he still upheld the

---

[1] Asquith, op. cit., p. 229.
[2] *Parl. Deb.*, 4th ser., vol. xxxiv, p. 1454.
[3] *The Times*, 19 June 1895. See the comments of *Baner ac Amserau Cymru*, 26 June 1895. (There is a note on this in Ellis's writing in N.L.W., Ellis Papers, 3215.)
[4] J. L. Garvin, op. cit., vol. ii, p. 604; Eluned E. Owen, op. cit., pp. 188–9.
[5] Archbishop of Wales, op. cit., pp. 171–2.
[6] *The Times*, 28 May 1895.
[7] Ibid., 2 Oct. 1891.

principle of disestablishment, and Gladstone replied assuring him of his support.[1] It was quite consistent that he should approve of the Bill in principle, but consider also that some of the disendowment provisions were too severe. Many others on the Liberal side shared this view, in 1912 as in 1895, among them the ex-premier's grandson, W. G. C. Gladstone (Kilmarnock). The 1895 measure was by far the most stringent of the various disestablishment measures introduced, and the Bill that eventually became law in 1919 was in its financial provisions much more favourable to the Church.

The death-blow to the government, however, was intimately bound up with the activities of the Welsh members. On 18 June D. A. Thomas moved an amendment to vest some Church property in a national council.[2] A Liberationist, A. Illingworth (West Bradford), supported him, and the government majority fell to thirteen. Meanwhile Lloyd George was busily negotiating about his amendment to the ninth clause to set up a national council. He informed Asquith that the Local Government Act allowed for councils of this nature.[3] Lloyd George had also been active in the counsels of the Liberation Society: 'an expression of opinion from the Liberation Society would certainly assist us with a certain class of people', he wrote, and urged Herbert Lewis to write a letter of support.[4] On 17 June Lloyd George attended a meeting of the Society, his first for eighteen months even though he was, with Ellis, Sam Evans, and Herbert Lewis, a committee member. It was reported there that Asquith had promised to consider Lloyd George's amendment to the ninth clause, and Carvell Williams was instructed to communicate with Asquith in favour of the amendment.[5] In his letter to Asquith on 19 June, Williams claimed that 'the representatives of the Welsh people will be better acquainted with local wants and feelings than the Commissioners'.[6] The succeeding events are mysteriously obscure. Lloyd George's enemies subsequently alleged that he had intrigued with the Opposition to compel the government to accept his amendment, and he found difficulty in clearing himself of the charge. Early on 20 June some Welsh members were told by Asquith that he had not yet accepted Lloyd George's amendment to the ninth clause.[7] Later that day, D. A. Thomas moved an amendment to omit clause six of the

[1] *Y Goleuad*, 3 July 1895.   [2] *Parl. Deb.*, 4th ser., vol. xxxiv, pp. 1395 ff.
[3] Lloyd George to Asquith, 19 June 1895 (Bodleian, Asquith Papers, box 14).
[4] Lloyd George to Herbert Lewis, 13 June 1895 (Penucha MSS.).
[5] Liberation Society MSS., 17 June 1895.
[6] Carvell Williams to Asquith, 19 June 1895 (Bodleian, Asquith Papers, box 14).
[7] *South Wales Daily News*, 21 June 1895.

Bill, to enable tithe to be reallocated nationally.[1] Asquith was absent at a dinner, and the government tottered as Unionist speakers enthusiastically supported the amendment. Bryce floundered helplessly against Gorst, Gibbs, Hicks-Beach, D. A. Thomas, and, for the first time at this critical stage, Joseph Chamberlain. Asquith returned in time to save the situation, but his amended version of the clause was carried by only seven, Thomas telling with Webster against the government. Now the government was clearly doomed, and the next day a snap vote moved by Brodrick to censure Campbell-Bannerman for his alleged mishandling of cordite supplies was carried by seven votes. Only four Welsh members were present in the government lobby.[2] Although the matter was hardly an issue of confidence, Harcourt and Rosebery, in harmony for once, persuaded their colleagues of the need to resign.

The fall of the Liberal government became something of a *cause célèbre* in Wales for some months to come. It was clear that the real defeat had been on 20 June on Thomas's amendment, and not over the trivial 'cordite vote' on 21 June. During the elections that followed, Bryn Roberts refused to speak on behalf of Lloyd George, alleging that the resignation of the government was due to the disloyalty of Lloyd George and D. A. Thomas, particularly the former, and their underhand alliance with Tories and Parnellites to overthrow the government because their amendments were not accepted. He returned to this theme in his election address, which he issued in the form of a fifty-page booklet.[3] Sir Henry Fowler also told his constituents at Wolverhampton that the fall of the government was due to Lloyd George's machinations.

The most comprehensive attack, however, was made in the following autumn by the Methodist journal, *Y Goleuad*.[4] Its editor, E. W. Evans, was very friendly with Bryn Roberts, another staunch Metho-

---

[1] *Parl. Deb.*, 4th ser., vol. xxxiv, pp. 1598 ff.

[2] They were A. Spicer (Monmouth Dist.), D. Randell, C. F. E. Allen (Pembroke Dist.), and the 'revolter', Frank Edwards. Ellis was much criticized for allowing this defeat to take place. Dilke voted against the government.

[3] In Bryn Roberts Papers (N.L.W.). Cf. Bryn Roberts to Fowler, 5 Oct. 1895 (N.L.W., Bryn Roberts Papers, 236).

[4] *Y Goleuad*, 25 Sept. 1895 (Editorial—'Cleon') and subsequent issues to 27 Nov. 1895. The *Goleuad*'s reporting of the crisis the previous June had been curious. Its correspondent, writing on 26 June 1895, at first strongly condemned Lloyd George and D. A. Thomas for undermining the government—'ceisio gormod, colli'r cwbl' (wanting too much, losing everything). But, in an addendum, he reported that he had now learnt that the government had in fact accepted Lloyd George's amendment to the ninth clause, and concluded that Wales was much indebted to Lloyd George for his initiative on behalf of Welsh home rule.

dist. In a series of hostile leading articles, he alleged that Lloyd George had conspired with the Opposition on two occasions. On the first, on 20 May, the government stood firm. But on the second, more pressure was imposed. At a meeting of some Welsh members with Asquith at midnight on 20 June, he alleged, Asquith had still not accepted Lloyd George's amendment, and the first notification that he had done so was given to a handful of Welsh members at 4 p.m. on 21 June.[1] The defeat on the 'cordite vote' a few hours later gave the government an opportunity to escape from the dilemma. The Liberals were thrown out of office and Welsh disestablishment set back a decade, owing to Lloyd George's 'foolish vanity'.

After a surprising delay, Lloyd George dealt contemptuously with these charges. 'I would not think it worth taking any notice of such an accusation, were it not that it is perfectly clear from internal evidence supplied by the articles themselves that the *Goleuad* writer is simply a poor tool in the hands of one of the Welsh members.'[2] He almost certainly had Roberts in mind. His defence was simply that Asquith had accepted his amendment to the ninth clause before the government resigned, and that 'every available' (he deleted 'the majority of the') Welsh member save one approved of this. At New-bridge in 1898 he pointed out that both parties had accepted his amendment. Ellis, who derived some private amusement from the controversy, made a speech defending Lloyd George from the impu-tation of treachery and stating that his amendment had been accepted by Asquith. This view has been uncompromisingly accepted by all Lloyd George's biographers, who have treated the attacks of the *Goleuad* as simply motivated by petty spleen.[3]

But the evidence throws doubt on Lloyd George's plea of inno-cence. Asquith refused to enter the controversy. The editor of the *Goleuad* wrote to Asquith to confirm the charges made, stating them to be based on evidence 'of the most reliable character'.[4] Asquith then wrote to Ellis: 'As a matter of fact, the only amendments in Clause 9 which the Govt. were prepared to make or accept were those put down in my name on the evening of 21 June . . . I read your

[1] Ibid., 13 Nov. 1895.
[2] Lloyd George to Ellis, 4 Nov. 1895 (N.L.W., Ellis Papers, 690). *Baner ac Amserau Cymru*, 16 Nov. 1895, noted that Lloyd George's disclaimers, and the confirmatory letters of Ellis and Herbert Lewis, were not published in the *South Wales Daily News*.
[3] For example, du Parcq, vol. ii, p. 166; J. Hugh Edwards, vol. iii, pp. 134–7; Frank Owen, pp. 83–84.
[4] E. W. Evans to Asquith, 23 Nov. 1895 (N.L.W., Ellis Papers, 74). This letter has been mutilated but it remains legible.

published letter and substantially agreed with it. It is not, however, strictly accurate to say that we "accepted" Ll. George's amendment, and I think you showed rather too great a tendency to whitewash him, after the underhand and disloyal way in wh(ich) he undoubtedly acted.'[1] There is also the view of Fowler that the real defeat of the government came on 20 June, when its majority fell to seven. 'If the Welsh members had been guided by you', he told Bryn Roberts, 'my *private* opinion (but of course I could not say this publicly) is that the late Govt. would not have been defeated in the late Parliament.'[2]

There is, therefore, at least a degree of doubt as to whether Lloyd George's amendment had been accepted by the government. Contemporaries in Wales clearly believed that it had: on 21 June Gee congratulated Herbert Lewis 'on your success over the 9th Clause'.[3] Again, in 1909, when the controversy was long forgotten, Asquith appeared to admit that the amendment had been accepted after all, in contradiction to his earlier view.[4] Even so, there is no doubt that Lloyd George's activities did materially weaken his own government, even if the charge of consorting with the Opposition remains unproved. After its first warm acceptance of Lloyd George's admission, the Welsh press began to have doubts, and both *Y Faner* and the *South Wales Daily News* adopted a critical attitude. An observant reporter, Henry Lucy of the *Daily News*, believed that on the Monday, when the ninth clause was to be discussed, the government might well have been in a minority, and this was also the retrospective view of Boscawen, secretary of the Church Party.[5] There is thus presumptive evidence for believing that Lloyd George and D. A. Thomas, acting independently, largely helped to undermine their own government, and thus retard the progress of disestablishment.

The ensuing general election in July was disastrous for the Liberal Party. There seemed little agreement among its leaders as to the main issue at stake. Rosebery said it was the House of Lords; Harcourt suggested local option, and John Morley, Irish home rule, while in Wales disestablishment played its traditional role. The result was the return of 411 Unionists against only 177 Liberals and 82 Nationalists, a Unionist majority of 152.

[1] Asquith to Ellis, 30 Nov. 1895 (N.L.W., Ellis Papers, 74), 'Private'.
[2] Fowler to Bryn Roberts, 14 Oct. 1895 (N.L.W., Bryn Roberts Papers, 64), 'Private and Confidential'.   [3] Gee to Herbert Lewis, 21 June 1895 (Penucha MSS.).
[4] Memorandum on 'The Differences between the present (1909) Bill and the Bill of 1895, as amended' (Bodleian, Asquith Papers, box 3).
[5] H. W. Lucy, op. cit., p. 479. Griffith-Boscawen, op. cit., p. 71.

In Wales the results had special significance. Disestablishment figures on every Liberal election address, usually followed by agriculture or temperance. Welsh home rule, however, is mentioned by only five candidates out of thirty-four.[1] Eight addresses deal solely with Welsh affairs. On the other hand, the Unionists made their most concerted attempt yet to make inroads on the Liberal strongholds. All save two refer to the Disestablishment Bill in their addresses which are notable for their unprecedented attention to Welsh affairs. The Church Defence Committee was active in many constituencies, as the Duke of Westminster, Lord Penrhyn, Lord Emlyn, and others flung in their resources. Registration was carefully organized in urban areas.[2] The general weakness of the Liberal position gave the Church Defenders a great opportunity. Osborne Morgan admitted to Asquith that some seats were 'in the lap of the gods'.[3]

The results gave Welsh Unionists much heart. While the majority of Welsh seats were still impregnably Liberal, some remarkable gains were made. The Unionist vote rose by 16,000 and six seats were gained from the Liberals. In all, the Unionists won nine seats, a total not equalled since. For the first time since 1880, the tide of Liberalism in Wales had been stemmed. There were some surprising gains. Cardiff and Swansea Town went Unionist, Sir J. T. Dillwyn-Llewelyn increasing his poll by nearly 1,000 in the latter constituency. General Laurie, a veteran of the Indian Mutiny and the Crimea, won the dockyard seat of Pembroke, while Sir John Jones Jenkins, a popular local industrialist and owner of the Beaufort tinplate works, captured Carmarthen Boroughs, a constituency much affected by the depression in the tinplate industry. Major Jones's American connexions stood him in poor stead here, when linked with the hated name of McKinley. Anglicized South Glamorgan and Radnorshire were won by two landowners. The Liberal nucleus was thus reduced to twenty-five, and, while some seats were retained by large majorities, others saw a striking decline. In Montgomeryshire, where much depended on whether 'enough of the old nonconformist spirit has been roused to counter the discontent and unrest which the bad times have instilled into the farmers',[4] Humphreys-Owen retained the seat by only twenty-seven. In Flintshire, where the Church Defence

[1] Lloyd George, Brynmor Jones, Herbert Lewis, Pritchard Morgan, Samuel Smith.
[2] *Young Wales*, Aug. 1895, pp. 186–8.
[3] Osborne Morgan to Asquith, 6 July 1895 (Bodleian, Asquith Papers, box 19).
[4] Humphreys-Owen to Rendel, 19 July 1895 (N.L.W., Rendel Papers, xiv. 667).

Committee had been active, Samuel Smith's majority fell by 1,000, while in Merthyr Tydfil, D. A. Thomas and Pritchard Morgan saw their majorities slashed by the astonishing margin of 7,000. In these circumstances, it is surprising that there were not further disasters. Lloyd George, with a popular opponent and much local hostility after his recent tactics, did well to hold his seat at Caernarvon. The overall setback to Welsh Liberalism gave *The Times* much satisfaction: 'the progress of Unionism in Wales is bound up with that of education and enlightenment'.[1]

The Liberal government of 1892–5 left a bitter taste among the radicals of Wales. On paper, there were impressive memorials. Education and land reform had been materially advanced, while a Welsh Disestablishment Bill, highly radical in scope, had been piloted through most of its stages in the Commons, to form a pattern for later years. Nevertheless, there was profound disillusionment at the outcome. It became clear that Wales was strong only when the Liberal Party was weak and that such strength was illusory. Some tried to attach the stigma of guilt to individuals, to Tom Ellis in accepting the loaves and fishes of office, to Lloyd George in destroying confidence in the party leadership and party discipline, to Stuart Rendel in accepting Gladstone's equivocations at face value and succumbing to his obsession with Irish home rule. There were numerous candidates for the role of Judas. But the cause of failure lay far deeper than any breach of faith, real or imaginary, by individuals. Rather did it reside in basic conflict between Liberalism and nationalism in the minds of Welsh radicals, which fatally compromised their appreciation of the realities of political power.

(v) *The Collapse of* Cymru Fydd

Disillusion at Westminster was accompanied by disaster in Wales itself. *Cymru Fydd* suddenly collapsed, leaving a disintegration that was total and complete. Since 1891 *Cymru Fydd* branches had penetrated to all parts of Wales, under the dynamic stimulus of Lloyd George. To an ever-increasing extent, its original objective of preserving the Welsh language and revitalizing Welsh culture was being subordinated to the political aim of national self-government. Only thus it seemed, could unity and direction be imposed on the various individual expressions of nationality in political and cultural life, that had shown such impressive momentum in the past quarter of

[1] *The Times*, 12 Aug. 1895.

a century. On 23 August 1894 a meeting was held at Llandrindod Wells to frame a constitution of a national *Cymru Fydd* league, amalgamating all the different branches in all parts of Wales. The main initiative now came from the North, but Lloyd George was not discouraged at the reluctance of South Wales to join the new movement. 'It is only a question of getting a thoroughly good organizer', and Beriah Gwynfe Evans was appointed to fulfil this role.[1] The new tide seemed to be sweeping all before it in the constituencies: in Arfon, William Jones, an attractive and eloquent young patriot, intimate with Tom Ellis and Lloyd George, was pushed into the Liberal candidature by *Cymru Fydd* forces over the head of the official Liberal nominee, D. P. Williams of Llanberis.[2] This sentiment was finding its way into Parliament also. In April 1894 Herbert Lewis, as a Welsh home ruler, spoke in support of Dalziel and on behalf of Scottish home rule, while on 29 March 1895 Dalziel and Lloyd George carried a motion for 'home rule all round' by twenty-six votes.[3] The sympathy for local devolution shown by Rosebery at the Cardiff meeting of the National Liberal Federation seemed to be another encouraging portent. Finally, a vigorous new nationalist journal, *Young Wales*, was launched in January 1895, under the editorship of a former Independent minister, later to be Lloyd George's biographer, John Hugh Edwards, with the object of 'conserving and strengthening the individuality of Wales'.[4]

But already there were ominous signs that all was not well with the movement. The fragile unity of Wales seemed already in flux. Above all, a dangerous rift had appeared between the Liberals of the North and the South Wales Liberal Federation, dominated by the powerful and cosmopolitan Liberal Association of Cardiff. It was the South Wales Federation, through its President, D. A. Thomas, which had previously taken the lead in urging Welsh separatism, and had been scarcely less ardent than the North in welcoming the rebellion of the 'Four'. But gradually a distinct attitude had emerged in Glamorgan and Monmouth, a realization that the wealthiest and most populous counties might have interests that might diverge from those of the rest of Wales, that the concept of Welsh nationality required

[1] Lloyd George to Herbert Lewis, 22 June 1894 (Penucha MSS.).
[2] Lloyd George to Ellis, ? 1894 (B.M., Herbert Gladstone Papers, Add. MSS., 46022, ff. 96). The struggle for the Liberal nomination in Arfon is illustrated by Bangor MSS., 1124, ff. 135–69.
[3] *Parl. Deb.*, 4th ser., vol. xxii, pp. 1300 ff.; ibid., vol. xxxii, pp. 523 ff.
[4] *Young Wales*, Jan. 1895, p. 1.

reappraisal, if not revision. This divergence had already been noticeable in the discussions over Alfred Thomas's National Institutions
Bill in 1891–2. Now it hardened into definite hostility, as the control
of Lloyd George and his friends of the rural North over the growing
structure of *Cymru Fydd* became ever more evident. In the autumn of
1894 Lloyd George openly avowed the growing personal and political rift between himself and D. A. Thomas. A meeting at Cardiff on
4 January 1895, between the *Cymru Fydd* leaders and the spokesmen
of the South Wales Liberal Federation, failed to reach agreement
over the crucial questions as to whether there should be one Federation for the whole of Wales or four subordinate ones, of which Glamorgan and Monmouth should constitute one, and also whether the
proposed national council should have effective, or merely nominal,
supremacy.[1] Although the North Wales Liberal Federation took the
ultimate step of amalgamating itself with the *Cymru Fydd* League,
the South Wales Federation refused to do so. When a convention
was held at Aberystwyth on 18 April to form a unified 'Welsh National
Federation' (*Cynghrair Cenedlaethol Cymru Fydd*), the South Wales
Liberals were ostentatiously absent.[2] Although the new body tact-
fully elected Alfred Thomas and Beriah Gwynfe Evans, two South
Wales representatives, as its first President and secretary, the gulf
was clearly widening.

Nevertheless, the progress of the *Cymru Fydd* movement was the
overriding factor in Welsh politics in 1895. As has been noted, its
influence was far-reaching on the Committee stages of the Disestablishment Bill and the famous controversy over Lloyd George's
amendment to the ninth clause reflected its significance. The movement derived its impetus almost entirely from the leadership of Lloyd
George. To him the lesson of the recent Liberal ministries was that
the dominance of England in the Imperial Parliament made it impossible for the requirements of Wales to receive adequate treatment.
'I maintain strongly', he wrote, 'that all our demands for reform,
whether in Church, Land, Education, Temperance or otherwise,
ought to be concentrated in one great agitation for national self-
government.' Echoing Joseph Chamberlain in 1886, he believed that
the very threat of disestablishment being settled by a local assembly
would force the Church into a compromise, in the same way that the

[1] *South Wales Daily News*, 5 Jan. 1895. *Baner ac Amserau Cymru*, 9 Jan. 1895.
[2] See the letter by D. A. Thomas in *South Wales Daily News*, 18 Apr. 1895; cf. Gee
to Herbert Lewis, 24 Apr. 1895 (Penucha MSS.), and *Baner ac Amserau Cymru*,
24 Apr. 1895.

fear of home rule was bringing a settlement of the Irish land question steadily nearer.[1] A revitalized national Church could become a most powerful force for unity in Wales. The veteran Gee lent him powerful support in the *Baner*, while Lord Rosebery announced his support for 'home rule all round' on 14 November. On the other hand, English Liberationists attacked Lloyd George's proposals as prejudicial to disestablishment.[2] D. A. Thomas pointed out that they were tantamount to an avowal that Ireland was no longer the crucial question of political life.

The decisive clash between the *Cymru Fydd* League and the South Wales Federation came at the notorious conference at Newport on 16 January.[3] Lloyd George had spoken optimistically of the support of the press and public. 'When the people are roused to the point of interest they are with us. . . . We have neither paper nor politician of any great influence actively hostile.'[4] But at Newport, Lloyd George was to meet with the first great rebuff of his political career. On a motion to create one national Federation, a bitter dispute broke out between Lloyd George and the South Wales leaders, headed by D. A. Thomas. Robert Bird, a Cardiff alderman, a Wesleyan, and a sober and moderate politician, told Lloyd George that the cosmopolitan population of the great towns of South Wales would never submit to Welsh domination. Amid uproar, Lloyd George was howled down, and the prospect of national unity vanished. The *Cymru Fydd* leaders were still optimistic. Lloyd George maintained the next day: 'Wales is with us—the Rhondda proved that'. He asserted that the Newport meeting 'was disgracefully packed with Newport Englishmen', and that only seven out of twenty South Wales constituencies were represented.[5] Herbert Lewis noted in his diary, 'As we anticipated, a packed meeting. C. F. defeated and Lloyd George shut up. This will be the end of the negotiations with them and the W.N.F. will go ahead.'[6] But, while the skeleton of the Welsh National Federation survived, it was clear that the ideal of *Cymru Fydd* was moribund.[7]

---

[1] Lloyd George to Gee, 9 Oct. 1895 (N.L.W., Gee MSS., 8310E, 501). Also see his article on 'Home Rule All Round', *Young Wales*, Oct. 1895, pp. 231–5.

[2] *British Weekly*, 31 Oct. 1895.

[3] There are full accounts in the *South Wales Daily News*, and the *Western Mail*, 17 Jan. 1896. Cf. *Y Tyst*, 24 Jan. 1896, and Llewelyn Williams, 'Through Welsh Spectacles', *Young Wales*, Feb. 1896, pp. 30–31.

[4] Lloyd George to Herbert Lewis, 13 Dec. 1895 (Penucha MSS.).

[5] Lloyd George to Herbert Lewis, 16 Jan. 1896 (Penucha MSS.).

[6] Herbert Lewis's Diary, 16 Jan. 1896 (Penucha MSS.).

[7] There is no adequate account of the *Cymru Fydd* movement. William George, *Cymru Fydd: Hanes y Mudiad Cenedlaethol Cyntaf* (Liverpool, 1945), is very slight.

The break-up of *Cymru Fydd*, combined with the disillusion of the Welsh Party at Westminster, introduced a new phase in the history of Welsh radicalism, as it had developed since 1868. The sentiment of national separatism was genuine enough, but when translated into political organization as opposed to cultural activity alone, it foundered on certain inevitable practical obstacles. The most obvious was the growing divergence of outlook between the rural areas and the industrial coalfield, and this was indeed the immediate cause of the collapse of *Cymru Fydd*. But, more fundamentally, there was the contradiction between the realities of influence within the Liberal Party, which had provided the key to political advancement since 1868, and the impotence of isolated independence. By breaking with the Liberal Party, Welsh radicals would lose their one avenue of political persuasion.[1] Tom Ellis came to perceive this harsh truth, and he played little part in the *Cymru Fydd* campaign from 1890. He perceived that it was the nonconformity of Wales that created the unity of Wales, rather than any spontaneous national demand for home rule. Even Thomas Gee was anxious to disavow that Welsh home rule would retard, or even precede, disestablishment. In later years, Lloyd George himself tacitly came to accept these unpalatable truths, but during the *Cymru Fydd* period he was guilty of much self-deception. After 1891 there is an unreality about *Cymru Fydd*; it becomes a network of paper organizations rather than a reflection of a genuine national call for home rule, as were the Home Rule Conventions in Ireland. Lloyd George justifiably condemned the South Wales Liberal Federation as an unrepresentative and narrow caucus, but it is questionable whether his own *Cymru Fydd* had any broader popular basis, particularly as in so many districts the personnel of *Cymru Fydd* and of the local Liberal associations were interchangeable. The presence of loyal Liberal politicians such as Alfred Thomas and Mabon upon *Cymru Fydd* platforms demonstrated that this was separatism in only a nominal form. There was not in Wales that self-generating demand for an ever-increasing degree of exclusion from the British political system that stamped the nationalist movement in Ireland. Indeed, such a movement in Wales would

The account by Llewelyn Williams in Viscountess Rhondda (ed.), *D. A. Thomas, Viscount Rhondda*, pp. 69–77, is distorted by an overpowering animus against Lloyd George. There are some personal reminiscences in Beriah Gwynfe Evans, *The Life Romance of David Lloyd George* (London, n.d. (1915)), pp. 68–73.

[1] *Mutatis mutandis*, the broad outlines of the argument by F. S. L. Lyons in his *Fall of Parnell* (London, 1959), pp. 174–6, in connexion with the position of the Irish Party after 1886, can be applied equally to the Welsh members.

have condemned Welsh radicalism to oblivion. After 1896, therefore, Welsh Liberalism underwent a slow, reluctant, and unwelcome self-analysis. It had reached the parting of the ways. At Westminster as in Wales itself, attention turned away from the seductive vision of home rule and 'revolt'. Instead, there returned the old radical programme, of religious equality in all its aspects, gradually shedding its nationalist pretensions, with only a bitter memory to poison future recollection of the grandiose ideals of the recent past. Welsh radicalism had entered upon its Silver Age.

V

THE WELSH REVOLT
1896–1906

(i) *The Silver Age of Radicalism: the Boer War*

'THE main feature of Welsh politics today is its stagnation.'[1] These bitter words by the Liberal lawyer, Artemus Jones, written in 1903, amply illustrate the despair and disillusion almost universal in Welsh radical circles in the years after the fiasco of *Cymru Fydd*. The golden glow appeared to have departed. Even such treasured achievements as the University of Wales were failing to measure up to the national aspirations of many of its creators: Arthur Price observed that ' You could have had a real Cymru Fydd party if the University had backed Lloyd George and Ll.[ewelyn] Williams.'[2] On all sides, there was apathy and disenchantment. At the height of the South African War a Welsh writer could observe that 'not for many a long year have Welsh politics been so dull and uninteresting'.[3] In the words of Arthur Price, ' Welsh Nationalism in our day is in a hopeless plight'.[4]

This general disillusion was equally marked at Westminster and in the constituencies. In Parliament, the general election of 1895 had left the Liberal Party in a highly critical situation. Salisbury's power-ful cabinet, including for the first time Joseph Chamberlain, was backed by a majority of 152, while the Opposition, torn by disagree-ments between its leaders, was uncertain over the lines of future policy. On a smaller scale, the Welsh Parliamentary Party mirrored this situation. In personnel, they followed the customary pattern. Twenty-two out of their reduced ranks came from business or the law, while all save four claimed to be nonconformists. Sixteen were considered to speak Welsh with a fair degree of fluency. There were some most able recruits in Ellis Griffith (Anglesey), William Jones (Arfon), and Brynmor Jones (Swansea District)[5], all associated with

---

[1] *Young Wales*, June 1903, p. 123.
[2] J. Arthur Price to J. E. Lloyd, 4 Dec. 1902 (Bangor, Lloyd Papers, MSS. 314, no. 455).
[3] 'Y Gwyn o Ddyfed': 'Welsh Politics in 1899', *Young Wales*, Jan. 1900, p. 7.
[4] J. Arthur Price to J. E. Lloyd, 6 July 1903 (Bangor, Lloyd Papers, MSS. 314, no .456).
[5] Brynmor Jones had been member for Stroud, 1892–5.

the *Cymru Fydd* campaign, Welsh in outlook and, in the cases of
Ellis Griffith and William Jones, in speech also. Reginald McKenna,
a young London barrister who had been patronized by Sir Charles
Dilke, greatly strengthened the debating powers of the Welsh Party
as member for North Monmouthshire. Yet, in spite of this infusion
of new blood, the Welsh Party seemed to present a confused and ineffective image. There were bitter quarrels over tactics. 'A small but
very noisy section of Welsh politicians, led by Mr. Lloyd George,
have for years past been trying to introduce Mr. Parnell's tactics
among us', wrote Bryn Roberts,[1] and the relation of the Welsh
members to the Liberal Party as a whole continued to provoke bitter
disputes. Until 1902 the Welsh Party was at its lowest ebb. Many of
its members were of little account, particularly the 'elderly and commercial section' represented by such men as Alfred Thomas, Herbert
Roberts (West Denbighshire), and Vaughan Davies (Cardiganshire).[2]
Several of the men of real ability were mutually antagonistic—Lloyd
George, D. A. Thomas, Bryn Roberts for instance—while Tom Ellis,
with his health rapidly deteriorating, gradually withdrew from the
Welsh political scene. There were separate initiatives by individuals,
for instance by Herbert Lewis on behalf of a national museum and
library, and for the provision of Private Bill facilities for Wales. But
there was little concerted action, and less general agreement on the
main lines of approach. In 1899 even Lloyd George himself was
reluctant to support a Welsh amendment to the Address, to the surprise of Herbert Lewis: 'it was curious that I should have had to argue
the subject in such a quarter'.[3] Alfred Thomas, elected chairman of
the Welsh Party in 1897 on Osborne Morgan's death when Lloyd
George declined to stand, was a reluctant revolutionary, and hardly
a militant leader. In 1901 Humphreys-Owen lamented that the Welsh
Party 'committed suicide when it put that worthy old pantaloon
Alfred Thomas into the Chair'. Lloyd George had now become 'a
below the gangway English radical—nothing more'.[4]

This decline of the Party at Westminster was paralleled by a steady
deterioration of Liberalism within Wales itself. On the surface, the ascendancy of nonconformist radicalism still seemed beyond challenge.

---

[1] Bryn Roberts to Sir Henry Fowler, 5 Oct. 1895 (N.L.W., Bryn Roberts Papers,
no. 236).

[2] For a general survey of the Welsh Party in these years see Sir Ben Bowen Thomas,
'Agwedd ar Wleidyddiaeth Cymru, 1900–14', *Y Llenor*, xii (1943), pp. 72–80.

[3] Herbert Lewis's Diary, 6 Feb. 1899 (Penucha MSS.).

[4] Humphreys-Owen to Rendel, 23 Mar. 1901 (N.L.W., Rendel Papers, xiv. 689a).

By-elections at East Denbighshire in 1897 and Pembrokeshire in 1898 showed the traditional Liberal plurality. Nevertheless, all over Wales the structure of local Liberalism in the constituencies after 1895 shows a consistent picture of disintegration of organization and morale. Even in the large towns of Swansea and Cardiff, where powerful Liberal associations met regularly and arranged an intense programme of registration, new tensions were emerging at the local level. New cross-currents were complicating the bizarre coalition which made up Cardiff Liberalism. The Welsh Protestant League, headed by Clifford Cory, was imperilling the Liberal position in municipal elections, particularly in wards such as Adamsdown and Grangetown where the support of the United Irish League, and its powerful leaders, Father Hayde, Dr. Buist, and Dr. Mullins, was vital for the Liberal cause.[1] Again, while the heterogeneous nature of the labour force in Cardiff made working-class organization difficult to organize, the rise of 'Labour' candidates, sponsored by the Trades Council, in municipal elections was an ominous portent. In 1897 John Chappell of the Coal-Trimmers Union, previously regarded as a 'masters' union', defeated the Liberal councillor, Jacob Comley, in Splott ward, which became 'the Gibraltar of Labour'.[2] This could have dangerous implications when so much power rested on Liberal business men and shipowners in the Chamber of Commerce. In any case, the size and election expenses of Cardiff, the largest single-member constituency in the Kingdom, made selection of a candidate a most difficult exercise.[3]

In Swansea there was similar confusion. Much acrimony surrounded the renomination of R. D. Burnie as Liberal candidate in 1898. Here, as in Cardiff, there was a complex coalition to keep together, the nonconformists of Capel Gomer with the Irish of Greenhill, industrialists such as Cory Yeo and Morgan Tutton with the growing power of labour as revealed at local elections from 1898 onwards. Burnie's renomination in preference to Morgan Tutton in 1898 brought many of these conflicts out into the open, since

---

[1] *South Wales Daily News*, 19 Jan. 1899; *Welsh Catholic Herald*, 10 Oct. 1900. Dissension between the Protestant League and the United Irish League imperilled the Liberal position in the Roath by-election for the Cardiff Council in January 1899. Even so, C. H. Bird, the Liberal candidate, gained the seat.

[2] *South Wales Daily News*, 11 Mar. 1898; *Labour Pioneer*, Oct. 1900. The Cardiff Labour Church was an active force in these years. There is some interesting material on Cardiff politics in the period 1897–9 in three scrap-books kept by the secretary of the Cardiff Liberal Association, H. G. C. Allgood (Cardiff, MS. 4.488, 1/3–3/3).

[3] William Sanders to Alfred Thomas, 1 July 1899 (Cardiff, Pontypridd Papers).

Burnie was suspect for his radical attitude to social policy, his anti-imperialism, and his sympathy for Irish home rule.[1] Again, he was a man of modest means, and Swansea was no constituency for the poor man. In time, his opposition to the Boer War cost Burnie his candidature, and he was to be followed by the largesse and patronage of great industrialists such as Sir George Newnes, and later Sir Alfred Mond.[2]

In the county constituencies, this Liberal disintegration was still more emphatic. All over Wales, local Liberal machinery seemed on the point of collapse. Gower was a typical case. The Liberal Association did not meet once between the elections of 1895 and 1900: as its secretary remarked, 'it had been allowed to become practically extinct, the only sign of life being shown at election time'.[3] In spite of a strong challenge by Labour in the 1900 election, the Gower Liberals resumed their hibernation after 1900 and did not meet again until 1905. After a confused meeting in Swansea Liberal Club, it was discovered that the president of the Association had retired from politics, while the chairman and treasurer were both dead![4] It is not surprising that Labour spokesmen should condemn the Association as an unrepresentative 'clique of wirepullers'.[5] The same story can be seen in many other constituencies. In Cardiganshire the party machinery almost disappeared after 1895, and virtually no sub-scriptions were received from district associations. The resources of Cardiganshire Liberalism amounted to £11. 2s. 6d., and financial disaster was averted only when the sitting member, Vaughan Davies, a landowner who had been a Conservative until 1892, personally took over the debt of the Association.[6] This dangerous extension of personal influence caused widespread alarm. The same ominous trend to succumb to local patronage, rather than submit to demo-cratic procedure, appeared in Carmarthen Boroughs where rivalry between Carmarthen and Llanelli had been traditional. The nomina-tion in 1899 of Alfred Davies, a wealthy industrialist who was later to be rejected after flagrant bribery of the electorate, in place of

[1] *Cambria Daily Leader*, 18 Feb. 1898.
[2] *South Wales Daily News*, 3 July 1900; *Cardiff Times*, 13 Oct. 1900; *Cambria Daily Leader*, 13 Sept. 1900. It was pointedly noted that Newnes had provided a Free Library for Putney and a Town Hall for Lynton. 'That was the stamp of man they had in their midst'!
[3] *Mumbles Weekly Press and Gower News*, 23 June 1905.
[4] *South Wales Daily News*, 21 Aug. 1905.
[5] *Llais Llafur*, 20 Oct. 1900.
[6] *South Wales Daily News*, 8 Jan. 1897, 10 June 1898.

Thomas Hughes, a leading figure in the Tinplaters' Union, amid scenes of great turbulence, caused intense anger in Labour circles.[1] In such constituencies as South Glamorgan, South Monmouthshire, West and East Carmarthenshire, Merthyr Tydfil, East Glamorgan, and Anglesey, Liberal machinery crumbled into obsolescence. Finally, in Merioneth the death of Ellis in April 1899 produced a period of crisis, in which the corrupted and unrepresentative nature of Liberalism in the county was fully illustrated. The first crisis was averted eventually by the nomination of the historian and *litterateur*, Owen M. Edwards, largely on the initiative of the more working-class sections of the county, Ffestiniog and Corris.[2] But Edwards's retirement in 1900, after a nominal membership during which he never made a speech in the House, provoked more disagreement. When the initiative of the nineteen vice-presidents secured the nomination of Osmond Williams, a Liberal landowner from Penrhyndeudraeth and son of a former member, there were angry criticisms of the structure and function of the Association. After intense local acrimony, the entire Association was reconstituted. A writer in the *Genedl* wrote, somewhat optimistically, 'the eyes of Britain have been on Ffestiniog'.[3] The situation in Merioneth reproduced the confusion general throughout Wales.

The disappearance of the Welsh National Federation after the fall of *Cymru Fydd* left Welsh Liberals without any national co-ordination beyond that afforded by the Welsh Party at Westminster. Lloyd George's fertile mind attempted to remedy this deficiency in 1898 when he proposed a 'Welsh National Liberal Council', on which all Welsh constituencies should be represented. The inaugural meeting was to be held at Cardiff in February 1898, and most of the Welsh members of Parliament wired their support. But there were powerful dissentients, Bryn Roberts, D. A. Thomas, and Humphreys-Owen among them. Above all, the embers of the unhappy *Cymru Fydd* episode were again stirred. Cardiff Liberal Association attacked the proposal to give each constituency equal weight on the new Council, and also that to leave a majority of non-elected members on the executive by thirty-four to thirty-two, so reminiscent of the 'wire-pulling' of *Cymru Fydd*. The *South Wales Daily News* supported this

---

[1] *South Wales Daily News*, 6 May 1899.

[2] Ibid., 22 Apr. 1899; E. W. Evans to Herbert Lewis, 20 Apr. 1899 (Penucha MSS.). Herbert Lewis himself was also approached.

[3] *Y Genedl Gymreig*, 23 Oct. 1900. There are full accounts of the crisis in the Merioneth Liberal Association in the *Genedl*, 4 Sept.–30 Oct. 1900.

view, and revived the scheme of four regional bodies. At the Cardiff
meeting, with Lloyd George's dazzling genius for conciliation, a
façade of unity was maintained. In deference to the Cardiff Liberals,
it was agreed that constituency associations would nominate one
member per 3,000 electors. But clearly all the teeth of the new 'Welsh
National Liberal Federation' had been removed. It could possess no
personality of its own, and was now no more than a body for co-
ordinating propaganda, the mouthpiece of English Liberalism in
Wales and a quite different body from *Cymru Fydd*.[1] Still Cardiff
Liberals remained incurably suspicious, and at the second convention in 1899 they succeeded in striking out a minor provision for
the representation of non-elective bodies such as the *Cymru Fydd* of
London (name of ill-omen!) in which some of Lloyd George's friends
such as Timothy Davies were prominent.[2] Lloyd George harangued
'Cochfarf' to little effect.[3] The Cardiff Liberals continued to adopt
an attitude of stubborn reluctance towards the new 'Welsh National
Liberal Federation' for years to come, and it failed to impose any
initiative in political affairs. In 1899 Lloyd George told them 'they
had been in existence for eighteen months, and the sum total of their
work was the appointment of a secretary (laughter)'.[4] Officials of
the Federation told publicly and privately of their frustration in their
work.[5] Not until 1908 did the Federation take an independent part
in a by-election.[6] Efforts to create a unified and coherent structure
for Welsh Liberalism seemed doomed to frustration.

In these circumstances, the various Welsh causes in politics
attracted little attention. Welsh disestablishment receded from the
forefront of national politics after the excitements of 1895. The
Liberation Society was concerned to rebut a rumour that disestablishment had been dropped entirely.[7] On only two occasions did disestablishment come before Parliament. The first was in February
1897, on a private member's motion for a general disestablishment

---

[1] *South Wales Daily News*, 29 Jan.–5 Feb. 1898; *Western Mail*, 28 Jan.–5 Feb.,
gives a hostile and often distorted account. Also cf. Lloyd George to Alfred Thomas,
30 Nov. 1897 (Cardiff, Pontypridd Papers).
[2] *South Wales Daily News*, 1 Aug. 1899. It is intriguing to note that Timothy Davies
was nevertheless present at this meeting as a delegate from East Carmarthenshire,
presumably a piece of sleight of hand by Lloyd George.
[3] Lloyd George to Edward Thomas, 15 July 1899 (Cardiff, Cochfarf Papers),
'Private'.
[4] *South Wales Daily News*, 2 Feb. 1899.
[5] e.g. C. E. Breese to Edward Thomas, 12 Dec. 1904, 3 Jan. 1905.
[6] In the Pembrokeshire by-election of July 1908.
[7] Liberation Society MSS., 6 Jan. 1902.

all round, by Samuel Smith (Flintshire), whose entire political creed at this time centred on apprehension at the growth of Roman Catholicism. But the motion was poorly supported and mustered only eighty-six votes.[1]

A more notable debate came in 1902, on a motion by William Jones, member for Arfon.[2] No longer did his motion state that the Church had 'failed to fulfil its objects' as Dillwyn had so often alleged, but simply asserted disestablishment to be 'in the best interests of the Welsh nation and of the Church'. Jones's eloquent and charming speech, whose 'silvery tones' caught the fancy of *Punch*, stressed the anti-national character of the Church in the past, and referred to the views of three Welsh clergymen who had recently advocated the restoration of the óld British Church, separate from Canterbury.[3] The seconder, Alfred Thomas, advocated the removal of the state connexion on simple Liberationist grounds. The motion was supported by both Asquith and Harcourt, being an issue that both the imperialist and Gladstonian wings of the divided Liberal Party could endorse. The government offered little defence, Ritchie, the Home Secretary, being patently unfamiliar with the subject. The government majority as a result was a mere forty-one, much reduced from its usual size.

Thereafter, Welsh disestablishment slumbered until 1906, although it could still raise profound passions in press and pulpit in Wales. During these years, nonconformist leaders were alarmed at a loss of impetus, and in 1900 they had actually to report a drop in membership among all the leading denominations save for the Methodists.[4] Chapel debts soared ever upwards, from £332,877 in 1896 to £668,429 in 1908, and it was less easy than in the past to interpret this as a sign of vitality.[5] In the industrial South, a variety of pressures, the growth of new leisure-time activities such as rugby football and boxing, the influence of the ʻnew theology' of R. J. Campbell, and above all the failure of the churches to adapt themselves to the social problems of an industrial community, were combining to undermine the traditional ascendancy of the chapel.[6] A particularly serious factor was

[1] *Parl. Deb.*, 4th ser., vol. xlvi, pp. 27 ff.
[2] Ibid., vol. cii, pp. 379 ff.
[3] The vicars of Bangor, Welshpool, Llanidloes (the Revs. T. Edwin Jones, D. Grimaldi Davis, Edmund O. Jones).
[4] *Young Wales*, Jan. 1900, p. 22. The total of nonconformist members was given as 434,856.
[5] *Royal Commission on the Church and other Religious Bodies in Wales, Memorandum to Report*, 1910, p. 129.
[6] These points are discussed by C. R. Williams, 'The Welsh Religious Revival,

the relative decline in the use of the Welsh language. Nonconformity was most firmly rooted in the Welsh-speaking areas: over 75 per cent. of Welsh nonconformists attended Welsh chapels—among the Methodists the proportion was much higher. But whereas in 1891 54·4 per cent. of the Welsh people spoke their native tongue, by 1901 this proportion was down to 49·9 per cent.[1]

Churchmen claimed that the ground being lost by nonconformity was being regained by the Church. They pointed out how communicants at Easter service rose from 114,885 in 1895 to 193,081 in 1905.[2] The figures of rebuilt churches and mission rooms, of Sunday scholars, confirmations, marriages, and baptisms all showed marked progress. The need to adapt the Church to Welsh conditions was now fully appreciated: the Bishop of St. Asaph was strongly attacked by his own chapter for patronizing English incumbents.[3] The Church was further strengthened by the appointment of John Owen as Bishop of St. David's in 1897. Owen, a more endearing personality than the truculent Bishop of St. Asaph, spoke Welsh fluently, and indeed had been brought up as a nonconformist in the Llŷn peninsula.[4] But it was apparent that the members lost to the denominations were for the most part lost to all religious bodies. Secularism was gaining far more emphatically than the established Church; as the population of Wales soared over the million mark, and immigrants poured into the coalfield almost as freely as into the United States, church membership failed to keep pace. Many chapels and churches were almost empty, left behind by changes in patterns of population and by changes in ideas. The great revival of 1904 thus came at a vital moment to infuse new life into the religious bodies of Wales.

As disestablishment was apparently a dying cause after 1895 so, too, Welsh home rule aroused little interest. After the disappearance of *Cymru Fydd* there seemed no prospect of a united Welsh movement. When Lloyd George convened a meeting of Liberal members in the House to sponsor federal devolution, it was criticized by Robson and Channing, and the meeting adjourned without a

---

1904–5 ', *British Journal of Sociology*, 1952, but this article tends to apply to Wales in general conditions peculiar to the South Wales coalfield.

[1] *Census of England and Wales*, 1891 and 1901. The 1891 census was the first to include a statement on the extent of the Welsh language.

[2] *Royal Commission, Report*, 1910, p. 20.

[3] G. Lerry, *Life of A. G. Edwards, Archbishop of Wales* (Oswestry, 1940), p. 71.

[4] For Owen, see Eluned E. Owen, *The Early Life of Bishop Owen* (Llandyssul, 1958) and *The Later Life of Bishop Owen* (1961).

decision.[1] Finally, a motion by Herbert Roberts in March 1898, urging 'home rule all round' in the cause of lightening the pressure of business on the House, proved a fiasco. Haldane and D. A. Thomas, Dillon and Redmond, all criticized the motion on the grounds that it would remove paramountcy from the more urgent case of Ireland. Thomas, in particular, made some savage attacks on his Welsh colleagues. Conversely, Balfour opposed the motion on the usual grounds that it would lead to separatism and disunion. The issue attracted no general interest and the debate was ignominiously counted out.[2]

In subsequent years, a few indirect approaches were made towards home rule, though mainly of a formal and academic character. In 1902 and 1903 Welsh members introduced motions in favour of Welsh self-government, using the familiar arguments about the inadequate treatment of Welsh affairs in an over-burdened Parliament, and the established right of Wales to separate legislation. On these occasions even D. A. Thomas supported them.[3] But the government, in the person of Walter Long, steadfastly refused to discriminate between Welsh and English legislation, and each motion was easily defeated. A more subtle approach came in 1902, when Frank Edwards introduced a Bill to transfer certain administrative functions to Welsh county councils, and to set up a joint board under Clause 81 of the 1888 Local Government Act. On the Second Reading on 16 April, Harcourt and Asquith spoke in favour, but the Welsh Unionists, as well as the government, regarded it as a revolutionary precedent which would weaken the powers of the central government. The Bill was thrown out by 201 to 163. Welsh home rule seemed farther away than ever.[4]

In one respect, it might have seemed possible that the political parties would take some action in Welsh affairs. The Report of the Land Commission appeared early in 1896, and seemed to present a case for urgent action. The condition of agriculture in Wales, and in the United Kingdom as a whole, was now critical. The nadir was reached in 1895, when the prices of meat and wool fell to a disastrously low level. The impact on Wales was especially serious, with its meagre smallholdings, largely unscientifically farmed, and its peasant proprietors frequently made bankrupt in the attempt to redeem mortgages on their holdings.

[1] *The Times*, 25 Mar. 1896.   [2] *Parl. Deb.*, 4th ser., vol. liv, pp. 1680 ff.
[3] Ibid., vol. ci, pp. 239 ff.; vol. cxix, pp. 1171 ff.
[4] Ibid., vol. cvi, pp. 383 ff.

The Report of the Land Commission was mainly concerned with the position of the tenant-occupiers, who farmed 87·4 per cent. of the cultivated land of Wales.[1] Here, a remarkable number of the recommendations of the Commissioners were unanimous. They urged a more sympathetic and efficient system of estate management, with more Welsh land agents and a more impartial attitude towards the political or religious outlook of the tenants. The law relating to landlord and tenant should be amended, with a simplification of the machinery of the Agricultural Holdings Acts. There should be compensation for unexhausted improvements and for disturbances after capricious eviction, together with a stable rental when estates changed hands. The Game Laws should be amended, and the small class of occupying freeholders should be offered state loans to pay off mortgages. Finally, the 1892 Witnesses Protection Act needed extension.[2]

But the crux of the Report showed a basic divergence. The Majority Report, signed by six Commissioners, urged the creation of judicial rents, fixed by county courts, to which all parties to a contract of tenancy could appeal. This fulfilled the old demand of Gee and nearly all Liberals, on the lines of the Irish Land Act of 1881 and the Scottish Crofters Act of 1886. It was, equally, condemned by all landlords as an intolerable interference with freedom of contract. Thus the Minority Report, signed by the two landowners, Lord Kenyon and Sir John Dillwyn-Llewelyn, M.P., and by Seebohm, the historian, opposed the demand for a land court. It would impair the relationship between landlord and tenant, lessen the landlord's interest in repairs and improvements, and lead to an unwarranted extension of the powers of the state into the rights of private property. Instead of a land court, the Minority Report suggested mediation by the Board of Agriculture.[3]

Even under a Unionist government, sympathetic to the landed interest, there were hopes of legislation to implement some of the unanimous recommendations. The Welsh members were eager to bring them before Parliament. It was significant that when the government introduced an Agricultural Land Rating Bill in April 1896, it was the Welsh members, particularly Lloyd George, who led the attack.[4] They claimed that the provision to remit the rates was

---

[1] *Land Commission, Report*, p. 271. [2] Ibid., pp. 900 ff.
[3] Ibid., pp. 937–46. Cf. J. E. Vincent, *The Land Question in South Wales* (Cardiff, 1897).
[4] Lloyd 'George's speech on Second Reading (*Parl. Deb.*, 4th ser., vol. xl, pp. 237 ff.).

a present of £1,550,000 to the landlords by the taxpayer. Lloyd George successfully demonstrated that the members of the government would themselves benefit personally by many thousands. He tried unsuccessfully to have Wales omitted from the operation of the Bill, and the long, hard fight in Committee, which delayed the Third Reading until 1 July, gave new heart to the disconsolate Liberal Party.

However, the main object of the Welsh members was to put forward some of the Commissioners' proposals. The first attempt was made by J. Lloyd Morgan (West Carmarthenshire) in February 1897, when he tabled a resolution proposing the advance of state loans to the small class of occupying freeholders. But, despite the support of several Welsh Unionists, the motion mustered a mere forty-three votes.[1] A more determined effort came with a Bill brought forward by M. Vaughan Davies, the ex-Conservative Liberal member for Cardiganshire, and a landowner whose own malpractices had evoked the censure of the Land Commissioners. His Land Tenure Bill, which came up for Second Reading on 19 May 1897, was the culmination of a great agitation within Wales, and brought the last major debate on Welsh land. The Bill aimed at instituting a land court, with a judge appointed by the Board of Agriculture to fix a fair rent for five years and reasonable conditions of tenancy. Once again, Welsh Liberal members rehearsed the land hunger, insecurity, and excessive rental, which were the lot of the Welsh farmer. Lloyd George perceptively pointed out that the state already widely interfered in free contract, for example in boards of conciliation in industrial disputes. But Welsh Unionists, more articulate in this debate than ever before, were adamant in their hostility to a land court. The irrepressible Stanley Leighton made great play with the irrelevant information contained in the Report about the flora and fauna of Wales. Walter Long was as intransigent as ever, and the Bill was inevitably rejected by a large margin, in spite of the support of the official Liberal leadership and the Irish Nationalists.[2]

The later history of the Welsh land question was uneventful, and it was no surprise when Salisbury told Lord Carrington in the Lords in 1899 that the Welsh agrarian question could not be dealt with in that or any other session.[3] A final flurry came in 1903 when Herbert Roberts moved that the unanimous recommendations of the Land

---

[1] *Parl. Deb.*, 4th ser., vol. xlvi, pp. 1014 ff.
[2] Ibid., 4th ser., vol. xlix, pp. 817 ff.   [3] Ibid., vol. lxxiii, p. 387.

Commission be given effect. Both sides of the House produced support for this moderate proposal. At the Board of Agriculture, Hanbury proved more conciliatory than Long. He accepted the resolution in principle, but no legislation was forthcoming.[1]

Gradually, the Welsh land question began to lose its urgency. After 1900 agricultural distress became less acute, as prices for dairy farmers again began to rise. The Agricultural Holdings Act of 1900 gave some guarantee of arbitration over the compensation of tenants, and so mollified Welsh Liberals to some degree. Thus, the seven bulky volumes of the Land Commission lingered on the shelves of public libraries, unheeded and unread. In time, the idea of a land court itself began to lose its appeal in radical circles. Llewelyn Williams asserted that it would turn Wales into a 'litigating Hades'.[2] He maintained that a judicial rental would lead to the evil of free sale, while landlords would be able to claim bonuses to make up the difference between the judicial rent and the real competitive rent. Even more serious, it would make tenancy a permanent condition: tenants would be '*adscripti glebae*—once a tenant, always a tenant'.[3]

Above all, the very appointment of the Land Commission had itself had a beneficial effect in the country-side. It acted as a safety-valve for rural discontent, and did not, on the whole, paint an unfavourable picture of the relations of landlords and tenants. The cases of oppression and unjust eviction receded into the distant past, and Liberal witnesses before the Commission were unable to quote more than a few alleged cases of intimidation or political pressure since the Ballot Act twenty-five years earlier. In any case, the land question was a social just as much as an economic phenomenon, and the Local Government Act of 1888 had gone far to removing the primacy of the gentry in local politics and society. On the other hand, the economic base of Welsh agriculture remained poor, save for the case of labourers whose numbers rapidly diminished after 1850 and whose wages rose steadily down to 1914.[4] To a great extent, the problem eased itself by its sheer insolubility. Emigration from rural areas to the coalfield relieved the pressure of population, while the gradual

---

[1] Ibid., vol. cxx, pp. 135 ff.
[2] *South Wales Daily News*, 12 Jan. 1901.
[3] Llewelyn Williams, 'The Needs of Wales: Land Law Reform', *Young Wales*, Jan.–Mar. 1903.
[4] J. H. Clapham, *Economic History of Great Britain* (London, 1925), vol. iii, p. 99. Although it is significant that the census of 1911 showed an increase in the number of persons employed on the land, the first increase since 1851, and, indeed the only increase recorded between 1851 and the present day.

spread of the English language greatly increased social mobility. By the general election of 1906, therefore, the Welsh land question was not a major issue.[1]

In all these spheres, the Welsh members had little enough to show for their efforts in the Parliament of 1895. A crucial decision came in 1899, when Tom Ellis died at the age of forty, still secure in the affections of most of his compatriots. The vacancy in the Whips' office brought about a major crisis for the Welsh Party. After reluctantly appointing Herbert Gladstone to succeed Ellis, Campbell-Bannerman offered a junior Whipship to a Welsh member. On Rendel's advice, Herbert Lewis was approached. Most of his colleagues, including apparently Lloyd George, seemed to favour acceptance, but on 27 April Lewis announced that he had declined.[2] The offer of a junior Whipship was renewed by Herbert Gladstone a fortnight later, and the Welsh members discussed this invitation anxiously in Committee Room 7 on 18 May. Clearly, acceptance of the offer of a junior Whipship would explode the fiction of 'independence' for ever. Characteristically, ten of their number were absent from this crucial debate. Lloyd George proposed that the position should be clearly defined, and that they constitute themselves forthwith an independent party on the lines of the Irish. But every other member save for Herbert Lewis, as usual Lloyd George's *fidus Achates*, opposed this suggestion. In the words of Vincent Evans in the *South Wales Daily News*, 'a great deal of desultory conversation followed', and the meeting ended indecisively.[3] In fact, a fundamental decision had been taken. It was the end of the idea of an independent Welsh Party at Westminster, and the end of Lloyd George's 'Parnellite' career as an independent Welsh nationalist. The 'Welsh Revolt' was off.

The confusion and divisions of the Welsh members were intensified still further by the advent of the South African War in October 1899. One of the many myths of modern Welsh history is that Wales, with its fellow-feeling for small nations, was united in support of the Boers. In fact, the 'pro-Boers' were in a minority in Wales as everywhere else, although Lloyd George made them an unusually vocal

---

[1] In the general election of 1906, only seven Liberal candidates referred to it in their election addresses. There are some useful articles on the Welsh land question after 1895 in *Cwrs y Byd*, edited by the Rev. Pan Jones.

[2] Herbert Lewis's Diary, 20, 25, 27 Apr. 1899 (Penucha MSS.). Lewis to Alfred Thomas, 21 Apr. 1899 (Penucha MSS.). 'Strictly private and confidential'.

[3] *South Wales Daily News*, 19 May 1899; *Western Mail*, loc. cit.

minority. Despite its radical tradition, Wales was much attracted to imperialism. Tom Ellis, with his Fabian associations, had been an admirer of Cecil Rhodes and the friend of Rosebery. Such staunch nonconformist members as Ellis Griffith, Lloyd Morgan, and Brynmor Jones strongly supported the imperial cause, as did other prominent Liberals such as Beriah Gwynfe Evans and the Rev. Thomas Johns of Llanelly. On the crucial vote moved by Sir Wilfrid Lawson on 25 July 1900, to reduce the Colonial Secretary's salary by £100, only three Welsh members were in the 'Aye' lobby, Lloyd George, Bryn Roberts, and Humphreys-Owen. Mafeking was celebrated with the same wild frenzy from Bangor to Aberdare.[1] Lloyd George advised Herbert Lewis against attending a meeting at Caernarvon. 'I thought one broken head a sufficient sacrifice to Moloch. . . . The mob was seized with a drunken madness and the police were helpless.'[2] Welsh sentiment took irrational pride in the deeds of the Royal Welsh Fusiliers at Paardeberg and the Welch Regiment on the Tugela, in Sir George White (born at Glasinfryn) and General Sir James Hills-Johnes of Dolaucothi, in Dr. Mills Roberts, who had once known fame as goalkeeper for the Preston North End 'Invincibles', now in charge of the Welsh Field Hospital. Lord Roberts and Baden-Powell, both of whom were claimed to have Welsh blood, were subsequently made honorary freemen of Cardiff, and indeed imperialism was rife in the South Wales metropolis. In one constituency after another, 'Little Englanders' were rejected as candidates by Liberal Associations, Bird at Cardiff, Burnie at Swansea, Lleufer Thomas at Gower.[3] The English language press reverberated with fulsome accounts of 'What Wales has done in the War'.[4]

On the other hand, the nonconformist and predominantly Welsh-speaking areas were far more circumspect. They were less prone to 'jingoism' and more insulated from the imperialist currents surging through England and Scotland. The Welsh language press, *Y Faner, Y Genedl, Y Cymro, Y Traethodydd, Yr Herald Cymraeg*, and *Y Tyst* were strongly hostile to the war; so too was the Wesleyan Methodist *Gwyliedydd*, in marked contrast to the *Methodist Times* in England. Many of the giants of the pulpit, Rev. Evan Jones, Rev. Towyn

---

[1] See the *Aberdare Times*, 26 May 1900, for a description of the wild celebrations in Aberdare.
[2] Lloyd George to Herbert Lewis, 22 Apr. 1900 (Penucha MSS.).
[3] *South Wales Daily News*, 3 July, 22 Aug., 28 Sept. 1900.
[4] e.g. *Young Wales*, Jan. 1901.

Jones, Rev. J. 'Gomer' Lewis opposed the Boer War as they opposed
all war, and extolled the virtues of such pious Calvinists as President
Paul Kruger.[1] Lloyd George had great influence here, and he found
a new ally in his old enemy, Bryn Roberts, who regarded Liberal
imperialists as no less disloyal to the Liberal tradition than were
Welsh home rulers. Herbert Lewis was another staunch opponent of
the war, in spite of hostility from his local Association. From the
isolation of the Lords, Rendel urged a national campaign against the
'Salem Chapel Jingo' and 'the Imperial Perks element'.[2] In these
areas, sympathy with struggling nationalities still had some currency,
dating from the days of 'Hiraethog'. 'While England and Scotland
are drunk with blood, the brain of Wales remains clear, and she
advances with steady step on the road to progress and liberty.'[3]
There is evidence, too, that in the later stages of the war, when
Campbell-Bannerman shrewdly switched the Liberal attack from
the principles of the war to its conduct, in the period of the concentration camps and the so-called 'methods of barbarism', no part
of the United Kingdom responded more readily to his appeal than
did Wales.

In the 'khaki' election of October 1900, however, the disunity of
Welsh Liberalism was painfully apparent. The traditional Liberal
programme was curiously unobtrusive: only fifteen Liberal candidates even refer to the cause of disestablishment in their election
addresses. Only ten Liberal candidates can be classed as being
definitely hostile to the war, and of these nine were returned.[4] On
the other hand, Welsh Unionists, some of whom were away at the
front, make the war their sole concern.

It was, in the circumstances, a remarkable testimony to the resilience of the old radical appeal that, whereas the Liberal Party in
Britain as a whole made little headway and remained in a minority
of 132, in Wales much of the ground lost in 1895 was recaptured. At
election times, Welsh Liberals could regroup their scattered forces,
however divided previously. Radnorshire, Swansea Town, and even

---

[1] E. Foulkes, 'Y Rhyfel, Myfyrdodau "dyn y stryd"', *Y Geninen*, Apr. 1900, pp. 76-81.
John Owen, 'Y cyn-Arlywydd Kruger', *Y Traethodydd*, Jan. 1902, pp. 35-39. The editor
of the *Traethodydd* at this time (1900-5) was the Rev. Evan Jones, Caernarvon.

[2] Rendel to Humphreys-Owen, 29 Mar. 1901 (N.L.W., Glansevern MSS., 704).

[3] Lloyd George's speech (quoted, J. Hugh Edwards, *From Village Green to Downing
Street: the Life of the Rt. Hon. D. Lloyd George*, London 1908, p. 121). There is a breakdown of Lloyd George's poll in the *Cardiff Times*, 13 Oct. 1900.

[4] The exception was J. A. Bright, a former Liberal Unionist, defeated in the highly
marginal seat of Montgomery District.

Carmarthen District were recaptured, the last a considerable triumph in view of the local eminence of the late member, Sir John Jones Jenkins. In Cardiff, Sir Edward Reed, running as a highly individual Liberal, reformed the Liberal coalition. His enthusiasm for disestablishment had waned, yet he obtained a solid nonconformist vote. He vacillated over Irish home rule, and finally came out in opposition, yet the O'Connell branch of the United Irish League voted for him to a man.[1] He had bitterly attacked the Amalgamated Society of Engineers' strike in 1897, yet the Cardiff Trades Council declared in his favour. Reed carried the day by 801, thus showing that personal influence was still a potent factor in elections and that politics could still be largely a nexus of personal loyalties and relationships in the twentieth century as in the eighteenth.[2] The sole Unionist success came in Monmouth Boroughs, where Dr. Rutherfoord Harris, an eminent imperialist and the friend of Rhodes and Jameson, defeated the sitting Liberal, Spicer, in a contest of spectacular corruption.[3] Thus Wales in all returned twenty-eight Liberals (eleven unopposed) to six Unionists. The 'khaki' election in Wales is difficult to assess. The normal issues were in the background. There are perhaps only two clear-cut cases of revulsion against imperialism—Lloyd George's triumph over local opposition at Caernarvon and Keir Hardie's defeat of Pritchard Morgan at Merthyr Tydfil, to become the first independent Labour member for Wales. The election left the Welsh members numerically stronger but still far from a cohesive body. Far more was needed than the customary 'ceremony of congratulation' at the polls to provide Welsh Liberalism with a sense of purpose, and to wipe away the paralysis of despair that gripped Welsh political life.

(ii) *The Education Act of 1902*

At a time when Welsh political nationalism and its representatives in Parliament seemed to be lapsing into impotence, they were suddenly galvanized into violent action by strange developments in a field which had remained largely tranquil for thirty years, that of

[1] *Welsh Catholic Herald*, 12 Oct. 1900; *Western Mail*, 22, 23 Oct. 1900; *Evening Express*, 11 Oct. 1900.

[2] Reed soon proved troublesome. On 18 Dec. 1900 he wrote to *The Times*, condemning Campbell-Bannerman's attitude to the war. He supported the Education Act of 1902, and finally joined the Unionists over Tariff Reform in 1904.

[3] Harris was unseated on petition for corruption, but J. Lawrence retained the seat for the Unionists in the by-election (cf. *Report on the Trial of the Parliamentary Election Petition for the Monmouth Boroughs*, 1902, p. 414). In Newport, unlike Cardiff and Swansea, the Catholic vote went Unionist.

education. Under the aegis of conciliatory governments, Welsh education had flourished, free from the passions of political debate. Under the presiding genius of Viriamu Jones, the University of Wales had expanded rapidly, until by 1900 there were 1,310 students undergoing courses, in part or in entirety, at the three constituent colleges.[1] The development of intermediate education was equally impressive. After the Act of 1889, local education joint committees had forwarded a series of schemes successively to the Charity Commissioners, the Department of Education, and the Privy Council, before receiving parliamentary approval. The delaying tactics of the House of Lords bore little fruit. In May 1896 the edifice was crowned by the creation of a Central Welsh Board to direct the system, with Humphreys-Owen as chairman and Viriamu Jones as vice-chairman. From this time dates that multitude of 'County' schools which still forms such a striking feature of the Welsh educational scene. By 1903 there were ninety-five of these schools with a total of 8,789 pupils: seven years later the total had risen to 13,729.[2]

The religious problem in these schools was solved by what the Bishop of St. Asaph termed 'rigid undenominationalism'.[3] As under the Cowper–Temple clause in Forster's Act of 1870, Clause 45 of the Intermediate Education Act had laid down that no catechism or formulary peculiar to any denomination would be taught at these intermediate schools, while a 'conscience clause' permitted any pupil to be withdrawn. In effect, the new schools became increasingly secular.

In elementary education, however, the bitterness of religious controversy could not be quelled. It had emerged again during the discussion of the intermediate school schemes. It appeared also in nonconformist complaints that two of the four teachers' training colleges in Wales were the monopoly of the established Church.[4] But above all, it centred on the position of voluntary schools. After 1870 Wales had proved a fertile ground for the new Board Schools. By

[1] *Report of the Board of Education: Higher Education, 1902* (Cd. 845), pp. 404, 457, 504.
[2] J. Vyrnwy Morgan, *A Study in Nationality* (London, 1911), p. 387.
[3] Archbishop of Wales, *Memories*, p. 178.
[4] *Second Report of the Commissioners appointed to inquire into the Elementary Education Acts*, 1887, qu. 39,409. See also *Parl. Deb.*, 3rd ser., vol. cclxxxii, pp. 609 ff. The two colleges under attack were those at Caernarvon and at Carmarthen. The High Church proclivities of the principal of Caernarvon training college were especially resented. The Caernarvon training college later transferred to Bangor, to become St. Mary's, Bangor. The other two colleges were the Normal College, Bangor, and a women's college at Swansea.

1897 there were 326 School Boards in Wales, and 379 Boards by 1902. The dominance of voluntary schools was fast disappearing. Against 840 voluntary schools, with an average attendance of 96,000 (71,940 of them at Anglican National Schools), were arrayed 821 Board Schools, with an attendance of 171,507.[1] By 1906, after the passage of the Balfour Act, 'provided' state schools were in a considerable majority, numbering 1,028 as against 746 voluntary 'nonprovided' schools, of which 650 were Anglican and 53 Roman Catholic.[2] Church spokesmen noted with alarm the growing tendency of Welsh School Boards to favour an entirely secular system of instruction. Even so, there were still hundreds of 'single-school areas' in Wales, rural parishes where Church Schools alone catered for primary education, and they were bitterly resented by nonconformists. The new militancy and vigour of the Church in the second half of the nineteenth century served to make these anomalies the more keenly felt. Nonconformists had very few voluntary schools of their own, the Wesleyan body being small, and largely an alien importation.[3] Thus any proposal to sustain the schools of a church long felt to be 'alien' and class-conscious would be certain of a largely united opposition.

It was clear to all that the elementary education system and its relationship with secondary education were in urgent need of reform. At the Education Department at this time were a curiously diverse pair, Sir John Gorst and the Duke of Devonshire, and it seemed inevitable that their early efforts to deal with the education problem should be indecisive.[4] In 1896 Gorst made the first attempt.[5] He introduced a Bill which would have set up an education authority in each county, largely composed of county councillors. In Wales, the local authorities created under the 1889 Act would become the new committees. The 17s. 6d. limit on grants to schools would be abolished and an additional 4s. grant made to Church Schools. The Welsh were vehement in opposition, Sir George Osborne Morgan stating that Wales was 'a land of Board Schools'. The Second Reading was carried by a huge margin, Herbert Lewis noting in his diary, 'Irish all against us—sickening'.[6] But the Liberals fought hard in

---

[1] *Parl. Deb.*, 4th ser., vol. xlvi, p. 208 (Herbert Roberts's speech).
[2] *List of Public Elementary Schools in Wales on 1st August 1906* (C. 3640).
[3] It claimed only 40,811 communicants in 1905.
[4] See Sir George Kekewich, *The Education Department and After* (London, 1920).
[5] *Parl. Deb.*, 4th ser., vol. xxxix, pp. 526 ff.
[6] Herbert Lewis's Diary, 12 May 1896 (Penucha MSS.).

Committee, and on 22 June Balfour announced the withdrawal of the measure.

A new Bill in 1897, aimed at granting 5*s*. per pupil to voluntary schools, again had a stormy passage. Ellis raged: 'It is so outrageously and comprehensively bad that one does not know on what vicious points to concentrate.'[1] Two Welsh members, Herbert Roberts and Reginald McKenna, tried to include Board Schools within the measure. The main feature of the committee stage was the manner in which Welsh members led the attack, Lloyd George, Herbert Lewis, Sam Evans, Ellis Griffith, and others proposing a long series of amendments. On 18 March Lewis unsuccessfully attempted to exclude Wales from the Bill, Tom Ellis making almost his last major speech on this amendment. The Bill finally went through with Irish support, Balfour commenting that 'Wales and Scotland have had an almost undue share of the Debate'.[2]

On a number of subsequent occasions, Welsh educational grievances were again aired at Westminster. In 1898 and 1899 Lloyd George, supported by many of his colleagues, moved resolutions condemning the elementary education system.[3] The motion by Samuel Smith (Flintshire) on 28 May 1900, to draw attention to romanizing influences in Church Schools, one which received the surprising support of H. O. Arnold-Forster (Unionist, West Belfast), afforded the Welsh Party an opportunity to refer to cases in Flintshire and other counties.[4] However, recent events in education, particularly the decision reached by T. B. Cockerton at the expense of the London School Board, made it imperative to undertake a wholesale reorganization, and Morant at the Board of Education was working to this end.

On 24 March 1902 Balfour introduced his great Education Bill. Its major provisions were that authority over primary, technical, and secondary education would be given to local committees of county or county borough councils, while larger boroughs and urban districts would also be given committees. The distinction between Board and voluntary schools would disappear, all being financed from the rates. The local education authority would have rights of inspection

---

[1] Ellis to R. A. Hudson, 5 Apr. 1898 (quoted, J. A. Spender, *Sir Robert Hudson*, p. 60).

[2] *Parl. Deb.*, 4th ser., vol. xlvii, p. 1409. Cf. Griffith-Boscawen, *Fourteen Years in Parliament*, p. 117.

[3] *Parl. Deb.*, 4th ser., vol. lvi, pp. 479 ff.; vol. lxviii, pp. 55 ff.

[4] Ibid., vol. lxxxiii, pp. 1525 ff.

in voluntary (or, in the new jargon, 'non-provided') schools, with the power to appoint two out of six managers, in return for assistance from the rates. Finally, in Wales, the secondary authorities set up under the Act of 1889 would become the new local authorities.[1]

The very comprehensiveness of the measure left the Liberal Opposition somewhat nonplussed. Haldane, the disciple of Hegel, ardently welcomed the Bill, while Macnamara criticized the fact that its adoption was left to local option. A Welsh Liberal, Humphreys-Owen, also showed some enthusiasm. The First Reading was unexpectedly opposed by twenty-three critics (including four Welsh members),[2] a motley array of squires who feared an increase in the rates, and of nonconformists who were beginning to perceive the dangers to their educational standing. Except for some churchmen who objected to the retention of the Cowper-Temple clause in provided schools, Unionist reaction was generally favourable.

But by the time the Second Reading was due in May a tremendous opposition had welled up. The *British Weekly* led the outcry against the maintenance of Church Schools on the rates, schools which in 8,000 parishes were the only ones open to nonconformists: it openly advocated passive resistance, calling in the authorities of Bunyan, Baxter, Brown, and the other Puritan heroes. A great meeting at St. James's Hall on 15 April, addressed by Dr. Clifford, Dr. Parker, the Rev. Hugh Price Hughes, Dr. Guinness Rogers, R. W. Perks, M.P., and many others, advocated the most strenuous opposition.[3] It was 'Rome on the rates'. In the Commons, Bryce bitterly attacked the 'Voluntary Schools Relief Bill'. It would, he claimed, exacerbate the religious controversy and deny popular control over schools maintained by public funds. But the most notable attack on the Bill came from Lloyd George. His speech testified to his class antagonism to Church and clergy: as he remarked later to D. R. Daniel, 'I hate a priest, Daniel, whenever I see one'.[4] He cogently expressed the hardships felt by nonconformists in rural areas, with the religious

---

[1] Ibid., vol. cv, pp. 846 ff. The most recent survey of the controversy over the Education Act of 1902 is Benjamin Sacks, *The Religious Issue in the State Schools of England and Wales, 1902–14* (Albuquerque, New Mexico, 1961). He has, however, little to say on Wales. A very useful periodical source for the 'Revolt' from 1903 is the *Welsh Leader*.

[2] They were Ellis Griffith, Charles Morley (Brecon), D. A. Thomas, and Osmond Williams (Merioneth), the last an Anglican.

[3] *British Weekly*, 17 Apr. 1902 and subsequent issues; *Church Times*, 18 Apr. 1902; the *Guardian*, 16, 23 Apr. 1902. Sacks, op. cit., pp. 36 ff.

[4] Memoir by D. R. Daniel, 'D. Lloyd George: Canghellor y Trysorlys' (N.L.W., Daniel MSS., 2912, p. 52).

tests on teachers and the church formularies for pupils. The 'clerical yoke' would be riveted on thousands of parishes, and none would suffer more than the people of Wales.[1] The Welsh members opposed the Second Reading by twenty-three to two, but it was carried by a majority of 237, in Herbert Lewis's rather confused view, 'the lowest point that the nonconformist cause has reached politically for a long time to come'.[2]

In the later tumultuous passage of the Bill, the case of Wales was merged in the general nonconformist protest. After their 'war to the knife and fork' during the South African War, Liberals and nonconformists could again unite against the common clerical enemy. During the prolonged Committee stage, which occupied forty-nine days, the Bill was widely altered. On 22 June a new grant of 4s. per scholar, with a further £900,000 from the exchequer, replaced the former voluntary and Board School grants. On 9 July, with the support of Haldane, Macnamara, and some other Liberals, and in the absence of Chamberlain owing to a cab accident, the Bill was made compulsory rather than optional, on a free vote. William Jones (Arfon), a professional educationalist, was the only Welsh Liberal to vote in favour, as he had been previously (23 March 1900) the only supporter of a Catholic University in Ireland. On 31 October the 'Kenyon–Slaney Clause', an attempt to make teaching in non-provided schools conform to the trust deeds, and aimed at ritualist practices, was carried against the opposition of High Churchmen.[3]

Welsh members were prominent in leading the Liberal counter-attack. In particular, Lloyd George showed great resource and persistence in committee. The nonconformist demagogue who inveighed against the 'retinue of acolytes' in voluntary schools could also receive a graceful tribute from Balfour, in the closing stages of the Bill, as 'an eminent Parliamentarian'.[4] It was Lloyd George who inspired a significant amendment concerning Wales, when, on 12 November, at his instigation, Sir Alfred Thomas, Chairman of the Welsh Party, moved to transfer the powers of the local authorities in Wales under the 1889 Act to the new local authorities constituted under Balfour's Bill. The Welsh members had been divided over the

---

[1] *Parl. Deb.*, 4th ser., vol. cvii, pp. 1098 ff.

[2] Herbert Lewis's Diary, 8 May 1902 (Penucha MSS.).

[3] See the angry comments of the *Church Times*, 7–21 Nov. 1902, and of the *Guardian*, 5 and 12 Nov. 1902. The *Guardian*, however, was much more moderate than the *Church Times*: it still thought the Bill essentially sound, whereas the *Church Times* urged that 'the bill for the destruction of Church Schools' should be abandoned.

[4] *Parl. Deb.*, 4th ser., vol. cxv, p. 1173.

proposal at the private meeting of their Party, but 'Lloyd George swept everything before him in the most peremptory fashion, and carried them in favour of the English plan'.[1] In debate, the Welsh Party took divergent views. The amendment was supported by Brynmor Jones and the Hon. George Kenyon (Unionist, Denbigh District), but Humphreys-Owen, Bryn Roberts, and Samuel Moss (Liberal, East Denbighshire) all attacked the break-up of the harmonious undenominational secondary system that had endured since 1889. Balfour accepted the amendment with understandable pleasure. The amendment was strongly attacked by the *British Weekly*, which failed to understand its purpose. Privately, Lloyd George told Herbert Lewis that his object was to preserve uniformity throughout Wales to enable a central board to be set up for elementary as well as for secondary education. In addition, by using the county councils, Lloyd George gave himself a most powerful weapon with which to operate his policy in opposition to the Balfour Act. Herbert Lewis concluded, 'Ll. G. showed tremendous determination and driving force in carrying the thing through'.[2]

On 18 December the Bill received the Royal Assent. Hitherto, Wales had simply followed the general nonconformist plan of campaign, with its members active in opposition. William Jones was reprimanded for his silence over the debates,[3] while Artemus Jones belaboured 'the fat merchants and squires' for not helping Lloyd George more vigorously.[4] Eleven Welsh county councils passed 'no-rate' resolutions, declaring that they would not administer the Act. But on 17 January 1903 Lloyd George introduced a totally new phase. In a manifesto to the Welsh people, he declared that refusal to administer the Act would neglect the great opportunity afforded by Sir Alfred Thomas's sub-clause.[5] The Education Act should be operated, but on certain important conditions. Voluntary schools should be brought under public control, religious tests for pupil teachers should be abolished, and the 'Colonial Compromise' should be offered over denominational instruction.[6] Only if these terms were

[1] Herbert Lewis's Diary, 11 Nov. 1902 (Penucha MSS.).

[2] Ibid. *Parl. Deb.*, 4th ser., vol. cxiv, pp. 765 ff. Cf. *British Weekly*, 27 Nov. 1902.

[3] Jane Jones to William Jones, ? 1902 (Bangor, William Jones Papers, MSS. 5466, no. 10) (in Welsh).

[4] T. Artemus Jones, 'The Welsh Struggle against the Education Bill', *Young Wales*, Dec. 1902, pp. 266–7.

[5] *South Wales Daily News*, 17 Jan. 1903; *Baner ac Amserau Cymru*, 24 Jan. 1903.

[6] A compromise over religious instruction in many of the colonies (e.g. Canada) whereby general undenominational instruction based on simple Bible teaching was amplified by denominational 'right of entry' one or more days a week.

refused should nonconformists refuse to pay rates. This new strategy would be peculiar to Wales, where the Liberal preponderance in county councils was overwhelming. In the popular phrase of the day, Lloyd George asserted, 'No control, no cash'. This manifesto marks the genesis of what came to be called the 'Welsh Revolt'. Some Welsh Liberals had at first advocated that the Bill, 'which sinned against Religious Equality and Popular Control', should be prevented from applying to Wales at all.[1] Lloyd George now argued convincingly that the more effective policy would be to operate the Act, but in such a way that 'equality of citizenship, equality of creed, equality of opportunity and equality of nationality' would be made secure for all.

Subsequent events were largely determined by Lloyd George's personal direction. The Welsh National Liberal Council formally adopted his policy on 25 January, and, on 25 February, a Report was issued by a sub-committee of Welsh members, including Lloyd George, Humphreys-Owen, and Bryn Roberts, which urged that voluntary schools be brought under public control and brought up to a full state of efficiency.[2] At the same time, Lloyd George had proved characteristically flexible in his attitude. He had not yet lost hope of a compromise and attempted to begin negotiations with Church leaders through the Board of Education. To the general surprise, he found the warmest response from his greatest adversary, the Bishop of St. Asaph. The 'fighting bishop' had mellowed with years. He admitted the nonconformist grievances over public control and religious tests, while with no less than 50 per cent. of the children of the diocese of St. Asaph educated in Anglican schools, he was anxious to find a compromise, or, in the jargon of the day, a 'concordat'.[3]

The initial approach had been through Morant himself. The architect of the Balfour Act was apprehensive at the possibility of his scheme being frustrated by the Welsh county councils, and, after discussions with Lloyd George and Herbert Lewis, he communicated with the Bishop of St. Asaph. Thus, on 27 February 1903, an im-

[1] A. C. Humphreys-Owen to the Rev. Josiah Jones, 21 June 1902 (N.L.W., MSS. 6412B). Cf. Daniel Rowland, 'Mesur Addysg Mr. Balfour', *Y Traethodydd*, Jan. 1903, pp. 24 ff.

[2] *Baner ac Amserau Cymru*, 28 Feb. 1903.

[3] For the bishop's attitude see his autobiography, *Memories*, pp. 176–203. Also see Eluned Owen, *Later Life of Bishop Owen*, pp. 36 ff. The proportion of children educated in Church Schools in St. Asaph was far above the national average. For Wales as a whole, the figure was only 16 per cent. (*Church Times*, 1 May 1903).

portant conference was held at Llandrindod Wells, when Lloyd
George and several other Liberal members met Lord Kenyon, as
a representative of the diocese of St. Asaph. As Herbert Lewis noted,
'an excellent spirit prevailed', and a further conference was arranged
to discuss the possibility of public control of voluntary schools, with
facilities for religious instruction on the 'colonial plan'.[1] But the
majority of Welsh Church leaders proved incurably suspicious of
any scheme associated with Lloyd George, and the Bishops of St.
David's, Llandaff, and Bangor declined to enter the discussions.
Bishop Owen of St. David's made it clear that he regarded the prohibition of denominational teaching in school hours and the sacrifice of the right of the Church managers to appoint teachers as quite
impossible terms. Wales, he held, was less ripe for compromise than
was England, in view of its plethora of Board Schools without religious instruction of any kind. Thus the conference which met at the
Palace Hotel, Westminster, on 24 March, contained representatives
from one diocese only, St. Asaph. Those present included the bishop,
Lord Kenyon, and Lord Mostyn, with, on the Liberal side, Lloyd
George, Herbert Lewis, and Frank Edwards. Another member of
the conference was the Roman Catholic Bishop of Menevia.[2]

The discussion was amicable, and terms were discussed, which
included the teaching of the Anglican religion in Church schools one
day per week from 9.0 to 9.30 a.m. Bishop Edwards himself favoured
acceptance of the concordat, but his diocese was intransigent. On
28 April the St. Asaph diocesan Board of Education rejected the
terms offered, and declared that any further negotiations would be
impossible.[3] In retrospect, it is remarkable how much agreement was
reached, including an acceptance of the syllabus of religious instruction given by the London School Board for all provided and non-
provided schools.

Henceforth, Lloyd George was compelled to advise outright
resistance to the Act. At Swansea on 19 May he urged local education authorities not to administer rate-aid until the government
amended the Act. A large national convention at Cardiff on 3 June,
with representatives present from free churches, Liberal organizations, and trade unions, from all parts of Wales, heard a series of

---

[1] *South Wales Daily News*, 28 Feb. 1903; Herbert Lewis's Diary, 27 Feb. 1903
(Penucha MSS.).
[2] *South Wales Daily News*, 25 Mar. 1903; Herbert Lewis's Diary, 24 Mar. 1903.
Lewis notes in pencil, 'Ll. G. answered all the questions'.
[3] *South Wales Dai   News*, 29 Apr. 1903; Eluned Owen, op. cit., pp. 42–44.

aggressive speeches from Welsh members of Parliament, all urging complete passive resistance to the Act.[1] But an entirely united front was hard to maintain. Not only had the Radnorshire and Brecknockshire councils, which both had narrow 'Sectarian' (i.e. Unionist) majorities, already voted rate aid; even nonconformist Carmarthenshire proved recalcitrant. Its chairman, Professor D. E. Jones, a prominent Independent, described Lloyd George's Cardiff policy as 'immoral and un-Christian', and he entered into negotiations with the Bishop of St. David's. After immense pressure by Lloyd George and his associates, a motion denying rate-aid to non-provided schools was eventually forced through Carmarthenshire County Council on 22 July by thirty-eight votes to thirteen.[2] Merioneth and Montgomeryshire Councils also attempted private concordats with Church leaders, but by the end of 1903 both had fallen through. In Wales, there seemed to be a complete stalemate, with the Act itself virtually suspended. Herbert Lewis commented, 'I think the Govt. are anxious to wash their hands of Wales educationally. But will they be allowed to do it?'[3]

The political parties viewed these developments with detachment, Wales appearing to follow a course peculiar to itself. On the Unionist side, the great virtue of the Balfour Act had been its grant of maintenance to Church Schools, and any compromise which might imperil this great achievement was necessarily suspect. The particular complexion of Welsh opinion made Welsh national movements of any kind automatically distrusted. In the debates on the Education Act, Lord Hugh Cecil had opined that 'there was a certain virulence about the Celtic temperament'.[4] The *Church Times* and the *Guardian*, no less than the *Western Mail*, applauded the refusal of the three Welsh dioceses to attend the Westminster conference.[5] The proposal to appoint teachers by a joint board seemed especially obnoxious, and Churchmen showed deep relief when the proposed concordat fell through. For the Liberals, nonconformist spokesmen were no less intransigent. Robertson Nicoll showed great alarm at Lloyd George's January manifesto, which ran counter to his proposal for complete passive resistance, and he was as relieved as Church leaders at the

---

[1] *South Wales Daily News*, 4 June 1903. Ben Tillett sent a letter of apology.

[2] *South Wales Dai y News*, 27 June, 23 July 1903. Cf. Llewelyn Williams, 'Wales in 1903', *Young Wales*, Feb. 1904, and *Y Tyst*, 29 July 1903, for the Welsh Independent viewpoint.

[3] Herbert Lewis's Diary, 26 Nov. 1903 (Penucha MSS.).

[4] *Parl. Deb.*, 4th ser., vol. cxiii, p. 418.

[5] *Church Times*, 24 Apr. 1903; *Guardian*, 6 May, 1903; *Western Mail*, 23 Mar. 1903.

failure of the St. Asaph concordat and the subsequent falling into line by the Welsh councils.[1] By December, all the councils save Brecknockshire and Radnorshire had refused rate-aid to voluntary schools. However, in the Liberal League, the imperialist wing of the Party, Lloyd George met with strong and unexpected support. Their 'constructive', almost Fabian, attitude to domestic legislation was alienated by the nihilism of passive resistance. In February 1903 Sir Edward Grey strongly upheld the Welsh policy of offering to take over Church Schools, with facilities for denominational instruction.[2] Rosebery was also favourable, while Haldane later made clear his support for the St. Asaph concordat.[3] When it fell through, the Liberal League felt that resistance to the payment of rates had a far more plausible justification.

By the beginning of 1904 it was clear that the government had to take action. Sir William Anson, at the Board of Education, had long flinched from coercion, and had simply delayed the 'appointed day', when the Act would come into force, later and later, until 1 February 1904. But this tactic merely played into Lloyd George's hands. He had been temporizing until the county council elections, which were now due. Now he flung in all his resources. Throughout February he and his associates, notably Herbert Lewis, Frank Edwards, and Humphreys-Owen, campaigned up and down Wales, fighting exclusively on the Act, and the results were brilliantly successful. Every council went 'Progressive' by a clear margin. Even Radnorshire and Brecknockshire, which had formerly had 'Sectarian' majorities, now elected 'Progressive' councils, by 22—10 and 39—21 respectively. In place of 543 'Progressives' and 252 'Sectarians', the thirteen Welsh councils now comprised 639 'Progressives' and 157 'Sectarians'. The Liberal triumph was complete and overwhelming.[4]

The elections were unquestionably a personal triumph for Lloyd George. They marked, said the Unionist *Morning Post*, 'the beginning of the real conflict between the Board of Education and the Welsh Councils'.[5] They formed a clear and unmistakable verdict on

---

[1] *British Weekly*, 22 Jan., 7 May 1903.

[2] Speech at a Liberal League dinner, reported in *South Wales Daily News*, 27 Feb. 1903.

[3] There is a very interesting comment on this in Herbert Lewis's Diary, 26 Feb. 1903 (Penucha MSS.). For Haldane's view, see *Parl. Deb.*, 4th ser., vol. cxxxi, pp. 1017 ff.

[4] The individual county results were: Anglesey, 48 Progressives and 8 Sectarians; Brecon, 39—21; Caernarvon, 59—6; Cardigan, 54—10; Carmarthen, 60—8; Denbigh, 53—11; Flint, 40—16; Glamorgan, 75—13; Merioneth, 52—3; Montgomery, 37—19; Monmouth, 50—18; Pembroke, 50—14; Radnor, 22—10 (*Y Genedl*, 15 Mar. 1904).

[5] *Morning Post*, 11 Mar. 1904.

the Balfour Act. Indeed, Herbert Lewis was told that, had it not been for the Act, the Liberals might have failed to carry Flintshire. 'We suffer much from the fact that almost all the schoolmasters etc. are Church. How different from what it is in Merionethshire. . . .'[1] Lloyd George was not slow to point out the moral of the results. On 14 March he moved to reduce the Education vote by £500 to draw attention to the administration of the Education Act and the injustice of its operation in Wales. Interestingly, his support came mainly from the Liberal Imperialists. Haldane stated that the Board could not 'mandamus a nation', while Grey urged a compromise over religious instruction. From the government benches, Lord Hugh Cecil indicated that a compromise over denominational teaching based on the wishes of parents, was not impossible, but Anson failed to respond.[2]

Once again, therefore, Wales had become a major cause of political contention. The government was gravely embarrassed by the policy of the Welsh councils. In theory they were operating the Act, but in practice they claimed that structural defects in the voluntary schools should first be repaired. Indeed, Carmarthen Town Council went further, and independently refused either to appoint managers or pay the salaries of teachers in voluntary schools. An inquiry by A. T. Lawrence, K.C., on 25 and 26 March found this action illegal. But few cases were met as easily as this. Morant was particularly alarmed by the threatening situation, and urged a renewed attempt at a concordat. Lloyd George found both him and Anson 'humble and conciliatory'.[3] Humphreys-Owen pointed out the wisdom of allowing the Tories to settle the question. 'It is not one on which we could get up a sufficiently strong popular agitation to impress the House of Lords.'[4]

The government's response eventually came on 26 April in the form of the Education (Local Authority Default) Bill, largely devised by Morant. It consisted of one clause only. It empowered the Board to take over the administration of the 1902 Act where a local authority was in default, and from the first its passage was stormy.[5] Lloyd George declared that it converted the Board into a debt-collecting

[1] John Owen to Herbert Lewis, 31 May 1904 (N.L.W., Herbert Lewis Papers, no. 73).

[2] Parl. Deb., 4th ser., vol. cxxxi, pp. 1004 ff. Cf. Y Tyst, 16 Mar. 1904.

[3] Lloyd George to Herbert Lewis, 16 Mar. 1904 (Penucha MSS.). Morant to Lewis, 13 Mar., 4 Sept. 1904 (Penucha MSS.).

[4] Humphreys-Owen to Lewis, 31 Mar. 1904 (Penucha MSS.).

[5] Parl. Deb., 4th ser., vol. ccxxxiii, pp. 1203 ff.

agency. The Opposition divided on the First Reading. On the Second Reading, on 15 July, the Bill was subjected to powerful criticism. The Welsh members, backed up by Bryce, Macnamara, and Campbell-Bannerman, inveighed against it. Anson replied that its introduction was essential to ensure enforcement of the law. Bitterness reached its peak on the committee stage on 5 August. After two amendments had been discussed, Balfour moved the closure, thus virtually suspending discussion of the Bill. Several members protested, and twenty-one, including thirteen Welshmen, refused to participate in the vote on the closure, and were thus 'named' by the Deputy Speaker. The burly Mabon suggested that he himself would have to be removed forcibly from the Chamber. In protest, Asquith led the Opposition from the House and refused to debate the measure further.[1] This turbulent scene provoked a nation-wide reaction. While the Labour M.P., Will Crooks, denounced this 'outrage on the people's liberty', the Unionist press unanimously condemned the un-parliamentary behaviour of Lloyd George and his friends.[2] In the Lords, the Bill had a prompt passage, and received the Royal Assent on 15 August.

Thus came into being what the *Daily News* termed the 'Coercion of Wales Bill'.[3] In Wales, it became known as *Y Mesur Gormes*. It was a simple and skilful scheme, which could be operated with ease. But many hazards still lay ahead, for the initiative lay still with the Welsh county councils. By appearing to administer the Act according to the letter, they could avoid any suggestion of being declared in default.

The excitement over the Default Act diverted attention from another attempt at compromise. Again, the initiative came from the Bishop of St. Asaph, who had persisted in his personal efforts to reach a settlement on the lines of the concordat proposed in 1903. On 28 January 1904 he met Morant, who gave his approval to the scheme he proposed, as later did Lloyd George.[4] This formed the basis of the Education (Transferred Schools) Bill which the bishop introduced in the Lords on 9 May 1904.[5] This would allow non-provided schools to be transferred to local authorities where desired,

---

[1] Ibid., vol. cxxxix, pp. 1220 ff.
[2] Will Crooks to Edward Thomas, 9 Aug. 1904 (Cardiff, Cochfarf Papers); *The Times*, 6 Aug. 1904; *Morning Post*, 6 Aug. 1904.
[3] *Daily News*, 27 Apr. 1904.
[4] Archbishop of Wales, op. cit., pp. 193–4.
[5] *Parl. Deb.*, 4th ser., vol. cxxxiv, pp. 704 ff.

with arrangements to be made later between the local authorities and the governing bodies over the appointment of teachers and a syllabus of instruction according to the wishes of the parents. The Bill received the cautious endorsement of Archbishop Randall Davidson, Earl Cawdor, and Lord Londonderry. On 4 July, in a somewhat tepid debate, it received an unopposed Second Reading.[1] But it progressed no further, Londonderry declining to give the official blessing of the government. Like many compromises, it left both sides dissatisfied. Nonconformists considered it inadequate in being merely permissive, while the great majority of Free Churchmen opposed 'any clerical right of entry in school hours'.[2] Churchmen, on the other hand, held that the scheme gave too little scope for denominational instruction, and that it 'endowed undenominationalism'.[3] Thus an honest attempt to reconcile popular control with religious education was doomed to failure.

After the passage of the Default Act, the fertile legal brain of Lloyd George was active in devising new policies to evade the law. More and more he assumed sole command. He was now President of the Welsh National Council, chairman of the national executive appointed at Llandrindod, chairman of the Welsh national convention of education. Wales, he claimed, was near 'a national revolution'.[4] Of thirty local authorities, only the Town Councils of Wrexham and Caernarvon refused to carry out his policy. When the Methodists of Merioneth County Council protested, and complained that they would have to resort to the rates, Lloyd George and his associates met the Merioneth Education Committee on 1 October, and forced them into line.[5] Finally, a remarkable national convention was held at the Park Hall, Cardiff, on 6 October, with delegates present representing local education authorities and Free Church organizations. Thirteen members of Parliament were in attendance. After a stirring bi-lingual address from Lloyd George, resolutions were adopted, stating that when the Default Act was applied, education authorities would refuse to maintain any elementary schools. Nonconformist parents of children at non-provided schools, would then withdraw them and they would be educated, out of voluntary

[1] *Parl. Deb.*, 4th ser., vol. cxxxvii, pp. 393 ff.
[2] *British Weekly*, 12 May 1904. R. W. Perks to Asquith, 23 Dec. 1903 (Bodleian, Asquith Papers, box 19).
[3] *Church Times*, 13 May 1904. Cf. *Guardian*, 11 May 1904.
[4] *South Wales Daily News*, 9 Aug. 1904.
[5] Ibid., 3 Oct. 1904. *Y Genedl*, 4, 11 Oct. 1904. H. Haydn Jones to Bryn Roberts, 8 Feb. 1905 (N.L.W., Bryn Roberts Papers, no. 107), 'Private'.

effort, in chapels and vestries. Representatives of the Free Church Council, Clifford, Meyer, Scott Lidgett, all pledged the support of English nonconformists for their co-religionists.[1]

Had the government not been toppling to its fall, it is difficult to see what solution could have been found to a virtual mass abdication by Welsh local authorities. The Default Act was not the dead letter implied by some writers[2] but was operated in several cases. In Merioneth, where the County Council consisted of fifty-two Progressive and only three Sectarian members, Lord Londonderry informed the Council on 1 April 1905 that they were in default over non-provided schools, and thus grants of £2,000, due to the Council from October 1903, were withheld by the Board.[3] A great conference at Bala on 2 May, strongly coloured by the evangelical fervour that followed the religious revival then sweeping throughout Wales, urged nonconformist parents to withdraw their children from Church Schools. These numbered 896 out of some 1,600 pupils in Merioneth and a withdrawal gradually took place. Lloyd George told the assembled company at Bala that 'the present revival would make the people of Wales stronger to encounter the children of Amalek in Whitehall and the sons of Ammon who dwelt nearer home (laughter and applause)'.[4] At Shrewsbury, on 18 May, he urged that the Welsh National Council raise a fund of £12,000 to meet the expenses of educating the nonconformist children of Merioneth.[5] In the Commons, Osmond Williams, the Merioneth member and himself an Anglican landowner, moved a motion on the Adjournment, maintaining that the Merioneth Council had been wrongly declared in default, and that the unrepaired Church Schools were themselves in default. Against Lloyd George and the other Welsh members, Anson was hesitant and unconvincing.[6]

The situation rapidly seemed to be getting out of hand. A series of county conventions was held to endorse the 'Cardiff policy' and Lord Rendel donated £500 to the campaign fund. Although the majority of local authorities were still careful enough to avoid being technically in default, those of Montgomeryshire, Barry, Mountain Ash, and finally Glamorgan were all found in default, and had their

[1] *South Wales Daily News*, 7 Oct. 1904.
[2] e.g. Frank Owen, op. cit., p. 130; Sacks, op. cit., pp. 53–54.
[3] *South Wales Daily News*, 13 Mar.–8 Apr. 1905.
[4] Ibid., 3 May 1905.
[5] Ibid., 19 May 1905.
[6] *Parl. Deb.*, 4th ser., vol. cxlvi, pp. 363 ff. Cf. *Y Tyst*, 17 May 1905.

funds withheld by the Board.[1] Only in Montgomeryshire, of these councils, did an education committee still exist by September, the Conservative minority of nineteen here being just sufficient to form a quorum. However, the Liberals had at least the satisfaction of leaving a deficit of £3,670 to be met by their opponents.[2] At this crucial stage, the Unionist government resigned, on 4 December 1905, and Birrell, the new Liberal minister under Campbell-Bannerman, intimated at once that he would not apply the Default Act.[3] The 'Welsh Revolt' thus came suddenly to an end.

The history of the administration of the Education Act of 1902 in Wales seems to present a resurgence of the old nonconformist radical tradition, a rebirth of the nationalist sentiment which had receded since 1895. Certainly, the 'Revolt' has received inadequate attention from historians. It was far more effective than the indiscriminate passive resistance of English nonconformists, and until the election of 1906 public maintenance of voluntary schools in Wales was reduced to a minimum. Although there was disagreement in the nonconformist ranks over the question of secular education, where the Methodists were generally in opposition to the older sects, the Baptists and Independents,[4] to a remarkable extent sectarian rivalry was welded into unity. On the Cardiff convention platform in October 1904 were the Rev. Evan Jones, a Methodist, the Rev. Elvet Lewis, an Independent, Lloyd George, a Baptist, Osmond Williams, an Anglican, Col. Ivor Herbert, a Roman Catholic, and William Brace, vice-president of the South Wales Miners' Federation. *Llais Llafur* and the other Labour organs were no less ardent in the protest than was the Liberal press.[5] It seemed that the Liberal and nonconformist forces in Wales were combining to present the semblance of the most organized national rebellion since the days of Glyn-dŵr in the fifteenth century.

[1] *South Wales Daily News*, 7 June, 27 July, 20 Sept., 20 Oct., 1905. In Barry the only 'non-provided' school was the large Roman Catholic school, St. Joseph's.

[2] Ibid., 21 Sept. 1905.   [3] *British Weekly*, 21 Dec. 1905.

[4] This division persisted from the days of Forster's Act of 1870. Humphreys-Owen pointed out to Rendel that forty-eight of the fifty-two School Boards in Wales which pursued a secular policy in 1894 were in the southern counties where the Baptists and Independents predominated. In the North, where the Methodists were most numerous, there were only two secular Boards, one each in Anglesey and Denbighshire (N.L.W., Rendel Papers, xiv. 710). The issue to some extent split denominations. Thus amongst the Baptists, Lloyd George supported religious instruction in schools while Sir Alfred Thomas opposed it. See letter from Ellis Davies, *North Wales Observer*, 1 Jan. 1904.

[5] For example, see *Llais Llafur*, 29 Mar., 31 May 1902. This reflected the attitude of the Labour movement as a whole: the trade unions and the I.L.P. joined the Liberals in condemning the Act, while the Fabians ardently welcomed it. For Keir Hardie's views, see *Aberdare Times*, 7 June 1902.

In reality, this unity was to a great degree superficial, and the extent of public interest exaggerated. The 'Revolt' did not mark a revival of the Welsh Party, which still, said the *South Wales Daily News*, lacked 'cohesion and effectiveness'.[1] The revolt, in appearance united, sprang essentially from the genius and driving-power of Lloyd George alone, and not from the combined action of the Party as a whole. Working closely with Lloyd George were only Herbert Lewis, Frank Edwards, and Humphreys-Owen, the last two being churchmen. The remainder were largely carried along as passive sup-porters, and Sir Alfred Thomas was patently a figure-head. Even some of Lloyd George's closest allies were apprehensive at the implications of his policy. 'Having had no literary education himself he is unable to realize the needs of the education system. He regards it simply as a political scaffolding and so long as he can see his way to set up the scaffolding he does not trouble himself with the charac-ter of the edifice.' Humphreys-Owen concluded, 'My best hope is that the Revival may produce another Ellis'.[2]

Some Liberals were frankly hostile. D. A. Thomas believed the Cardiff policy to be illusory,[3] and many other fissures appeared after Lloyd George declared opposition to the Default Act. Lloyd Morgan (West Carmarthenshire), an Independent, was another critic, declar-ing the policy financially unworkable,[4] and with reason. Bryn Roberts, a Methodist, was another constant opponent. He thought Lloyd George's 'extreme policy' to be 'unwise from every point of view' and favoured a compromise over 'inside facilities', although his constituency association in Eifion condemned his attitude.[5] Many, particularly among the Methodists, believed the 'Revolt' would bring discredit on Wales, among them Tom Ellis's brother-in-law, H. Jones-Davies, while young nonconformists such as W. J. Gruffydd thought that the 'Revolt' was a superficial distraction from the more fundamental social and spiritual tasks confronting the churches.[6] Lloyd George kept up a façade of unity with the utmost difficulty. At various times, Montgomeryshire, Merioneth, Pembrokeshire, and even his own Caernarvonshire, broke away and were won back with

[1] *South Wales Daily News*, 17 Aug. 1904; cf. *Church Times*, 11 Nov. 1904.
[2] Humphreys-Owen to Rendel, 18 June 1905 (N.L.W., Rendel Papers, xiv. 704*a*).
[3] Lady Rhondda (ed.), *Viscount Rhondda*, pp. 78 ff.
[4] *South Wales Daily News*, 14 Nov. 1904.
[5] Bryn Roberts to —, 25 Oct. 1904 (N.L.W., Bryn Roberts Papers, no. 239). *North Wales Observer*, 21 Oct. 1904; 6 Jan., 20 Oct. 1905.
[6] W. J. Gruffydd, *Hen Atgofion* (Aberystwyth, 1936). Ll. Hugh Jones to Bryn Roberts, 19 Oct. 1904 (N.L.W., Bryn Roberts Papers, no. 124).

the greatest difficulty. When the Liberals took office, Lloyd George had gained immensely in personal prestige, but the nonconformist grievances remained without remedy. Thousands of pounds, collected to finance the voluntary nonconformist schools, remained and remain uninvested and locked up in country banks down to the present day.[1] The revolt over the Education Act recalled a vanishing past, a tradition of political dissent that was weakening fast, in spite of the temporary stimulus of the religious revival. The privileged position of Church Schools was keenly felt in many quarters, but the politically minded ministers who proclaimed it in 1902 spoke for a diminishing section of Welsh opinion.

There is a postscript to the 'Welsh Revolt'. Although it was inspired by denominational rather than by national motives, there was, contemporary with the most bitter phase of the struggle, a prospect of a real advance in Welsh educational autonomy. In August 1903 Anson proposed a joint board of Welsh county councils for educational purposes, a proposal which Lloyd George enthusiastically adopted, and negotiations were begun with the Hon. W. N. Bruce, for the Board. All the Welsh local authorities, save only Carmarthenshire which had its own idiosyncratic position, agreed to the proposals, but by the fall of the Unionist government, no active steps had been taken to implement them.[2]

(iii) *The Labour Movement in Wales*

While the embattled forces of Church and Dissent were waging their traditional struggle over denominational schools, a powerful new force was emerging which threatened to transform the existing political pattern. To the alarm of the older parties, industrial workers began to form an organization and a party of their own.

The growth of the Labour movement within Wales remains a subject the outlines of which are still far from clear.[3] But it seems beyond

---

[1] William George, *My Brother and I*, p. 193; A. T. Davies, *The Lloyd George I Knew* (London, 1948), p. 48.

[2] *South Wales Daily News*, 5 Aug. 1903. Carmarthenshire objected on the grounds that (i) the new Joint Board resembled in structure the Central Welsh Board, which had failed to foster the Welsh language; (ii) Biblical instruction was not safeguarded.

[3] The sketch of the early Labour movement in Wales which follows is necessarily incomplete. As the new edition of the *Bibliography of Welsh History* indicates, there is virtually no published material on the political wing of the movement in Wales and very little on the industrial. The story needs to be pieced together from fragmentary evidence in local newspapers, and the records of local trade unions, trades councils, I.L.P. branches, &c. It is to be hoped that the new *Dictionary of Labour Biography* will succeed in unearthing material of this kind that might otherwise be destroyed. In the meantime, only an interim summary can be attempted.

dispute that Wales played a negligible part in the revival of the British Labour movement, both in the political and the industrial spheres, that featured the troubled years after 1880. The political and cultural isolation that suffused Welsh affairs with a peculiar character of their own left Wales detached from the metropolitan activities of the Fabian Society or the Social Democratic Federation. Men felt more immediate loyalty to their village or valley than to their class. Even the Independent Labour Party, in many respects a rebellion of the provinces and intrinsically regional in character, was slow to penetrate into Wales: the Bradford conference of January 1893, which saw the foundation of the Party contained no delegate from Wales.[1] By the summer of 1897, only four weak branches seem to have been founded in Wales, at Cardiff, Treharris, Merthyr Tydfil, and in Wrexham in the North.[2] At the 1895 election, 'Independent Labour' candidates stood at Swansea District and Merthyr Tydfil, but with little success.

This earlier feebleness of the Labour movement is paralleled by the course of industrial relations.[3] Trade unionism in Wales presented a confused and fragmentary appearance until the last decade of the nineteenth century. There were individual strongholds of some of the 'new model' unions, notably the Cardiff, Barry, Swansea, and Newport branches of the Amalgamated Society of Engineers, 'the best organized towns in the engineering trade'.[4] Railway unionism had also become established and there were effective branches of the two major railway unions in South Wales, the branches of the Amalgamated Society of Locomotive Engineers and Firemen at Neath and Pontypool and the branches of the Amalgamated Society of Railway Servants at Cardiff and Barry being particularly active. There had been several delegates from South Wales at the founda-

[1] Although Henry Pelling has shown (*Origins of the Labour Party*, London, 1954, p. 122 n.) that there was a delegate from South Wales, S. G. Hobson, who missed his train. Tom Mann had conducted an early missionary campaign for the I.L.P. in South Wales in 1894 (*South Wales Daily News*, 6–28 June 1894).

[2] *Fourth Annual Report of the I.L.P. Conference, 1897*, p. 10. *I.L.P.: Directory and Branch Returns for 3 months ending 31 May 1896* (Glasgow, 1896). The *I.L.P. News*, Apr. 1897, also records a branch in existence at Maes-y-cwmer. One delegate from Wales attended the 1897 Conference, Dan Osborne from 'Glamorgan East', which was stated to have twenty-five members.

[3] The account which follows is based largely on MSS. in the Webb Trade Union Collection in the London School of Economics Library. There is a good account of the 'new unionism' in Swansea in P. S. Thomas, *Industrial Relations: a short study of the relations between employers and employed in Swansea and neighbourhood, from about 1800 to recent times* (Cardiff, 1940), pp. 72 ff.

[4] Webb T.U. Collection, section A, vol. xvi, f. 191. There were 976 members in Cardiff, 410 in Newport, 280 in Swansea, and 160 in Barry in 1892.

tion meeting of the A.S.R.S. in London in 1872, while three of its
early general secretaries had Welsh connexions, Fred Evans, Edward
Harford, and, from 1897, Richard Bell from Merthyr Tydfil.[1] But
trade unionism generally in industrial Wales was feeble and ill-
organized, in the large coastal towns and the inland valleys alike.
A considerable impetus, however, came from the militant 'new
unionism' at the end of the 1880's, which appealed to unskilled
workers through the programme of a 'general union' embracing
several trades. Sidney Webb noted that Newport, 'like most of the
towns in South Wales, owes almost the whole of its importance as
a Trade Union town to the new Unionism'.[2] New trades councils
were formed between 1891 and 1893 at Newport, Barry, Neath,
Merthyr Tydfil, and Pontypridd, while the older councils at Cardiff
(formed in 1884) and at Swansea (founded as early as 1873) were
totally transformed after years of obsolescence. Trade unionism here,
stated Webb, 'was all quite new and consequently full of fight'.[3] In
Cardiff, membership of the Dockers' and Seamen's Unions soared
to many thousands, with the assistance of national union leaders
such as Ben Tillett, Tom Mann, and Havelock Wilson, while the
National Amalgamated Labourers' Union, based at Cardiff, penetrated throughout the South Wales ports. By 1891 over 20,000
workers were affiliated to the Cardiff Trades Council.[4] At Newport
there was a similar resurgence among unskilled labour, as the rapid
growth of the new unions infused life into older craft unions such as
the Wheelwrights and the Wagonbuilders.[5] At Swansea the new
Labourers' Union formed in the town grew to 2,000 members in
a few months, while the Dockers' Union also numbered over 2,000
men in a variety of employments by 1891.[6] Older unions were also
galvanized into new action. The A.S.R.S. formed new branches at
Tondu and Pontypridd in 1890 and effectively demonstrated its
strength in a successful strike on the Taff Vale railway.[7] The new
trades councils gradually began to secure the election of their representatives to local governing boards, Burial Boards, and School

[1] G. W. Alcock, *Fifty Years of Railway Trade Unionism* (London, 1922), pp. 82,
112 ff., 225 ff., 287 ff. Fred Evans was general secretary, 1874–83; Harford, 1883–97;
Bell, 1897–1909. Another Welshman, J. H. Thomas, was general secretary from 1916
after the merger of the A.S.R.S. into the National Union of Railwaymen in 1913.
[2] Webb T.U. Collection, section A, vol. iv, f. 191.
[3] Ibid., f. 176.   [4] Ibid., ff. 75–90.   [5] Ibid., ff. 185–92.
[6] Ibid., ff. 271–7; P. S. Thomas, op. cit., pp. 73–77. Webb noted that 'a very strong
feeling of Wales for the Welsh' was the dominant feature of Swansea trades unionism.
[7] *South Wales Daily News*, 13 Jan., 25 Feb. 1890. The A.S.R.S. strike lasted for
eight days, 6–14 Aug. 1890.

Boards, and it seemed that a new militancy and drive were transforming the structure of industrial relations in the ports of South Wales.

But the extent of the 'new unionism' remained limited. Some of
the new trades councils, those at Neath, Merthyr, and Pontypridd,
remained small and struggling for many years. Even in the large
towns of Cardiff, Newport, and Swansea, a series of disastrous strikes
in the years 1891–2 among dockers and seamen and in the building
trades caused a serious recession in the strength of trade unionism.
By 1893 the Dockers' and Seamen's Unions were largely moribund
throughout South Wales.[1] The Labourers Unions gradually dissipated their strength, while in other unskilled trades such as the
Gasworkers there was never much coherent organization.[2] In two
years after 1891 the union membership affiliated to Cardiff Trades
Council fell from 20,000 to 9,700; in Newport there was a similar
recession, while in Swansea and Neath, with their more obviously
Welsh characteristics, trade unionism was hidebound by a cautious
attitude towards industrial action and by hostility to unions based in
England. In any case, the 'new unions' had made little enough
penetration inland, and in the mining valleys trade unionists continued to form a small minority of the total labour force. Thus, in the
tinplate industry, the Association of Tinplate Workers steadily disintegrated during the severe trade depression of the 1890's which left
at least two-fifths of the labour force of the industry unemployed.
By 1900 the tinplaters were scattered throughout half a dozen different unions, of whom the Steel Smelters and the Tin and Sheet
Millmen were bitter rivals over wages policy, as the enduring antagonism between their respective secretaries, John Hodge and Tom
Phillips, demonstrated.[3] In the iron and steel industry trade unionism
was no less feeble. The ephemeral Amalgamated Association of
Iron and Steel Workers, formed in 1888 and which at one time
claimed over 7,000 members in six of the seven great works of the
South, gradually declined in the 1890's under the impact of the prolonged depression which closed the mighty works at Rhymney and
Tredegar. In any case, its claim to be regarded as a trade union at all
was highly doubtful: it possessed no branch organization and no
funds, contributions being deducted from wages by the employers.
The successful strike of the Engineers and Boilermen at Ebbw Vale

---

[1] Webb T.U. Collection, section A, vol. xlii, ff. 170–5.
[2] Ibid., ff. 46–55.
[3] W. E. Minchinton, *The British Tinplate Industry* (Oxford, 1957), pp. 108 ff.

in 1892 was the first effective demonstration for the ironmasters of the potentialities of active trade unionism.[1]

Above all, the dominant elements in the industrial labour force of Wales, the miners, who numbered over 150,000 by 1900, were extremely slow to combine and their leaders anxious to compromise. Twenty years earlier it had seemed that a new militancy was invading the coalfield. Under the leadership of Thomas Halliday, the Amalgamated Association of Miners spread rapidly, its membership reaching a peak of 45,000. But a series of long strikes between 1871 and 1875 left the A.A.M. bankrupt and broken. In its place, a new agreement was negotiated, which set up a sliding scale of wages based on the selling price of coal. A change of one shilling a ton in price would involve a change of $7\frac{1}{2}$ per cent. in wages. The agreement could be terminated with six months notice on either side. To administer the system, a joint committee was set up, the five owners' representatives being headed by W. T. Lewis (later Lord Merthyr), 'the best hated man in the principality', and the five miners' leaders by William Abraham (Mabon), the vice-president of the Sliding Scale Committee.[2]

For twenty years the sliding scale controlled wages, and its operation provoked bitter criticism from miners in other parts of the United Kingdom. In spite of a new agreement in 1880, basing the wage level on that of 1879, the wage level remained depressed. The price of conciliation was found in infrequent audits, striking increases in wages followed by massive reductions. The system proved a direct incentive to employers to under-sell and to over-produce, since the sliding scale guaranteed that profits would be maintained intact. Constant wage adjustments caused constant disputes with the Coal-Owners Association, whose chairman, W. T. Lewis, 'the last of the industrial barons',[3] had scant sympathy with the miners' demands. Eventually, a new adjustment of the scale was negotiated in 1892, entailing a $7\frac{1}{2}$ per cent. reduction, followed by a further $2\frac{1}{2}$ per cent. reduction. By 1897 wages had fallen to a level only 10·94 per cent. above that of 1879 and thousands of miners faced near starvation.

An equally serious consequence of the scale mechanism was its tendency to intensify divisions between the various mining unions.

[1] Webb T.U. Collection, section A, vol. xxiii, ff. 152–64.
[2] Eric Wyn Evans, *Mabon*, pp. 13–15. The text of the sliding scale agreement is printed in Ness Edwards, *History of the South Wales Miners* (London, 1926), pp. 74–76.
[3] Lady Rhondda (ed.), op. cit., p. 118.

Eight small localized bodies existed simultaneously, of which only three were bona fide trades unions with their own independent organization and funds.[1] The small South Wales branch of the Miners' Federation of Great Britain, of which William Brace was the secretary, never numbered more than 6,000. By 1893 barely 45,000 out of 120,000 miners in South Wales were organized in trade unions. The dominant voice among the Welsh miners during this period was that of William Abraham (Mabon), secretary of the Cambrian Miners Association. A characteristic product of industrial nonconformity, deacon of Capel Nazareth, Pentre, Mabon founded his adherence to the sliding scale essentially on ethical rather than on economic considerations. The apostle of industrial peace, he believed that there was no essential conflict of interest between capital and labour, and that mutual adjustment would secure an agreement satisfactory to both sides. The scale symbolized this harmonious relationship. To Mabon, strikes and lock-outs were primitive and unnecessary. Until the turn of the century, he could command a unique authority over the Welsh mining community. With a homely parable and his fine tenor voice which won fame at the *eisteddfod*, he could enthral multitudes and charm away all dissent. But increasingly he was under fire. Two miners' associations, those of Neath, Swansea, and Llanelly and of Monmouthshire, refused to sign the new scale of 1892, while Isaac Evans, secretary of the Neath, Swansea, and Llanelly men, virulently attacked Mabon for his subservience.[2] The employers, he alleged, 'give him [Mabon] a good feed, some good wine and good cigars and then can do what they like with him', while Mabon's son was employed personally in the office of W. T. Lewis himself. Above all, William Brace vigorously condemned the sliding scale and urged the cause of Federation.[3] In the savage Hauliers' strike of 1893, which was specifically directed against the sliding scale, the ominous 'English influence' was noted for the first time, a menace to Mabon's ascendancy. The advocates of the M.F.G.B. pointed out how Mabon's own professions of the need for a general union throughout the Welsh mining community were stultified by his adherence to a system of collective bargaining which fatally compromised the growth of unionism.

[1] Webb T.U. Collection, section A, vol. xxvi, ff. 155–205.
[2] Ibid., f. 196.
[3] See Brace's letter in *South Wales Daily News*, 20 Aug. 1893. The climax to the duel between Brace and Mabon was reached in this month when Mabon was awarded damages of £500 at Swansea assizes after suing Brace for libel.

In 1898 the situation was transformed by the six-months' coal stoppage, which begins a new era in the history of South Wales. On 30 September 1897 the miners' representatives had given the required six months' notice to terminate the sliding scale, demanding instead a 10 per cent. wage increase and a basic minimum wage. Before the six months had elapsed, on 26 February 1898, Sir W. T. Lewis declared that negotiations were suspended, and all individual contracts terminated. For six months nearly 100,000 men were idle, and poverty was widespread throughout the coalfield. The Home Office conciliator, Sir Edward Fry, was refused permission to intervene by Sir W. T. Lewis, while dissension among the miners' leaders made their position constantly weaker. The final settlement reached on 1 September was a complete victory for the owners.[1] A 5 per cent. wage increase was granted, but the hated sliding scale was to remain until 1902. In addition, the monthly holiday, 'Mabon's Day', was abolished, and it seemed that much of Mabon's own ascendancy passed away with it. He had 'fought tooth and nail for his day' but to no avail. Yet, despite this disastrous conclusion, 1898 proved to be the 1868 of the coalfield. The old disunity and apathy evaporated in the bitter awakening of defeat. From 1898, therefore, dates the effective origin of the Labour movement in Welsh history.

In political developments, the immediate significance of the stoppage of 1898 lay in the impetus provided for the Independent Labour Party. During the stoppage, Wales had become for the first time a missionary centre for the organized Labour movement. I.L.P. spokesmen were dispatched to the valleys, and William Wright of Mexborough made South Wales organizer.[2] In an active campaign, several I.L.P. branches were formed, mostly in the East Glamorgan coalfield, but as far West as Gwaun-cae-gurwen and Ystalyfera. The *Labour Leader* organized a relief fund to feed the starving children and dependents of the unemployed miners, to which trade unions all over the country contributed. By September 1898 the fund had swelled to £327.[3] Even more important, during the strike, Keir Hardie had arrived in South Wales. He had long considered that the passionate temperament of the Welsh and their community con-

---

[1] *South Wales Daily News*, 2 Sept. 1898. Three miners' representatives refused to sign the settlement, including John Williams, agent of the Western District and later M.P. for Gower, 1906–22.

[2] *Labour Leader*, 28 May, 16 July 1898.

[3] Ibid., 10 Sept. 1898. Sir Thomas Lipton donated 2,000 lb. of sugar and George Cadbury £100 of cocoa (Emrys Hughes, *Keir Hardie*, London, 1956, p. 91).

sciousness made them potentially enthusiastic converts. 'Like all
true Celts, they are Socialists by instinct.'[1] Soon he had gained a wide
following, his meetings often resembling religious gatherings in their
messianic fervour, for instance at Penydarren, notwithstanding the
sixty armed constables lying in ambush in the event of a riot. In the
Labour Leader, a series of passionate articles by Hardie depicted in
simple and compelling terms the living conditions of miners' families,
and bitterly criticized the compromise tactics of Mabon and the
other miners' leaders.[2] Robert Williams even contributed some
articles in Welsh, which proclaimed the imminent downfall of
capitalism. The deep impression left by the miners' defeat was seen
in the growth of thirty-one I.L.P. branches by the end of 1898.[3]
Keir Hardie, Wright, Alpass, and Grady became familiar figures,
and thirty delegates at Porth on 3 September participated in the
most important Socialist conference yet held in Wales. The membership of the I.L.P. totalled 1,704.

The majority of these branches proved ephemeral. By January 1899
they had declined to twenty-six in number and by December to
eleven. But the hold gained proved ineradicable. Already there were
I.L.P. members on the Newport Board of Guardians and the urban
district councils of Merthyr and Ystalyfera.[4] The press was also
influential in the Labour cause. In the western valleys, more homo-
geneous in population and far from the impact of the new immigrant,
Llais Llafur of Ystalyfera, edited by D. J. Rees, was gaining a wide
circulation in the Swansea valley with its vigorous, even scurrilous,
style. Elsewhere, the 'Carolyne Martyn Van' found a ready sale for
Blatchford's *Clarion* in the coalfield.[5]

These circumstances emboldened Keir Hardie to stand for a Welsh
seat in the 'khaki election' of 1900. In September 1900 he was
nominated by the Aberdare and Merthyr Trades Council as Labour
candidate, defeating such well-known Welshmen as William Brace
and Tom Richards.[6] Hardie was officially sponsored by the Labour

[1] Ibid., 9 July 1898. [2] Ibid., 2, 9 July 1898.
[3] *I.L.P. News*, Sept. 1898. Willie Wright attended the I.L.P. conference of 1899 on
behalf of the branches of Cardiff, Glamorgan East, Gower, Monmouth West, and
Rhondda (*Seventh Annual Conference Report, 1899*).
[4] C. Thomas sat on the Newport Board of Guardians as a Labour member from
1897 to 1901. C. E. G. Simmons sat on the Merthyr U.D.C., 1898–1900; Daniel
Daniels and John Thomas sat on the Ystalyfera U.D.C., 1899–1900.
[5] *Labour Leader*, 29 July 1899.
[6] *Tarian y Gweithiwr*, 27 Sept. 1900; *Aberdare Times*, 29 Sept. 1900; *South Wales
Daily News*, 23 Sept. 1900. Hardie's adoption followed a heated dispute in the Merthyr
and Aberdare Trades Council. Aberdare had proposed Tom Mann, while Mountain

Representation Committee, formed in London the preceding February. Hardie seems to have considered his chances more favourable in Preston, where he was also candidate, but following defeat there he returned to South Wales. Local circumstances were in his favour. The senior member, D. A. Thomas, although a coal-owner himself, encouraged Hardie's candidature, and Thomas's personal patronage was the decisive factor still in the politics of Merthyr Tydfil. His colleague, Pritchard Morgan, was on bad terms with Thomas, and much criticized in his constituency for his long absences pursuing gold-mining ventures in China. It was even alleged that he had indulged in 'Chinese slavery'.[1] He proved a militant imperialist and decorated Merthyr with posters which urged, 'Vote for D. A. Thomas and Keir Hardie, both pro-Boers'.[2] Had Hardie not faced so disorganized an opposition, his return would have been highly problematical. His programme was scarcely nationalist in tone. 'My programme is the programme of Labour; my cause is the cause of Labour—the cause of Humanity—the cause of God.' In the event, while Thomas easily headed the poll, Hardie polled 5,745 against Morgan's 4,004 in spite of the disfranchisement of those miners who had received poor relief in 1898, and thus became the first independent Labour member for Wales. He himself attributed his success to his personal reputation, to the influence of the I.L.P. since 1898, and the hatred of imperialism and war in the seat once held by Henry Richard.[3] More fortuitous elements must also be considered—the weakness of the Liberal machine, the unpopularity of Pritchard Morgan, his support by the Merthyr licensed victuallers, his gold and his adventures in China. Finally, Merthyr and Aberdare possessed a unique tradition in working-class history. They had been the last active centres of Welsh Chartism, while working-class support had formed the basis of Richard's triumph in 1868. Aberdare in particular had powerful radical associations. It had been the centre of the first Welsh Co-operative Society, at Cwmbach in 1860, while its trades council had advocated the nomination of the fiery Tom Mann at the last election. The revolutionary Socialist, C. B. Stanton, had been elected overwhelmingly as miners' agent for Aberdare just before the poll, in succession to the venerable David Morgan ('Dai

---

Ash and Dowlais had favoured William Brace. Hardie was eventually adopted by thirty-two votes to seven, Brace's supporters having left the meeting in disgust.

[1] *Tarian y Gweithiwr*, 21 June 1900. The *Tarian* was a pro-Liberal miners' journal.
[2] S. D. Shallard, 'Merthyr Tydfil', *Labour Leader*, 20 Oct. 1900.
[3] *Labour Leader*, 13 Oct. 1900.

o'r Nant'). As a result of these personal and sociological factors, Hardie triumphed, and retained the Merthyr seat until his death in 1915.[1]

In 1900, however, the Merthyr election represented a solitary breach with the older radical background. Nowhere else did Socialism so completely transform the cause of Labour. Elsewhere, the progress of Labour candidates is distinguished less by doctrine than by a vague insistence on the need for more working-class representatives. This was the case at Gower, the other seat in 1900 where Liberal and Labour candidates were in opposition.[2] Here, John Hodge of the Steel Smelters ran against a local capitalist, Aeron Thomas, an ex-mayor of Swansea. Hodge's programme was nebulous in the extreme —he described it as 'Labour first, politics second'[3]—and he decided to fight Thomas only after first being rejected by the narrowly un-representative Gower Liberal Association.[4] The combined weight of nonconformity and local industrial paternalism were too powerful a combination for Hodge, while several local Labour leaders, includ-ing Hodge's rival, Tom Phillips (Tin and Sheet Millmen), and John Williams, miners' agent for the Western District, mounted Liberal platforms to deplore Hodge's division of the progressive and nationalist vote.[5] Even so, the narrowness of Aeron Thomas's margin was to many an ominous portent. In 1903 the secretary of Cardiff Liberal Association noted that Gower would be 'lost to Labour'.[6] In most parts of Wales, working men's organizations showed extreme reluctance to challenge their Liberal inheritance and the emergence of Labour must be pictured as a partial and localized crystallization from a much older system of thought. In Cardiff, where there were 10,000 trade unionists in all trades by 1900,[7] the heterogeneity of the labour force militated against unity. The three 'Labour' councillors, Chappell, Jenkins, Crossman, all took their places in the Cardiff Liberal Association, and the trades council in

[1] He joined the Welsh Parliamentary Party at the start of the new session (*South Wales Daily News*, 7 Dec. 1900).
[2] See my article, 'The Khaki Election in Gower', *Gower*, xiii (1961).
[3] *Cambria Daily Leader*, 29 Sept. 1900.
[4] *South Wales Daily News*, 28 Sept. 1900.
[5] This produced acrimonious exchanges in the local press subsequently, particularly between John Williams and Henry Davies (Tin and Sheet Millmen), who had favoured Hodge (*Llais Llafur*, 20 Oct.–10 Nov. 1900). The *Labour Leader*, 20 Oct. 1900, also commented bitterly on the election and reviled the 'coalmaster, moneylender, brewer and employer of women dockers', Aeron Thomas, with a brave artistic licence.
[6] Memorandum by H. G. C. Allgood (Cochfarf Papers, Cardiff Public Library).
[7] *Labour Pioneer*, June 1900.

1900 wired its support for even such a dubious ally as Sir Edward Reed.[1] In Newport, a Labour Representation Committee was formed in 1901, but the trades council still endorsed the Liberal employer, Albert Spicer, at the polls.[2] However, in Swansea, where Ben Tillett was an influential figure within the Dockers' Union, the progress of Labour representation was dramatic. In 1898 David Williams was returned as the first Labour member of the borough council, and in 1900 Labour representation increased to five. A Labour Representation Committee was formed in Swansea in 1901.[3] In subsequent years, from Newport to Pontardulais, in municipal elections and contests for county and town councils, School Boards and Boards of Guardians, Labour candidates gained repeated successes. In November 1905 there were gains in a host of municipal elections. The most striking result of all was in Merthyr Tydfil, where all twelve Labour candidates were returned, eleven of them miners or checkweighers, while Enoch Morrell followed Timothy Owen at Aberavon and W. S. Crossman at Cardiff to become the Labour mayor of Merthyr.[4] By 1905 there were twenty-seven I.L.P. branches in South Wales.[5]

In the industrial field, the impact of the stoppage of 1898 was equally decisive. The complete absence of united purpose among the miners' leaders had caused comment even by the Board of Trade's industrial conciliator, Sir Edward Fry,[6] and the position of Mabon and the older leaders became far less secure as a result. At once, decades of dissension were forgotten, and on 24 October 1898, the scattered pithead lodges were shaken into the unity of the South Wales Miners' Federation, with Abraham as president and Brace as vice-president. The following January, the S.W.M.F. was admitted to the Miners' Federation of Great Britain, the sliding scale necessitating their admission on a different basis. By the end of 1899 S.W.M.F. membership totalled 104,212. In December 1902 the miners again gave notice to terminate the hated sliding scale, and in March 1903 the scale disappeared, the new agreement including

[1] *Western Mail*, 3 Oct. 1900. W. M. Thompson, editor of *Reynolds News*, had declined an offer to stand as Labour candidate (*Llais Llafur*, 29 Sept. 1900).
[2] *Labour Pioneer*, May 1901. *South Wales Daily News*, 27 Apr. 1901.
[3] Stan Awbery, *Labour's Early Struggles in Swansea* (Swansea, 1949), pp. 33 ff. *Cambria Daily Leader*, 2 Nov. 1900.
[4] *Labour Leader*, 10 Nov. 1905. For a portrait of Enoch Morrell, see *Glamorgan Free Press*, 11 Nov. 1905.
[5] *Thirteenth Annual I.L.P. Conference Report*, 1905, pp. 60 ff.
[6] *Labour Leader*, 3 Sept. 1898.

a maximum and minimum wage rate and a conciliation board to regulate wages. This new settlement was still unsatisfactory to Smillie and the M.F.G.B., but the existing agreement was virtually re-enacted in December 1905. Nevertheless, it was evident that the surface harmony since 1875 had disappeared and the whole fabric of industrial relations was fast deteriorating.

This new unity among Welsh miners greatly stimulated their political activity. The miners' unions remained unaffiliated to the Labour Representation Committee, and the growing Socialism of local lodges had yet to penetrate the circle of leadership. But a sense of vulnerability was impelling the miners' unions to collective self-defence. In particular, the decision of Mr. Justice Farwell against the Amalgamated Society of Railway Servants in the Taff Vale case in 1900, which made unions liable for the tortious actions of their agents, seemed to threaten an ominous employers' counter-offensive on the American pattern. In 1902, therefore, the Miners' Federation set up a fund to return its own representatives to Parliament, and in Wales this was especially effective. Clearly, they were laying claim to every industrial seat in South Wales, as soon as a vacancy occurred.[1] In Gower, where such a vigorous challenge had been made in 1900, John Williams, the erstwhile opponent of the Labour cause, was nominated as miners' Labour candidate in 1903, by a body whose representative nature was as suspect as the ridiculed Gower Liberal Association itself.[2] A more crucial case came in South Glamorgan, where William Brace had been nominated as candidate by the 'South Glamorgan Labour Representation League', a body dominated by the Barry branch of the A.S.R.S. The claims of Labour in South Glamorgan were disputed by the shipping employers who dominated the Liberal Five Hundred: they showed that miners comprised barely a fifth of the electorate. But, after pressure from Herbert Gladstone, the Liberal Chief Whip, who had recently completed a secret electoral pact with the Labour Representation Committee, the Liberal Association gave way: after all, Brace's Liberal credentials as Vice-President of the Welsh National Liberal Federation were unimpeachable, and he openly avowed his antipathy to Socialism.[3]

[1] Pickard had arranged a scheme whereby the miners would be allocated one seat per 10,000 union members. On this basis, the S.W.M.F. claimed all the seats in South Wales, including such dubious 'mining' constituencies as Brecknockshire and South Glamorgan. (Cf. R. Page Arnot, *The Miners*, London, 1948, pp. 360–1.)

[2] *South Wales Daily News*, 19 Oct. 1903. Vernon Hartshorn was howled down at this stormy meeting.

[3] *South Wales Daily News*, 28 July, 7 Aug., 12, 29 Sept., 22, 29 Oct. 1903. Notes of

A more urgent case came in 1904 when, on Harcourt's retirement, Tom Richards, their treasurer, had been nominated by the Miners' Federation. After much equivocation, the West Monmouthshire Association decided by 116 votes to 66 that the time was 'not ripe' for Labour representation. Again, there was pressure by Herbert Gladstone, but the decisive factor was the refusal of the Liberal nominee, Warmington, the old member up to 1895, to oppose a Labour candidate. After Richards had made clear his intention to accept the Liberal whip in the House, he was narrowly nominated by sixty-two votes to fifty-one.[1] Richards triumphed over his protectionist opponent by over 4,500. By 1906 the miners' fund totalled nearly £12,000 and further candidacies were threatened in Mid-Glamorgan, Brecknockshire, Carmarthen District, and East Carmarthen. In Monmouthshire, the Newport Trades Council nominated James Winstone, a miners' agent, with L.R.C. backing. The detachment of the Miners' Federation towards the Labour Party was increasingly under strain. In 1906, while the M.F.G.B. as a whole voted against affiliation to the Labour Party, South Wales voted strongly in favour by 41,843 to 31,527.[2] In the course of seven years, the political pattern of industrial Wales had become transformed. Wales, said Mrs. Snowden fiercely, 'a hot-bed of Liberalism and Nonconformity in the past, . . . would become a hot-bed of Socialism and real religion in the future'.[3]

This last observation reveals the conflict that was emerging between the radicalism of the past and the Socialism of the future. The traditional struggles—disestablishment, education, land reform, temperance—were class struggles of a kind, representing the uprising of nonconformity against social inferiority. In origin, they derived from the social structure of the country-side, where the 'unholy Trinity' of the bishop, the brewer, and the squire had long formed the entrenched opposition. But to the problems of an industrial community—the low living standards and purchasing power of the industrial worker, the bitter conflict of capital and labour, the rootless society of a vast sprawling industrial proletariat—to such issues

an interview of Herbert Gladstone with A. J. Williams, 7 Nov. 1903 (B.M., Herbert Gladstone Papers, Add. MSS., 46106, ff. 38–42).
[1] *South Wales Daily News*, 7 June–12 July 1904. *Llais Llafur*, 25 June, 3 Sept. 1904. Also see 'Some Plain Talk about the West Monmouth campaign' (Leader), *Glamorgan Free Press*, 14 May 1904. The Unionist candidate was Sir John Cockburn, former Premier of South Australia.
[2] *South Wales Daily News*, 5 Oct. 1906.
[3] Mrs. Snowden, 'Socialism in South Wales', *Labour Leader*, 27 Oct. 1905.

as these, the old Liberal platform had no solution and its Welsh national character little relevance. Welsh nonconformity had retained its close contact with working-class life, and still provided the framework for communal association within every village. Abraham, John Williams, Tom Richards, representative of the old type of Labour leader, were staunch nonconformists, with a background of the Sunday School and the local *eisteddfod*: John Williams celebrated his election for Gower in 1906 by preaching the sermon at Capel Gomer.[1] Their election programmes in 1906 were essentially Liberal. But the old issues, which could combine the 'Whiggery of the Big Pew' in alliance with unskilled workers against the common ecclesiastical enemy, were losing their significance, and the narrow sectarianism which insulated Welsh thought was gradually being displaced. Such prominent capitalists as D. A. Thomas, David Davies, T. W. David, C. J. Cory, Henry Radcliffe, W. Thomas (Maerdy), and W. Jenkins (Ocean Colliery) were all Liberals in politics, Welsh by birth, nonconformists by religion. But the growth of new class alignments made these qualifications irrelevant. Nonconformist ministers inveighed against the materialism and atheism of Socialist propaganda, and many young militants left their congregations.[2] As nonconformity lost its hold, the new social gospel took its place. Its meetings employed the language and mystique of traditional religion, but it was the miners' agent and not the minister who gained from the new fervour.

The conduct of the Welsh members of Parliament is instructive here. They represented the new Welsh bourgeoisie of the later nineteenth century, the professional and business classes. Their fire was still directed at the unholy alliance of 'Beer and the Bible': one searches in vain, even among the speeches of Lloyd George, for reference to the basic issues of unemployment, depressed wages, and inadequate housing in the industrial South. The great coal stoppage of 1898 evoked little interest from the members from South Wales. Brynmor Jones did move a motion on the adjournment in June 1898, in which S. T. Evans and others spoke, but, beyond exhorting the government to settle the dispute, scant sympathy was shown towards the miners' demands.[3] The Penrhyn Quarry dispute, however,

[1] *Cambria Daily Leader*, 29 Jan. 1906.
[2] *Y Geninen*, Oct. 1909, p. 261. Also see 'Gwerinwr', 'Eglwysi Cymru a Phlaid Lafur', *Geninen*, Oct. 1910, pp. 258–60. Also see the comments of the *Commission of Enquiry into Industrial Unrest: No. 7 Division. Report of the Commissioners for Wales, including Monmouthshire*, 1917 (Cd. 8668), pp. 15 ff.
[3] *Parl. Deb.*, 4th ser., vol. lx, pp. 44 ff.

affords an interesting contrast. The two great strikes of 1896–8 and 1900–3, fundamentally provoked by Lord Penrhyn's refusal to recognize the Quarrymen's Committee, aroused immediate interest and sympathy. For this was the kind of issue that the Welsh members thoroughly understood.[1] Bryn Roberts and Lloyd George were active in defending the suspended quarrymen and demanded wide powers of state intervention. Here was a small community of 10,000 which was, and remains today, intensely religious and closely knit, ranged against a great autocratic landowner, who refused equally to grant the workmen a minimum wage or to grant them chapel leases. The motions moved by William Jones and Asquith in 1897 and 1903 revealed an instinctive and sympathetic appreciation of the small, chapel-going rural community fighting for its status.[2] The *Daily Chronicle* vied with the *Labour Leader* in collecting funds for the strikers. But the broader question of the class struggle in an industrial society found no such response.

At this early stage, Socialism still seemed an alien growth in Wales: the very word *Sosialaeth* had an imported ring—*Cymdeithasaeth* would have been less alien.[3] Its assaults on the 'gloomy, narrow and unaesthetic religion of Wales' seemed to threaten the very fabric of Welsh life.[4] But the new movement spread as it adapted itself to the temper and mystique of Wales, and soon found indigenous roots. Hardie regarded the Welsh as temperamentally sympathetic to Socialism, as did Michael Davitt who campaigned for him at Merthyr Tydfil in 1906. Nowhere was the class division more marked than in Wales, with most of the land owned by a nexus of anglicized churchmen. Nowhere were the teachings of Henry George more applicable. Tom Ellis himself had noted the Welsh tradition of ' *Cyfraith, Cyfar,*

---

[1] The basic issue was that Lord Penrhyn refused to recognize the Quarrymen's Committee, which demanded a 4s. 6d. daily minimum wage and protested against the subletting of portions of the quarry to contractors (and thus to unskilled labourers). On 28 Sept. 1896 he suspended seventy-one men and refused both government arbitration and the proposed terms of Sir Edward Clarke in 1903. See *North Wales Clarion,* 31 Oct. 1896; *South Wales Daily News,* 22 Nov. 1900; *Y Genedl,* 4 Dec. 1900 and following issues; *Penrhyn Quarry* (1903), a pamphlet published privately in April 1903 by Lord Penrhyn. Also W. J. Williams to Sydney Webb, 27 Feb. 1894 (Webb T.U. Collection, section A, vol. xxviii, ff. 283–4). W. J. Williams was the secretary of the North Wales Quarrymen's Union, which was formed in 1874, and absorbed only recently into the Transport and General Workers' Union. There is also a good deal of material on trade unionism in the slate quarries in the W. J. Parry Papers in the National Library of Wales. Parry's tract, *The Penrhyn Lock-out* (1901), cost him £500 in damages. (See N.L.W., MSS. 8733–67.)

[2] *Parl. Deb.,* 4th ser., vol. xlv, pp. 691 ff.; vol. cxxi, pp. 482 ff.

[3] Edward Foulkes, 'Sosialaeth', *Y Geninen,* Jan. 1908, p. 21.

[4] *Labour Leader,* 6 Jan. 1905.

Cyfnawdd, Cymorthau and *Cymanfaoedd'*, the tradition of social co-operation from Robert Owen to R. J. Derfel.[1] Soon Socialism was acquiring Welsh characteristics. The poetry of R. J. Derfel was infused equally by the rights of labour and by Welsh patriotism. *Llais Llafur*, firmly rooted in the village industry of the Swansea valley, began to oust *Tarian y Gweithiwr* in the coalfield. Several nonconformist ministers, Dr. Pan Jones, Rev. J. Nicholas, Tonypandy, Rev. T. Nicholas, Glais, among them, sought to unite 'the red dragon and the red flag'. In the 'Mecca of nonconformity', Swansea, Dr. 'Gomer' Lewis swung his mighty influence behind the Labour cause. 'Who was their Saviour but a Labour man?'[2] A few vestries were gradually opened to Labour spokesmen, and even the radical Socialist, C. B. Stanton, was quick to deprecate attacks by members of the Aberdare Trades Council on the nonconformist clergy.[3] Keir Hardie himself always showed a sensitive appreciation for Welsh sentiment, even to the extent of attending the *eisteddfod* and learning the Welsh national anthem.[4] He co-operated with his colleagues in sponsoring Welsh disestablishment and advocated Welsh home rule on Socialist grounds. He maintained that the Labour Party alone was truly nationalist for it alone wanted the land of Wales to belong to the people of Wales. Able young Welshmen such as Silyn Roberts, the pioneer of workers' education in North Wales, followed his lead. The success of Labour spokesmen in harmonizing their programme with the national self-consciousness of Wales goes far towards explaining their success in the subsequent general election.

(iv) *The General Election of 1906*

On 4 December 1905 the Liberal and Labour parties were afforded an unexpected and decisive opportunity. Hoping to profit from Liberal dissension after Rosebery's recent speech at Bodmin, Balfour suddenly resigned, and Campbell-Bannerman headed the new Liberal administration. There was much speculation in Wales as to its representation in the new ministry. A few sentimentalists may have imagined that Lloyd George would become Minister for Wales,[5] but

---

[1] *Addresses and Speeches*, p. 22.
[2] T. E. Nicholas, 'Y Ddraig Goch a'r Faner Goch', *Y Geninen*, Jan. 1912. Speech by Dr. 'Gomer' Lewis at Gorseinon (*South Wales Daily News*, 22 Jan. 1906).
[3] *Merthyr Express*, 11 June 1904.
[4] David Lowe, *From Pit to Parliament: the early life of Keir Hardie* (London, 1923), p. 187.
[5] As stated in J. Hugh Edwards, *From Village Green to Downing Street: the Life of Rt. Hon. D. Lloyd George* (London, 1908), p. 139.

it was generally anticipated that he would receive an office commensurate with the great part he had played in the Liberal revival since 1900. His appointment as President of the Board of Trade, and that of Herbert Lewis as junior Whip, brought general satisfaction to all parties in Wales, as an impressive testimony to the growing prominence of Wales in political life.

In January the general election duly followed, and nowhere was revulsion against the late Unionist government more marked than in Wales. A series of issues combined to produce a cataclysmic rout for the Unionist Party, which was defeated in every contest.

In 1906 Welsh politics followed far more closely than in previous years the course of events in Britain as a whole. Thus, the leading question in the election, the tariff reform campaign begun by Joseph Chamberlain and the play made by Liberals with the 'small loaf' that protection would bring, had great effect in Wales as elsewhere. Wales was a stronghold of free trade. The rural areas had remained faithful to orthodox economics despite the agricultural depression, although 'fair trade' Unionists had made headway in some border constituencies in 1895.[1] While it was admitted that the imports of foreign produce were the major source of depression, the Land Commissioners of 1896 had declared firmly against tariffs.[2] Conditions on the land thereafter began to improve. In 1897 a popular Unionist protectionist, the Hon. G. T. Kenyon, was heavily defeated in the East Denbigh by-election, and generally Unionist candidates in 1906 show extreme caution in dealing with the issue of food taxes. In the industrial South there had been immense industrial expansion under free trade, particularly since 1850, while the large urban centres were strongholds of classical economic orthodoxy. In Cardiff and Swansea, the local chambers of commerce had a strong Liberal leaven. The Cardiff body in particular, of which D. A. Thomas was for years the president, was deeply wedded to the free trade of 'finance imperialism': to the shipping community and those mercantile interests which throve on insurance on freights, dividends and discounts on foreign loans, and the export of capital, protection represented a direct threat to their primacy in the financial markets of the world. The South Wales chambers of commerce vied with the Miners' Federation in their denunciation of Hicks-Beach's export duty on coal in

<hr>

[1] Notably in Montgomeryshire and Flintshire. See Samuel Smith, *My Life Work*, pp. 334 ff.
[2] *Report*, p. 846.

1901 as a menace to coal exports.[1] Chamberlain, therefore, made only
a brief incursion into South Wales during his tariff reform campaign.
In speeches at Cardiff (20 November) and Newport (21 November)
in 1903, he dwelt on the depression in the steel and tinplate industries
and the need for retaliatory tariffs to prevent dumping. Lysaght's of
Newport had, he stated, imported 50,000 tons of steel in 1902. But
he was careful to make little allusion tō the coal trade, and he made
comparatively slight impression. He was followed in successive weeks
by Campbell-Bannerman, Churchill, Harcourt, and finally Asquith.
Although Chamberlain won over the Cardiff member, Sir Edward
Reed, to the cause of imperial preference, at the general election of
1906 the Unionist candidate, Sir Fortescue Flannery, a northern
industrialist, was heavily defeated by the Hon. Ivor Guest, himself
a recent convert to Liberalism.

In one Welsh industry, the effect of overseas protection was very
marked. Tinplate had been virtually a Welsh monopoly, and the
McKinley tariff in the United States in 1891 had a grave effect in
Wales. Of 500 mills at work in 1891, only 261 were working in 1896,
while the labour force contracted from 25,000 men to 16,000 over the
same period.[2] But subsequently the tinplate industry revived markedly.
Other markets were found in the colonies and South America, home
consumption increased, and there was much re-export to the United
States. The petroleum industry absorbed much of the tin lost to the
canning industry, and by 1900 there were again 412 mills at work.
The labour force rose steadily to 29,000 by 1913, while a new conciliation board in 1905 largely removed the causes of friction over
wages that had embittered industrial relations in the industry over
the past quarter of a century. One prominent tinplate owner, Sir
John Jones Jenkins, rejoined the Liberal Party he had left in 1886 in
view of Chamberlain's attacks on the tinplate industry, the prosperity
of which, he maintained, rested on the free importation of foodstuffs.

In other Welsh industries, the effect of foreign tariffs was much less
clear. Chamberlain made play with the 'dumping' of foreign steel in
South Wales: in 1903, he said, 250,000 tons would find their way into
the country. The United States and Germany had both overhauled

[1] *South Wales Daily News*, 20 Apr. 1901.
[2] Articles by Sir J. J. Jenkins in *South Wales Daily News*, 20 Nov. 1901, 9 Jan. 1906.
Llewelyn Williams, 'The Tinplate Industry', *British Industries under Free Trade* (ed.
Harold Cox), London, 1903, pp. 163 ff. Minchinton, op. cit., pp. 108 ff.; P. S. Thomas,
op. cit., pp. 80 ff.

Britain in steel production by 1902. But total British production was still rising steadily, reaching 4,850,000 tons in 1902, and after the conclusion of the Russo-Japanese War in 1905 British trade began to revive. The Welsh shipping industry had grown prosperous under free trade and Chamberlain's jeremiads, which warned of the 1,700,000 increased tonnage of foreign shipping, caused little alarm. On one major subject, coal, Chamberlain had significantly little to say. Coal exports had continued to rise impressively, reaching nearly 50,000,000 tons f.o.b.[1] in 1905. Half of this had been exported from Welsh ports. Industrialists such as D. A. Thomas and trade union leaders such as Mabon averred that free trade, by providing cheap fuel, made the best use of the geographical and economic advantages of South Wales.

Thus the onslaught on the free trade system was one major factor in the Liberal triumph in Wales. The other issues that preceded the election have already been examined. In particular, the outcry against the Balfour Education Act gave immense impetus to Welsh Liberalism. If the election of 1906 was first a triumph for the apostles of free trade, it was next the greatest nonconformist triumph since the days of Cromwell. In Wales, nonconformist ministers toured the land, breathing life into traditional issues. Disestablishment, the fundamental demand, was not as prominent as in the past: barely half the thirty-two Liberal candidates refer to it in their election addresses. On the other hand, Sir Alfred Thomas, chairman of the Welsh Party, with unwonted initiative, declared in August 1905 that he could not support any government that did not put Welsh disestablishment prominently on its programme.[2] In the face of this somewhat unreal threat, Campbell-Bannerman gave a rather indefinite pledge of future action. At a national convention at Caernarvon on 2 January 1906 Lloyd George and several of his colleagues dwelt on the vital place of disestablishment among proposed Liberal legislation.[3] In addition, the disestablishment of the Church in France by the Rouvier ministry in December 1905 was a tremendous stimulus to all who favoured the separation of church and state. It is clear, therefore, that the issue was prominent during the campaign.

[1] Halevy, op. cit., vol. v, p. 341. See D. A. Thomas's article in Harold Cox (ed.), *British Industries under Free Trade* (1903), pp. 348 ff.

[2] *South Wales Daily News*, 30 Aug. 1905; *Glamorgan Free Press*, 18 Nov. 1905.

[3] This meeting was postponed for five days to accommodate one of Evan Roberts's revivalist meetings in the town.

The nonconformist cause had been provided with an immense and fortuitous inspiration by the religious revival which had been convulsing Wales for the past fifteen months. In October 1904 a young ex-miner, Evan Roberts, launched a revivalist movement at Loughor, near Llanelly, and it soon grew to massive proportions.[1] Throughout 1905, a rekindled religious fervour swept like a torrent throughout Wales. Chapel membership mounted rapidly: significantly, the increase was most marked in the Baptist denomination, whose religious attitude was, perhaps, least curbed by ecclesiastical formalism.[2] Temperance made spectacular headway in industrial areas. Even anglicized regions such as the Gower peninsula were engulfed by the new passions.[3] The 1904 revival has usually been regarded as a movement that distracted attention away from public affairs, and it is the spiritual impact of the revival in providing countless individuals with a new self-discipline and a sense of beauty which is most immediately apparent. Nevertheless, it would be superficial to ignore the profound political effect of the resurgence of nonconformity at this decisive moment. For ten years the statistics of the nonconformist bodies, which Welsh Liberals had watched as anxiously as industrial prices, had shown only sluggish progress. In ten years from 1893 to 1903 the four main bodies had increased their membership by only 66,000 and indeed in recent years there was evidence even of an absolute decline. The claim of nonconformity to represent the overwhelming mass of the Welsh people seemed increasingly doubtful. Now, nonconformist membership leaped ahead, increasing by a further 82,000 in the next two years alone, reaching 550,280 communicants for all denominations by 1905, at a time when the established Church was patently aloof from the new messianism.[4] This striking advance in Welsh nonconformity gave profound impetus to the later stages of the campaign

[1] See W. T. Stead, *The Revival of the West* (London, 1905). Spectacular accounts of the effects of the revival are given at length in all Welsh newspapers at this time. R. H. Heindel points out that the Welsh revival had been preceded by the Torrey–Alexander mission (*The American Impact on Great Britain, 1898–1914*, University of Pennsylvania, 1940, p. 370). See also Wyn Griffith, *Spring of Youth* (London, 1935), pp. 111 ff.

[2] The Baptists' total of communicants rose from 116,310 in 1903 to 143,835 in 1905. The total for the four major nonconformist denominations rose from 447,625 to 530,410 in the same period (*Royal Commission on the Church and other Religious Bodies in Wales*, Memorandum to *Report*, 1910, p. 133). The Baptists' total fell away almost as rapidly after 1905, declining to 127,226 in 1913.

[3] Cf. *Mumbles Weekly Press and Gower News*, 23 Dec. 1904 and 6 Jan. 1905, for the convulsive events in Mumbles.

[4] *Royal Commission, Report*, p. 20. Also see *Evidence*, vol. iv, Cd. 5435, qu. 48,498 (Bishop of Bangor's evidence).

against the Education Act of 1902. It required a sophisticated audience indeed to distinguish between the nonconformist minister as revivalist and as sectarian politician. It was noted in the press how frequently meetings directed against the Balfour Education Act would be transformed with a religious passion: *Marchog Iesu yn llwyddiannus*, the battle-hymn of the revival, rang out from many a Liberal platform. Lloyd George drove the connexion home. In the 'higher atmosphere' produced by the revival, the Welsh people would repel the attempt to enforce dogma through the county court. 'It was 1859 which made 1868 possible, and it was 1904–5 that would ·make the triumph of 1905–6 an accomplished fact in the history of the Welsh people.'[1] To Lloyd George, the lesson of the revival was not merely the need for temperance, but also for the Liberal programme of local option. He struck up a warm personal friendship with Evan Roberts himself, who stayed with Lloyd George at his home in Criccieth.[2] Dr. Clifford asserted openly his belief that the revival was the spiritual offspring of the 'Welsh Revolt': 'you cannot touch men in their consciences without affecting their whole religious life.'[3] The revival of 1904, the last in Welsh history, remained local to Wales: in spite of the enthusiasm of W. T. Stead, it made little penetration into England. Even in Wales, its effects proved much more ephemeral than in previous revivals: already by 1906 there were complaints in the Rhondda that the old laxity was returning and that drunkenness and sin in all its aspects were again disfiguring life in the valleys.[4] But, in the limited perspective of the 1906 election, this unexpected spiritual upheaval fundamentally reinforced the Liberal cause, and the nonconformist churches which gave it life.

In a variety of ways, Wales on the eve of the 1906 election presented a spectacle of national fulfilment, far removed from the disillusioned fatalism of 1895. There was Lloyd George in the cabinet, the first native Welshman to be so honoured. An old ambition had recently been attained in the passage of legislation to provide for a national Welsh Library and Museum,[5] even though Rendel sourly considered that 'this National Museum business is a friendly lift by

[1] *South Wales Daily News*, 3 May 1905.
[2] Mrs. Lloyd George to Mrs. D. R. Daniel, 12 Sept. 1905 (N.L.W., Daniel MSS., no. 2850), in which Mrs. Lloyd George boasts of having met Evan Roberts.
[3] *Cardiff Times*, 21 Oct. 1905.
[4] *South Wales Daily News*, 8 Feb. 1906.
[5] Much the best account of this movement is Thomas Parry's chapter in K. Idwal Jones (ed.), *Syr Herbert Lewis*. Rendel to Principal T. F. Roberts, 14 June 1905 (Penucha MSS.).

the Govt. to Welsh Tories in view of the General Election'. Even in the field of sport events conspired to lend national sentiment a new vitality when in December 1905 the Welsh rugby team gained a famous triumph over the all-conquering New Zealanders.[1] On a variety of levels, sentimental and profound, there was a new excitement and hope surging throughout rural and industrial Wales.

The effect in the general election of January 1906 was dramatic indeed. Nowhere was the national revulsion against the late Unionist ministry more pronounced than in Wales, where Liberal or Labour candidates carried all thirty-four seats. Allowing for unopposed returns, it was calculated by political statisticians that Liberal and Labour candidates polled 200,063 votes against the Unionists' 111,093, a proportion of 64:36.[2] All Unionist seats were regained. Guest triumphed in Cardiff by the record margin of over 3,000.[3] Colonel Ivor Herbert, a Roman Catholic landowner, captured South Monmouthshire for the first time, thus terminating the almost continuous tenure of the Morgans of Tredegar since 1659. Denbigh District, Monmouth District, and Montgomery District were other Liberal gains. In South Glamorgan the miners' representative, Brace, swept out the sitting member, Wyndham-Quin, by over 4,000. Labour had indeed cause to be grateful to the magnanimity of Herbert Gladstone in 1903. Three other miners' candidates were elected, Abraham, Tom Richards, both guaranteed a clear run by Gladstone, and John Williams, returned for Gower.[4] In the last constituency, a significant breach between the Gower Liberal Association and the Miners' Federation candidate saw Williams gain a decisive victory over a popular young tinplate employer.[5] In Merthyr Tydfil, Keir Hardie, the only successful L.R.C. candidate, narrowly defeated an unofficial last-minute candidate, Henry Radcliffe, a Methodist shipowner. It was notable that D. A. Thomas still dominated here,

[1] On 16 Dec. 1905 Wales defeated New Zealand, 3—0. See the effusive remarks of T. Watts-Dunton in the 1906 edition of Borrow's *Wild Wales*, pp. xxii–xxiii.

[2] *South Wales Daily News*, 29 Jan. 1910.

[3] This in spite of (or perhaps because of) the vitriolic criticism of D. A. Thomas who queried the sincerity of Guest's Liberalism, with good reason (*South Wales Daily News*, 2, 31 May 1904). Guest's victory was the more notable in view of the recent disaffection of many Irish voters over the Education Act, which had cost the Liberals control of Cardiff Council in the 1904 elections (*South Wales Daily News*, 1, 2 Nov. 1904).

[4] Notes by Herbert Gladstone, 1905 (B.M., Add. MSS., 46107, f. 60).

[5] I have described this election in 'The Gower Election of 1906', *Gower*, xii (1959); the most striking feature of the election was the confusion and acrimony of the Liberals of the constituency, contrasted with the careful preparation made by Labour since 1903.

polling 77 per cent. of the votes cast.[1] In Swansea District, pressure by the local education authority prevented a Labour candidature.[2] A curious episode of another kind took place in Montgomeryshire, where David Davies, the young squire of Llandinam and heir to the patrimony of the Ocean Collieries, was returned unopposed as a highly dubious Liberal, receiving the endorsement of both parties![3] In all, thirteen Liberal or Labour candidates were returned unopposed, while eleven others had majorities of over 2,000. Free trade and the Education Act had been the dominant features of their campaigns. The four miners' representatives also adopted a Liberal, and, indeed, nationalist, position. Brace described himself as a 'whole-hearted Welsh nationalist' and demanded a Welsh education council, home rule; and disestablishment. Also prominent on their platform was the necessity to repeal the notorious Taff Vale verdict and protect the status of trade unions. Keir Hardie alone adopted a Socialist standpoint: and he even advocated Welsh home rule.

In the English elections, Welsh affairs inevitably carried little weight, although a handful of Unionists, Balfour included, stressed the dangers of Welsh disestablishment.[4] Hart-Dyke at Dartford referred retrospectively to the Intermediate Education Act whose passage he had encouraged back in 1889.

There was much speculation in Wales as to the place of Welsh affairs in the crowded Liberal programme. As before, the Welsh members derived mainly from business and the bar: Oxford, Cambridge, and London had provided their higher education rather than the Welsh university colleges, at which only two members (S. T. Evans and Ellis Griffith) had been students. On the other hand, in a House of Commons that spoke eloquently of the political effectiveness of dissent, twenty-five Welsh members out of thirty-four were nonconformist.[5] Since the marginal triumphs of 1868 the wheel had

[1] *South Wales Daily News*, 27 Jan. 1906.
[2] Note by Herbert Gladstone (B.M., Add. MSS., 46106, f. 36). The candidate was J. Littlejohns.
[3] His highly eccentric programme included support for preferential tariffs, disestablishment and public control of education, together with opposition to Irish home rule. His father and grandfather had both been Liberal Unionists.
[4] Among others are L. Worthington-Evans (Colchester), A. Akers Douglas (Kent, St. Augustine's), and Lord Dunsany (W. Wiltshire).
[5] The *Free Church Year Book* for 1906, pp. 306–11, stated that 193 government supporters were nonconformists, in addition to 13 Scots Presbyterians or Unitarians, and about 7 Unionist nonconformists. The Welsh members consisted of 7 Methodists; 9 Congregationalists or Independents; 6 Baptists; 1 Wesleyan; 1 Presbyterian; and 1 nonconformist of dubious allegiance (D. A. Thomas), together with 8 Anglicans and 1 Roman Catholic.

come full circle. Intermittently over half a century the Welsh radicals had striven incessantly to force their programme upon the political parties, with only sporadic legislative success. If they failed now, with a unanimous representation, with a cabinet almost entirely from the Celtic countries, with the hero of Welsh nonconformity himself at the Board of Trade, flanked by such proven allies as Asquith and Morley, then it would be hard indeed for the heirs of the tradition of Thomas Charles, Henry Richard, añd Thomas Gee to repel the surging forces of working-class democracy. Those Socialists that Keir Hardie found among the cloisters of the theological colleges of Bala and Aberystwyth[1] might well impel the next generation into nationalism of a far more revolutionary nature.

[1] D. Lowe, op. cit., p. 108.

VI

THE LAST PHASE OF RADICALISM
1906–1914

In the eyes of radicals everywhere, the Liberal triumph at the polls seemed to usher in a new age of democracy and social advance. Nowhere were expectations higher than in Wales, with its unbroken array of Liberal and Labour representatives. But it was apparent that the situation was very different from that of 1892, the last occasion of a Liberal majority. Then, the very insecurity of the ministry had given prominence to the activities of the Welsh Party and thrown the Party's confusions into clearer relief. In 1906, however, the magnitude of the Liberal victory inevitably forced the interests of the small band of Welsh members into the background. As usual, Arthur Price was ready with a gloomy prognostication: 'in spite of the great apparent triumph, Welsh Liberalism is really doomed'.[1] Some Liberal journalists pointed hopefully to the fact that the phalanx of thirty-four had potential reinforcements in those members for English constituencies who were of Welsh birth. Over a dozen in number, they included such stalwarts of *Cymru Fydd* as Leif Jones (Appleby), George Hay Morgan (Truro), and Timothy Davies (Fulham), the last being an intimate of Lloyd George.[2] But it was beyond dispute that, in common with the eighty-four Irish Nationalists, the Welsh members must reconcile themselves to the prior passage of measures of general, rather than of local interest. In the debate on the Address, Ellis Griffith acknowledged that the King's Speech was compelled to deal with wider issues, such as education, unemployment, and the status of trade unions, in view of the arrears of legislation that formed the legacy of the Unionist government.[3] For several years after 1906, therefore, the distinctive problems of Wales occupied a modest place in political debate.

---

[1] Price to Daniel, 24 Jan. 1906 (N.L.W., Daniel Papers, 2150).
[2] Others included Col. Ivor Philipps (Southampton), W. H. Davies (Bristol), John Jenkins (Chatham), John Simon (Walthamstow), Richard Bell (Derby), Donald Maclean (Bath), L. Atherley-Jones (N.W. Durham).
[3] *Parl. Deb.*, 4th ser., vol. clii, p. 238.

(i) *The End of the Education Question*

Some of the measures proposed by the Campbell-Bannerman government, however, had a vital relevance for Wales. In particular, a settlement of the education controversy was essential after the bitter tension of the 'Welsh Revolt'. The general election had provided an incontestable mandate for the new government to amend Balfour's Act of 1902, and it was inevitable that this should be the first item on the ministerial programme.

The new Education Bill, introduced by Augustine Birrell in the Commons on 9 April 1906, bore the clear imprint of the nonconformist protest, even though Morant had laboured to reconcile it with the system laid down by Balfour's Act. A deputation from the Welsh National Liberal Council, led by Alderman T. J. Hughes, had seen Birrell on 29 March and impressed on him Welsh hostility to religious tests on teachers and to any denominational 'right of entry' in elementary schools.[1] A more notable influence, however, had come from a conference in Cardiff on 23 March, called by Lloyd George to discuss the establishment of a national council to co-ordinate the various levels of Welsh education. Under the Balfour government, Anson had proposed a joint committee of local authorities in 1903. The more revolutionary proposal of a national council for Wales had come from Lloyd George in a speech before the Cardiff Cymmrodorion Society on 3 March, and he succeeded in persuading the Bishops of St. Asaph, Llandaff, and St. David's, and the Roman Catholic Bishop of Menevia to attend, despite the protests of the Cardiff Liberal Association. Representatives of Welsh county councils and nonconformist bodies were also present. A resolution moved by Brynmor Jones, M.P., in favour of a Welsh national council to which the powers of the Board of Education in Wales and the educational powers of the Board of Agriculture and the Central Welsh Board should be delegated, was carried overwhelmingly. Lloyd George, fresh from his triumphs in obstructing the Act of 1902, was in a most conciliatory vein, and the spectacle of apparent national inter-denominational unity was impressive.[2] But it later became evident that Lloyd George had greatly exaggerated the degree of agreement reached. The Church representatives had consented to

---

[1] *South Wales Daily News*, 30 Mar. 1906; Walter H. Hughes to Edward Thomas, 28 Mar. 1906 (Cardiff, Cochfarf Papers). Hughes observes, 'English Free Churchmen are really leaning on us in Wales'.

[2] Ibid., 24 Mar. 1906.

a council only in very general terms, and were most reluctant to endorse any concrete proposal. Conversely, a nonconformist such as Professor Edward Anwyl of Aberystwyth saw in a national council a means of strengthening the Central Board at the expense of the University Court 'where the Church and Tory element is much more powerful' (*lle mae'r elfen eglwysig a Thoriaidd yn llawer iawn cryfach*).[1] It required far more than Lloyd George's diplomatic finesse to eradicate the reality of denominational hostility in Wales.

Birrell's Bill largely fulfilled nonconformist expectations.[2] All public elementary schools would be controlled by the local authority. Teachers would not be compelled to provide religious instruction, while only undenominational teaching of the 'Cowper-Temple' variety would be given during school hours in schools under public control, although 'extended facilities' for denominational teaching were to be allowed in certain transferred voluntary schools. In addition, Part IV of the Bill proposed a council for Wales with representatives from county and county borough councils and from urban district councils. This portion of the Bill, which clearly owed its origin to the President of the Board of Trade, was in response to the clear unanimity of the Welsh members, Birrell stated, and Sir Alfred Thomas, on their behalf, gave grateful acknowledgement. The *South Wales Daily News* joyfully proclaimed that it established Welsh home rule in education.[3]

It at once became apparent that there was scant prospect of unanimity over these proposals. The general lines of the Bill were bitterly denounced by churchmen for their threat to denominational teaching. Archbishop Davidson and Bishop Knox of Manchester led the counter-attack, but the Bishops of St. David's and St. Asaph were no less belligerent. To them, the council for Wales was as obnoxious as the rest of the Bill. It would inevitably be dominated by the Welsh councils, every one with a radical majority, whose recent behaviour in the 'Revolt' had aroused earnest clerical apprehension. Anson pointed out that the large majority of Welsh Unionists were totally unrepresented in the Commons, even though they had polled over 110,000 votes, and thus their opinions would be disregarded. The second national conference called by Lloyd George, which met at Llandrindod Wells on 1 June, was therefore very different in composition from that of Cardiff. It consisted almost

[1] Anwyl to T. Huws Davies, 10 Feb. 1906 (N.L.W., Huws Davies MSS., 16,354c).
[2] *Parl. Deb.*, 4th ser., vol. clv, pp. 1017 ff. Cf. Sacks, op. cit., pp. 62 ff.
[3] *South Wales Daily News*, 12 Apr. 1906.

entirely of Liberal and nonconformist spokesmen. As on other occasions, strong controversy broke out between the representatives of Glamorgan and Monmouthshire and those from the rest of Wales over the respective proportions of representatives on the council. Although Lloyd George shrewdly made P. P. Pennant, one of the very few Unionists present, chairman of the conference, he could not conceal the fact that the prospect of agreement in Wales was quite illusory.[1]

The attitude of the Unionist Party was made plain when the Bill came up for its Second Reading on 7 May. George Wyndham (Dover) and Lord Castlereagh (Maidstone), the latter a scion of the Vane-Tempest family of Machynlleth, condemned the proposal to hand over Church Schools to county councils which had been persecuting them for many years and which were sworn enemies of the establishment. Balfour objected on the grounds that it would lead to an incipient home rule for Wales. For the government, Lloyd George, in addition to making a strong defence of undenominational education as a solution for the difficulties of 'single-school areas', devoted a major part of his speech to justifying the proposed Welsh council, which, he claimed, was strongly advocated by the Unionists of Wales. The Bill was given a Second Reading by 410 votes to 204, the Welsh members being unanimous in its favour.[2]

From the first, several aspects of the Bill evoked strong criticism. The old division over secular instruction re-emerged on 28 May, when an amendment to create an entirely secular system of instruction was supported by eight Welsh members of various denominations, but it received a mere sixty-three votes. The Welsh council was early on made a target of attack in Committee. On 21 May Stuart-Wortley (Sheffield, Hallam) moved an Instruction to report Part IV as a separate measure. He expressed great alarm at a local authority being created without responsibility to Parliament. On the other hand, Redmond, for the Irish members, who were generally hostile to Birrell's measure, ardently welcomed the council as a stage towards devolution for his fellow Celts, and the Instruction was overwhelmingly rejected. A similar motion moved by W. C. Bridgeman (Oswestry) on 18 June, and supported by F. E. Smith, Anson, Long, and Lord Robert Cecil, mustered a mere eighty-one votes.[3]

---

[1] Ibid., 2 June 1906. Cf. *Church Times*, 8 June 1906.
[2] *Parl. Deb.*, 4th ser., vol. clvi, pp. 1014 ff.
[3] Ibid., vol. clvii, pp. 461 ff.; ibid., vol. clviii, pp. 1496 ff.

But, although the government were firm in support of the general principle of a national council, it was evident that they had devoted insufficient thought towards the machinery for its creation. They adopted a bewildering variety of expedients. On 17 July the original scheme for a separate national council, as laid down in Clause 37 of Birrell's Bill, was pungently criticized by F. E. Smith (Liverpool, Walton), who suggested the substitution of a consultative committee for whose actions the President of the Board of Education would be responsible to Parliament. Lloyd George, in a most conciliatory reply, suddenly proposed instead a special minister with financial and supervisory powers. Later in the debate, Lloyd George moved an amendment which, he claimed, contained the substance of Smith's demand, that a member of Parliament 'whether holding office or not' should be responsible to Parliament for the actions of the council. This unorthodox constitutional procedure was effectively criticized by Wyndham, Balfour, Cecil, and Carson.[1] Their passion for constitutional propriety was, doubtless, exaggerated, but the status and functions of the new minister were extremely vague, despite the government's appearance of willingness to conciliate. Lloyd George confessed to Campbell-Bannerman that the decision to create the new minister had been agreed hurriedly between himself, Birrell, and Asquith, without reference to the Prime Minister. He was at pains to reassure the King that the new post would entail neither the establishment of a new department nor any additional expenditure.[2] On 23 July the ephemeral minister disappeared as rapidly as he had emerged, Birrell now proposing to make the council responsible solely to the treasury, with a public audit of accounts. On this occasion, the Irish members voted against the government, the amendment being carried by 133 votes.[3] In this modified form, the Welsh council, as clause 26, was incorporated in the Bill which eventually passed its Third Reading on 30 July, by 369 to 177, the twenty-eight Welsh members present all voting in support. Lloyd George demonstrated that the five main requests of the Opposition concerning the Welsh council, including parliamentary control, a public audit, and the reservation of religious questions to the Board of Education, had all been conceded. Nevertheless, the handling of the matter by the government had lacked sure direction, which a surface geniality could

[1] *Parl. Deb.*, 4th ser., vol. clxi, p. 41 ff.
[2] Lloyd George to Campbell-Bannerman, 19 July 1906 (B.M., Add. MSS., 41239, f.96).
[3] *Parl. Deb.*, 4th ser., vol. clxi, pp. 741 ff.

not conceal, and it was increasingly difficult to take seriously the projected council for Wales.

The Bill faced its inevitable nemesis in the Lords. Lansdowne had intransigently refused Archbishop Randall Davidson's suggestions for a compromise. Never was the anomalous relationship of the two Houses more obvious. The Bill, passed by a huge majority in the Commons and with an unquestioned popular mandate behind it, found a mere handful of supporters in the Upper House. Crewe, the Lord President, had to undertake the defence almost alone, with little assistance from his colleagues.[1] The transformed Welsh council was scarcely likely to escape the holocaust. In the Second Reading in the Lords, Bishop Edwards of St. Asaph showed how slight was agreement over the council in Wales itself. Earl Cawdor, for many years a Welsh member as Viscount Emlyn, attacked the analogies drawn between the council and the Central Welsh Board, whose function was purely consultative. The entire scheme was, he alleged, 'one step further in the direction of Home Rule for Wales'.[2]

Amid the general destruction of Birrell's measure, the Welsh council was included. On 21 November Cawdor moved that it be omitted from the Bill. It would hand over voluntary schools to those who had robbed them, without the safeguard of control by the Board of Education. He was supported by another Welsh landowner, the Marquis of Londonderry, who upheld the position of Church Schools in the most inflexible manner and claimed that the Welsh council was but one latent stage on the road to disestablishment. The Bishop of St. David's denied that there was that unanimity in Wales claimed by Lloyd George and Birrell. On the Liberal side, a defence of national devolution came from Rendel (in a long-delayed maiden speech) and the Liberal Bishop of Hereford, but the amendment was carried by 109 to 44, the Bishops of St. David's and Bangor voting in the majority.[3] The eventual return of the Bill to the Commons in a totally distorted form provoked immense Liberal bitterness. The issue between the Upper and Lower Houses, between 'the Peers and the People', seemed clear-cut. On 10 December Birrell moved the rejection of the Lords' amendments en bloc, and this was carried by 416 to 107, three Welsh members, Col. Ivor Herbert, Tom Richards, and Herbert Roberts, strongly attacking the

[1] G. K. A. Bell, *Randall Davidson, Archbishop of Canterbury* (London, 1935), vol. i, p. 523.
[2] *Parl. Deb.*, 4th ser., vol. clxii, p. 1287.
[3] Ibid., vol. clxv, pp. 779 ff.

Lords for rejecting the Welsh council.[1] A final attempt at compromise by Archbishop Davidson was turned down by Balfour and Lansdowne; the Lords insisted on their amendments and on 20 December Campbell-Bannerman, in solemn tones, announced the withdrawal of the Education Bill. This marked the demise of any possible settlement over elementary education in general, and of a Welsh council in particular. Few mourned the 'rapid extinction of this half-baked project', said Balfour.[2] But Welsh journals bore the headlines, 'Welsh nation flouted by the Peers'.[3]

As a consolation, the government brought forward the moderate scheme for a Welsh department in the Board of Education in February 1907. A. T. Davies, a solicitor, was appointed permanent secretary, with the distinguished scholar, Owen M. Edwards, as chief inspector of schools. Even this mild proposal provoked party acrimony, particularly since Birrell had now been succeeded at the Board of Education by Reginald McKenna, a Welsh member. In the debate on the civil estimates in March, Lord Robert Cecil indulged in passionate attacks on the constitutional dangers involved, alleging the existence of a conspiracy between McKenna, Lloyd George, and the new officials, to destroy Church Schools. He professed the greatest suspicion of the new appointments. Owen Edwards, a Methodist, was former Liberal member for Merioneth (1899–1900), while Davies had not only been prominent in the 'Revolt' on the Denbighshire County Council but had even been at one time election agent for Herbert Lewis and Lloyd George.[4] Y Faner denounced Cecil's 'shabby' conduct.[5] Undeterred, Cecil returned to the theme in the debate on the Address in 1908, even implying financial collusion between A. T. Davies and McKenna, but his charges carried little conviction.[6]

Although ardently welcomed by the Welsh press, the new department carried few dangers of separatism. It failed to capture the imagination of patriotic Welshmen, who complained that it was failing in its duty to stimulate instruction in Welsh culture and the Welsh language. The department was to fight a long and largely inconclusive battle with the Central Welsh Board, to their mutual detri-

---

[1] *Parl. Deb.*, 4th ser., vol. clxvii, pp. 214 ff.   [2] Ibid., pp. 1735 ff.
[3] *South Wales Daily News*, 23 Nov. 1906.
[4] *Parl. Deb.*, 4th ser., vol. clxxi, pp. 95 ff. Cf. A. T. Davies, op. cit., pp. 51 ff. Also see T. Rees, 'Bwrdd Addysg Newydd Cymru', *Y Geninen*, July 1907, pp. 151–5.
[5] *Baner ac Amserau Cymru*, 20 Mar. 1907.
[6] *Parl. Deb.*, 4th ser., vol. clxxxiii, pp. 897–8.

ment. As the Welsh secondary education system became more professional, the ideals of the 1880's gradually receded. Increasingly, the
educational structure came to acquire an alien and anglicized character, out of harmony with nationalist sentiment and serving only to
accentuate the disenchantment felt towards the institutions created
by the national movement.[1]

After 1906 the education question, even in Wales, receded from
the forefront of politics. Successive attempts at a settlement proved
inconclusive. After consultation with Lloyd George and McKenna
in March 1908, the Bishop of St. Asaph, as in 1904, introduced
a compromise measure in the Lords. It was based on his previous
Bill and proposed the transference of all schools to the local authorities, with facilities for denomination instruction three days a week.
Archbishop Davidson, Crewe, and Lansdowne gave it a cautious
blessing, but the Second Reading debate was adjourned *sine die*.[2]
Meanwhile the government were themselves attempting to grapple
with the problem. On 18 May McKenna brought forward a similar
measure himself for Second Reading. It recognized only one type of
school, with increased exchequer grants to certain non-provided
schools. In debate Llewelyn Williams (Carmarthen District) advocated the secular solution, but the Welsh members eventually voted
in favour by twenty-nine to one, the one being D. A. Thomas, ever
the individualist, who had written that he thought it 'a very poor
thing'. This Bill also lapsed.[3]

After long negotiations with religious leaders, the new President
of the Board of Education, Walter Runciman, introduced yet another
Bill on 25 November, which represented a final attempt at compromise. Its complicated provisions contained the vital concession
of denominational instruction within school hours in schools publicly
controlled. There was some cross-voting here, Anson supporting the
Bill, while Balfour opposed it. Some nonconformists also opposed
the Bill, Clement Edwards (Denbigh District) pungently attacking
'right of entry'. The Second Reading was carried by 323 to 157, the
Welsh members voting twenty-three to three (Clement Edwards,
D. A. Thomas, Keir Hardie) in favour. But all hopes of success lay

---

[1] Webster, op. cit., pp. 509 ff. Beriah Evans to E. T. John, 28 July 1913 (N.L.W.,
John Papers).
[2] *Parl. Deb.*, 4th ser., vol. clxxxvii, pp. 3 ff.; Archbishop of Wales, op. cit., pp. 205 ff.
[3] *Parl. Deb.*, 4th ser., vol. clxxxviii, pp. 1676 ff. For Thomas's view, see D. A.
Thomas to ? Price, 13 Mar. 1908 (Cardiff, Cochfarf Papers). For Llewelyn Williams's
view, see *Manchester Guardian*, 22 July 1909.

in discussions outside the House. On 3 December, against the advice of Archbishop Davidson, the Representative Church Council voted against Runciman's Bill by a large majority, and it was withdrawn.[1]

The decline in the political impetus of the forces of Church and dissent alike drew public attention away from the traditional education question. Without the guidance of Lloyd George, there was scant prospect of the Welsh county councils reviving the 'Revolt' or receiving popular support for such a move. Disillusion with the aftermath of the 'Revolt' was believed to menace Liberal seats on the Montgomeryshire County Council in the 1907 elections, even in the Welsh-speaking Liberal strongholds in the western half of the county.[2] A few local authorities attempted resistance, however, even after the shock of the West Riding judgement, which Lloyd George himself deplored.[3] The Merioneth council refused to maintain Church Schools until the end of 1907, and McKenna had to consider the distasteful possibility of applying Anson's Default Act himself. On the other hand, Lloyd George, declared emphatically that if the Coercion Act were applied to Wales he would be compelled to resign, and Herbert Lewis followed his lead.[4] The crisis in Merioneth gradually dissolved. But a more serious case came in Swansea where the local authority had declined to increase the salaries of teachers in the Oxford Street school. The attitude of the government aroused the gravest suspicions. After the Board of Education's commissioner, Hamilton, had reported in 1908 that the local authority was in default, Runciman set aside his recommendation, for which he was strongly condemned in a debate on a motion moved by W. Joynson-Hicks on 11 March 1909. Even J. H. Yoxall, a Liberal and the representative of the National Union of Teachers, criticized Runciman's policy. The managers of the Church Schools took legal action and judgement was successively found in their favour by King's Bench, the Court of Appeal, and finally in April 1911 by the House of Lords. In the *Board of Education v. Rice and others*, a case notable for its recognizing the evolution of an administrative department as

---

[1] The details of these negotiations are provided in Bell, op. cit., vol. i, pp. 533 ff.; Archbishop of Wales, op. cit., pp. 208 ff.; Eluned E. Owen, op. cit., pp. 117–30.

[2] Richard Jones to William Jones, 21 Feb. 1907 (Bangor, William Jones Papers, MSS. 5470, no. 57).

[3] Lloyd George to Campbell-Bannerman, 22 Oct. 1906 (B.M., Add. MSS., 41239, f. 148). In Dec. 1906 the House of Lords pronounced the action of the West Riding County Council, who had refused to pay teachers in non-provided schools the portion of their salary remunerating them for denominational instruction, to be illegal.

[4] Herbert Lewis's Dairy, 30 June 1907 (Penucha MSS.).

a judicial tribunal and by implication justifying the growth of delegated legislation, the Lord Chancellor, Loreburn, criticized the conduct of his ministerial colleagues.[1]

The last embers of the 'Revolt' had died out and the Act of 1902 was henceforth administered legally and without friction. In practice, Welsh nonconformists found that it afforded a greater measure of public control than they had anticipated, and in fact a gradual transference of voluntary schools was taking place. In 1903 there had been 926 public 'council' schools as against 800 Church Schools: in 1913 the respective totals were 1,218 'council' schools (accommodation 421,950) as against 649 voluntary (accommodation 105,167).[2] The priest was indeed being extruded from the schools, but by less overt means than those visualized by the older generation of nonconformists.

The other major aspect of the education question in Wales, the campaign for a national council, likewise fell into obscurity. At a further conference at Shrewsbury in September 1908, a scheme drafted by Brynmor Jones and Professor Anwyl failed to gain acceptance, even when Lloyd George implied that it might prove the forerunner of a 'Minister for Wales'. A similar story was seen in further conferences in 1913 and 1914. Their endeavours were mainly of academic interest. Among the Liberals, every discussion foundered on the same rock, the balance of representation between Glamorgan and Monmouth and the rest of the country. As the disestablishment controversy was resumed after 1910, Church spokesmen were implacably hostile towards a council which Bishop Owen of St. David's averred would be inevitably partisan.[3] Thus at the outbreak of war in 1914 Welsh education remained incomplete, immune from the warfare of sects, but deficient through the dualism of its organization and its relation to the social life of Wales. As a politically contentious issue, the Welsh education system had shed all significance.

(ii) *The Church Commission*

In the field of education, the demands of Wales merged into those

---

[1] *Parl. Deb.*, 5th ser., vol. ii, pp. 525 ff. *The Times*, 7 Apr. 1911. A full account of the controversy is given in Eluned E. Owen, op. cit., pp. 109–11; also see *South Wales Evening Post*, 27 Apr. 1959 for some reminiscences. The constitutional implications are discussed in W. A. Robson, *Justice and Administrative Law* (London, 3rd ed. 1951), pp. 471–3; C. T. Carr, *Concerning English Administrative Law* (London, 1941), p. 110.

[2] *Report of the Board of Education for the year 1912–1913* (Cd. 7341), p. 93.

[3] *South Wales Daily News*, 6 Jan. 1909. Cf. E. L. Chappell, *Wake Up! Wales* (London, 1943), pp. 31–49. Edward Anwyl to William Jones, 10 Mar. 1908 (Bangor, William Jones Papers, MSS. 5475, no. 42).

of nonconformity in general. But the main channel of the national movement, into which all the traditional currents of popular feeling were canalized, remained the question of Welsh disestablishment. Although the King's Speech had made no mention of disestablishment during the 1906 session, the government could hardly avoid action of some kind, in view of the lengthy series of Liberal commitments since 1887, culminating in Campbell-Bannerman's pledge to Sir Alfred Thomas just prior to the late election that disestablishment remained an essential part of the Liberal programme. Lloyd George himself had confirmed this before a meeting of the Welsh members, and it was widely assumed that he had demanded a pledge of some kind before taking office in the new government. Even so, elementary realism forced the Welsh Party to acknowledge that a Welsh Disestablishment Bill was highly unlikely in the 1906 session. Thus the Party decided instead to give immediate support to bills dealing with the land, temperance, the enfranchisement of places of worship (designed to secure freehold rights for nonconformist chapels), and an eight-hour day for miners. But over disestablishment there was at once disunity. Samuel Evans proposed on his own initiative to introduce a Church Suspensory Bill on the lines of Asquith's Bill of 1893. After strong criticism from his colleagues, he agreed to withdraw it, but some other Welshmen, notably Ellis Griffith and D. A. Thomas, were already concerned with the 'ominous silence' from the government.[1]

When the response of the government was finally announced, it scarcely allayed the fears of Welsh nonconformists. In place of legislation, Campbell-Bannerman proposed a royal commission to inquire into the position of the Church and other religious bodies in Wales. For, in private, ministers made it clear that they were anxious to settle the Welsh Church question, with all its complications, on a compromise basis. Particularly was this true of Lloyd George, from whom the issue would derive its main momentum in the cabinet. The years since the break-up of the *Cymru Fydd* movement had greatly extended his political horizon. The Welsh questions which had been the overriding passion of his early youth dwindled in significance before the great social and economic questions that beckoned to the ambitious young President of the Board of Trade. This was seen in 1908 when he and D. R. Daniel tried in vain to persuade Llewellyn Williams that disestablishment was no longer a crucial issue for the

[1] *South Wales Daily News*, 15 Feb. 1906; *Church Times*, 9 Mar. 1906.

people of Wales.[1] To achieve a compromise settlement, Lloyd George had approached the Bishop of St. Asaph in February 1906 and had suggested an extremely moderate Welsh disestablishment measure in which the Church would retain all its endowments save for the tithe—a scheme which, if known, would have instantly forfeited the confidence of Welsh radicals in Lloyd George. The Bishop of St. Asaph told Randall Davidson that Lloyd George 'would rather like to get Disestablishment carried with a minimum of friction'.[2] On 22 February 1906 Lloyd George saw the bishop and Davidson in the Lords and made the proposal for a royal commission to inquire into the provision for spiritual needs made in Wales by the Church and by nonconformity. After some hesitation, Davidson agreed, and Lloyd George wrote that 'he hoped that a Bill of a moderate kind might be the outcome'.[3]

In May the government therefore announced the appointment of a Commission of nine, under the chairmanship of Lord Justice Vaughan Williams, formerly a judge on the Queen's Bench and now in the Court of Appeal. Four were churchmen, Lord Hugh Cecil, Archdeacon Owen Evans, J. E. Greaves (the Liberal Unionist lord-lieutenant of Caernarvonshire), and Frank Edwards, a Liberal M.P. The other four were nonconformists, Samuel Evans, M.P., Sir John Williams, Dr. Fairbairn (principal of Mansfield Congregational College, Oxford), and Professor Henry Jones of Glasgow University. In reply to D. A. Thomas in the Commons, Campbell-Bannerman justified the appointment of the Commission on the grounds that there was a deficiency of accurate information and that this had gravely embarrassed the Liberal governments of 1894–5 in framing their disestablishment measures. But clearly it served the additional purpose of shelving a controversial question while the ministry turned to social and economic matters of more general urgency.

From the first, the Royal Commission was most unpopular in Wales. In D. A. Thomas's words, it was taking evidence after the verdict had been given.[4] There had been no consultation with the Welsh Party over its appointment, while nonconformists in Wales had traditionally shown an aversion from an official compilation of statistics, preferring to rely on their own figures. Before the

---

[1] Memoir by D. R. Daniel, 'D. Lloyd George: Canghellaur y Trysorlys' (N.L.W., Daniel MSS., 2912, pp. 72–77).
[2] Bell, op. cit., vol. i, p. 504.
[3] Ibid., p. 505.
[4] British Weekly, 8 Nov. 1906.

Commission began its inquiries, there were sharp exchanges between Vaughan Williams and the Nonconformist Central Evidence Committee over the procedure to be adopted in the taking of evidence.[1] The appointment of the Commission was unanimously condemned by the Welsh Liberal press, and Liberal spokesmen found it necessary to deny informed rumours that the idea of a Commission had originated with Lloyd George.[2] Churchmen, on the other hand, were generally favourable to the Commission. It would provide an opportunity to demonstrate, with reliable statistics, the revival of the Church, and a committee was appointed to prepare evidence, with Frank Morgan of Keble College, Oxford, as secretary.

When the Commission began work in October 1906, it soon confirmed the worst fears of nonconformists. Its chairman, Judge Vaughan Williams, began to interpret the terms of reference very rigidly and to exclude much evidence brought by nonconformists showing the general impact of nonconformity on the social life and culture of Wales. Both the Bishop of St. Asaph and his colleague, Sir John Williams, had to admit that Vaughan Williams's manner was querulous and brusque, and his personality created great friction within the Commission. He had a tendency to interpolate long and irrelevant personal reminiscences, and there were frequent clashes with the belligerent nonconformist members.[3] Sir Henry Jones later recalled: 'I learnt for the first time how much ill-feeling religious men can entertain towards one another. Such an atmosphere of distrust, suspicion and pious malice I never breathed before or since.'[4] In the Commons in March 1907 Welsh Liberal and Labour members condemned the Commission in the strongest terms. In an attempt to conciliate the two sides, Lloyd George and Loreburn, the Lord Chancellor, tried to mediate between Vaughan Williams and Samuel Evans, but even Lloyd George's bewitching genius for diplomacy was of no avail. In April three nonconformists, Jones, Evans, and Fairbairn, resigned, being replaced by J. H. Davies, Brynmor Jones, M.P., and the Rev. J. Morgan Gibbon.[5] Still the Commission was

---

[1] *Royal Commission on the Church and other Religious Bodies in Wales, Evidence*, vol. iv (Cd. 5435), pp. 543 ff.

[2] *Cambrian News*, 3 May 1907; *Manchester Guardian*, 21 May 1907.

[3] Archbishop of Wales, op. cit., pp. 224 ff. For Sir John Williams's view, see Herbert Lewis's Diary, 7 Mar. 1907 (Penucha MSS.). The biography of Judge Vaughan Williams in the *Dictionary of National Biography* (1912–21 supplement) is quite misleading: Williams is incomprehensibly given the credit for the tranquil passage of Welsh disestablishment.

[4] H. J. Hetherington, *Life and Letters of Sir Henry Jones* (London, 1924), p. 95.

[5] Herbert Lewis's Diary, 7 Mar. 1907; *Y Tyst*, 24 Apr. 1907. *Baner ac Amserau*

torn by acrimony, and in 1909 J. H. Davies and Sir John Williams tried to offer Huws Davies, its diligent secretary, financial induce-ment to leave the Commission. J. H. Davies reinforced this offer by abusing Vaughan Williams vigorously in Welsh. However, the Bishop of St. Asaph succeeded in demonstrating to Huws Davies that 'the Chairman is not the man to appreciate the significance of your resignation' although sympathizing with him over the insults he had received.[1] Amid universal execration and ridicule, the Com-mission continued its slow and stormy passage.

As the 1907 session progressed, with the Commission in near dead-lock and disestablishment still apparently far off, much unrest be-came evident in Wales. After forty years of struggle, victory seemed as remote as ever. The first signs of this discontent followed Lloyd George's so-called 'guard-room' speech at Caernarvon on 17 Janu-ary, in which he appeared to imply that Welsh disestablishment would be withheld until the House of Lords question was disposed of. But Ellis Griffith, Llewelyn Williams, and others questioned this attitude, not without justice. If an Education Bill and an Irish Land Bill were to be included in 'filling up the cup' or 'ploughing the sands', it was hard to see why Wales should be left out. The record of the Commission seemed to indicate that the government were betraying their trust. By May, of forty-nine witnesses called, twenty-three were churchmen, and only twenty-six represented the various nonconformist bodies.[2] As on other occasions, the Independents led the outcry, through their organ Y Tyst. The Union of Welsh Independ-ents recorded their support for the three Commissioners who had resigned and stated that they would forward no further evidence until the Commission gave a guarantee that it would be fairly received. On 4 June the Congregational Association of North Caernarvonshire demanded that the Welsh members should refuse their support to the government unless a Welsh Disestablishment Bill was introduced in the 1908 session. Another 'Welsh Revolt' seemed in prospect.[3]

It was given fresh impetus on 22 June when Campbell-Bannerman announced in the Commons that a disestablishment measure was

Cymru, 27 Mar., 8 May 1907. In 1919 J. H. Davies was appointed the third principal of the University College of Wales, Aberystwyth.

[1] J. H. Davies to T. Huws Davies, undated; Bishop of St. Asaph to Huws Davies, 26 Oct. 1909 (N.L.W., Huws Davies MSS., 16,354c).
[2] South Wales Daily News, 6 May 1907.
[3] Y Tyst, 8 May 1907; Baner ac Amserau Cymru, 8, 15 May 1907; South Wales Daily News, 5 June 1907.

most unlikely in 1908. Herbert Lewis, while feeling the answer to be 'honest and inevitable', was nevertheless 'amazed at the form in which the reply was given and at once felt that it would create a great sensation in Wales'.[1] Nonconformist associations in all parts of the country carried motions strongly critical of the government's attitude. The Union of Welsh Independents at Neath on 25 June demanded a definite pledge from the Prime Minister, and this was reiterated by the Welsh Baptist Union on 3 September. Many Welsh correspondents wrote anonymously to the *British Weekly*, abusing Lloyd George for a breach of faith.[2] But it was a different matter to compel the Welsh Party to take action, particularly in view of its profound deference to Lloyd George, by far its most powerful member. On 12 June motions by Ellis Griffith and D. A. Thomas in favour of a more independent course failed even to find a seconder. Even when Campbell-Bannerman and Asquith told a Welsh deputation on 17 June in the clearest manner that, as long as the Lords question remained, there could be no pledge over Welsh disestablishment, there was no sign of a rebellion at Westminster, least of all from the amiable Welsh chairman, Sir Alfred Thomas. Another meeting of the Party on 25 July saw another motion by Ellis Griffith, that the government be urged to introduce a bill not later than the fourth session, again fail to find a single supporter.[3] In speeches at Shrewsbury (15 June), the Reform Club (1 July), and Pontypridd (20 July), Lloyd George made his own position clear. The Lords blocked the way towards disestablishment, while in any case education, and not disestablishment, had been the foremost Welsh demand in 1906.

But even Lloyd George's immense prestige could not stem the undercurrent of protest which was welling up from radicals in Wales; it culminated in the organization of a great nonconformist convention at Cardiff on 10 October, which, as originally conceived, was to articulate the disappointment and indignation of Welsh nonconformity at its betrayal. The *British Weekly* belligerently proclaimed that it would bring the government to heel, and particularly Lloyd George, who had 'yielded to the breath of officialdom'.[4] However, when 10 October arrived, the purpose of the meeting had undergone a subtle transmutation. The accents of revolt were being

---

[1] Herbert Lewis's Diary, 11 June 1907 (Penucha MSS.).
[2] Ibid., 7 Aug. 1907; cf. *British Weekly*, 6, 13, 20, 27 June, 4 July 1907.
[3] *South Wales Daily News*, 26 July 1907.   [4] *British Weekly*, 26 Sept. 1907.

stilled and the great convention had become merely a nonconformist rally in favour of disestablishment, similar to countless others in the past. Lloyd George had made careful preparations beforehand. He had written to the Prime Minister that the Welsh agitation was 'becoming a little menacing' and urged that he send a message to the convention to placate it: 'you have no better friends than these half-insurgent Welsh ministers'.[1] He had also arranged through Sir Alfred Thomas to meet certain key delegates beforehand: 'we want to avoid a row if we possibly can'.[2] In the early part of the meeting the speakers were subdued, and one, Principal William Edwards of Cardiff Baptist College, totally disavowed any intention of criticizing either Lloyd George or the government. There was a brief defiance from the veteran Methodist, the Rev. Evan Jones, Caernarvon, but the emotional oratory of Lloyd George (whose presence there was quite unofficial)[3] soon turned the meeting into the customary personal triumph. He showed that the main interest of Wales lay in a settlement of the position of the Lords, but, amid passionate references to his own personal sacrifices of life and property in the past, appeared also to promise a Welsh Disestablishment Bill in the fourth session of the present Parliament. As D. A. Thomas showed, Lloyd George's personal magnetism had confused the issue and the national cause was no more advanced. Lloyd George himself stated that he had given no specific pledge: 'the government will not be worried much more on the subject of Welsh Disestablishment until the time comes to arrange the programme for 1909', he wrote.[4] But in the autumn of 1907 Welsh radicals were satisfied. The *British Weekly* and *Y Tyst* again fell into line.[5] When Ellis Griffith attempted to introduce a note of criticism into the proceedings of the Welsh National Liberal Council at Rhyl on 30 October, he was angrily shouted down.

It is clear that the 'Revolt' of 1907 was a very mild affair. Lloyd George throughout maintained a firm grip on the Welsh Party: he was entitled to attend their meetings and he used this privilege to the full. The Welsh press was generally favourable to him, particularly influential newspapers such as *Y Faner, Yr Herald Cymraeg, Y*

[1] Lloyd George to Campbell-Bannerman, 5 Oct. 1907 (B.M., Add. MSS., 41240, f. 86).

[2] Lloyd George to Sir Alfred Thomas, 7 Oct. 1907 (Cardiff, Pontypridd Papers).

[3] *Baner ac Amserau Cymru*, 16 Oct. 1907.

[4] Lloyd George to Campbell-Bannerman, 19 Oct. 1907 (B.M., Add. MSS., 41240, f. 105).

[5] *British Weekly*, 17 Oct. 1907; *Y Tyst*, 16 Oct. 1907. Cf. *Y Genedl Gymreig*, 15, 22 Oct. 1907.

Genedl, and the *Cambrian News*. Even the belligerent Welsh Baptist Union was to compromise itself by electing Lloyd George as its president for 1908–9.[1] The picture of nation-wide opposition painted by some of Lloyd George's biographers, while artistically effective, is historically much exaggerated.[2] Perhaps the most perceptive attitude was that adopted by the Caernarvon journal, *Y Genedl*. It showed that, while the position of the establishment was an injustice, it was scarcely the most serious evil from which Wales suffered. It was hardly comparable with such issues as malnutrition or unemployment (now rising to 10 per cent. of the total labour force), in the settlement of which England and Wales must co-operate.[3]

The affairs of Wales, however, could not wholly be lost sight of, as deadlock with the House of Lords became imminent. Amid the vicissitudes of governmental fortunes, Welsh Liberalism remained as impregnable as ever. By-elections at East Denbighshire (August 1906), Pembrokeshire (July 1908), and East Denbighshire again (April 1909) showed little weakening in the Liberals' overwhelming strength. The county council elections showed an inevitable recession after the remarkable victories of 1904, but every county retained its 'Progressive' majority, despite landlord pressure in many counties.[4] The position of Wales in the government was much enhanced by the ministerial changes following Campbell-Bannerman's retirement in April 1908). The new Premier, Asquith, had introduced the first Disestablishment Bill in 1894, while Lloyd George, to appease the radical wing of the Liberal Party, was now elevated to the rank of Chancellor of the Exchequer. In addition, Samuel Evans entered the government as Solicitor-General. Thus it was, with the Parliament of 1906 visibly drawing to its stormy close, Welsh disestablishment at last appeared in the King's Speech in 1909. On 21 April 1909 Asquith himself introduced the Bill in the Commons.

In the Methodist *Goleuad*, the Rev. Evan Jones of Caernarvon, the erstwhile rebel, welcomed the Bill as an earnest of good faith.[5] But other nonconformists in Wales were critical of a measure that had demonstrably little prospect of becoming law. This was in fact Asquith's own view. He wrote to the King that the Bill 'probably

---

[1] *South Wales Daily News*, 29 Sept. 1908. Lloyd George made a point of conducting proceedings at the conference entirely in Welsh (ibid., 6 Nov. 1909).

[2] For example, du Parcq, vol. iii, pp. 463 ff.; Frank Owen, pp. 152–3; J. Hugh Edwards, vol. iv, pp. 78 ff.

[3] *Y Genedl Gymreig*, 1 Oct. 1907 (leading article: 'Pa Ffordd').

[4] The result in 1907 was the return of 401 'Progressives' to 200 'Sectarians'.

[5] *Y Goleuad*, 28 Apr. 1909 (leading article by Rev. Evan Jones, dated 22 Apr.).

will not proceed beyond the affirmation of the principle by a second reading in the House of Commons',[1] and it was clearly designed to pacify the nonconformist bodies. It was a remarkable and ironic commentary on the Royal Commission on the Welsh Churches that Asquith was introducing a Bill before its report had been issued; but Herbert Lewis, now a junior Whip, had forwarded him statistics from 'that astounding body', thus emulating the function performed by Ellis in 1894.[2]

The First Reading debate was brief and uneventful. The measure closely resembled that of 1895.[3] The four Welsh dioceses would be disestablished on 1 January 1911, and ecclesiastical corporations would be dissolved. The disendowment provisions were more moderate than those of 1895, the Church representative body retaining cathedrals, fabrics, burial grounds, and benefactions obtained since 1662. The main difference from the previous measure was that the commissioners would now be only temporary. After 1915 a council of Wales with representatives from every county, borough, and urban district council would apply the secularized endowments, mainly tithe and glebe. Thus Lloyd George's momentous amendment of 1895 received retrospective sanction. Asquith justified his Bill on the grounds of nonconformist predominance in Wales and the opinion of the Welsh people, as shown repeatedly in elections since 1880. The Opposition were much embarrassed at not having a single Welsh representative on their benches. As a substitute, a border member, W. C. Bridgeman (Oswestry), moved that the Bill be delayed until the Report of the Royal Commission. F. E. Smith, Lord Robert Cecil, and others attacked the acquisition of Church property, and the Unionists took the unusual step of dividing on the First Reading, but the Bill was easily carried by a majority of 172 votes.

The Bill aroused little excitement. The *Morning Post* noted that the House was sparsely filled and the debate had an air of unreality.[4] The *Manchester Guardian* believed it would be futile to proceed to a Second Reading.[5] The force of this view was seen a few days later when Lloyd George introduced the celebrated 'People's Budget'

---

[1] Asquith to the King, 26 Jan. 1909 (Bodleian, Asquith Papers, box 4).

[2] Herbert Lewis to Asquith, 13 Apr. 1909 (Bodleian, Asquith Papers, box 3).

[3] *Parl. Deb.*, 5th ser., vol. iii, pp. 1525 ff. Cf. Memorandum on 'Differences between the present Bill (1909) and the Bill of 1895 as amended' (Asquith Papers, box 3).

[4] *Morning Post*, 22 Apr. 1909.

[5] *Manchester Guardian*, 22 Apr. 1909.

which so aroused the Lords and the Unionist Party as to sweep other issues into oblivion. The Church Defence Committee organized a number of token protest meetings, but there was little sense of danger. On 10 June Asquith intimated that the Bill would not proceed beyond a Second Reading, and announced its withdrawal on 15 June. Again there were protests in Wales: Herbert Lewis described a meeting of the Welsh members with Asquith on 8 June as 'perfectly stormy' and a turbulent meeting of the Welsh Party rang with cries of rebellion.[1] But, as before, Lloyd George served to soothe the ruffled feelings of his compatriots and only Clement Edwards (Denbigh District) staged a brief, solitary rebellion. The Independents at their annual congress expressed their strong disappointment through the matchless rhetoric of the Rev. Towyn Jones, but few heeded them. Increasingly, the time-honoured issue of the 'alien Church' was beginning to lose its primacy in Welsh political life. As a writer in *Y Geninen* suggested, the legislation of the later Victorian period, from the Ballot Act of 1872 down to the Parish Councils Act of 1894, had made 'religious equality' a reality, and the issue of disestablishment had therefore lost its significance. On many social issues, he pointed out, the Methodists were far more obstructive than was the established Church.[2] In any case, it was beyond question that Welsh disestablishment, in common with every other measure, would stand or fall by the success of the ministry in dealing with the Lords' veto. As the pungent rhetoric of Lloyd George drove his adversaries onwards towards constitutional crisis, the hopes and suspicions of radicals, in Wales as elsewhere, awaited the verdict of 'the great assize of the people'.[3]

(iii) *Liberals and Labour, 1906–12*

The repeated disappointments over disestablishment between 1906 and 1910 further intensified the disillusion of Welsh radicals in their parliamentary representatives, even though few could suggest any practical alternative policy. D. A. Thomas, who played an increasingly lonely role in politics, bitterly criticized his colleagues, comparing the multitude of Scottish and Irish measures with the total absence of legislation for Wales. The Welsh Party seemed to him 'a fraud and a failure . . . the laughing stock of the Commons' while

[1] Herbert Lewis's Diary, 8 June 1909 (Penucha MSS.); *South Wales Daily News*, 12 June 1909.
[2] 'Elphin': Dadgysylltiad i Gymru: A Oes Brys?' (*Y Geninen*, Apr. 1907, pp. 89–90).
[3] From a speech by Lloyd George, 3 Dec. 1909, quoted in *Better Times* (London, 1910), pp. 176 ff.

the Welsh National Council was 'a mere annex of the Hotel Carnarvon'.[1] The very magnitude of the electoral victory in 1906 seemed to have led to the extinction of the Welsh Party as a political force, and in the following years its disintegration was increasingly marked. Lloyd George, McKenna, Herbert Lewis, and Samuel Evans withdrew into higher realms, while Lloyd George easily secured the compliance of his colleagues by remote control. Most of the other Welsh members were undistinguished: they included several practising barristers who were irregular in their attendance. The only other Welsh members at all prominent in debate were Llewelyn Williams, one of the last links with the idealism of *Cymru Fydd*, William Brace (mainly on mining affairs), and the egregious J. D. Rees (Montgomery District), an importunate questioner on subjects great and small, a fanatical foe of women's suffrage and, in due course, a Unionist member. When Herbert Lewis became Secretary to the Local Government Board in July 1909, Asquith selected another Welsh member, William Jones (Arfon), to succeed him as junior Whip. It was a pleasant gesture, but it scarcely carried political significance.

Even the departure of their quiescent and picturesque chairman, Sir Alfred Thomas, to the Lords in 1910 under the title of Baron Pontypridd did little to stimulate the Welsh Party. He was succeeded in 1911 by a far more positive figure, Ellis Griffith, but even he was powerless to do more than create an impression of activity and influence. In a mood of temporary irritation in 1910, even such a conformist member as Brynmor Jones was moved to protest against the insignificance of the Welsh representatives. 'I can see now we ought in 1906 to have made the Welsh Party a real power, instead of allowing ourselves to be a mere appanage of the Whips' office.'[2] But he offered no suggestion as to how this might have been accomplished.

It would be wrong, however, totally to disregard the activities of the Welsh Party in this period. At least one potentially important achievement had been secured almost accidentally in March 1907, with the creation of a Welsh Standing Committee in the Commons. Campbell-Bannerman, in restoring the Scottish Standing Committee of Gladstone's days, was moved to establish a similar body for Wales.[3] It was to comprise all thirty-four members for Wales and

---

[1] *Merthyr Express*, 16 Jan. 1909; *South Wales Daily News*, 3 Dec. 1908.

[2] Brynmor Jones to Alfred Thomas, 8 Aug. 1910 (Cardiff, Pontypridd Papers).

[3] *Parl. Deb.*, 4th ser., vol. clxxii, pp. 669 ff. Cf. J. F. Redlich, *Procedure of the House of Commons* (London, 1908), vol. iii, pp. 215–16. The dormant Welsh Standing Committee was used for the Marriages (Wales and Monmouthshire) Bill in March 1962.

Monmouthshire. Subsequently, the Welsh Committee rapidly became obsolete until its resurrection in the form of a Welsh 'Grand Committee' by the Macmillan government in 1960, but its symbolic importance was considerable. Another issue that arose in the same year, 1907, concerned Haldane's military reorganization. Amid his overhaul of the structure of the British army, he had promised a distinctively Welsh division and confirmed this before the Welsh National Liberal Council at Rhyl in November. But the scheme he forwarded later included several of the English border counties, while the headquarters of the division was to be established at Shrewsbury. There were strong protests from South Wales, especially from Cardiff, and Haldane was persuaded to concede a Welsh commander and headquarters for the new division.[1] This still appeared insufficient, and in 1908 Colonel Ivor Herbert (South Monmouthshire) moved a reduction of the army estimates by £1,000 in protest against Haldane's refusal to make Wales a separate command, but to no avail.[2]

Another demonstration of the separate claims of Wales appeared in the abortive Licensing Bill of 1908. Stringent temperance reform had been a consistent demand by Welsh nonconformity, while the Sunday Closing Act of 1881 had formed the first legislative recognition of Welsh nationality. Asquith's Bill of 1908 therefore made special provision for Wales. On the one hand, it included Monmouthshire in the operation of the Welsh Sunday Closing Act, as had been recommended by the Peel Commission in 1899. On the other hand, it allowed for much wider powers of reduction of licences by direct veto than in England. Licences, which would statutorily be reduced from 7,102 to 4,659 in number, could be diminished still further in Wales to 3,104 or even to a mere 1,584.[3] In Committee, G. Cave (Unionist, Kingston) moved an amendment to omit these special Welsh provisions. F. E. Smith stated that direct veto by a bare majority would be tyrannous, while Earl Winterton attacked any suggestion that Wales should be treated as a separate nation.[4] The Welsh clause was upheld by a large majority, as was the provision relating to Monmouthshire, but the Bill was eventually thrown out by the Lords on the Second Reading in November.

[1] *South Wales Daily News*, 4–9 Dec. 1907.
[2] *Parl. Deb.*, vol. clxxxv, pp. 1786 ff.
[3] *The Government Licensing Bill and what it will do for Wales* (Liberal Publication Department, 1908). Cf. *Parl. Deb.*, 4th ser., vol. clxxxvii, pp. 1714 ff. (Herbert Roberts's speech).
[4] *Parl. Deb.*, 4th ser., vol. cxciv, pp. 1391 ff.

The relative tranquillity of Wales at Westminster faithfully reflected the political atmosphere in the constituencies, where the
deceptive calm of the last twenty years continued to prevail. The
annual conventions of the Welsh National Liberal Council were still
enveloped in ineffective complacency, as the avowed frustration of
the treasurer and the secretary of the Council, C. E. Breese and
W. H. Hughes, indicated.[1] In 1907 an attempt was made, inspired by
Lloyd George, to reconstitute the Council on a broader basis. He
criticized the Council as it had existed since 1898 as little more than
a committee drawn from the locality of wherever it happened to
meet, and recommended strengthening the skeleton framework of
local constituency associations with representatives from the Women's Liberal Federation, Labour, free church and temperance
organizations, Liberal organizations in England, and from the Welsh
Party. Despite renewed protests from the Cardiff Liberal Association that these changes would gravely weaken the democratic character of the Council, they were carried out and Lord St. David's
made president of the newly constituted body.[2] The effect, however,
was to deprive the Council of what little individuality it still possessed
and to reduce it totally to the status of a functional electioneering
machine. The Pembrokeshire by-election of July 1908 was the first
occasion for the Council to intervene independently at election time.[3]

A fundamental weakness of the Welsh National Liberal Council
continued to be the crumbling machinery of Liberalism in the constituencies after decades of apparent invincibility. In some constituencies no local association existed, while in several others the
machinery was largely nominal. In the first category, Merthyr Boroughs was a clear example. Since 1888 the Merthyr Liberal Association had ceased to function; in 1902 D. A. Thomas had reproved the
secretary of the Brecon Road Liberal Association for claiming to
represent Merthyr as a whole.[4] The main surviving recognition of
Liberalism was the survival of Liberal clubs at Merthyr and Aberdare, whose major purpose seems to have been refreshment—not
that that was without electoral significance! In 1900 Keir Hardie had

[1] e.g. Breese to Edward Thomas, 3 Jan. 1905 (Cardiff, Cochfarf Papers). Hughes to
William Jones, 23 Feb. 1911 (Bangor, William Jones Papers, MSS. 5473, no. 1). In
1911 Hughes was succeeded as secretary by Cyrus Evans who retained his post until
the Liberal split after 1918.
[2] *South Wales Daily News*, 31 Oct. 1907, 3 Oct. 1908.
[3] Ibid., 14 July 1908.
[4] D. A. Thomas to T. J. Rice, 11 Nov. 1902 (Glamorgan Record Office MSS.,
D/D Xes, 6).

found a largely disorganized opposition. Merthyr politics were dominated by the personal influence of D. A. Thomas, who maintained private election agents at Merthyr and Aberdare and whose ascendancy in the district had passed beyond challenge, even democratic challenge, as his control over the South Wales coal industry was consolidated. The rivalry of Merthyr and Aberdare was another force for disunity. When in the autumn of 1909 Thomas announced his adoption as Liberal candidate for Cardiff after twenty-two years at Merthyr, there was immense local confusion. A series of hurriedly convened meetings selected *ad hoc* representatives for a general meeting, and the Merthyr Liberal Association was hastily reconstituted, under the presidency of W. Rees Edmunds, a Cardiff solicitor, with D. M. Richards as registration agent.[1] Yet, in spite of this disorganization the official Liberal candidate, Edgar Jones, comfortably headed the poll with Keir Hardie 1,500 votes behind, at the general election in January. The following June, a further step forward was taken when a full-time agent was appointed at a salary of £80 per annum, in the person of O. T. Hopkins, the secretary of Ynys-hir and Wattstown Co-operative Society,[2] and, their forces regrouped, the Merthyr and Aberdare Liberals reassembled to meet the challenge of Labour.

In other constituencies, local Liberal machinery was only slightly less perfunctory than in Merthyr. In the Rhondda and East Glamorgan divisions, local 'Labour and Liberal Associations' met annually to 'report progress' and little else. A similar body was constituted in Mid-Glamorgan in 1908, to counter the influence of the I.L.P. in the constituency, particularly in the Garw Valley.[3] In South Glamorgan, those Cardiff shipping owners who predominated in local Liberal circles reconstituted the Liberal Five Hundred in December 1908, 'as it had been in a state of suspended animation for years', in the words of its president, Alderman T. W. David.[4] In these and other constituencies, a curious feature of the structure of politics was the persistence of a traditional pattern of influence side by side with the organized caucus of a democratic system. Thus in the critical East

---

[1] *Merthyr Express*, 1909 and 1910 *passim*. See particularly issues of 21 Aug. and 23 Oct. 1909, and 26 Mar. 1910. M. J. Rees and others to William Jones, 6 Dec. 1909–29 Nov. 1911 (Bangor, William Jones Papers, MSS. 5472, nos. 74–79). MS. recollections of Sir Edgar Jones, 9 Mar. 1961 (I am grateful to Mr. Ieuan Gwynedd Jones and Dr. A. Seaman for the use of this source). There is some ephemeral material relating to Merthyr politics at this time in the D. M. Richards MSS. in the National Library of Wales, MSS. 3293F, 3470F.   [2] *Merthyr Express*, 8 Oct. 1910.
[3] *South Wales Daily News*, 24 Sept. 1908.   [4] ibid., 5 Dec. 1908.

Carmarthenshire by-election in August 1912, at a crucial period in the fortunes of the Asquith ministry, it was discovered that the local Liberal Association was profoundly swayed by those few landed families in the county who still adhered to Liberalism, notably the Stepneys of Llanelly and the Hughes family of Tre-gib. Only by openly challenging the narrow and unrepresentative Association, which had not met for almost three years, did the fiery Independent minister, the Rev. J. Towyn Jones, succeed in ousting aristocratic Whigs such as Sir Stafford Howard or Sir Courtenay Mansel from the nomination as Liberal candidate for nonconformist East Carmarthenshire. Even in the Wales of the twentieth century, the politics of connexion and of territorial influence were still in evidence, even on the Liberal side, where recollections of the evictions of 1868 were still vividly rehearsed.[1]

It was, however, external pressure rather than internal decay that formed the major threat to Liberal predominance in Wales in the years after 1906, as the growth of the Labour movement assumed alarming proportions. The threat from organized Labour was a constant preoccupation of Welsh Liberals from 1906 onwards. This was immediately demonstrated in the first session of the new Parliament. Twenty-five Welsh members voted for the Trades Disputes Bill, moved privately by the Labour Party in March 1906, which afforded trade unions complete immunity from damages in civil actions—an impressive testimony to the power of the working-class vote at the polls. Even such a conservative Liberal as the Hon. Ivor Guest (Cardiff) protested that his election pledges compelled him to support the Labour members' Bill.[2] At the Welsh National Liberal Council at Cardiff in October, Lloyd George devoted most of his speech to a defence of the Liberal Party as the party of the working man. Temperance, education, disestablishment, and Welsh self-government on an extended scale were all, he claimed, essential for the well-being of the Welsh proletariat. Cunningly, he suggested that agitation on Socialist lines might well scare employers into adopting an extreme Tory position.[3] All over Wales Liberal and nonconformist conventions

---

[1] For this episode, see *Western Mail*, 31 July–24 Aug. 1912; *South Wales Daily News*, 31 July–28 Aug. 1912. Territorial influence was still an important factor in rural areas, forty years after the Ballot Act. In 1914 the Liberal candidate for Radnorshire could complain: 'Every squire in the county is a rampant Tory, and every conceivable influence brought to bear on the voters' (William Lewis to William Jones, 6 Mar. 1914; Bangor, William Jones Papers, MSS. 5472, no. 83).
[2] *Parl. Deb.*, 4th ser., vol. cliv, pp. 1342–4 (Guest's speech).
[3] *South Wales Daily News*, 12 Oct. 1906; *Church Times*, 5 Oct. 1906.

were increasingly preoccupied with the threat from organized
Labour, industrial and political, and with revision of their attitude
towards social and economic problems in an industrial community.
A minority adhered to the 'new theology' popularized by R. J.
Campbell, although its effect on the Welsh ministry was restricted.
Symptomatic of the new unease was a meeting of the Calvinistic
Methodist assembly at Caernarvon in 1908, when, in a discussion
on 'Christianity and Society', a succession of speakers condemned
the churches for an excessively and narrowly theological outlook,
and the eminent preacher and theologian, the Rev. J. Cynddylan
Jones, caused a sensation by revealing that he had been voting Labour
for years.[1] Many nonconformist Liberals, Daniel Lleufer Thomas and
the Rev. Gwilym Davies notable among them, devoted themselves to
co-operative enterprises and schools of 'social service', the germ of a
new 'Forward Movement' throughout rural and industrial Wales.[2]

The political machinery of Labour in Wales, however, continued
to present almost as fragmentary and disunited an appearance as
that of the Liberals themselves. The I.L.P. penetrated into new
areas, the mining valleys of the Rhondda (where three branches were
formed early in 1906), the tinplate villages of West Wales and even in
North Wales, in the slate-quarrying districts of Ffestiniog and Llanberis. By 1910 it claimed ninety-five branches in South Wales and
nine in the North, but the depth of its penetration is difficult to determine.[3] Much the most remarkable feature after 1906 is a growing
tendency towards independent action among the mining community.
A new militancy was surging through the S.W.M.F., based on the
I.L.P. stronghold of Aberdare, whose agent was the fiery C. B. Stanton. The annual conference of the S.W.M.F. in 1906 saw the older
leaders such as Mabon and Brace subjected to unprecedented criticism for their adherence to Liberalism. Although the M.F.G.B. as
a whole voted against affiliation to the Labour Party in 1906, South
Wales voted strongly in favour, by 41,843 votes to 31,527.[4] The

---

[1] *Y Goleuad*, 2 Sept. 1908. Also see *Y Geninen*, 1908–14 *passim*. The *Goleuad*
published a series of articles on 'Yr Eglwysi a Sosialaeth', 26 Aug.–16 Sept. 1908.

[2] See article on Lleufer Thomas by David Williams, *Dictionary of Welsh Biography*
(London, 1959). Cf. *South Wales Daily News*, 8 Sept. 1911. Lleufer Thomas remained
chairman of the Welsh School of Social Service until 1923.

[3] *Report of the Eighteenth Annual Conference of the I.L.P.*, 1910. For the growth of
the I.L.P. in the Rhondda, see E. D. Lewis, op. cit., pp. 172–9; also see letter by Noah
Ablett in *Rhondda Leader*, 2 June 1906. For South West Wales, see *Llais Llafur*, 1900,
1906, 1910 *passim*. For North Wales, see *Y Genedl Gymreig*, 29 Sept., 3 Dec. 1908; also
David Thomas, *Silyn* (Liverpool, 1956), pp. 73 ff.

[4] *South Wales Daily News*, 13 Mar., 5 Oct. 1906.

Federation laid claim to every seat in South Wales when the sitting member retired. In some constituencies there was a threat of an immediate breach with Liberalism. In Mid-Glamorgan, an *ad hoc* conference of trades councils, miners' lodges, and I.L.P. branches at Aberavon, claiming to represent nearly 10,000 working men, elected Vernon Hartshorn, miners' agent and I.L.P. member, as their candidate in 1907.[1] In East Glamorgan, Evan Thomas, miners' agent and an ordained Baptist minister, was nominated to fight the seat on Sir Alfred Thomas's retirement.[2] In distant East Carmarthen, David Morgan, another nonconformist miners' representative, was nominated to succeed Abel Thomas, the elderly and silent barrister who had held the seat since 1890.[3] Even in Cardiff, with its immense diversity of trades, the trades council voted overwhelmingly in favour of contesting the next election.[4] Gradually a coherent vision of a Labour Party was emerging. In 1905 David Watts Morgan had echoed the old attitude of 'Labour first, politics second' when he informed the Rhondda miners that a S.W.M.F. nominee 'could call himself what he liked—Liberal, Conservative, Democratic, or Socialist—and was only pledged to the Labour programme of the Federation'.[5] But events were rapidly making this political eclecticism outmoded. In 1908 the miners of South Wales (and of North Wales also) voted heavily for affiliation to the Labour Party once again, and on this occasion they were supported by a majority of the miners throughout Britain. In 1909, therefore, even such reluctant revolutionaries as Mabon, Brace, Richards, and John Williams were projected unwillingly on to the Labour benches side by side with Keir Hardie. The dream of industrial co-operation had faded as a cumulative series of bitter disputes poisoned relations between capital and labour from 1908 onwards.[6] In that year a strike of 6,000 Powell

---

[1] Ibid., 8 Oct. 1906.
[2] Ibid., 26 Nov. 1907.
[3] Ibid., 18 Nov. 1907.
[4] Ibid., 28 Nov. 1907.
[5] *Rhondda Leader*, 5 Jan. 1905.
[6] There is no satisfactory account of the industrial unrest in South Wales during these years. David Evans, *Labour Strife in the South Wales Coalfield* (Cardiff, 1911), while informative, is highly prejudiced on the side of the owners. Ness Edwards, *History of the South Wales Miners' Federation*, vol. i (London, 1938), is equally distorted on behalf of the miners. E. D. Lewis, op. cit., gives only a general outline. A full account of the details of collective bargaining is given in Eric Wyn Evans, *Mabon* (Cardiff, 1959) and *The Miners of South Wales* (Cardiff, 1961) and in the same author's two theses on 'Mabon' (Univ. of Wales M.A., 1945) and 'Industrial Relations in the South Wales Coal Industry', 1800–1912' (Univ. of Wales Ph.D., 1952), but he has little to say on the wider social and economic forces making for unrest. There are some

Duffryn men brought work in the Aberdare valley to a standstill, and unrest rapidly spread to neighbouring areas. The tangible and immediate causes of deadlock concerned the attempts of coalowners to circumvent the effects of the Eight Hours Bill of 1909, with resultant disputes over the double-shift system and the rate of payment in 'abnormal places' in the Naval Collieries, Tonypandy. More fundamental was the deep apprehension aroused by the growth of the massive oligopoly of the Cambrian Combine with its £2,000,000 share capital, under the control of D. A. Thomas, which provoked an increasing revulsion against the entire structure of capitalism among the mining community. From 1909 the syndicalists of the Plebs League were active in the Rhondda and Aberdare valleys, advocating direct industrial action in place of the constitutional method, and in the prolonged Cambrian strike of 1910–11 their influence in the counsels of the S.W.M.F. became increasingly powerful. In four short years the alliance of Liberals and Labour in Wales, in the joint causes of radical reform and Welsh nationality, seemed to have disintegrated. Indeed, the main immediate opposition to the miners' demands came from the Liberals themselves. Chief among the detested coalowners was D. A. Thomas himself, triumphant at the polls for twenty years but now, even to so moderate a Labour spokesman as Watts Morgan, as great a criminal as the Russian Tsar (the ultimate comparison in Labour circles), for his liability for the Clydach Vale disaster.[1] Symbol of the long series of hostile judicial decisions against trade unions was Judge Bryn Roberts, Calvinist Methodist, Liberal M.P. for twenty years, but now reviled as 'a boss Union smasher', out to destroy organized labour.[2] Above all, Mabon, Brace, and Richards, older leaders and apostles of the Liberal alliance, were losing their ascendancy in the coalfield. The pioneers of the Miners' Federation were told that 'they must move on or move out', by the demagogic Stanton, amid the passions of the Cambrian stoppage.

interesting recollections of this period in Sir Nevil Macready, *Annals of an Active Life* (London, 1924), vol. i, pp. 136–57, and Arthur Horner, *Incorrigible Rebel* (London, 1960), pp. 15–16. Cf. Michael Foot, *Aneurin Bevan* (London, 1962), pp. 27–29.

Full details are given in contemporary newspapers, particularly *South Wales Daily News*, *Western Mail*, and *Rhondda Leader*, but they are generally strongly prejudiced against the miners (cf. Macready, op. cit., p. 149). There are interesting comments in the *Labour Leader*, 18, 25 Nov. 1910. A valuable collection of newspaper cuttings has been deposited in the Glamorgan Record Office (D/DNCB, vols. vi–xiv). The entire subject still awaits its historian.

[1] *Rhondda Leader*, 3 Nov. 1906.

[2] *South Wales Daily News*, 30 July 1908. See also C. B. Stanton's speech to the Pontypridd miners (*Merthyr Express*, 21 Aug. 1909).

'They [the miners] were going in for an industrial union and were going to use it for political purposes in a way which had never been done before (Cheers).'[1]

In view of the ferment and tension in the coalfield, it is a remarkable testimony to the tenacity of the older radical tradition that so few inroads were made into Liberal strength in Wales before 1914. The passion of Labour was slow to assume political form. The elections of January and December 1910 were dominated less by the emergence of the Labour challenge than by the excitement surrounding the legislation of the outgoing Liberal government, and in particular Lloyd George's celebrated 'People's Budget' of 1909. Nowhere was the budget more popular than in Wales. Apart from the sentimental appeal of the 'first Welsh budget', its provisions were inevitably extremely popular throughout the Principality, particularly the taxes on licences, the 5 per cent. tax on mineral rents, and the land increment duties. In South Wales the growth of unearned profits through mining royalties would be checked, while in the rural areas the great landowners were accepted objects of popular hostility. The speeches of some opponents of the budget were calculated to fan Welsh passions, revealing as they did the apprehension of many Englishmen of the mysterious Welsh attorney. The Duke of Marlborough spoke of the 'demagogue from Wales'; Lord George Hamilton objected to 'this Welshman' managing the finances of Englishmen, while the Archbishop of York (Cosmo Lang) attributed the Limehouse speech to 'that mysterious possession affecting the Celtic temperament which is called the "hwyl", which makes the speaker say he knows not what, and excites the audience they know not why'.[2] Lloyd George's eloquent justification of his Welsh origin afforded scope for some of his most effective campaign speeches and gave a personal and intimate interest in the election to Welshmen that they were later to recapture in the First World War.

This was reflected in the election results of January 1910. While there were heavy Liberal losses in England, in Wales Liberal preponderance was, if anything, more marked even than in 1906. While two insecure border seats, Denbigh District and Radnorshire, were lost, in twenty-three seats the Liberal or Labour majority was the highest ever, higher even than in 1906. The combined Liberal-Labour vote totalled 260,876 against 121,521 Unionist votes: in 1906 the

[1] *Merthyr Express*, 17 Oct. 1909.
[2] J. Hugh Edwards, *Life of David Lloyd George*, vol. iv (London, 1913), p. 126.

estimated totals had been 200,063 against 111,093.[1] The most notable newcomer to the ranks of the Welsh Party was Alfred Mond. Unionists who had for years borne taunts at the 'alien Church' were quick to indicate the anomaly of a German-Jewish industrialist sitting for Swansea and becoming treasurer of the Disestablishment Campaign Committee. 'Vales for the Velsh' screamed from every hoarding, and F. E. Smith dwelt bitingly on 'this fiery crusader crying out in the accents of his native Wales', but Mond easily headed the poll, nevertheless.[2] On the other side of the House, William Ormsby-Gore, returned for Denbigh District by eight votes as one of the two Unionist members, was to prove by far the most able and articulate Conservative yet returned for a Welsh constituency.[3]

The Labour challenge was easily contained. At Swansea, the dockers' nominee, Ben Tillett, finished well at the bottom of the poll, his poor showing contrasting sharply with the success of Labour candidates in local elections in recent years. The largesse and power of Mond were the dominant factor here. At Merthyr Tydfil, Keir Hardie was headed by the popular and eloquent local candidate, Edgar Jones, a Welsh-speaking Baptist, who polled more votes among the miners than did Hardie himself.[4]

As the constitutional crisis over the Lords remained unresolved, with the failure of the conference of the party leaders in the summer of 1910, another general election became imminent over the terms of the proposed Parliament Bill. Again there was much apprehension as to the effect on the Liberal vote of the growing tension with Labour. In the far North, William Jones was told in Arfon of the urgent need to placate the angry quarrymen of Caernarvonshire over the Osborne Judgement.[5] In the southern coalfield, industrial strife had reached a new pitch of bitterness during the Cambrian dispute in which over 20,000 men were idle. The riots at Tonypandy in November 1910, in which serious damage was caused, a miner was killed, and squadrons of Hussars patrolled the coalfield, appeared the prelude to a total social convulsion and provided an ominous background to the general election in the following month.

[1] *South Wales Daily News*, 29 Jan. 1910.
[2] A. Griffith-Boscawen, *Memories* (London, 1925), p. 59; Frank Owen, op. cit., p. 135. There is some interesting ephemeral election literature on Mond's campaigns in Swansea, 1910–23, in Swansea Public Library. [3] Now Lord Harlech.
[4] For Swansea, see Stan Awberry, op. cit., pp. 33 ff. For Merthyr, see recollection of Sir Edgar Jones (cf. p. 244, n. 1); *Merthyr Express*, 29 Jan. 1910.
[5] R. E. Jones to William Jones, 3 Apr., 25 Nov., 21 Dec. 1910 (Bangor, William Jones Papers, MSS. 5468, nos. 66, 77, 79).

Again, however, the threat of the Labour challenge proved more alarming than the reality, although conflict with Liberalism was far more intense than in January. Two more constituencies saw Labour and Liberal candidates in opposition, with the Liberals in each case victorious. In East Glamorgan, C. B. Stanton, on the threshold of his conversion from revolutionary syndicalist to bellicose imperialist, failed to receive the endorsement of the M.F.G.B. executive, and, with organized nonconformity strongly hostile, was well beaten by Clement Edwards. More significant was a breach in Mid-Glamorgan. In a by-election the preceding March the local Liberal caucus had rejected an appeal by the Master of Elibank, the Liberal Chief Whip, to concede the seat to Labour, and F. W. Gibbins, a local tinplate owner, had narrowly defeated Vernon Hartshorn, the Labour candidate. In December Hartshorn was again defeated even in this overwhelmingly working-class constituency by the Liberal journalist, J. Hugh Edwards, in the name of nonconformity and Welsh nationalism.[1] The only consolation for Labour was the result in Gower, where John Williams, the sitting member, narrowly beat off the unexpected challenge of a last-minute Liberal opponent, W. F. Phillips, a virulent opponent of Socialism, by 953 votes. Even here, the presence on Williams's platform of such respected local patriarchs as Dr. 'Gomer' Lewis of Capel Gomer was as much a tribute to the older social pattern as reaction against it.[2]

In Wales as elsewhere, the general election of December 1910 was fought almost entirely on the question of the Parliament Bill. Even the time-honoured issue of disestablishment appeared on barely half a dozen Liberal addresses, thus giving rise to later Unionist claims that the government had no mandate to deal with Welsh disestablishment. Thirteen out of twenty Unionist candidates referred to the question. The election results in general showed little variation from those of January: the overall Liberal majority rose from 122 to 126, with Irish and Labour support included. In Wales, two more seats were lost by the Liberals, the border constituency of Montgomery District to its former member, and, more surprisingly, Cardiff. Here,

---

[1] *South Wales Daily News*, Mar. and Nov.–Dec. 1910 *passim*; *Labour Leader*, 8 Apr. 1910.

[2] *Llais Llafur, Cambria Daily Leader, Mumbles Weekly Press and Gower News*, Nov.–Dec. 1910 *passim*. For Phillips's attitude towards Socialism, see his article 'Cymru a Sosialaeth', *Y Geninen*, Jan. 1911. He also edited the *Y Gwerinwr: Monthly Democrat*, a journal founded in 1912 to counter the Socialist elements in the S.W.M.F. Phillips was much embarrassed in the 1910 election by the revelation that he had been a member of the Newport branch of the I.L.P. as recently as May (*Llais Llafur*, 10 Dec. 1910).

Sir Clarendon Hyde, a last-minute choice as Liberal candidate and a stranger to the constituency, was defeated by Lord Ninian Crichton-Stuart, son of Lord Bute. The Liberal coalition in Cardiff was slowly dissolving. On the other hand, Sir Francis Edwards (Liberal) regained Radnorshire for the second time. Otherwise, the position remained the same, with eleven ministerialists returned unopposed, and reduced government majorities on generally lower polls.

Even after 1910 there were few indications that the political ascendancy of Liberalism would be overthrown, even in the coalfield. As the old Liberal system became static and artificial, its mystique remained. A final example before the First World War came in 1912 in a striking by-election in East Carmarthenshire. The prospects were inauspicious for the Liberals. At a time of several Unionist by-election successes, their machinery was antiquated and they were themselves divided between aristocratic official nominees and the personal dynamism of the powerful Independent minister, the Rev. Towyn Jones. In addition, there was a large and rapidly growing Labour vote in the anthracite coalfields of the Gwendraeth and Amman valleys, which had been developed considerably in the last decade. Of the electorate of 12,258, 8,000 lived in the industrial belt south of Llandebïe. Even Towyn Jones himself was careful not to offend the Labour element by introducing known opponents of the Labour Party such as Clement Edwards and J. Hugh Edwards.[1] Yet, once again the Labour challenge was ineffective, and its candidate, Dr. J. H. Williams of Burry Port, finished ignominiously bottom of the poll. The traditional programme of disestablishment and land reform, advocated with passionate imprecision by the burning eloquence of Towyn Jones, one of the giants of the Welsh pulpit, dominated the campaign. In contrast, Labour, based almost exclusively in the Llanelli and Burry Port area, failed to develop a distinctive image throughout the campaign. Indeed, it owed much of its election machinery to the assistance of the Women's Social and Political Union, which worked closely with the Labour Party.[2] Until 1914, therefore, in East Carmarthenshire as elsewhere in Wales, the ascendancy of Liberal politicians, Liberal associations, and Liberal newspapers remained almost unshaken.

[1] Towyn Jones to William Jones, 26 July, 10 Aug. 1912 (Bangor, William Jones Papers, MS. 5472, nos. 39 and 41).
[2] I am grateful to the Rt. Hon. James Griffiths, M.P., who was active in this by-election, for this information. This account of the Carmarthenshire East by-election is based on the *South Wales Daily News* and *Llais Llafur*.

In the relations between Liberals and Labour in the years after 1906 there is a strange contrast between industrial tension and political quiesence. By 1914 the coalfield was apparently seething with unrest. The year 1911 had seen the eclipse of Mabon and Brace on the executive of the Miners' Federation in favour of avowed Socialists such as Stanton, Barker, and Hartshorn. Noah Ablett's *Miners' Next Step*, published by the 'Unofficial Reform Committee', contemplated the violent overthrow of industrial capitalism and its replacement not by nationalization but by a syndicalist structure of workers' control. Power would be vested in workers' lodges, instead of in an irresponsible, bureaucratic executive. Only thus would the oppression of 'wage slavery' be terminated and working men 'have leisure and inclination to really live as men, and not as the beasts which perish'.[1] A series of colliery disasters, culminating in the appalling tragedy of Senghenydd in 1913, which cost the lives of 439 men, further inflamed a vast sprawling population, already in the throes of profound sociological upheaval. Yet this industrial militancy was slow to express itself at the polling booths. A number of technical explanations may be advanced. There were still obstacles to working-class representation—universal manhood suffrage was still far from a reality, with disqualification on receipt of Poor Law relief and complicated registration provisions which often disfranchised those younger immigrants who provided the impetus for the movement towards industrial action. The high cost of the maintenance of members was a severe burden until the Payment of Members Act in 1911, while the Osborne Judgement appeared to undermine the whole financial basis of the struggling Labour Party. More important still, the basic structure of Labour Party organization was still highly indeterminate. Those local assemblies which nominated John Williams in Gower or Vernon Hartshorn in Mid-Glamorgan were scarcely more representative than were the reviled 'Liberal Associations' themselves, and this sorely undermined the cohesion of the Labour movement as a political force until the new constitution of 1918 established a Labour Party in every constituency. In any case, constitutional politics were increasingly out of favour. The growing pressure in favour of 'direct' industrial action, particularly among miners and railwaymen and in unskilled trades, served to reinforce that trend to unconstitutional violence ominously revealed in the Britain of the Limehouse speech and the Curragh 'mutiny', no less than in France, Italy, and the United States.

[1] *Miners' Next Step* (Tonypandy, 1912), p. 30.

These are, however, only partial explanations. The basic cause of the continuing ascendancy of Liberalism lay in the unity of outlook which persisted between those professional and mercantile Liberals who had dominated Welsh life since the 1880's, and the working-class mind. They shared the same animosities—the bishop and the squire, the alien Church and the dear loaf—and they inherited the same nonconformist tradition, sanctified by the 'martyrs' of 1868. Accounts of the Labour unrest in South Wales in the years before 1914 constantly underestimate the persistence of the radical tradition. If new ideologies were penetrating into the eastern valleys, bringing the philosophy of Sorel, Bakunin, and de Leon into Welsh mining valleys, through the Labour College movement and journals such as the *Rhondda Socialist* and the *South Wales Worker*, aided by the fiery advocacy of *déraciné* Englishmen such as A. J. Cook, there were still many areas that remained largely unaffected. Here working men were still more ready to respond to the appeal of community rather than to the appeal of class, still profoundly attached to the cultural and social values of a closely knit Welsh environment. The very advance of Labour into South Wales itself reinforces this impression: the evangelicalism of Keir Hardie, rooted in the mystique and social ethos of nonconformity, proved far more effective at the polls than the crude materialism of C. B. Stanton. Syndicalism itself, in South Wales as in Clydeside, was profoundly shot through with an integrated sense of community, in some sense insulated from the English world outside: the young Arthur Horner, a Baptist lay preacher in Merthyr Tydfil, was to undergo his first experience of violent conflict in Jim Connolly's 'Citizen Army', on behalf of the cause of Celtic nationalism in Ireland.[1] Up to 1914, indeed, the major centres of industrial militancy in the coalfield were few and localized, and its extent has often been exaggerated. Away from the storm centres of the Rhondda and Aberdare there were many areas where Socialism was at best static if not in decline. Only in two districts, Aberdare and Maesteg, did the miners vote for a general stoppage in October 1910.[2] In 1912, when the British miners in general narrowly voted to continue the strike on behalf of a minimum wage, the South Wales miners as a whole voted for a return to work. If there was a complete reaction against the older leaders in the election of the Welsh

---

[1] Horner, op. cit., pp. 25–26.
[2] *South Wales Daily News*, 1 Oct. 1910. The total vote was 73,345–42,817 against a general stoppage.

members on the M.F.G.B. executive in 1911, the following year saw
William Brace again returned ·easily at the head of the poll, at the
expense of C. B. Stanton, while the re-election of Vernon Hartshorn,
a known opponent of syndicalism, was itself almost a vote for moderation.[1] Thousands of miners who voted for affiliation to the Labour
Party in 1908 must have returned to their traditional Liberal allegiance
when confronted with a direct personal choice at the polls in 1910.
Some characteristic forms of Labour organization owed much to the
leadership and initiative of local Liberals. This was often the case in
the Co-operative movement, whose South Wales branches increased
their membership rapidly in this period from 19,772 in 1892 to
117,858 in 1915: for example, the Liberal alderman W. H. Brown
was a pioneer in Co-operation in Newport and presided over the Cardiff Co-operative congress of 1900.[2] Down to 1914, therefore, Liberal nonconformity remained in the ascendant. To achieve a political
revolution in Wales, a sociological revolution was first necessary, to
suggest new values and wider loyalties. It was here that the effect of
the First World War had such a convulsive impact upon the industrial South, particularly on the younger generation. Only then did
the working class of Wales seize decisively the political power that
had been theirs since the Reform Act of 1884. Until that time, even
amid the evident ineffectiveness of the Welsh Party, the feebleness of
Liberal Associations and the increasing irrelevance of Welsh disestablishment as the centre-piece of any political creed, Labour in
Wales remained largely rooted in the local issues of the villages and
valleys rather than in the international cause of social revolution.

(iv) *The Second Welsh Home Rule Movement*

In the stormy interval between the two general elections of 1910,
as the cause of disestablishment reached a critical phase and labour
relations in the coalfield rapidly deteriorated during the Cambrian
stoppage, interest was unexpectedly revived in the dormant issue of
Welsh home rule. Its resurgence was due solely to the efforts of one
man, E. T. John (1857–1931), a manufacturer in Middlesbrough, who
had returned to Wales in middle age after nearly forty years in the
commercial and political life of the North-east. John had joined forces

[1] Ibid., 1 Oct. 1912. The figures were Brace, 40,991; Hartshorn, 35,649; Barker,
32,082, elected. For Hartshorn's views on syndicalism, see *South Wales Daily News*,
13 Sept. 1912.
[2] *Swansea Co-operative Congress: Souvenir, 1917* (Manchester, 1917), pp. 182–3,
200–2.

with the experienced journalist, Beriah Gwynfe Evans, basing his tactics on 'a persistent and well-directed newspaper campaign'.[1] In a series of letters to the press, they expounded the need for Welsh self-government, as part of a general system of federal devolution. Even the Unionist *Western Mail* lent unexpected support.[2] In addition, John kept in close touch with the newly formed Scottish National Committee, with which forty-four Scottish M.P.'s under the general leadership of W. H. Cowan (East Aberdeen) were associated.[3]

John's immediate task, however, lay in the conversion of Welsh opinion, and he began in Anglesey, where he resided. On 29 September 1910 he carried a resolution in favour of federal devolution in the Anglesey Liberal Association, which urged 'similarity and spontaneity' of treatment of Scotland and Wales with Ireland. After an unsuccessful attempt to 'capture' the Welsh National Liberal Council at Mountain Ash on 20 October, several other Liberal Associations declared in favour of Welsh home rule in 1911. On 13 August 1911 the Welsh National Liberal Council also passed a resolution to this effect. John's position was much enhanced by his return as Liberal member for East Denbighshire in the election of December 1910. He emphasized the cause of Welsh self-government during his campaign and was elected by the large majority of 3,263. However, the significance of this should not be exaggerated, as the East Denbighshire constituency, with its large nonconformist and mining vote, was an immensely secure Liberal stronghold.

It was clear that John had to undertake a revolution in political thinking on Welsh affairs. Some modest progress had been made in providing separate administrative treatment for Wales, but only to a limited extent. An unexpected extension had come during the debates on Lloyd George's National Insurance Bill of 1911. After the Irish members had successfully agitated for a separate commission for Ireland, the Scottish and Welsh members belatedly demanded separate administrations for their countries also. With Lloyd George taking no interest in the issue, new commissions came into being for Scotland and Wales. Many civil servants regarded this as entailing the total destruction of the National Insurance scheme, but experience belied their fears. Under the active chairmanship of T. J. Hughes, the Welsh Commissioners succeeded in emerging unscathed from

---

[1] Beriah Evans to John, 15 Apr. 1913 (N.L.W., E. T. John Papers).
[2] Beriah Evans to John, 22 Aug. 1913 (N.L.W., E. T. John Papers).
[3] John to W. H. Cowan, 5 Oct. 1910 (N.L.W., E. T. John Papers).

defeatism in London and nationalist criticism in Wales and played a most effective part in helping to operate Lloyd George's revolutionary experiment in welfare legislation. In the words of Sir Henry Bunbury, 'it was not only a necessary but a very successful experiment in applied home rule'.[1]

In the field of agriculture, after great pressure in Wales, Runciman, President of the Board of Agriculture, agreed in 1912 to create a Council of Agriculturists for Wales, with a Welsh-speaking inspector and an agricultural commissioner in the person of Professor Bryner Jones. Although its creation provided further evidence of the distinct economic problems of Wales, the new Council failed to satisfy Welsh opinion. It possessed no powers and no funds. Instead, the Welsh National Committee, under John's presidency, demanded a fully autonomous Welsh Board of Agriculture.[2] This demand was reiterated by a sub-committee of the Welsh Party under the chairmanship of Alfred Mond which reported in July 1914. Again the depressed, insecure condition of Welsh agriculture was rehearsed and, it was claimed, only a Welsh Board of Agriculture, by establishing state land banks and co-operative credit associations to lend money to tenant farmers on easy terms, could rehabilitate Welsh rural life.[3]

The campaign for Welsh devolution was greatly assisted by the general trend of current political discussion. At the constitutional conference between June and November 1910, among the many proposals canvassed was that of federal devolution, as a solution to the Irish question. This was the theme of an inspired series of articles in *The Times* in October and November by 'Pacificus', widely supposed to be Lord Esher, but who was in fact F. S. Oliver, the biographer of Alexander Hamilton.[4] Among the Unionists who favoured a settlement of the Irish question on these lines were the Hon. Edward Wood, Leopold Amery, and J. A. R. Marriott. At the same time, several government spokesmen also began cautiously to advocate a federal solution. Lloyd George had always preferred this

---

[1] Bunbury (ed.), *Lloyd George's Ambulance Wagon* (London, 1957), pp. 30–31. Also see pp. 148, 222–6, 272. Also see *Daily Chronicle*, 13 Nov. 1911, and *Wales*, Jan. 1912. There is a comment in Beriah Evans to John, 28 July 1913 (N.L.W., E. T. John Papers). The Welsh commissioners were Ald. T. J. Hughes (Chairman), J. Rowland, Dr. Harold Richards, with Prof. Thomas Jones as secretary.

[2] *Western Mail*, 31 May, 18 June, 21 Sept. 1912.

[3] *Welsh Land. Report of the Welsh Land Committee: Rural* (London, 1914), particularly chapters xiii–xv. For further discussions of the Welsh land question at this time, see *Wales*, 1911–14, for articles by Ellis Davies, Brynmor Jones, and others; Llewelyn Williams, 'Pwnc y tir yng Nghymru', *Y Geninen*, Jan. 1914.

[4] *The Times*, 20 Oct.–2 Nov. 1910.

to outright Irish autonomy, ever since his flirtation with Joseph Chamberlain back in 1886, and both Lloyd George and the Master of Elibank appeared to endorse Welsh and Scottish home rule in speeches at Bala, the native town of Tom Ellis, on 20 September 1910. More significant still, there was even a hint that some Irish leaders might be prepared to accept such a policy, even though it would clearly retard home rule for Ireland alone. An interview with Redmond in New York on 5 October 1910 (which he was soon forced to disavow) and a letter by T. P. O'Connor appeared to point the way. John was told that they 'should help forward your movement immensely'.[1]

Although both Irish Nationalist and Unionist opinion soon proved quite intransigent, the Liberal government continued to proclaim the need for a full application of 'home rule all round'. Asquith, in introducing the third Irish Home Rule Bill on 11 April 1912, asserted it to be 'the first step in a larger and more comprehensive policy', and Brynmor Jones, as chairman of the Welsh Party, looked forward to its extension to Wales.[2] Shortly afterwards, on 6 May, Asquith reiterated to a deputation of Scottish members that the government intended to transmit 'the process of devolution, so as to apply to all the different parts of the United Kingdom', and that the case of Ireland was not isolated.[3]

John continued his earnest efforts to win over his reluctant colleagues to the cause of Welsh home rule. Some Welsh members were apprehensive that it would still further retard the progress of disestablishment, but John did succeed in persuading the Welsh Party to set up a sub-committee to consider self-government.[4] His own position was strengthened by his election as president of the newly formed Welsh National League. The cause of devolution was kept alive in a series of Scottish Home Rule Bills introduced privately by Scottish back-bench members between 1908 and 1914, which John supported in debate and for which he acted as teller. Finally in March 1914 John himself introduced a Welsh Home Rule Bill in the Commons, the first such measure ever to be discussed.[5] In the terms of

[1] Beriah Evans to John, 7 Oct. 1910 (N.L.W., E. T. John Papers). Beriah Evans to William Jones, 10 Oct. 1910 (Bangor, William Jones Papers, 5472, no. 51).
[2] *Parl. Deb.*, 5th ser., vol. xxxvi, p. 1403; ibid., vol. xxxvii, p. 121 (Brynmor Jones's speech).
[3] Asquith's interview with Scottish home rule deputation (Bodleian, Asquith Papers, box 3).
[4] John to J. E. Powell, 18 Mar. 1911 (N.L.W., E. T. John Papers).
[5] *Parl. Deb.*, 5th ser., vol. lix, pp. 1235–8.

this Bill, while the Imperial Parliament would retain control of foreign policy, defence, postal services, and customs and excise, a single-chamber Welsh legislature would be set up, with ninety full members elected by complete adult suffrage, to govern Welsh affairs. Its province would include pensions, insurance, labour exchanges, and taxation. The executive would include a Lord President, as the King's representative, while the Welsh members in the Commons would be reduced to twenty-seven in number, elected by proportional representation.

John's brief and able speech quoted Lloyd George's earlier declarations in support of Welsh home rule, but his bill aroused scant interest and did not progress beyond the formal First Reading. The World War soon extinguished all interest in the subject. The second home rule movement was far less heroic and visionary than the campaign of Tom Ellis and Lloyd George a generation earlier, and extended to a far narrower audience. It seemed that since the break-up of *Cymru Fydd* most Welshmen had lost faith in the nationalist panacea. The earnest sincerity of John, industrious but pedestrian, was not calculated to inflame the subdued passions of nationalism, particularly since Lloyd George lent him no assistance. It seemed that optimistic comparisons of Wales with Ireland had little foundation now. Their problems were far from identical, while opinion in Wales was much more divided by sectional, regional, or class antagonisms than it was unified by the appeal of autonomy.

(v) *The Triumph of Disestablishment*

The dominating factor in Welsh politics on the eve of the First World War, however, was the passage of the Parliament Act. After fifty years of struggle, Welsh disestablishment was at last made an active reality, the culmination of the efforts of Welsh radicalism. During the prolonged constitutional conflict between the Lords and the Commons between 1909 and 1911, Welsh disestablishment had made steady progress. Asquith had included an imprecise reference to 'religious equality' in Wales as one of the measures over which constitutional 'safeguards' must be demanded by a Liberal government in future, in his important Albert Hall speech in December 1909. In the January elections following, disestablishment had appeared on the addresses of twenty-six Welsh Liberal candidates, and Winston Churchill, the new Home Secretary, announced fiercely that it was the intention of the government 'to free Wales from its alien Church'.

Even at this critical stage, however, a compromise was not completely ruled out, particularly by the fertile mind of Lloyd George. In the constitutional conference of 1910, Lloyd George was active in promoting the idea of a coalition ministry, drawn from all parties, which would reach an accommodation on all the decisive political issues of the day. These included Welsh disestablishment, together with imperial preference, conscription, Irish home rule, and an increase in armaments, all of which Lloyd George curiously termed 'non-controversial questions', a description that emphasizes that impression of political irresponsibility which he aroused in some of his colleagues. Over Welsh disestablishment, he proposed a compromise over endowments as in 1906, together with a referendum of the Welsh people, both anathema to his nonconformist supporters in Wales.[1] However, the conference broke up on the question of Ulster, and the dissolution of Parliament on 28 November introduced the final phase of the crisis.

The subsequent progress of the Parliament Bill brought Welsh disestablishment gradually nearer. On 7 March 1911 a deputation from the Welsh Party was assured by Asquith that when the Parliament Bill became law a Disestablishment Bill would be given a position that would enable it to override the Lords' veto during the 1910 Parliament.[2] The fears of a section in Wales, led by such experienced campaigners as 'Cochfarf' and Beriah Gwynfe Evans, that once again the Welsh cause would be postponed were thus allayed.[3] An attempt by Unionist members to remove both Welsh disestablishment and Irish home rule from the scope of the Parliament Bill failed, and, after Asquith had finally revealed the King's promise to create sufficient peers to ensure the passage of the Parliament Bill, the Lords eventually narrowly passed it on 10 August. So the ground was cleared for another massive struggle. The new Home Secretary, McKenna, transferred from his unhappy sojourn at the Admiralty, opened the Liberal campaign at the Queen's Hall on 25 January 1912, in which he justified disestablishment in Wales on the grounds of the numerical inferiority of the Church and its lack of harmony with Welsh national life. Shortly afterwards, Ellis Griffith received long-overdue promo-

[1] Lucy Masterman, *C. F. G. Masterman* (London, 1939), pp. 164–5. Bell, op. cit., vol. i, p. 617.
[2] *South Wales Daily News*, 8 Mar. 1911.
[3] Beriah Evans to Edward Thomas, 17, 21 Jan. 1911 (Cardiff, Cochfarf Papers).

tion as Under Secretary to the Home Office, to help prepare the Bill.[1]
Brynmor Jones succeeded him as chairman of the Welsh Party.

The disestablishment controversy was given new momentum when,
after countless delays, the Report of the Royal Commission on the
churches finally appeared. Its appearance was characteristic of the entire history of the Commission. Only two members, the chairman
and J. E. Greaves, signed the Report without reservation. Lord Hugh
Cecil and Archdeacon Owen Evans appended a memorandum mainly
critical of the nonconformist statistics provided. Conversely, Sir
John Williams, Brynmor Jones, Sir Francis Edwards, J. H. Davies,
and Rev. J. Morgan Gibbon, all Liberals, appended notes and memo-
randa casting doubt on the accuracy of the Church figures, while
Gibbon in fact did not sign the Report at all and submitted an additional memorandum criticizing the conduct of the inquiry and the
way in which nonconformist evidence had been excluded by the
chairman, Vaughan Williams. Amid these reverberating disagree-
ments, the Report proper was a bald, attenuated document of sixty-
seven pages, a tiny mouse after years of mountainous labour. One
caustic critic considered it 'an amazing volume to anyone who was
not behind the scenes. . . The dullness of the thing will be its main
protection from criticism for the possible critic will be choked off by
the thickness of formless matter through which he would have to
work to get at the vitals, if any there are. . . . '[2] The Report avoided
the major controversy of the disendowment question altogether,
namely the origin of the title to Church property. This was, it said,
'almost impossible and very controversial'.[3] But it did serve the one
vital function of providing some statistical basis for the numerical
claims of Church and nonconformity.[4] It gave nonconformist communicants as 550,280 as against 193,081 for the Church. There were
4,526 chapels with sittings for 1,538,364 against 1,546 Anglican
churches, with accommodation for 458,917 worshippers. Roman
Catholics of all ages were given as roughly 64,800. Church spokesmen pointed out with justice that these figures related to the year
1905, when the nonconformist revival was at its height and that since
then there had been a recession, but the clear nonconformist preponderance of almost three to one was ample confirmation for the
claims of Liberal spokesmen and much exploited by them.

[1] Asquith to Ellis Griffith, 17 Feb. 1912 (N.L.W., Ellis Griffith Papers, 301).
[2] R. M. Thomas to T. Huws Davies, 27 Dec. 1910 (N.L.W., Huws Davies MSS., 16,354c).
[3] *Report*, p. 7.   [4] Ibid., p. 20.

The eight bulky volumes which comprise all the evidence and statistics garnered by the Commission during four years and in over 48,000 questions, are less revealing than the evidence of the Land Commission of 1893–6, because of the more restricted nature of the inquiries. Nevertheless, the picture of the condition of Welsh religious life gained from them is a valuable one. They depict a nonconformity which was already losing the brief messianic fervour of the revival of 1904, but which was still firmly rooted in the areas most truly Welsh in speech and outlook. It was much weakened by wasteful denominational rivalry, which led to an unnecessary multiplication of chapels in every village and hamlet, in spite of the fact that doctrinal variations between the various denominations, save for the Baptist theory of immersion, were almost non-existent.[1] Such differences as did exist lay rather in matters of government and organization. Church spokesmen, even in such populous areas as the Rhondda and Aberdare valleys, testified to the growing vitality of the established Church and its increasing adaptability to Welsh culture, an impression which many nonconformists confirmed, but it remained a minority creed, albeit an active one. There was still little co-operation in spiritual matters between Church and chapel, in part owing to class differences.[2] On all sides there was concern at the diminishing influence of all religious bodies, particularly among nonconformist bodies— by 1912 there was a total loss of 19,538 communicants since 1905 in spite of the rapid growth of the population. It was this which was leading the Methodists to abandon their traditional itinerant system in favour of the more settled pastorate of the Independents, and indeed the Methodists proved the most successful denomination in maintaining their membership during the period 1905–14.[3] A great gulf of hostility or prejudice, of which the Establishment was the symbol rather than the cause, still kept the ministers of religion apart, and diverted them from their spiritual mission.

As the prospect of a long and bitter struggle over disestablishment appeared inevitable, there were final efforts at a compromise. The 'Round Table Conference', convened by Sir Henry Lunn in December 1911, contained many distinguished men of moderate views, and aimed at securing a settlement over disendowment. The twelve Church representatives included Bishop Gore of Oxford, Bishop

---

[1] *Royal Commission, Evidence*, vol. ii, qu. 16,981–2; vol. iii, qu. 29,088.
[2] Ibid., vol. iv, qu. 48,095.
[3] Ibid., vol. ii, qu. 13,834; vol. iv, qu. 37,866. See Appendix C below.

Hicks of Lincoln, Canon Scott Holland, and Canon Hensley Henson, while the twelve nonconformists contained among their number the Rev. J. Scott Lidgett (Wesleyan), the Rev. J. H. Shakespeare (Baptist), and Sir Edward Fry (Quaker).[1] But the leaders of neither side were prepared to compromise. The young Edgar Jones, member for Merthyr Tydfil, was strongly reprimanded for suggesting at the Welsh Baptist Union that the terms of disendowment might be 'charitable and generous'.[2] On the other side, the *Church Times* belligerently warned its readers of 'The Coming Fight'.[3] The Church Defence Committee reassembled its forces, and in the Upper House of Convocation at Canterbury a resolution by Archbishop Randall Davidson in strong opposition to the Bill was carried overwhelmingly, Bishop Gore of Oxford alone dissenting.

Shortly after, McKenna introduced the third Welsh Disestablishment Bill on 23 April 1912.[4] Its provisions over disendowment closely resembled those of its predecessors. Of the endowments of the Church, £87,000 would be retained, while £173,000 derived from parochial endowments, Queen Anne's Bounty, and various parliamentary grants would be secularized and allocated by the Church Commissioners to national purposes. In the subsequent First Reading debate, which extended over two days, the Unionist Opposition made clear its determination to fight the Bill hard on every stage. Herbert Lewis had noted that, even during McKenna's 'careful but lifeless speech', the Opposition 'were extremely rude throughout'.[5] The main opposition came from the back benches, since the two leading Unionist front-bench spokesmen, Bonar Law and Austen Chamberlain, were both nonconformists and therefore felt less deeply over disestablishment than did their Anglican colleagues. The Church Parliamentary Committee had been reconstituted, with Alfred Lyttelton as chairman and Arthur Griffith-Boscawen as secretary.[6] Among its able array of speakers were Sir Alfred Cripps, Lord Wolmer, Sir E. Pollock, Samuel Hoare, Ormsby-Gore, the Hon. Edward Wood, and the formidable Cecils. Lyttelton led off for the Opposition in a dignified and moderate speech in which he made a theoretical defence of the concept of the Establishment and condemned violation

[1] *Church Times*, 22 Dec. 1911.
[2] *South Wales Daily News*, 13–23 Sept. 1911.
[3] *Church Times*, 2–16 Feb. 1912.
[4] *Parl. Deb.*, 5th ser., vol. xxxvii, pp. 944 ff. Cf. Stephen McKenna, *Reginald McKenna* (London, 1948), pp. 132 ff.
[5] Herbert Lewis's Diary, 23 Apr. 1912 (Penucha MSS.).
[6] Griffith-Boscawen, op. cit., p. 76.

of its property. Subsequent speeches were able and effective, displayed much learning, and were in the main free from passion. An interesting feature of the debate was a speech on each side by two Welsh Roman Catholic members, Col. Sir Ivor Herbert (Liberal, South Monmouth) and Lord Ninian Crichton-Stuart (Unionist, Cardiff). The 'Church Brigade' was represented by Lord Robert Cecil, Cripps, Ormsby-Gore, and Boscawen, while Joynson-Hicks, an evangelical Erastian, made a flamboyant attack on the idea of Welsh nationality and on Welsh children who would never 'lisp in their own wild language'. Liberal spokesmen, inevitably, came mainly from Wales and they were generally most temperate. A characteristic exception was Lloyd George who, said Herbert Lewis, 'gave the Bill a lift which it greatly needed'.[1] In the words of a London newspaper, he 'spurred the sluggish interest of the House'[2] with a vigorous onslaught on the Cecils, in which he appeared to imply that the critics of Welsh disendowment were themselves the beneficiaries of disendowment in the sixteenth century. This statement caused a robust controversy in *The Times* between Lord Hugh Cecil and the eminent historian, Professor A. F. Pollard, a Liberal who opposed disendowment, Pollard concluding waspishly that Cecil's view was 'that the guilt of theft is wiped out by prolonged enjoyment of the proceeds'.[3] Ellis Griffith wound up for the government and the First Reading was carried by a reduced government majority of seventy-eight. One Liberal, George Harwood (Bolton), voted against the Bill.

The Times commented, not inaccurately, that 'it would be an exaggeration to describe the attitude of the country towards the Welsh Church Bill as one of interest, or even of concern',[4] and the emptiness of the House during much of the debate appeared to confirm this. A brief, curious interlude before the Second Reading was a Bill introduced by Griffith-Boscawen to provide for a religious census. It was given a First Reading in the House on 8 May, several junior ministers, a number of Labour members, and even three Welsh members, William Jones, Keir Hardie, and Major Guest (Liberal, Pembroke District), supporting it, while two Ulster Unionists told against it. However, it progressed no farther.

[1] Herbert Lewis's Diary, 25 Apr. 1912 (Penucha MSS.).
[2] *Daily Graphic*, 26 Apr. 1912.
[3] *The Times*, 26 Apr.–1 May 1912. Cf. Viscount Cecil of Chelwood, *All the Way* (London, 1949), p. 120.
[4] *The Times*, 30 Apr. 1912.

The Second Reading debate occupied four days (13–16 May).[1] It was highly learned, even academic, at times, as the authorities of Stubbs, Maitland, Freeman, and even of Giraldus Cambrensis were bandied across the floor of the House. The Opposition attack was launched by an aggressive speech by F. E. Smith, a Methodist by up-bringing who cared little about disestablishment, but who now alleged that disendowment was deeply offensive to the Christian conscience —for which he was faithfully dealt with by G. K. Chesterton.[2] In a generally tedious debate, some of the speeches are of individual interest. Those supporting the measure included Keir Hardie, who embarrassingly welcomed disendowment as a prelude towards the total expropriation of landlords. Hobhouse (Chancellor of the Duchy of Lancaster) spoke eloquently, as a Liberal churchman, of the bene-fit the Church would derive from disestablishment, as later did C. F. G. Masterman (Bethnal Green), the searching critic of the 'condi-tion of England'. Asquith intervened on the third day, to justify the Bill solely on the grounds of Welsh opinion. On the final day, Lloyd George again enlivened proceedings by an attack on the Duke of Devonshire who had accused the government of 'robbery of God'. The Duke's fortunes, said Lloyd George with tremulous emphasis, 'were laid deep in sacrilege'. His ancestors had pillaged the poor and 'their hands were dripping with the fat of sacrilege'. The Church spokesmen, of whom Lord Hugh Cecil made perhaps the ablest con-tribution, concentrated mainly on the disendowment provisions. A curious contribution came from Sir John Rees (Unionist, East Not-tingham) who had voted as a Welsh Liberal for disestablishment as recently as 1909, and now tried to justify his change of front. Two Liberal members, Harwood and Sir Edward Beauchamp (Lowestoft), announced that they would vote against the Bill. The final contribu-tions came from Bonar Law and McKenna, neither particularly effec-tive, and the Second Reading was carried by 348 votes to 267. Two Liberals voted against, while nine others were absent unpaired. Seventy-five Irish members voted with the government. The Welsh members, by thirty-one to three, voted for the Second Reading.

At a time when party feelings were very inflamed after the Parlia-ment Act, the Welsh Disestablishment Bill became a topic of national

---

[1] *Parl. Deb.*, 5th ser., vol. xxxviii, pp. 801 ff. For an analysis of the vote, see *Manchester Guardian*, 17 May 1912.
[2] Earl of Birkenhead, '*F. E.*': *F. E. Smith, first Earl of Birkenhead* (new edition, London, 1959), pp. 135–6, 217. He provoked Chesterton's famous poem 'Anti-Christ', with the refrain 'Chuck it! Smith!'

controversy. The Church Defence Committee, as in the past, campaigned throughout the land, with two notable meetings, one at Caernarvon on 22 April addressed by Archbishop Davidson, and another, a combined protest march and meeting, at the Albert Hall on 12 June. Viscount Halifax stated that in the north of England Welsh disestablishment aroused far more antagonism than did Irish home rule.[1] The Bill aroused deep feelings among many Unionists, particularly for its apparent threat to private property. Yet the campaign aroused scant concern in the country at large. Since the 1890's the influence of great ecclesiastical meetings had greatly diminished: in the world of the suffragettes and the syndicalists they had a somewhat faded air. The debate on the Welsh Bill at the Church Congress in October, it was noticed, was poorly attended and much less vigorous than in the past.[2] Further, there were prominent dissentients among the clergy, including three bishops. The support of the Liberal Bishop Percival of Hereford for the Bill was anticipated, but the attitude of Bishop Hicks of Lincoln, himself half-Welsh by blood, was more surprising. He based the issue on the Welsh claim to nationality.[3] Above all, Bishop Charles Gore of Oxford, as an Anglo-Catholic, advocated disestablishment as a means of restoring the discipline and independence of the Church, and urged that Welsh opinion be heeded—an attitude for which he was strongly criticized within his own diocese.[4]

If there was a lessening enthusiasm among churchmen, on the government side the Bill was received with reluctance. Even on the First Reading, it had been noted that 'many Liberal members are apathetic and even hostile to the passage of the Bill. They say it will do a great deal of harm in their constituencies.' Herbert Lewis was alarmed at the reaction of English Liberals 'who know nothing about Wales' and feared a revolt of at least thirty Liberals in Committee.[5] The Liberal churchmen included many opponents of the Bill, notably the Bishop of Birmingham and the Dean of Lincoln, while over sixty Liberal and Labour members of Parliament, including some nonconformists, formed a committee to secure more generous treatment of endowments. C. P. Scott, the editor of the *Manchester Guardian*,

[1] J. G. Lockhart, *Charles Lindley, Viscount Halifax* (London, 1936), vol. ii, p. 201.
[2] *Church Times*, 4 Oct. 1912.
[3] *Manchester Guardian*, 15 June 1912.
[4] G. L. Prestige, *Life of Charles Gore* (1935), pp. 553–4. Hensley Henson, *Retrospect of an Unimportant Life* (London, 1942), vol. i, pp. 209–10.
[5] Herbert Lewis's Diary, 23 Apr., 22 May 1912 (Penucha MSS.).

even favoured dropping the disendowment provisions entirely: he held that 'nobody has been able to appeal to English opinion with the same earnestness and effect as Lloyd George did in 1895'.[1] The Liberation Society, while in general control of the campaign in England,[2] had lost much of its political vigour, while 'political dissent' was a declining force. Even the militant Congregationalists made only the briefest reference to the Bill at their annual conference in June.[3] In Wales itself, there were signs that this traditional issue was losing its immediacy if not its urgency, and was less easily identified as an injustice. A prominent Methodist Liberal, the shipowner, Henry Radcliffe, a lavish contributor to nonconformist charities, announced his opposition to the Bill, and other ministers from the same denomination expressed concern at the disendowment provisions.[4]

Throughout the summer and autumn of 1912 the Welsh Bill took a modest place in political debate, far behind such subjects as the Insurance Act, free trade, the Osborne Judgement, and Irish home rule. The Liberal record in by-elections at this time was disastrous, and, so far as the Welsh Church Bill had any influence on them, it was to lose the Liberals votes from their Anglican supporters. One interesting exception seems to be the Bolton by-election of November 1912, caused by the death of George Harwood, a Liberal churchman who had voted twice against the Welsh Disestablishment Bill. The Liberal candidate, T. C. Taylor, another Liberal churchman, made the Bill a prominent feature of his campaign, and his relatively large majority of 1,176 was quoted by nonconformists as indicative of support for their measure.[5] Another campaign in which the Disestablishment Bill played an important part was the East Carmarthen by-election of August 1912, where Towyn Jones was comfortably returned over Unionist and Labour.

After some bitter discussions over three resolutions by Asquith to arrange the allocation of time for the measure, the Committee stage of the Welsh Disestablishment Bill began on 29 November 1912. By this time, 5,365 petitions had been handed in against the Bill, with

[1] C. P. Scott to J. Arthur Price, 25 Apr. 1912 (N.L.W., Huws Davies MSS., 16,354B).
[2] Liberation Society MSS., 15 Oct. 1911.
[3] *British Weekly*, 9 May 1912.
[4] *Western Mail*, 31 Oct. 1912. Cf. articles by Radcliffe in issues of 16 Dec. 1912 and 19 July 1913. Radcliffe had fought Keir Hardie as a Liberal at Merthyr Tydfil in 1906, with Welsh disestablishment foremost on his programme.
[5] *Manchester Guardian*, 16 Nov. 1912. In Dec. 1910 the Liberal majority had been 1,661.

1,442,880 signatories.[1] Liberals were indignant at the tactics employed by the landladies of Borth and others to secure signatures.[2]
The early stages in Committee, dealing with disestablishment, were
uneventful, but, when the disendowment sections were reached,
a crisis arose. The alarm felt by many Liberals showed itself in an
amendment moved on 13 December by two Liberals, G. France
(Morley), a Wesleyan Methodist, and W. G. C. Gladstone (Kilmarnock), grandson of the former Prime Minister.[3] This proposed
alienating only tithe (£126,000 per annum) and restoring the balance
of £47,000 to the Church, including all glebe. For the government,
Lloyd George and Simon opposed the amendment, but the government majority, normally 106, fell to fifty. Eleven Liberals voted
against the government,[4] while sixty-eight Irish members voted for
the clause as it stood. The government had escaped, 'saved by the
Irish', in the opinion of Unionists, but they could not ignore the
strong feelings of many of their supporters. In view of the 'substan-
tial division of opinion', Asquith determined that concessions must
be made, even at the risk of a threatened 'Welsh Revolt'.[5]

Henceforth a series of concessions was made by the government,
amid indignation in Wales. On 18 December McKenna announced
that the Church would be left sums from Queen Anne's Bounty and
parliamentary grants received since 1800, a combined total of £15,000.
This concession was mildly attacked by Brynmor Jones and Sir Herbert Roberts, and criticized with immense bitterness by Llewelyn Williams, who condemned 'the revolt of the private secretaries' which
had caused it. Nevertheless, the amendment was carried without
a division.[6] The following day, on an amendment that the Church
retain the glebe, the government majority slumped to fifty-five. The
ceding of some endowments again caused accents of revolt to be
heard in Wales. Y Genedl and Y Tyst condemned the Welsh Party for
accepting them and urged the Bill be dropped.[7] But they found little
support. Many English nonconformist leaders, notably the Rev.
F. B. Meyer (Methodist), secretary of the Free Church Council, were

[1] The Times, 7 Dec. 1912.
[2] T. Closs to William Jones, 20 Nov. 1912 (Bangor, William Jones Papers, MSS.
5471, no. 84). The reference is to 'Y Borth', Menai Bridge.
[3] Parl. Deb., 5th ser., vol. xlv, pp. 965 ff.
[4] They were Sir H. Havelock Allan, R. Armitage, Sir G. Agnew, Sir J. Barran,
Sir E. Beauchamp, W. Pearce, Sir G. Nicholson, Hon. Guy Wilson, J. W. Wilson, and
G. France and W. G. C. Gladstone (tellers).
[5] Asquith to the King, 18 Dec. 1912 (Bodleian, Asquith Papers, box 4).
[6] Parl. Deb., 5th ser., vol. xlv, pp. 1555 ff.
[7] Y Tyst, 25 Dec. 1912 (leading article, 'Brâd y Saeson').

urging a compromise, while in the *Manchester Guardian* C. P. Scott had written that 'apart from tithe we should be glad to see the rest of the disendowment proposals dropped'.[1] A further concession came on 10 January 1913, when an amendment by W. G. C. Gladstone advocating a scheme for the commutation of life interests, as had been suggested by Lord Rendel and the Bishop of Hereford, was accepted in spite of the protests of the Welsh Party. A later amendment to provide for the compensation of curates, which was supported by many Labour members, was, however, rejected by the government.[2]

The internal disagreements of the Liberals were eventually resolved by the intransigence of their opponents. No concession made the Unionists more conciliatory. They fought the Bill on every clause and on every division. Eventually, by persistent use of the guillotine, the Committee stage was finally concluded on 4 February, and the following day the Third Reading was carried by 107 votes, a significantly large majority in view of the small margins on some of the individual clauses. One Liberal (Beauchamp) voted against and three abstained.[3]

In any case, the debates in the Commons were a formal preliminary to the rejection of the Bill by the Lords. In the Second Reading debate of 11–13 February, few peers supported the measure.[4] Earl Beauchamp and the Marquis of Crewe spoke for the government, and the Bill received the powerful support of the Bishop of Oxford. In a remarkable speech, he reiterated the strength of feeling among Welsh nonconformists and the effect of the establishment in alienating the mass of working-class people from the Church. His was almost a lone voice. The Archbishops of Canterbury and York, the Bishops of St. Asaph, London, and St. David's, Lord Salisbury and numerous other Unionists, dwelt on the strength and tradition of the Welsh Church. The Bill was rejected by 252 to 51, the episcopal bench voting it down by eighteen to two. Henceforth the Welsh Disestablishment Bill would require the full process of a three session passage, as required by the Parliament Act.

In due course, on 16 June 1913, McKenna introduced the Bill a second time.[5] In a two-day debate, the familiar arguments were

---

[1] *Manchester Guardian*, 18 Dec. 1912.
[2] *Parl. Deb.*, 5th ser., vol. xlvi, pp. 1549 ff.
[3] The abstainers were W. G. C. Gladstone, G. France, and Hon. E. Fiennes.
[4] *Parl. Deb.*, 5th ser., vol. xiii, pp. 1014 ff.
[5] Ibid., vol. liv, pp. 59 ff.

reiterated if not substantiated. Lord Hugh Cecil moved the rejection of the Bill in a passionate speech in which he claimed that it was being forced through in defiance of public opinion. Bonar Law, in a speech with 'plenty of edge and hook in it' in Herbert Lewis's view,[1] appeared to threaten that the Opposition would repeal the Bill when they were returned to power. Supporters of the Bill included Ramsay Mac-Donald, in a philosophical disquisition, Asquith and Runciman, together with the erstwhile rebel, W. G. C. Gladstone. The Second Reading was carried by 357 to 258; the Bill was reported without amendment and on 8 July it was read a third time by a majority of 103. The Third Reading debate was enlivened by a speech of lurid eloquence by Towyn Jones, whose references to nonconformity wading through 'tears and blood' serve to explain his lack of success at Westminster after his triumphs in Independent pulpits.[2] Again, the Bill received short shrift in the Lords. After a powerful appeal in favour by the Lord Chancellor, Haldane, Lord Salisbury's negative motion was carried by 243 votes to 48, the Bishops of Oxford and Hereford again supporting the Bill. Thus the full mechanism of the Parliament Act would have to be applied. The Church Defence Committee again organized a series of protest meetings, led by Bishop Owen of St. David's who repeatedly denounced 'this mean little Bill'. But the *Manchester Guardian* correctly observed that the predominant feeling was one of indifference.[3] The matter was one for Welshmen to settle.

For the third time, the Bill came up in monotonous fashion before the Commons on 20 April 1914, for its Second Reading.[4] Not even the frenzy of partisanship kindled by the Curragh crisis could lend passion to debates, in which every argument had been long since exhausted. Keir Hardie urged that the issue be speedily settled, that attention might be turned to graver social issues. The Bill passed on the Second Reading by eighty-four, and on 12 May Asquith carried resolutions that the Irish Home Rule, Welsh Church, and Franchise Bills be reported without amendment. A two-day debate on the Third Reading was distinguished by a remarkable oration by William Jones, which kept even Lord Hugh Cecil riveted to his place.[5] After

---

[1] Herbert Lewis's Diary, 17 June 1913 (Penucha MSS.).
[2] *Parl. Deb.*, 5th ser., vol. lv, pp. 339–40.
[3] *Manchester Guardian*, 18 June 1913.
[4] *Parl. Deb.*, 5th ser., vol. lxi, pp. 601 ff.
[5] Mrs. Lloyd George to William Jones, ? 1914 (Bangor, William Jones Papers, MSS. 5466, no. 151).

a torpid discussion, the Welsh Church Bill was read a third time on 19 May, and passed.

The final stages of the passage of the Bill were overshadowed by the deepening international crisis. In the Second Reading in the Lords, the debate was adjourned *sine die*, and a committee appointed, on the motion of Lord St. Aldwyn, to inquire into nonconformist petitions in Wales against the Bill and into the structure of Convocation. Before it had completed its laborious findings, the outbreak of war made it necessary to suspend party controversy. On 15 September, therefore, Asquith moved the suspension of the Irish Home Rule and Welsh Disestablishment Bills for a period of twelve months. A distinction was made between the two measures, however; in the case of the Welsh Bill only the date of disestablishment was postponed, and the three commissioners would proceed with their work. Bonar Law protested at this, but it is clear from his speech that his gesture in leading his party out of the Commons was inspired by the Irish Home Rule and not by the Welsh Disestablishment Bill, as implied by the Archbishop of Wales.[1] There was a final flurry in the cabinet on 17 September when Lloyd George and McKenna, in opposition to Asquith and Simon, successfully resisted the Lords' amendments to the Suspensory Bills, and on 18 September both the Welsh Disestablishment Bill and its attendant Suspensory Bill were passed and duly received the Royal Assent.[2]

The culminating achievement of Welsh nonconformist radicalism was thus carried out in an atmosphere of profound anticlimax, in an empty Commons and with the minds of all on the international crisis. It was not an inappropriate ending to the later stages of the Welsh Disestablishment Bill. The political parties maintained a constant agitation, but more and more it resembled a formal and unreal pageant, which left the great mass of the population unmoved. The feelings of many Unionists were, indeed, passionate. Bonar Law's reluctance to reach a settlement over the Ulster question in October 1913 was due in part to a fear that it would facilitate the passage of the Welsh Church Bill. 'It is my belief', he wrote, 'that a very much larger number of our members in the House of Commons would, if they had to choose, prefer Home Rule rather than disestablish the Church.'[3]

---

[1] *Parl. Deb.*, 5th ser., vol. lxvi, pp. 882 ff.; Archbishop of Wales, op. cit., p. 268; Eluned E. Owen, op. cit., pp. 236–42.

[2] Herbert Lewis's Diary, 17 Sept. 1914 (Penucha MSS.).

[3] 'Notes on a Conversation with Asquith, 15 October 1913', quoted in Robert Blake, *The Unknown Prime Minister* (London, 1955), p. 161 n.

Later events made this view seem greatly exaggerated. While the Unionist candidates at by-elections railed against the 'robbery of religion', the electorate was clearly more interested in Ireland and insurance, although the campaigns of the Church Defence Committee may have influenced the results at Flint District (January 1913) and at Newmarket (May 1913). One Unionist member has since admitted that 'no permanent harm was done either to religion or to the Church of England in Wales by disestablishment'.[1] The Liberals showed even less pugnacity. Political nonconformity was losing its old impetus: it had always relied excessively on a concentration of strength in a few key areas. The Liberation Society was a mere shadow, while the disappointingly inactive attitude of the Free Church Council revived the demand for a National Free Church Council for Wales alone.[2] While the Welsh Bill was before Parliament, in three successive annual conferences of the Congregational Union, 'the most political and republican of the sects', only the briefest reference was made to it.[3] The anxiety of nonconformist leaders to compromise over endowments testified to their sense of weakness. The arguments employed by each side show a significant change from those employed in the debates of 1893–5. The Liberals had now jettisoned entirely the old 'Liberationist' and 'alien Church' arguments, and relied instead simply on the nonconformist numerical majority in Wales and the persistent expression of Welsh opinion, as revealed in elections. The Unionists, for their part, no longer condemned the principle of special legislation for Wales and relied more on general theoretical arguments, although they could never decide whether disestablishment or disendowment were the greater evil. The conflict here between F. E. Smith and the Cecils was absolute. Thus the Liberals chose more empirical arguments; the Union-

[1] Earl Winterton, *Orders of the Day* (London, 1953), p. 64.

[2] For the campaign for a Welsh National Free Church Council, see Beriah Evans to E. T. John, 26 Sept. 1913 (N.L.W., John Papers); *South Wales Daily News*, 6 Nov. 1909, 8 July 1911. The Free Church Council was variously criticized for the inadequate representation afforded to the four Welsh Federations on its executive and for its neglect of the Welsh language. An annual convention of the Welsh free churches had met since 1906, but its deliberations had excited little interest. The Rev. F. B. Meyer and the Free Church Council executive had shown great reluctance towards 'disestablishing' the Welsh nonconformist churches, as churchmen such as Griffith-Boscawen were quick to point out. The first Welshman to be elected president of the Free Church Council was the Rev. Evan Jones, Caernarvon, in 1909 (cf. J. Hugh Edwards, 'The National Free Church Council at Swansea', *British Weekly*, 11, 18 Mar. 1909).

[3] *British Weekly*, 14 May 1914. This famous description of the Congregationalists comes from Elie Halévy, *History of the English People in the Nineteenth Century* (London, new edition, 1952), vol. vi, pp. 64–65.

ists adopted a more general standpoint. Both testified to the force of Welsh nationality. Bishops denounced, pamphlets flooded the land,[1] but the British public remained unimpressed.

Even in Wales, the old enthusiasm was waning. In 1912 Lloyd George organized great disestablishment meetings at Caernarvon and Swansea (on the anniversary of the great Liberationist assembly of 1862) but the popular rallies of the past were absent. Lord Pontypridd, formerly Sir Alfred Thomas, for whom disestablishment and disendowment had once formed the centre-piece of his political creed, had difficulty in subduing his 'qualms of conscience' over disendowment.[2] In the crucial by-election in Flint Boroughs in January 1913, a seat represented in the past by such ardent Liberationists as Eyton, John Roberts, and Herbert Lewis, the Liberal candidate was advised 'to direct the attention of the electors to the danger of Food Taxes, and thus divert their attention to some extent from Welsh Disestablishment'.[3] For the motive power of the controversy was disappearing. Nonconformists had long ceased to be an under-privileged class, and Ellis Griffith had difficulty in explaining to the Commons precisely wherein lay the injustices of the establishment. With Lloyd George, Samuel Evans, and others aspiring to the highest offices in the land, Welsh nonconformists obviously had attained political and social equality. The memory of 1868 conveyed little to a generation brought up amid the ascendancy of nonconformist county councils. 'Religious equality' became little more than a slogan, although a slogan that had occupied much of three sessions of Parliament. The main objective of Welsh radicalism had thus lost its significance. Particularly was this in evidence in South Wales, torn by the passions of

[1] There is a multitude of pamphlets on the disestablishment controversy in this period. Among the most able are the following:
For the Bil : D. Caird, *Church and State in Wales* (1912).
      P. W. Wilson, *Welsh Disestablishment* (1912).
      J. Tudor Rees, *Welsh Disestablishment: Objections Answered* (1912).
      J. Theodore Dodd, *Welsh Disestablishment* (1912).
Against the Bill: Bishop of St. David's, *The Welsh Disestablishment Bill* (1911).
      J. Fovargue Bradley, *Nonconformists and the Welsh Church Bill* (1912).
      H. J. Clayton, *Indictment and Defence of the Church in Wales* (1912).
      W. Ormsby-Gore, *Welsh Disestablishment and Disendowment* (1912).
      Sir H. Lewis, *Is Disestablishment Just?* (1913).
There is also a full discussion of the Bill in the later chapters of the Bishop of St. Asaph, *Landmarks in the History of the Welsh Church* (1912).
[2] Lord Pontypridd to Huws Davies, 22 July 1913 (N.L.W., Huws Davies MSS., 16,354c).
[3] W. Allard to William Jones, 3 Jan. 1913 (Bangor, William Jones Papers, MSS. 5472, no. 67).

industrial strife. A 'Welsh Revolt' over disestablishment seemed a mere chimera here: an economic revolution seemed an imminent possibility.

The outbreak of the First World War in August 1914 dealt the final blow to the radical idealism which had sustained the Welsh national movement in its long struggle for recognition. The status of the Welsh nation was long since assured, with the University, the National Museum, and the National Library as its tangible symbols, recently sanctified by the colourful ceremonial of the investiture of the young Prince of Wales at Caernarvon. There seemed little left for which to fight. The political influence of radical nonconformity was fast evaporating, and its parliamentary spokesmen lacked the ability or the inclination to restore it to life. In Wales, as in France and in Italy, sectarian politics, the politics of 'dissidio', were becoming obsolescent. The First World War was to witness the zenith of the political career of David Lloyd George; but it also saw the death of Welsh radicalism as a major political force. Welshmen turned away to the economic and international questions of total war and of the post-war reconstruction, and an era was brought, sadly but decisively, to its close.

VII

EPILOGUE

(i) *Wales and the World War*

THE outbreak of world war in 1914 went far towards completing the demoralization of the radicals of Wales. The visionary idealism which had sustained them in their long struggle for national recognition was rapidly being extinguished. The first, and most obvious, factor in this process was the whole-hearted support that Welshmen of all parties and creeds gave to the war itself, in such striking contrast to the divisions of the recent past. That fellow-feeling for small nations overseas which had stimulated such widespread sympathy for the Boers in the South African War was now enlisted on behalf of the people of 'gallant little Belgium', of Serbia and Montenegro. Lloyd George, in a dramatic speech before a massed audience of London Welshmen at the Queen's Hall on 19 September, proclaimed that 'the world owed much to the little five-foot-five nations'.[1] He later stated that 'the invasion of Belgium made the vital difference, as far as I was concerned, between peace and war',[2] although it was surely the strategic dangers created by the German advance which swayed the one-time 'little Englander', rather than a purely sentimental sympathy. Ellis Griffith ardently flung himself into recruiting campaigns: he told an Aberystwyth audience that 'they were fighting for Wales on the plains of France'.[3] The plight of Serbia in particular made a deep impression in Wales; Lloyd George told the Serbian Society of his regard, as a Welshman, for 'the nation which can sing about its defeats', while David Davies, Lord Kenyon, and other public figures initiated a fund to assist the people of Serbia.[4]

The response of the Welsh people to the call to arms exceeded all expectations. Welshmen flocked to enlist in great numbers, relatively greater than the figures for England and Scotland. Over 280,000 eventually served in the forces.[5] Native patriotism was encouraged by

---

[1] *The Times*, 21 Sept. 1914.
[2] J. Saxon Mills, *Life of David Lloyd George*, vol. v (London, 1924), p. 71.
[3] Notes of a speech at Aberystwyth, Oct. 1914 (N.L.W., Ellis Griffith Papers).
[4] *The Times*, 8 Aug. 1917; cf. *Welsh Outlook*, July 1918.
[5] Ivor Nicholson and Lloyd Williams, *Wales: its part in the War* (London, 1919); p. 26. The proportions of troops to total populations were: Scotland, 13·02 per cent.; England, 13·30 per cent.; Wales, 13·82 per cent.

the creation of the Welsh Guards in February 1915, under the command of Col. Murray Threipland, and of a Welsh division under the Liberal member of Parliament, General Sir Ivor Philipps, of the famous Pembrokeshire family.[1] In this latter instance, as with the new Irish division, Lloyd George intervened personally to prevail over Kitchener's hostility.[2] Brigadier Sir Owen Thomas in North Wales and the 'London Welsh Committee', under Sir Vincent Evans, raised many battalions for the Royal Welsh Fusiliers. Even in the industrial South there was general enthusiasm for the war. Almost every leading miners' agent took part in the recruiting campaign, not merely moderates such as Brace, Richards, Gill, Hodges, and Watts Morgan, but even militants such as Stanton and Barker. *Llais Llafur*, the old organ of the I.L.P., bitterly denounced MacDonald, Snowden, and the 'pacifist clique'. Keir Hardie's 'peace meetings' at Aberdare in August 1914 were howled down by an angry mob, with Stanton, Aberdare miners' agent, at their head.[3] On Hardie's death, a crucial by-election took place in Merthyr in November 1915. The rival candidates were Stanton, who had now resigned as miners' agent and ran as 'Independent Labour' with Liberal and Conservative support, and James Winstone, president of the S.W.M.F. Winstone was no pacifist, but he was a member of the I.L.P. and unwisely invited Mac-Donald and Jowett down to speak on his behalf. In the event, Stanton won handsomely by 10,286 to 6,080. He claimed subsequently that he had been returned 'on the straight war ticket', to fight 'against the Huns for our homeland'.[4] In reality, however, Winstone's proportion of the vote was roughly Keir Hardie's basic Labour poll in Merthyr; the election merely underlined the continuing electoral weakness of Labour in a straight fight with the other parties.[5]

Even the introduction of conscription early in 1916 did not seriously diminish Welsh support for the prosecution of the war. The executive of the Miners' Federation declared against conscription, and hinted at a general strike throughout the coalfield.[6] Several non-

---

[1] *South Wales Daily News*, 19, 20 Feb. 1915. For Philipps, see *Dictionary of National Biography, 1931–40*. He sat as Liberal M.P. for Southampton, 1906–22.

[2] David Lloyd George, *War Memoirs* (new ed., 1938), vol. i, p. 452.

[3] *Merthyr Express*, 8 Aug. 1914; cf. J. E. Morgan, *A Village Workers' Council* (Pontypridd, 1956), pp. 37 ff.

[4] *Parl. Deb.*, 5th ser., vol. lxxvii, pp. 225–8.

[5] This account of the Merthyr by-election is based on *Merthyr Express*, 2 Oct.–4 Dec. 1915; *Llais Llafur*, 9 Oct.–4 Dec. 1915; *South Wales Daily News*, Oct.–Dec. 1915. See particularly the leading articles in the *Merthyr Express*, 4 Dec. 1915, and in *Llais Llafur*, 4 Dec. 1915.

[6] *South Wales Daily News*, 14 Jan. 1916.

conformist Liberals angrily threatened rebellion, particularly Llewelyn Williams, whose estrangement with Lloyd George dates from
this point. But in fact only four Welsh members voted against the
First Reading of the Conscription Bill on 6 January 1916, and only
three against the Second Reading on 12 January, and the protests in
Wales rapidly subsided.[1] Welsh soldiers distinguished themselves at
Ypres in October 1914, on the Somme in 1916, in the Palestine cam-
paign under Allenby, and in the capture of Pilkem Ridge in
September 1917, the crowning achievement of the Welsh Division.[2]
The melancholy poetry of the Merioneth shepherd, Hedd Wyn of
Trawsfynydd, invested their sufferings with a tragic grandeur, as did
that of Rupert Brooke for Englishmen.[3]

The enthusiasm of Wales for the war was heightened by the rapid
progress of Lloyd George, culminating in his succession to Asquith
as Prime Minister in December 1916. There was scant sympathy for
the fallen Premier, who had lost much of his early popularity in
Wales. Instead, Welshmen noted with pride the elevation of one of
their sons to world authority without loss of his national identity.
It was noticeable that even as Prime Minister, Lloyd George remained
aloof from London society, constantly harking back to his 'Tee-
total friends nagging me at Rhyl'.[4] His associates were rootless,
isolated men similar to himself, men such as Lord Riddell and
Philip Kerr. Even in Downing Street, Lloyd George remained in
some sense a provincial in politics. His premiership saw the introduction of many other Welshmen into his counsels, including J. T.
Davies (his private secretary), Thomas Jones (deputy secretary to the
cabinet), David Davies, M.P., and Captain Ernest Evans. At the same
time, Sir Alfred Mond was made First Commissioner for Works
and Herbert Lewis, Under-secretary to the Board of Education.
Towyn Jones became, however improbably, a government Whip.

---

[1] The dissentients on the First Reading were Llewelyn Williams, E. T. John, Tom
Richards, and G. Caradog Rees (Arfon); those on the Second Reading were E. T.
John, T. Richards, and Mabon. On the Second Reading five members who had
abstained on the First Reading (John Hinds, Haydn Jones, Ellis Davies, Towyn Jones,
and J. Hugh Edwards) voted with the government. Llewelyn Williams was very bitter
at being let down by several of his colleagues who had promised to support him in
opposition. See Llewelyn Williams to T. Huws Davies, 16 Jan. 1916 (N.L.W., Huws
Davies MSS., 16,354c). Also cf. South Wales Daily News, 7, 13 Jan. 1916.
[2] See the article by Major Wynn Wheldon, Welsh Outlook, Mar. 1919. Also Wyn
Griffith, Up to Mametz (London, 1936).
[3] Hedd Wyn was posthumously awarded the 'chair' at the Birkenhead Eisteddfod
of 1917, under the name of 'Fleur de Lys'.
[4] Lloyd George to William George, 29 Mar. 1915 (quoted in William George, My
Brother and I, p. 249).

Finally, Lord Rhondda, who as D. A. Thomas had conducted a twenty-year feud with Lloyd George since the *Cymru Fydd* fiasco in 1896, now entered the government as President of the Local Government Board, and later as Food Controller. If Welshmen were to look overseas, they saw William Hughes, born at Llansan-ffraid-ym-Mechain, as Labour Premier of Australia, while the fortunes of Charles Evans Hughes, son of a native of Tredegar, were anxiously followed in the 1916 Presidential election in the United States, in which he was very narrowly defeated by Woodrow Wilson.[1] It is not surprising that, on numerous counts, Welshmen felt a sense of personal identity with the great international conflict. After centuries of silent obscurity in the wings, they felt themselves to be in the limelight of world events.

During the war years, the traditional Welsh radical programme inevitably lapsed. Its most important feature, the newly passed Welsh Disestablishment Act, was in a somewhat difficult condition of suspended animation as a result of the war, and this caused Welsh churchmen much anxiety. To deal with this, after negotiations with the Welsh bishops, the government introduced a Welsh Church Postponement Bill in the Lords on 9 March 1915, designed to postpone the operation of the Act until six months after the end of war.[2] But at once there was a mighty protest. The Bill had been introduced without any consultation with the Welsh members and was strongly denounced by the National Free Church Council at Manchester the following day. The Welsh Party spoke out with unexpected independence, in spite of Lloyd George's private attempts to mollify it.[3] When the Bill came up before the Commons on 15 March, on a motion by Lord Robert Cecil, the Welsh members, headed by Sir Herbert Roberts, their Chairman, Ellis Griffith, who had recently resigned from the government, and Ellis Davies, vigorously attacked it.[4] As E. T. John pointed out privately, it would allow a general election, with the possible return of a Unionist ministry, bent on repeal, to take place before the six months had elapsed, and would hand over £40,000 in life interests to the Church.[5] Asquith, in a conciliatory

[1] Both William Hughes and Charles Evans Hughes are recorded in *Who's Who in Wales* (Cardiff, 1920). There is an effusive appreciation of William Hughes in J. Vyrnwy Morgan, *The War and Wales* (Cardiff, 1916), ch. 13.
[2] *Parl. Deb.* (Lords), 1st ser., vol. xviii, pp. 614 ff.
[3] Herbert Lewis's Diary, 15 Mar. 1915 (Penucha MSS.). John Massie to Ellis Griffith, 19 Mar. 1915 (N.L.W., Ellis Griffith MSS., 468). Eluned E. Owen, *The Later Life of Bishop Owen* (Llandyssul, 1961), pp. 268–87.
[4] *Parl. Deb.*, 5th ser., vol. lxx, pp. 1782 ff.
[5] E. T. John to Sir Herbert Roberts, 22 Mar. 1915 (N.L.W., John Papers).

speech, promised to begin negotiations with the Welsh Party, while Lloyd George emotionally appealed to his colleagues to 'push aside sectarian controversy' at a time when Welsh churchmen and non-conformists were dying side by side in the trenches.[1] But the following discussions proved inconclusive and the new coalition government had to announce the withdrawal of the Postponement Bill on 26 July.[2] It was an unexpectedly effective gesture of defiance by the Welsh Party, and one that caused much dismay among churchmen. In 1917 a further attempt to resolve the problem was broached. In the Lords, Lord Selborne moved a resolution to postpone the operation of the Welsh Church Act until at least twelve months after the end of hostilities, to enable the Church to overcome its financial difficulties. This was unexpectedly accepted by Lord Crawford, a somewhat obscure member of the government, but in the Commons Bonar Law, under pressure from Llewelyn Williams, disavowed his action.[3]

While these somewhat sterile controversies were continuing, the Welsh Church was at last taking a realistic view of the position, and taking steps to organize itself in preparation for the coming of dis-establishment. The advent to power of Lloyd George in December 1916 ironically encouraged the Welsh bishops to hope that the government would prove generous in compensating the Church in Wales for its losses over the commutation of life interests.[4] After intense and earnest negotiations, complicated by growing distrust between the Bishops of St. Asaph and St. David's, a large convention was held in Cardiff in October 1917.[5] Here steps were taken to establish a representative body and a governing body, while Sir John Sankey and Lord Justice Atkin undertook to assist the Welsh bishops in formulating a constitution. Thus by the end of the war the Welsh Church had reconciled itself to the coming of disestablishment, even though the nature of the disendowment provisions, after the unprecedented economic conditions of wartime, the lapse of vested interests and the enormous rise in the national debt, still remained highly uncertain.

The other traditional Welsh questions similarly languished in obscurity during the war years. In the field of education, the con-

---

[1] *Parl. Deb.*, loc. cit., p. 1818. Herbert Lewis commented, 'After all, but for him there would have been no Parliament Act and no Disestablishment Act' (Diary, 15 Mar. 1915, Penucha MSS.).

[2] Simon's speech, *Parl. Deb.*, 5th ser., vol. lxxiii, p. 1988.

[3] *Parl. Deb.* (Lords), 1st ser., vol. xxv, pp. 82 ff.; ibid., 5th ser., vol. xciii, pp. 1788–9; Owen, op. cit., pp. 328–34.

[4] Owen, pp. 321–3.

[5] Owen, pp. 348–59; *South Wales Daily News*, 3–6 Oct. 1917.

tentious movement for a Welsh national council was revived in a conference of local authorities at Llandrindod Wells in August 1917, but again there was dissension from Glamorgan and Monmouth over the proposed taxing bodies. The presence of Herbert Lewis at the Board of Education, as under-secretary to H. A. L. Fisher, aroused expectations in Wales, but the Fisher Education Act of 1918 proved a disappointment. While it allowed for further co-operation between central and local authorities and extended the provisions for further education, there was no reference to a Welsh national council: for this it was criticized by David Davies, now bidding hard for the leadership of the Welsh Liberal members.[1] The Welsh home rule movement lapsed in similar fashion, in spite of the indefatigable efforts of E. T. John, now president of the revived Celtic Congress. However, in the last year of the war interest revived in the cause of nationalism, in Wales as elsewhere. In June 1918 E. T. John and David Davies helped to convene a national conference at Llandrindod, with the avowed support of leaders of the Labour Party, including Ramsay MacDonald, Arthur Henderson, and George Lansbury.[2] However, even the sympathetic *Welsh Outlook* was compelled to admit that the conference was uninspiring and dominated by the quiescent old guard of Liberal nonconformity. The executive committee of the South Wales Labour Federation at Cardiff, while avowing its sympathy for the proposition of home rule for Wales, totally refused to associate with the Llandrindod conference, which it rightly regarded as a Liberal body.[3] On balance, the most successful of the traditional Welsh objectives, although not as a result of Welsh efforts, was the temperance movement. The Central Control Board for the liquor traffic, set up by Lloyd George in June 1915, was enthusiastically welcomed by nonconformists, as was the proposal that the Sunday Closing Act of 1881 be extended to Monmouthshire. Temperance reformers suggested a regional solution for Wales, based on immediate local option and ultimate state purchase.[4]

---

[1] Davies's speech, *Parl. Deb.*, 5th ser., vol. civ, pp. 777–9; cf. *Welsh Outlook*, July 1918, p. 208. For Davies's political outlook at this time, see Herbert Lewis's Diary, 9 May 1918, and Herbert Lewis to —, 28 Jan. 1918 (Penucha MSS.).

[2] *Welsh Outlook*, Mar.–July 1918, *passim*; E. L. Chappell, *Wake up! Wales* (London, 1943), pp. 75 ff.

[3] *Welsh Outlook*, July 1918, pp. 208–9.

[4] D. Lleufer Thomas, 'The Drink Problem: a Plea for Regional Treatment in Wales', *Welsh Outlook*, June 1918, pp. 189–91. Herbert Lewis to David Lloyd George, 27 Oct. 1917 (copy), (Penucha MSS.).

The war years further served to undermine what little militancy the Welsh Party still possessed. Its new leader, Sir Herbert Roberts, adopted unenthusiastically in 1915, was even less of a fighting man than his predecessor, Brynmor Jones. The Liberal split over the fall of Asquith in December 1916 cost the Welsh Party two of its most diligent members, E. T. John and Llewelyn Williams, who were to migrate to the Labour Party and the Asquithian Liberals respectively. The Maurice debate on 9 May 1918, a decisive moment in the political intrigues of the war, still further weakened the Welsh members, who supported the government by twenty to five, in the fateful division.[1] The compliance of the Welsh Party was apparently won over all too easily by political honours and appointments, with the massive expansion of bureaucracy during the coalition government. A significant episode came during the discussion of the Representation of the People Bill in November 1917. When David Davies moved that the University of Wales be given a member of Parliament, in view of the three members granted to the Scottish universities, he found a mere twelve supporters.[2] Ironically, the House of Lords provided the solution. The motion moved by Lord St. David's on behalf of a member for the Welsh University was accepted by the government, perhaps encouraged by his prophecy that it would prove a safe Conservative seat.[3]

As the successful outcome of the war became apparent in the autumn of 1918, Lloyd George took steps to continue the Coalition which had victoriously conducted the war. Among the issues which required negotiation with the Unionists was that of Welsh disestablishment. Lord Beaverbrook mischievously pointed this out in the *Daily Express* on 29 August; Lloyd George complained to Bonar Law: 'The reference to the Welsh Church is deliberately introduced to make it impossible for me to arrange matters with the Unionist leaders.'[4] On 2 November Lloyd George's published letter to Bonar Law, which was effectively an election manifesto, in addition to references to imperial preference and Irish home rule contained a general statement about the Welsh Church Act. Lloyd George stated that he did not believe that there was any desire to repeal it,

---

[1] The five dissentients were E. T. John, R. McKenna, Sidney Robinson, W. F. Roch, Llewelyn Williams. Robinson later was readmitted to the Coalition camp and received the 'coupon' in the 1918 election.

[2] *Parl. Deb.*, 5th ser., vol. xcix, pp. 2413 ff.

[3] Ibid. (Lords), 1st ser., vol. xxvii, pp. 1129 ff.; Herbert Lewis to Beriah Evans, 28 Jan. 1918 (Penucha MSS.). The prophecy was false (cf. p. 297, n. 1.).

[4] Frank Owen, op. cit., p. 492.

but 'I recognise that the long continuance of the war has created financial problems which must be taken into account'. This formula immediately satisfied the Bishop of St. Asaph, but Bishop Owen of St. David's remained sceptical.[1] His outlook seemed justified on 21 November when the election manifesto of the Coalition government contained no reference to the issue of the Welsh Church. The prospect of a final settlement based on the Act of 1914 proved impossible for Lord Robert Cecil. He announced his resignation from the government on the same day, owing to a fundamental objection to disendowment in any form, to the acquisition of churchyards, and to the exclusion of the Welsh clergy from the Convocation of Canterbury, even though he supported the government on every other point.[2] But his intransigent statement of principle found virtually no supporters in his own party: Bonar Law himself was well pleased to be rid of the interminable Welsh Church question on a compromise basis.

The so-called 'coupon election' of December 1918 was marked in Wales as elsewhere by intense patriotic frenzy. The Welsh elections were described as a 'great ceremony of congratulation', a national tribute to 'the greatest Welshman yet born'. Thus in Cardiff there were 'Hang the Kaiser' rituals, and in Cardiff Central three candidates, Unionist, Liberal, and Independent, claimed to possess the famous 'coupon'.[3] In Aberdare the newly enfranchised women electors were urged that a vote for the I.L.P. meant an acquittal for 'the filthy murderous Huns' who had defiled women and children, tortured Welsh troops, and strangled British trade. C. B. Stanton, representing the pro-coalition National Democratic Party, urged the immediate expulsion of all aliens from the country.[4] In the event, of twenty-two Liberals returned for the thirty-six re-distributed Welsh constituencies, twenty-one supported the coalition, Haydn Jones (Merioneth) being the sole Asquithian. The twenty-one included such wealthy industrialists as Sir D. S. Davies (Denbigh), Thomas Gee's son-in-law, Sir R. J. Thomas (Wrexham), Sir Evan Jones (Pembrokeshire), and Sir William Seager (Cardiff East). In addition, the four Unionists returned could all be expected to lend general support to Lloyd George. The Premier himself was triumphantly returned by the faithful electors of Caernarvon Boroughs by a majority of over 12,000 votes over Austin Harrison, editor of the *English Review* and

---

[1] Eluned Owen, op. cit., pp. 376–7. [2] *South Wales Daily News*, 23 Nov. 1918.
[3] Ibid.; *The Times*, 12 Dec. 1918. [4] *Merthyr Express*, 14 Dec. 1918.

an advocate of a negotiated peace in 1917. The rebel Asquithians were totally routed, Ellis Davies and E. T. John (now a Labour candidate) being bottom of the poll, as was Reginald McKenna at Pontypool, defeated by a Labour candidate on general economic grounds and not in retribution for his part in the Welsh Disestablishment Act, as alleged by the Archbishop of Wales.[1] An interesting contest was that in the newly formed University seat. After diligent academic intrigue within the Guild of Graduates, particularly in Aberystwyth, Sir Herbert Lewis was nominated as Coalition Liberal candidate and comfortably defeated the Labour candidate, Mrs. H. Millicent Mackenzie, on a 90 per cent. poll. Lewis possessed the 'coupon', but the most powerful element in his favour was the continuing influence of the shade of Tom Ellis among Welsh graduates.[2] Conversely, Ellis Griffith, another veteran of *Cymru Fydd*, was unexpectedly defeated in Anglesey, after twenty-three years in Parliament, by the war-time hero General Sir Owen Thomas, running as an erratic and very temporary member of the Labour Party and a supporter of the Lloyd George coalition.[3]

Even the Labour Party members returned in 1918 conform to the general pattern of the election. All ten were strong supporters of the late war, while the 'pacifists' were annihilated. But this served to conceal the effects of the war-time years which had been momentous ones for Labour, on the industrial and political fronts alike.[4] The Miners' Federation in particular had been seething with unrest as the government imposed an increasing number of controls on trade unionists. The Munitions of War Act of 1915, negotiated as a result of the famous 'treasury agreement' and designed to render strikes illegal, provoked violent resentment in South Wales. A delegate conference at Cardiff on 12 July defied the recommendation of their executive and voted heavily (by 94,700 to 51,850) for a stoppage throughout the coalfield.[5] After the personal intervention of Lloyd

[1] *Memories*, p. 284. Asquith himself, who was beaten in East Fife, had to contend with the aged W. Pritchard Morgan, fighting as an Independent.

[2] There is a wealth of correspondence on this election in the Penucha MSS. Mrs. Mackenzie was a former Professor of Education at the University College of South Wales and Monmouthshire, Cardiff.

[3] For an analysis of the curious contest in Anglesey, see the *Liverpool Daily Post*, 30 Nov.–5 Dec. 1918.

[4] For the general developments in the Labour movement during this period see G. D. H. Cole, *History of the Labour Party from 1914* (London, 1948); Branko Pribićević, *The Shop Stewards' Movement and Workers' Control, 1910–22* (Oxford, 1959). For Wales, see Ness Edwards, *History of the South Wales Miners' Federation*, vol. i (London, 1938), chs. vii and viii; E. D. Lewis, op. cit., pp. 248 ff.; Arthur Horner, op. cit.; Foot, op. cit., pp. 32–37.   [5] *Labour Voice*, 17 July 1915.

George, a new standard wage agreement was reached, 50 per cent. above the old rate, while a new clause was specifically directed at non-unionists. The effect was to give the miners' union much greater recognition. Even so, tension continued to mount and throughout the last two years of war there was a constant series of disputes over recruitment policy. The syndicalist 'Unofficial Reform Committee' led by Ablett and Cook was becoming influential enough to challenge Brace, Hartshorn, and the official leadership. The Commission of Inquiry into Industrial Unrest which sat under the chairmanship of Lleufer Thomas in the summer of 1917 painted a sombre picture of mounting tension throughout the coalfield.[1] The flood of new immigrants was helping to submerge older social institutions such as the chapels, and to erode what little community sense still prevailed in the sprawling mining valleys.[2] The messianic appeal of 'direct action' and 'workers' control', both in its syndicalist and guild socialist forms, was surging throughout trades councils, Labour colleges, and shop stewards' organizations. During the sociological turmoil of war, the class struggle in South Wales became a stark reality, with a polarization of economic forces. Massive industrial unions were confronted by massive oligopolistic combines as the pre-war trend towards industrial amalgamation was rapidly accelerated. In particular, those three groups associated with Lord Rhondda, United National, and T. Beynon expanded enormously in 1915–16 until their combined output amounted to over 40 per cent. of that of the coalfield as a whole.[3] In the face of this cleavage, the proposals of Lleufer Thomas and his colleagues to extend the conciliation board machinery, introduce the Whitley Councils into South Wales and equalize wage rates made inevitably little impact. The ideological excitement of the Russian Revolution provided a new stimulus to industrial unionism in all its diverse forms, and after 1918 South Wales was to become, along with Clydeside, the major breeding-ground for the Communist Party of Great Britain.[4] By contrast, the

[1] Commission of Inquiry into Industrial Unrest: no. 7 Division: report of the Commissioners for Wales including Monmouthshire, 1917 (Cd. 8668). The members of the Commission were Lleufer Thomas, Thomas Evans (Manager of Ocean Coal Co., &c.), and Vernon Hartshorn, with Edgar L. Chappell as secretary.

[2] Brinley Thomas has shown that in the period 1901–11, Wales had an annual gain of 45 per 10,000 in the rate of immigration, at a period when the English coalfield as a whole was losing population. See 'Wales and the Atlantic Economy', Scottish Journal of Political Economy, Nov. 1959, pp. 172 ff.

[3] Commission of Enquiry, p. 6. See also E. D. Lewis, op. cit., pp. 88–91, 253–4.

[4] Henry Pelling, The British Communist Party (London, 1958), pp. 16–17, 58–61, 84–87, 153–4.

political wing of the Labour Party remained patently ineffective until 1918, profoundly torn by the secession of MacDonald and his I.L.P. pacifist colleagues. It was this that had fatally split the Labour cause at Merthyr in the 1915 by-election. Then, in the last year of war, a new unity was forged: the Labour Party constitution of May 1918 provided a national machinery and a national programme for the first time. In South Wales, in areas such as Swansea,[1] much of the impetus came from local trades councils, even though the long-term effect of the new constitution was markedly to diminish their militant influence within the Party. In the general election in December, in Wales as elsewhere, the coalition nature of the Labour Party was still very apparent, but nevertheless the Labour campaign was more effective and the Labour image more distinct than ever before.

In Wales, therefore, Labour representation rose from four to ten. It included such men as Brace, Onions, Hartshorn, Watts Morgan, and the aged Mabon, whose 'patriotism' was beyond suspicion. Conversely the pacifist and I.L.P. candidates were heavily defeated. At Neath the Rev. Herbert Morgan, the former minister of Lloyd George's own chapel in London, and supported by his successor at Castle Street, the Rev. James Nicholas, was badly beaten by Hugh Edwards (Coalition Liberal). Here the hostility of the Miners' Federation to the Labour candidate was painfully clear.[2] At Aberdare the incorrigible Stanton, fighting on the programme of 'Make Germany pay', routed the Rev. Thomas Nicholas by 22,824 to 6,229. On the other hand, all over Wales, from Cardiff to rural Caernarvonshire, the Labour tide was visibly rising. The Labour vote rose to 180,875, the Liberal vote (Coalition and Independent) being 258,833.[3]

The 'coupon election' marks a further stage in the erosion of the Welsh national movement as a political force. The issues which determined the election were of general significance, national and international issues of peace and reconstruction, and not the old conflicts of church and chapel. The election, with the possible exception of the result in Anglesey, was in no sense a verdict on the Welsh Disestablishment Act, as has been claimed.[4] The Great War had

---

[1] Swansea Labour Party, Executive Committee minutes, 28 Nov. 1917 and 10 Dec. 1917.

[2] *Labour Voice*, 18 May 1918, 4 Jan. 1919; cf. Article in *British Weekly*, by J. Hugh Edwards, 2 Jan. 1919. Herbert Morgan had been minister at Castle Street, 1906–12, while Nicholas was minister from 1916 to 1935 (Walter P. John and Gwilym T. Hughes, *Hanes Castle Street a'r Bedyddwyr Cymraeg yn Llundain*, Llandyssul, 1959, pp. 68 ff.).

[3] Statistics in *Liberal Magazine*, Jan. 1919, p. 635.

[4] Archbishop of Wales, op. cit., p. 284; Eluned E. Owen, op. cit., p. 384. In Anglesey,

dealt a shattering blow to the social values and cultural pattern of Wales. Thousands of Welshmen serving at the front brought home the impact of world events to the remotest country villages, and produced a radical reassessment of the significance of Welsh affairs in the eyes of their countrymen. Some reacted with a contemptuous dismissal of the parochial jealousies of 'the Perfidious Celt', as did Caradog Evans. Others, such as Saunders Lewis, turned to a new and heightened nationalism, very different in quality from that born in the passions of 1868. But all seemed to agree that in the turbulent, revolutionary post-war world, Welsh radicalism, as traditionally conceived, could find no place.

(ii) *The New Outlook, 1918–22*

Among the immense political and economic problems facing the Coalition, the affairs of Wales ranked small. The most urgent question still remaining was a final settlement of the Disestablishment Act, still suspended in operation by the Act of 1914. The King's Speech in the new Parliament omitted any reference to it, and the question remained unresolved while Lloyd George was engaged in Paris. In April, a memorial was published, signed by twenty-seven members of Parliament, twenty-four Unionists, two Labour (Stephen Walsh and General Sir Owen Thomas, the new member for Anglesey), and one Coalition Liberal (Sir Edward Beauchamp), which proposed that the Welsh Church be reimbursed for its war losses by the exchequer and that it retain the use of churchyards.[1] But no more was heard of this memorial, which Asquith denounced as a proposal to re-endow the Church at the expense of the taxpayer.[2]

But Lloyd George had not forgotten the Welsh Church. In Paris he had discussed its problems with Lord Robert Cecil.[3] As Lloyd George had written to Bonar Law prior to the late election, there was little desire, even among Welsh churchmen, to reopen the disestablishment controversy. The Welsh Church had been active in framing its constitution anew, while on 24 May Archbishop Davidson had consented to the formation of a new ecclesiastical province of Wales.[4] The only question awaiting solution was that of a settlement

---

Sir Owen Thomas had promised to support revision of the Welsh Church Act, but it is difficult to estimate the part this played in the result (*Liverpool Daily Post*, 4 Dec. 1918).   [1] *Liberal Magazine*, May 1919, p. 219.

[2] *The Times*, 12 Apr. 1919. Also see the angry comments of Morgan Humphreys in *Y Genedl*, 1 Apr. 1919.

[3] Viscount Cecil of Chelwood, *All the Way* (London, 1949), p. 160.

[4] G. K. A. Bell, op. cit., vol. ii, p. 987.

of the complicated financial provisions relating to disendowment and the commutation of life interests. The Bishops of St. Asaph and St. David's had been in negotiation with Lloyd George and Bonar Law in the previous February, and when the Premier returned from Versailles in July he at once threw himself into discussions with the respective parties, employing all his familiar arts of diplomacy, charm, and erratic intuition.

He had already won over the leaders of the Welsh Church. The Bishop of St. Asaph had long reconciled himself to the passage of disestablishment and had formed a warm friendship with Lloyd George. Bishop Owen, with some reservations, was conciliated by the generosity of Lloyd George's financial proposals, particularly the promise of a treasury grant to cover the loss of ancient endowments: 'we shan't get all we ought to get, but we shall, I think, get a good deal'.[1] The bishops, reported Archbishop Davidson, were 'privately of opinion that the terms offered by the government were much better than they had anticipated',[2] and Welsh churchmen generally welcomed a rapid settlement. Similarly, Lloyd George propitiated with little difficulty the Welsh Free Church Council and almost all the Welsh members of Parliament. On the other hand, he proved to be as haphazard as ever in the drafting of specific proposals. By 24 July, with the session nearing its end, the government had still produced no Amending Bill, and the details of the measure were hurriedly worked out in the next forty-eight hours by the Welsh churchmen themselves.[3] The Home Secretary, Shortt, was left in almost total ignorance of the details of Lloyd George's confidential negotiations with the Welsh bishops and, almost up to the last moment, was very uncertain of the nature of the measure he was to introduce in the House.[4] Sir Henry Primrose, the former chairman of the Welsh Church Commissioners, complained of the 'ignorance and levity' with which Lloyd George rushed through complicated financial negotiations, while Huws Davies, secretary to the Commissioners, scathingly condemned the importunity of 'opportunist ecclesiastics'.[5] The whole episode was conducted with an extraordinary lack of public discussion.

[1] Eluned E. Owen, op. cit., p. 400.
[2] Bell, op. cit., vol. ii, p. 983.
[3] Owen, op. cit., pp. 400–4.
[4] Huws Davies to Sir Henry Primrose, 3 Aug. 1919 (N.L.W., Huws Davies MSS., 16,354c).
[5] Primrose to Huws Davies, 11 Aug. 1919; Huws Davies to Primrose, 3 Aug. 1919 (N.L.W., ibid.).

The fruits of these negotiations came in the Church (Temporalities) Bill, which Shortt brought up for Second Reading on 6 August.[1] Huws Davies noted that 'it was obviously regarded by Shortt as a purely Church product'.[2] Contrary to the opinions of many churchmen, Shortt argued, the Welsh Church had suffered little financial hardship during the war. It had enjoyed the proceeds of £744,000 in existing interests, while the interest on their capitalized value had risen from 3½ per cent. to 6 per cent. or more. In addition, the value of tithe had been inflated from £77 per £100 in 1914 to £136 in 1918, with again a corresponding increase in interest rates. On the other hand, to finance the commutation provisions, which were now made compulsory, the Welsh county councils and the three Church Commissioners had suffered great difficulties. Particularly was this the case with tithe: Welsh members had bitterly criticized Prothero's Tithe Act of November 1918 which forced the Welsh councils to pay £123 per £100 for tithe for commutation purposes,[3] whereas the Act fixed its value at only £109 in the open market. In all, the representative body had to be paid the huge sum of £3,400,000. Loans and a remittance of rates would provide £2,400,000 of this, while the balance of £1,000,000 would be made up by a grant from the treasury. The effect would be to make disendowment a gradual process. By 1950 the Welsh councils would be in possession of £212,000 per annum, but at the date of disestablishment (31 March 1920) only £48,000 of this would be immediately provided.

In the brief debate which followed, the embers of the old controversy were stirred. In a meeting of parliamentary churchmen the previous evening, the Welsh bishops had come in for heavy criticism from the High Church minority.[4] In the Commons debate, Lord Hugh Cecil continued his bitter attack on the general principle of disendowment, and savagely condemned Bonar Law for 'carrying out robbery, knowing it to be robbery'.[5] Ormsby-Gore, now member for Stafford, attacked the secularization of glebe and of churchyards: he stigmatized the measure as 'episcopal tyranny'.[6] Lord Robert Cecil claimed that the Bill would undermine belief in private property. On the other hand, a Welsh Liberal, Haydn Jones

---

[1] *Parl. Deb.*, 5th ser., vol. cxix, pp. 459 ff.
[2] Huws Davies to Primrose, 3 Aug. 1919 (N.L.W., ibid.).
[3] See *Parl. Deb.*, 5th ser., vol. cx, pp. 49 ff., 1521 ff., 2150 ff. Fifteen Welsh Liberals voted against the Second Reading of this Bill on 30 Oct. 1918.
[4] Owen, op. cit., p. 413.
[5] *Parl. Deb.*, 5th ser., vol. cxix, p. 470.
[6] Ibid., p. 482.

(Merioneth), criticized the terms as being too generous, particularly the grant of £1,000,000 from the treasury. But they were lone voices, attempting in vain to revive a controversy that had an antique ring in the world of 1919. The settlement was commended by such various speakers as Sir Owen Philipps (Chester), the chairman of the finance committee of the Welsh Church, Sir Donald Maclean (Peebles), the leader of the Asquithians, Sir Edgar Jones (Merthyr, Coalition Liberal), and Griffith-Boscawen, who accepted the Bill as a compromise after fighting Welsh disestablishment consistently since 1893. There was general agreement with the views of the Welsh steelworker, Tom Griffiths (Pontypool), who said that Church and non-conformist boys had been fighting together in the trenches and that it was wrong to revive the old bitterness now.[1] The Second Reading was carried by 182 to 37, the minority consisting of thirty-two Unionists, three Welsh Liberals (Haydn Jones, David Davies, Sidney Robinson), and two Labour members, the tellers being Ormsby-Gore and Sir Samuel Hoare (Chelsea). Seventeen Welsh members of all parties voted for the motion.

The Committee Stage was rapidly concluded, some attempted amendments by the three Welsh Liberal rebels being negatived, and the Third Reading was passed without dissent on 12 August. In the circumstances, the Lords could do little, however great their alarm at the passage of one of the great objects of radical policy. On the Second Reading, moved by Viscount Peel, the ecclesiastical spokesmen Archbishop Davidson and the Bishops of St. Asaph and St. David's all advised reluctant support to the Bill.[2] The discontent of the Cecils was voiced by Lord Salisbury, who deplored any compromise with the Act of 1914 and ridiculed the deluded Welsh bishops as being 'too simple-minded for this wicked world'.[3] After the Second Reading, however, a brief crisis arose. Lords Dynevor and Phillimore carried amendments in committee which would return churchyards to the Church and would make the withdrawal of the Welsh dioceses from the Convocation of Canterbury only optional. But in the Commons these proposals were firmly rejected, Lloyd George twice intervening to meet the criticism of the Cecils and Ormsby-Gore.[4] With the Welsh churchmen themselves anxious to have the Bill passed before the session ended, there was little the Lords could do. As the final stages were reached, the Unionist peers boycotted the Lords, leaving the

---

[1] Ibid., p. 493.
[2] *Parl. Deb.* (Lords), 1st ser., vol. xxxvi, pp. 882 ff.
[3] Ibid., p. 915.
[4] *Parl. Deb.*, 5th ser., vol. cxix, pp. 2101, 2108.

two senior Welsh bishops sitting alone in unhappy isolation.[1] On 19 August the Bill received the Royal Assent, and on 31 March 1920 the Welsh Church became formally disestablished.

The rapid settlement of the bitter controversy was generally applauded. *The Times* welcomed the ending of rivalry between Church and nonconformity,[2] and churchmen in general acquiesced. The *Church Times*, while approving the creation of a new Welsh province, still objected to the disendowment provision, which 'had behind it no principle whatsoever'; but by the end of the year it had decided that 'the Welsh Church has acted with great wisdom and that justification is unnecessary of an action which has already commended itself to the great mass of instructed opinion'.[3] Liberal opinion was equally favourable, even in Wales, where the bulk of nonconformity was solid in support of the Coalition. A few accents of revolt were heard. Llewelyn Williams, in whom a profound reverence for the ritual and tradition of the Catholic Church mingled incongruously with the most intransigent adherence to puritan nonconformity, was angrily fulminating at 'the great betrayal' of the fundamental principle that there should be no endowment by the state.[4] The *Genedl*, an Asquithian journal now, condemned the re-endowment (*ailwaddoliad*) of the Church at the instigation of Lloyd George.[5] The three rebel Liberals were similarly critical.[6] But they all found little response. Most Welshmen were weary of the old, sterile bitterness and wished the new Church of Wales well. Davidson pointed out that every Church leader in Wales approved of the settlement.[7] On 1 June 1920 Bishop Edwards of St. Asaph was invested as the new Archbishop of Wales, and the new Church quickly flourished, with the warm encouragement of Welsh nonconformist leaders. It was soon apparent that, in spite of disendowment, the financial position of the new Church was satisfactory. Increased funds were made available for stipends, pensions, and the endowment of ordinands, and the initial loss of

---

[1] Lord Salisbury to Archbishop of Canterbury, 22 Aug. 1919 (quoted, Bell, op. cit., vol. ii, p. 985).

[2] *The Times*, 6 Aug. 1919.

[3] *Church Times*, 8 Aug., 24 Dec. 1919.

[4] For his attitude, see articles in *Welsh Outlook*, Sept. 1919, p. 227, and *South Wales News*, 2 Aug. 1919. He had been a communicant of the Church of Wales briefly in his youth at Oxford, and was deeply attracted to the Catholicism of Tudor Wales, of which he wrote a great deal. The only minister to visit him on his death-bed in 1922 was a Roman Catholic priest (private information). Williams was deeply concerned at the spiritual vacuum in Wales between the Reformation and the Methodist Revival.

[5] *Y Genedl*, 12, 19 Aug. 1919.

[6] Letter in *The Times*, 12 Aug. 1919.

[7] Bell, op. cit., vol. ii, p. 986.

£48,000 was soon made good.[1] The Church also derived much benefit from its new organizational freedom and one immediate result
was the creation of two new bishoprics in South Wales, Monmouth,
and Swansea and Brecon. The Welsh Church Act of 1919 was perhaps more significant and less anachronistic than Professor R. T.
Jenkins has suggested.[2] It greatly increased the resilience of the
Church and brought it more into harmony with Welsh national
sentiment than in the past. The old tag of *Eglwys Loegr* lost its mean-
ing. More important, perhaps, it became more democratic in composition than in the past, more broadly based on popular support, and
less dependent on the small nexus of great landowners and squires.
In this sense, the 'loss of esteem' of which one writer complains was
a positive advantage.[3] Conversely, since the passage of disestablishment, Welsh nonconformity has lost much of its impetus. The great
ideal of the struggles of three generations was now attained; the
more intangible objectives, associated with the declining influence of
religious belief and observance, were less easy to define or to achieve.

The termination of the war, with its consequent wide recognition
of the principle of nationality, to some extent revived interest in the
question of federal home rule. On 3 June 1919 Major Edward
Wood (Ripon), the future Lord Halifax, moved a resolution to
establish a committee to inquire into devolution for England, Scotland, and Ireland and their existing differences in law and administration, and 'the extent to which these differences are applicable to
Welsh conditions and requirements'.[4] He was supported in debate
by three Welsh Liberals, Sir R. J. Thomas (Wrexham), T. A. Lewis
(Pontypridd), and John Hugh Edwards (Neath) who all criticized
the implied inferiority of Wales in the motion. On 4 June the
motion was carried by 187 to 34, all the seventeen Welsh members
present voting in favour. As a result, Lloyd George appointed the
so-called 'Speaker's conference', presided over by the Speaker, James
Lowther, and which included four Welsh members, Lord Aberdare,
John Hugh Edwards (Neath), Charles Edwards (Labour, Bedwellty),
and L. Forestier-Walker (Coalition Unionist, Monmouth).

The deliberations of the conference aroused little general interest,
and when its Report came out in May 1920 it was not calculated to

---

[1] See C. A. H. Green, *Disestablishment and Disendowment: the experience of the
Church in Wales* (London, 1935).
[2] He claimed that disestablishment had been postponed until it had become meaning-
less (*Sociological Review*, Apr. 1935, pp. 173–4).
[3] Hartwell Jones, op. cit., p. 61.   [4] *Parl. Deb.*, 5th ser., vol. cxvi, pp. 1873 ff.

stir public opinion.[1] The thirty-two members of the conference were almost equally divided between the Speaker's own scheme which proposed regional grand councils on the lines of Commons committees and Murray Macdonald's more ambitious scheme of subordinate Parliaments. Neither of these two interesting proposals for relieving parliamentary congestion had any real chance of implementation, and the Welsh press was generally lukewarm. Forestier-Walker signed Macdonald's scheme, while the other three Welsh representatives, perhaps unwisely, signed both, on the grounds that the Speaker's scheme afforded a practical short-term measure of devolution, while Macdonald's they approved in principle: it alone 'could satisfy the national aspirations of both Scotland and Wales'.[2] Another section of the Report of interest to Wales was the report of the sub-committee on the judiciary, which included John Hugh Edwards. It made cautious references to the proposed establishment of a Welsh judiciary, together with such technical reforms as the transference of Monmouth to the South Wales circuit. However, the Report of the conference remained a dead letter, as its proposals found little response from the political parties. Most Englishmen echoed the bland indifference of Lord Birkenhead who maintained that 'we had muddled along tolerably well for ten centuries',[3] and it was English opinion which required to be convinced.

Meanwhile, within Wales itself the movement for home rule showed signs of life. It was advocated by the magazine *Welsh Outlook*, edited at this time (1921–5) by Huws Davies, but whose effectiveness was minimized by its adulation of the Prime Minister, as befitted a journal founded by Thomas Jones.[4] The indefatigable E. T. John continued to compile statistics of Welsh economic and fiscal affairs, designed to illustrate the economic feasibility of Welsh home rule.[5] Some enthusiasm was, indeed, shown at a conference at Llandrindod Wells on 9 to 11 June 1919 at which many Welsh members of Parliament spoke, and Professor Alfred Zimmern, the new Professor of International Relations at Aberystwyth, delivered

---

[1] *Conference on Devolution, 1920: a letter from Mr. Speaker to the Prime Minister* (Cmd. 692).

[2] Ibid., p. 12.

[3] See the indignant comments of *Welsh Outlook*, Apr. 1919, and see Coupland, op. cit., pp. 315–17.

[4] Thomas Jones, *Welsh Broth* (London, 1950), pp. 144–5. Among the *Welsh Outlook*'s other editors were E. L. Chappell, W. Watkin Davies, and E. H. Jones.

[5] See John's pamphlet, *Wales: its Politics and Economics* (1919). One successful movement with which John was concerned was the National Farmers' Union of Wales, founded in 1919

an address. There were present representatives of all the major parties and denominations, but relatively few spokesmen of Labour. However, the movement would depend on the vigour of the Welsh members, and here little was to be hoped for. Their ineffectual representations for a Welsh Board of Agriculture and Board of Health were brushed aside. Lloyd George was too involved with wider issues to return to the home rule enthusiasm of his youth, although he did urge the Welsh members to 'go for the big thing' (i.e. home rule) rather than press for a Welsh Secretary of State. He refused to act on the Report of the Speaker's conference because it found no support in England.[1] When another conference on Welsh home rule was called at Shrewsbury on 31 March 1922, it was a pathetic failure. Very few local authorities attended, Herbert Lewis observing that this was caused by the fear of rural authorities that they would be dominated by Cardiff. Only fifty delegates were present in all. The meeting broke up on the usual dispute between Glamorgan and Monmouth and the other representatives.[2] When Sir Robert Thomas (Wrexham) attempted to follow up with a Government of Wales Bill in the Commons on 28 April, the result was a complete 'fiasco'. General Sir Owen Thomas denounced the measure and it was enthusiastically 'talked out' by that perennial breakwater against change, Sir Frederick Banbury.[3]

The cause of Welsh home rule was growing steadily weaker. The traditional conflict between North and South was being heightened by the growing strength of Labour in South Wales. Liberal enthusiasm and support waned when it was seen that the projected Welsh Parliament would only turn control over to the 'Bolsheviks of the South'.[4] E. T. John and Beriah Evans, the 'de Valeras of Welsh Home Rule',[5] were now associated with the Labour Party. John made attempts to enter Parliament as a Labour and Welsh Nationalist candidate for Brecon and Radnor (1922), Anglesey (1923), and Brecon and Radnor again (1924), each time with disastrous results. Many Welsh Labour members gave lip-service to the cause, particularly Will John (Rhondda West), Morgan Jones (Caerphilly), and D. R. Grenfell (Gower), but they did little to further it in any practical sense.

[1] *Welsh Outlook*, Jan. 1921, p. 302.
[2] Ernest Evans, 'The Shrewsbury Conference', *Welsh Outlook*, May 1922, p. 1074. Herbert Lewis's Diary, 31 Mar. 1922 (Penucha MSS.).
[3] *Parl. Deb.*, 5th ser., vol. ccliii, pp. 929 ff.; Beriah Evans to E. T. John, 2 May 1922 (N.L.W., E. T. John MSS.).
[4] D. R. Grenfell to John, 18 Dec. 1923 (ibid.) (in Welsh).
[5] Beriah Evans to John, 5 May 1922 (ibid.).

The same tale is to be told of the movement for a national council of education. A Departmental Committee under the Hon. W. N. Bruce, inquiring into Welsh secondary education, recommended a council of local authorities to replace the University Court and the Central Welsh Board, to which the Minister should delegate some of his powers. Its comprehensive criticism of the disorganization of the Welsh secondary education system, with its recommendation that the Intermediate Education Act of 1889 should be repealed, formed a depressing commentary on the outcome of the national movement for education.[1] In reality, progress in Wales towards a national council was halting. Conferences were held, inevitably at Llandrindod, in July 1921 and June 1922 to work out details. But the discussions showed little enthusiasm and there was profound disagreement as to the scope of the council, and whether it should be executive or merely advisory. Glamorgan was again concerned over its representation on the council. With the situation still fluid, the Lloyd George government broke up in October 1922, and the national council for education disappeared for ever.

The Coalition finally proclaimed the doom of the Welsh Party, whose members had largely been selected for their almost servile dependence on Lloyd George. They were now organized in two bodies. A group was formed from all parties under the chairmanship of Tom Richards (Labour, Ebbw Vale) until 1920, and then of John Hinds (Liberal, Carmarthen), while the Liberals alone were organized separately under the chairmanship of M. Vaughan Davies, an elderly Cardiganshire squire of mediocre ability. On his retirement there was no immediate replacement, several members declining the offer. Herbert Lewis reflected sadly: 'Neither in the House nor in the country does the chairman of the Welsh Party receive the support to which he is entitled.'[2] Welsh Liberalism, once inspired by a passionate, radical idealism, now seemed corrupted and decadent, far removed from the party of Ellis and the young Lloyd George.[3] It searched in vain for a programme to satisfy post-war Wales; its efforts were redolent of a fading past. Thus on 26 March 1920 Sidney Robinson (Brecon and Radnor) moved a Welsh Temperance Bill, designed to

---

[1] *Report of the Departmental Committee on the Organization of Secondary Education in Wales*, 1920 (Cmd. 967), pp. 109 ff.

[2] Herbert Lewis's Diary, 8 Feb. 1922 (Penucha MSS.).

[3] See *Welsh Outlook*, July 1918, Dec. 1918, Feb. 1919, Jan. 1920, for a critique of the Welsh Party. Also see the interesting reflections by Huws Davies, ibid., Dec. 1933, pp. 338–41.

extend extreme powers of prohibition of licences to Wales and to Monmouthshire. Despite the hostile attitude of H. A. L. Fisher, for the government, it was carried by eighty-six to eighty-four, but disappeared in Committee.[1] In August 1921 a new Licensing Act was passed, which permanently extended the operation of the Welsh Sunday Closing Act to Monmouthshire, as a result of the direct intervention of Lloyd George and of Lord Birkenhead in the Lords.[2] This aroused the warm enthusiasm of Lord Clwyd (formerly Herbert Roberts), a veteran temperance reformer, but it made slight impression on the Welsh political scene. Gradually the Welsh Party was fading into obsolescence. The great bulk of the Welsh press, *South Wales News*, *Baner ac Amserau Cymru*, *Y Tyst*, *Y Cymro*, *Cambrian News*, and *Yr Herald Cymraeg*, supported Lloyd George to the point of idolatry, and only the *Genedl*, edited by E. Morgan Humphreys, and the Baptist *Seren Cymru* were consistently hostile.

The general discontent with Welsh Coalition Liberalism provided an opportunity for the Asquithian wing of the divided Liberal Party, but the aloof Asquith, a former Liberal imperialist, was not a popular figure in Wales. Nevertheless, in January 1921 a new Welsh Liberal Federation was formed by some leading Welsh Asquithians, including Ellis Davies (its president), J. Aeron Thomas, Judge Bryn Roberts, Hopkin Morris, and H. Jones-Davies, the last the brother-in-law of Tom Ellis. It was designed to counter the Welsh National Council which Lloyd George controlled through Lord St. David's. Its manifesto attacked the government for re-endowing the Welsh Church, neglecting home rule and killing the Temperance Bill.[3] The issue was soon put to the test in a famous by-election at Cardiganshire in February 1921. Here the rival candidates were Captain Ernest Evans (Coalition Liberal), an Aberystwyth barrister and Lloyd George's private secretary, and Llewelyn Williams (Independent Liberal), the nominee of the Cardiganshire Liberal Association and a veteran Liberal and nationalist member who had developed an intense personal hostility to the 'tawdry rhetorician', Lloyd George, his one-time friend. This contest, fought with immense bitterness on both sides, made a deep impression in Wales and seems, superficially, to present a last flourish of the old national programme. But a study of the campaign reveals little by way of a consistent theme other than

[1] *Parl. Deb.*, 5th ser., vol. cxxvii, pp. 777 ff.
[2] Lord Clwyd to Sir Herbert Lewis, 12, 16, 17 Aug. 1921 (Penucha MSS.).
[3] *South Wales News*, 10 Jan. 1921. See also E. Morgan Humphreys, 'W. Llewelyn Williams', *Gwŷr Enwog Gynt: yr ail Gyfres*, pp. 62–70.

the personality and record of the Prime Minister. Lloyd George himself attempted to sway the election by blatant appeals to Welsh
sentimental regard for himself, and the main and most effective
Coalition speaker was Mrs. Lloyd George, whose Methodism proved
an additional asset.[1] Asquithian speakers, mainly from England,
tried in vain to rouse local indignation at the Disestablishment Act
of 1919. Clearly for them it was their most determined by-election
effort since Asquith's return at Paisley. Opinion in the county was
intensely divided. Sir Herbert Lewis summed up: 'Coast towns strongly
for Coalition. Uplands districts against. Unitarians against, Methodists and Independents said to be against: Baptists and Church for.'[2]
In the event, Captain Evans's local connexions, his nonconformity
and Conservative backing carried him to a narrow victory by 3,590,
thus representing a clear indication of Welsh unrest after the unsuccessful policies of the Coalition in Ireland and elsewhere. In
Cardiganshire the Asquithians carried on their vendetta through
Hopkin Morris in 1922 and 1923, until their triumph in the 1923
election, while intense cleavages in villages, chapels, and families
survived for some decades; but the issue on which the result turned,
perhaps, scarcely warranted such feeling.[3]

   The age of the particularist Welsh programme had passed, as
a force of political significance, and Lloyd George's premiership
proved deeply disappointing to those of his countrymen who hoped
for further recognition of their national characteristics. Wales emerged
now in the political spectrum above all through the industrial unrest
in the coalfield. No region reacted more violently to the bitter
aftermath of 'Black Friday' and the non-implementation of the

---

   [1] See particularly Lloyd George's speech at Westminster Hall, 8 Feb. 1921. Mrs.
Lloyd George, who made sixty-five speeches during the campaign, made play with
references to 'Dafydd yr Hwsmon' (David the Husbandman). One of the major issues
in the campaign was whether Lloyd George was, or was not, responsible for old-age
pensions in 1908!
   [2] Herbert Lewis's Diary, 18 Feb. 1921. Lewis's assessment of the Methodists'
attitude is surprising, as Evans was a Methodist.
   [3] This account of the Cardiganshire by-election has been based on the *Cambrian
News*, *South Wales News*, and *Y Genedl*. There were also full accounts in *The Times*,
24 Jan.–21 Feb. and in the *Manchester Guardian* for Feb. 1921. See particularly the
leading article in the *Guardian*, 21 Feb. I am also grateful to Mr. T. J. Evans, Carmarthen, for his recollections of the campaign. The results of the 1922 and 1923
elections in Cardiganshire were:
   1922. Evans (Nat. Lib.) 12,825; Hopkin Morris (Ind. Lib.) 12,310.
   1923. Hopkin Morris (Ind. Lib.) 12,649; Evans (Lib.) 7,391; Lord Lisburne (Cons.)
6,776.
The decision of the county Conservatives to contest Cardiganshire in 1923 was, therefore, fatal to Evans's cause.

Sankey Report than did South Wales, now under the spell of the
evangelical militancy of A. J. Cook. In rural and industrial Wales
alike, the older Liberalism was losing its appeal. Particularly was
this evident among the younger generation at the University, where
a ground swell was developing that was to secure the sensational
return of the Christian Pacifist, George Maitland Lloyd Davies, in
1923.[1] At the 1922 election, this growing revulsion was becoming
apparent. While Liberal membership dropped to eleven, eighteen
Labour members were returned, including nine gains. Labour
polled 363,421 votes, polling strongly even in rural Caernarvonshire
(which they won) and Merioneth. In the 1923 election, Labour representation rose to twenty-one and in 1929 to twenty-five. The
Labour members were unquestionably returned on general social and
economic grounds, reflecting the massive depression and unemployment which affected Wales more acutely than any other area. Welsh
political nationalism, it seemed, had found its own level; political
dissent was lost in the economic turmoil, and Welsh support for the
Labour Party proved as little affected by wider political trends as had
been its adherence to Liberalism in the six eventful decades after 1868.

(iii) *Conclusions*

With all its confusing cross-currents, the political history of Wales
between 1868 and 1922 possesses a unity of its own. It covers the
entire cycle of Welsh political nationalism as a major force in British
public life. The awakening and subsequent decline of this movement
can both be marked down with some precision. The election of 1868,
with the political evictions which followed, brought the distinctive
needs of Wales into the general context of British politics, after the
obscurity and isolation of centuries. Two forces, those of radicalism
and of nationalism, both quite novel in Welsh political experience
as coherent movements, were merged into a campaign for national
recognition. This campaign, of course, did not erupt suddenly in 1868.
There had been for seventy years previously an increasingly profound
and articulate national awareness in Wales in the aftermath of the

---

[1] *Welsh Outlook*, Sept. 1922, pp. 217–19. There is much material on the movement
in support of Maitland Lloyd Davies in the Bryn Roberts Papers in N.L.W. *The
Times* ranks Davies as a Labour member and he took the Labour whip. The result of
the election was:

Lloyd Davies, 570; Prof. J. Jones (Lib.) 560; Major J. Edwards (Ind. Lib.) 467.

Lloyd Davies, the grandson of a nonconformist minister, had been a conscientious
objector in the war. He died in 1949. Later members for the University of Wales were
Capt. Ernest Evans (1924–43) and Prof. W. J. Gruffydd (1943–50), both Liberals.

French Revolution. Usually ill-directed, often romanticized, this growing sense of nationality was none the less vigorous and alive. It found new expression as the extension of mass literacy under the twin impact of industrialism and of religious nonconformity created a public opinion of a new kind. The ignominy of the *Llyfrau Gleision* lent an added impetus. But it was after 1868 that this new awareness became articulate and effective. The advance of democracy—the extension of the franchise in 1867 and 1884, the protection of the Ballot and Corrupt Practices Acts, the creation of county councils— enabled political radicalism to become the major force in regenerating Welsh social and cultural life. A mounting wave of popular emotion found expression at Westminster in an organized Welsh Party, with apparent similarities to the militant obstructionists who were ranged behind Parnell. A remarkable group of young patriots, Tom Ellis and Lloyd George prominent among them, appeared as the prophets of a new era of national self-consciousness: their very name, 'Young Wales', in itself suggested a crusade of optimism and youthful re- bellion. The tide reached fullest flood in 1892 when the Welsh Party was presented with an unprecedented opportunity of effective power. The subsequent disillusion caused by the Liberal ministries of 1892–5, not in failing to introduce legislation or to undertake inquiry, but in declining to regard Welsh affairs as matters of urgency, left an in- eradicable imprint on the future course of Welsh nationalism. The relative impotence of the Welsh Party as the spokesman of a small national minority, dependent on the good offices of the Liberal leader- ship and fatally confused over the rival merits of intrusive pressure or external revolt, left a bitter memory. At the same time, the disintegra- tion of *Cymru Fydd* sharply underlined the basic divergence between radicalism and nationalism in Wales: it was this far more than the superficial cleavage between the rural North and the industrial South that caused *Cymru Fydd* to collapse. Since the 1890's, therefore, radicalism and nationalism have gradually parted company. Welsh national sentiment has often presented a conservative rather than a radical image. The shallowness of Lloyd George's claim that Welsh nationalism was merely 'an intensification of Liberalism' was in- creasingly emphasized by the course of the Liberal ministries after 1906. Democracy, which had helped to nationalize radicalism, now appeared to denationalize it by its very success. In the world of universal suffrage and mass literacy, of county councils and popular education, Welsh radicalism, its objectives realized, contained the

seeds of its own decay. Thereafter the forces of political nationalism
ebbed steadily until they were finally swamped in the collective en-
deavour of the First World War. The years since 1922 have seen no
real recovery.

In the subsequent recollections of Welsh writers and publicists,
the period after 1868 still lingers uneasily between history and myth.
Many of its major facets remain to be explored. Clearly it was a period
of convulsive and dramatic change. Economically, it witnessed the
astonishing industrial growth of South Wales, an explosive growth
of population both through external migration and through depopulation of the rural hinterland, the development of massive combines
and of mass trade unions. Culturally, it saw a remarkable literary
renaissance, the lyric poetry of Silyn Roberts, Gwynn Jones, and
W. J. Gruffydd, the classical prose of O. M. Edwards, the detached
scholarship of Sir John Rhŷs, Sir John Edward Lloyd, and Sir John
Morris-Jones, all coloured by an intense patriotism. Sociologically,
there came the gradual erosion of old landmarks, in particular the
institutions and the ethos of Protestant fundamentalism in the face
of the cumulative impact of Biblical criticism, scientific inquiry, and
change in the pattern of social culture. The impact of radicalism and
of nationalism was superimposed on these transformations, in the
course of which the place of Wales in British political and social life
was revolutionized. These different forces made for a growing excitement and uncertainty within Wales among what Gladstone laconi-
cally termed 'a singularly susceptible population'.[1] Further, they
were set against a background of upheaval in the history of Britain
as a whole. These years heralded the rapid dissolution of the serenity
and self-confidence of mid-Victorian Britain. They saw the first
break-up of Victorian prosperity, cyclical depression in industry and
collapse in agriculture. New tensions were released in political debate, with the rise of the Labour Party, the divisions over policy
towards Ireland and the class conflict with the House of Lords. The
brief hey-day of classical *laissez-faire* disappeared with the onrush
of new doctrines of collectivism, neo-Hegelianism, and imperialism.
Perhaps most significant of all, there was emerging a new sense of
vulnerability towards the world outside, a growing introspection
undermining belief in traditional institutions and the certainty of
moral values. In its different ways, the political history of Wales

[1] Gladstone to the Bishop of St. David's, 12 Jan. 1870 (B.M., Add. MSS., 44424
f. 88).

after 1868 reflects and emphasizes all these transformations. Even more, the fortunes of Wales illustrate some of the decisive factors in the evolution of the contemporary world. The idealism and later disillusion surrounding the idea of democracy; the political and ideological tension between Church and state; the rebellion of the farming community against an increasingly urban, capitalist society; the transition in the ideology of nationalism as it came to shed the liberal assumptions of 1789—these form the substance of the evolution of contemporary Wales. In embryo, the changing patterns of modern Wales provide a commentary on the development of the modern world.

It is, perhaps, not surprising that Welsh commentators have tended to look back on those tumultuous years with a strange blend of cynicism and nostalgia, sometimes indeed with anger. Idealism and frustration have been intermingled. Until the 1890's the writings and speeches of Welsh political leaders were suffused with a golden glow of optimism and hope. The advance of nationalism and of democracy in Wales seemed to form part of an irresistible world-wide movement. But since the 1890's there has been a growing dissatisfaction at the outcome of the national movement. The results and even the ambitions of Welsh nationalism are seen to have been incomplete and, indeed, self-defeating. There is a clear parallel here with the effect upon Welsh society of the Tudor innovations in government, over three centuries earlier. As with the Welsh gentry in the sixteenth century, the very political and social achievements which had formed the glorious outcome of the national movement, the new opportunities and mobility which had served to make Wales nationally self-conscious, have operated increasingly to the detriment of the national characteristics of Wales. The Welsh radicals, like the Welsh gentry three centuries earlier, succeeded only in de-Cymricizing themselves by their own success. But, unlike the sixteenth century, there is now no longer a vast, residual population, a submerged nine-tenths, to keep the Welsh culture and language alive and free from outside contamination. Inevitably, therefore, the leaders of the radical cause after 1868, like the Welsh Tudor gentry before them, have come under suspicion for neglecting the heritage of their forebears. The search for the 'Guilty Men' who betrayed the national cause has been an intense one. Even such national heroes as Ellis and Lloyd George have been regarded in an ambivalent way. Ellis, the 'Parnell of Wales', the youthful personification of the ideals of *Cymru Fydd*, was also the man who sacrificed his beliefs for the loaves and fishes of office.

Lloyd George, whose personal advancement symbolized the growing prominence of Wales in British political life, has come under fire for his political outlook no less than for his personal predilections, for neglecting after 1906 the Welsh questions that had formed the passion of his youth. More generally, the sword of censure has been turned against the Welsh people as a whole for failing to respond to the ideals of the visionaries of *Cymru Fydd*, as well as for palpable short-comings in the techniques of political unity. In the 1920's apostles of the national movement, such as Beriah Evans, Arthur Price, and Morgan Humphreys, surveyed the campaigns after 1868 with resignation and despair. In a famous monograph written in 1937 W. Hughes Jones looked back nostalgically to the period 1890–5. He contrasted the 'dull routine Liberalism of the Old Gang' with 'the National Liberalism of the new and young Wales of the nineties'.[1] But the vision had faded, Ellis and Lloyd George had been spurned, and Wales had 'dropped the Pilots'. A sentimental attachment to personalities such as Ellis has not disguised the melancholy appearance of recent interpretations of the past. 'Our history is a tragic one of prophets being ignored without honour; men of vision finding their countrymen blind. It is a succession of glorious starts that died with a whimper.'[2]

Clearly, since 1922 the older radicalism has become ever more irrelevant as a serious political force. The ethos of Liberal non-conformity remains a formidable force in Welsh life, a dormant giant, suddenly galvanized into action to resist the repeal of the Sunday Closing Act of 1881, to assist in preserving the federal University of Wales or in maintaining the proliferating structure of Welsh local government. But as an active political movement it is now of little significance. Welsh radicalism was the reflection of a particular stage of Welsh social development, but, under the impact of two world wars, the society which gave it birth has steadily faded away. Years before the passage of disestablishment 'religious equality' for non-conformity was a reality: the ostracism of the past remained no longer, leaving only a bitter memory to poison the efforts of the churches to secure inter-denominational co-operation. The hegemony of the squire is scarcely more significant than the dominance of the Angli-can parson. The social position of the landed classes was swept away

---

[1] W. Hughes Jones, *Wales Drops the Pilots* (Liverpool, 1937), p. 14. See also the same author's *A Challenge to Wales* (Liverpool, 1938), written under the pseudonym 'Elir Sais'.

[2] John Lloyd, review of *Wales through the Ages*, vol. ii, *Western Mail*, 29 Oct. 1960.

with the revolution of the Local Government Act of 1888; their economic foundations crumbled with the financial pressure of the two world wars, which broke up so many famous estates. The great houses of Golden Grove, Wynnstay, Gogerddan, and Penlle'r-gaer assumed a new role as student hostels and agricultural colleges, solitary landmarks of a by-gone hierarchical society. The 'decline of the gentry' is almost as elusive a concept as the 'rise of the gentry' in Welsh, as in English history, but clearly since 1922 this decline has been irremediable. With the fading of this society, the fortunes of the Liberal Party have steadily ebbed. Their eleven members of Parliament in 1922 dwindled to one alone, Emlyn Hooson (Montgomeryshire), by 1970. The revival of Liberalism in England and Scotland in the late 1950's and the early sixties, as shown in by-election victories at Torrington, Orpington, and Roxburgh and Selkirk, was significantly not paralleled in Wales. At the 1959 general election, there were a mere seven Liberal candidates for the thirty-six Welsh seats; in 1964, this total rose to only eleven. In the March 1966 general election, again only eleven Liberal candidates took the field, polling an average 8,000 votes each. One of the two remaining Liberal seats in Wales, Cardiganshire, held continuously by the Liberals since 1880, was lost to Labour. Alike in rural Denbighshire and in industrial Caerphilly, the old radical appeal had lost its magic. The decision in 1966 to create an entirely new Liberal organization in Wales, separate from the national party machine, had little apparent effect on the declining fortunes of Welsh Liberalism. In the 1970 general election, the Liberals (who now put up nineteen candidates) again met with scant success, and only narrowly clung on to their one remaining seat in Montgomeryshire. To many observers, the 1960's appeared indeed to have witnessed the 'strange death' of Liberal Wales. Its elderly spokesmen seemed more and more obviously the champions of *Cymru Fu* rather than of *Cymru Fydd*.

On the other hand, the attempts to create a new national movement on the ruins of the old radicalism for a long while showed relatively slight success. Much the most notable and interesting of these has been the Welsh Nationalist Party, *Plaid Cymru*, formed at the Pwllheli *Eisteddfod* in 1925 as a result of the fusion of two separate groups based on the University Colleges of Bangor and Aberystwyth.[1] From the start, *Plaid Cymru* sought to reject

[1] Gwynfor Evans, 'The Twentieth Century and Plaid Cymru', *The Historical Basis of Welsh Nationalism* (Cardiff, 1950), pp. 141 ff.

completely the older 'nationalist' radicalism and to cut adrift from all existing political parties. Saunders Lewis, its president until 1939 and a convert to Roman Catholicism who had reacted sharply against the unaesthetic puritanism of his youth, dwelt scathingly on the Welsh nationalism of the years before 1914, 'the spare-time hobby of corpulent and successful men'. He suggested a satirical obituary of such a 'Nationalist':

The deceased gentleman was also an ardent Welsh Nationalist, presided frequently on the platform of the National Eisteddfod, was a prominent figure in denominational assemblies, and attended regularly the annual dinner of the Honourable Society of Cymmrodorion.[1]

The reference to the Alfred Thomases and Brynmor Joneses of yore was all too apparent. Through Lewis, and still more through Dr. D. J. Davies, *Plaid Cymru* put forward a radical programme of social and economic reform—the regeneration of agriculture through co-operative farming and credit banks, the reorganization of the coal industry and the nationalization of royalties, a revised currency and banking system, and a separate customs unit. Saunders Lewis himself bitterly condemned the waste and inhumanity of twentieth-century monopoly capitalism.[2] Even so, the efforts of *Plaid Cymru* to create for itself a new radical image, quite distinct from that of 1868–1914, have been only partially successful. Inevitably the cultural and social aspects of its programme, its efforts to preserve the pattern of rural culture, to stimulate the Welsh language and to protect the Sunday Closing Act, have attracted many of the older nonconformists who sustained the national movement before 1914 and who associated the preservation of Welsh culture with the resilience of the nonconformist ethic. The *Blaid*'s opposition to 'imperialist' rearmament in the 1930's brought in many nonconformist ministers who regarded their mission as almost more social than spiritual. The incident at Penrhos aerodrome in 1936 enhanced its appeal among traditional pacifist, nonconformist elements.[3] The major centre of

---

[1] *The Welsh Nationalist*, Jan. 1932, p. 1.

[2] See D. J. Davies, *The Economics of Welsh Self-government* (Caernarvon, 1931), esp. ch. ii. Also see the same author's 'The Economic Case for Self-government', *The Welsh Nationalist*, Jan. 1932, pp. 2–3; 'The Labour Government's Betrayal of the Miners', ibid., Feb. 1932, p. 1; and Saunders Lewis's article, 'Some Economic Functions of a Welsh Government', ibid., Sept. 1933, p. 1.

[3] This arose out of attempted arson by Saunders Lewis, D. J. Williams, and the Rev. Lewis Edward Valentine at Penrhos aerodrome on 8 Sept. 1936; they were subsequently imprisoned for nine months. The place of anti-militarism in stimulating the cause of *Plaid Cymru* has again been seen in recent years in the progress of the Campaign for Nuclear Disarmament and the agitation against the stationing of German troops in Pembrokeshire in 1961.

Plaid Cymru has been the University of Wales, itself steeped in the mystique of *Cymru Fydd*.[1] Inevitably, while rejecting the radical past in theory, *Plaid Cymru* has been forced to embrace it in practice.

Partly as a result of this, its success as a pressure group within such bodies as the B.B.C. and the University Guild of Graduates was not matched by comparable success at the polls, even in areas where local depression and unemployment might have been expected to enhance the appeal of independent statehood and separation from the economy of England. In forty years, *Plaid Cymru* did not come appreciably near to winning a seat. In the election of 1964, it made its most ambitious attempt hitherto, putting up twenty-three candidates: in the event, twenty-one lost their deposits. While the party polled over 69,000 votes, no mean total, the proportion polled by each individual candidate showed a recession from the election of 1959. In the general election of March 1966, *Plaid Cymru* again put up twenty candidates and did well to maintain its previous share of the votes. Deposits were saved in Carmarthen and Caernarvonshire, but the party still seemed a very long way from winning a single parliamentary seat.

However, the disillusion with the Labour government that followed the 1966 general election brought an astonishing transformation. In a dramatic turn-round in votes, Gwynfor Evans, *Plaid Cymru*'s president, captured the Carmarthen seat from Labour in a by-election in July 1966, with a swing of 17 per cent in his favour. This by-election appeared to herald a complete change in the party's fortunes and, perhaps, a reversal of the main trends of Welsh politics since the end of the First World War. Membership of the *Blaid* rose sharply and it seemed to present for the first time a major threat to the ascendancy of the Labour Party. This triumph in a predominantly rural constituency like Carmarthen was followed by remarkably high polls in two more by-elections in industrial constituencies in South Wales. At Rhondda West in March 1967, there was a swing of 27·1 per cent from Labour to *Plaid Cymru;* in Caerphilly in July 1968, the swing to the Nationalists soared to 28·1 per cent, and the Labour majority collapsed from over 21,000 to a mere 1,874. The return of a Scottish Nationalist in a by-election in Hamilton also greatly heartened nationalist sympathizers in Wales. A new nationalist tide appeared to

---

[1] In 1959, sixteen of the twenty *Plaid Cymru* parliamentary candidates were university graduates, twelve of the University of Wales. Ten candidates were lecturers or schoolmasters by profession.

be sweeping through the land, and not even a series of alarming bomb explosions in government buildings in Cardiff and elsewhere (apparently the work of Welsh extremists) could stem its progress.

Even so, the extent to which these remarkable events did in fact reflect a revived support for separatism in Wales, rather than being merely a massive protest against the economic policies of the Wilson government, still seemed hard to determine. *Plaid Cymru*'s high polls in by-elections were not matched by comparable success in local government elections, while its organizational base, heavily dependent on students and the younger age-groups, remained relatively weak. In 1969 the party was embarrassed by widespread demonstrations of sympathy for the investiture of the Prince of Wales at Caernarvon, which put nationalists at an emotional disadvantage. Growing membership brought new and unfamiliar strains for the *Blaid*, especially in emphasizing the tension between the Welsh-speaking and the anglicized parts of Wales. The militant tactics of the Welsh Language Society (which resulted in some of its youthful members being briefly imprisoned in February 1970 for contempt of court) added to the party's difficulties. When the general election came in June 1970, for the first time *Plaid Cymru* fought every Welsh seat. However, the results showed a clear loss of momentum compared with the by-elections. *Plaid* candidates polled remarkably well in some rural and mining areas: in seven constituencies they gained over 20 per cent of the vote, and in three of these (Caernarvon, Aberdare and Carmarthen), over 30 per cent. The party's total poll amounted to 175,016, or 11·5 per cent of the Welsh total. Even so, this was well below the target set by the party's leaders. Twenty-five *Plaid* candidates lost their deposits, no new seats were captured, while, most disheartening of all, Gwynfor Evans was conclusively beaten by the Labour candidate at Carmarthen by nearly 4,000 votes. The election confirmed that *Plaid Cymru* had made some progress since 1966, especially in appealing to the enthusiasm of younger voters. But it still resembled a protest movement rather than a national party. The Welsh political scene was still dominated by Labour's big battalions. Not even a rejuvenated *Plaid Cymru* had yet succeeded in holding back the ebbing tide of Welsh nationalism.

In the light of this later reaction against it, in assessing the character and achievements of the Welsh national movement since 1868, a balance needs to be struck between the exaggerated hopes and still more exaggerated despair of many of its spokesmen and subsequent commentators. It is even more necessary not to take them at their own evaluation. The claim for national recognition that they were putting forward was, by its very nature, so novel, so striking a contrast with the recent past, that those who proclaimed it were often guilty of extremes of self-justification and exaggeration. Rendel, in the aftermath of disillusion after his retirement, wrote that 'in Welsh affairs there seems to be a conscious preference for unrealities'.[1] The most trivial issue, a regulation on a census form or a regimental cap-badge, would be magnified into the censure of a whole nation. Incidents from remote medieval history, legends of Llywelyn ab Iorwerth and Glyn-dŵr would be used as serious arguments to justify a line of practical policy.

Above all, there were the constant analogies drawn between Wales and Ireland after 1880. Inevitably these were emphasized by Unionists, but Lloyd George, Gee, and the Welsh home rulers gave them every encouragement. In fact, such comparisons were largely misleading. The political problems of Wales were not those of Ireland. While Catholic emancipation generated pressure within Ireland for a further degree of separatism, for repeal of the Union and later for home rule, in Wales disestablishment of the Church was an end in itself: it tended to divert support for self-government rather than to encourage it. In Wales, unlike Ireland, the squirearchy was anglicized but not alien. It was out of touch with nationalist movements, but was not in itself antagonistic to them. At the height of the land agitation in the 1880's and 1890's, they were still respected as patrons of *eisteddfodau* and as the framework of stability in the rural scene. Welsh landlords and clergy were too deeply integrated into the Welsh community to be the subject of boycotting. As dairy prices improved after 1895, the tithe agitation and agrarian unrest rapidly died away. The whole tenor of Welsh and Irish thinking was divergent, despite the protests of Lloyd George and his supporters. Even Tom Ellis's own avowals of sympathy for Thomas Davis and the ideals of Young Ireland half a century earlier have an *ex post facto* ring to them.[2] The ideal of Wales was to be recognized as a part of the British political and social structure: the ideal of Ireland was to

[1] Rendel to Humphreys-Owen, 4 Mar. 1894 (N.L.W., Glansevern MSS., 649).

[2] The inspiration that Ellis claimed to have drawn from Young Ireland is not evident in his letters previous to 1886. Indeed, he was a violent critic of the Parnellite nationalists up to 1885. Much of the belief in Ellis's debt to the writings of Thomas Davis rests on the article on Ellis written by J. Arthur Price in J. Vyrnwy Morgan (ed.), *Welsh Political and Educational Leaders in the Victorian Era* (London, 1908), a pietistic account written nine years after Ellis's death.

be severed from it. The object of the one was equality: the aim of the other was exclusion. Home rule in Wales, unlike home rule in Ireland, was indeed 'killed by kindness'. Wales was too much in contact with English influences. It felt conscious of geographical isolation, reinforced by religious and linguistic differences, yet without the insular self-consciousness of Ireland. The influence of the alien English, strong enough to be an irritant in the persons of estate managers or country rectors, was yet too deeply ingrained to be removed by the efforts or the optimism of a few young politicians and journalists. In practice, the great majority of Welsh people recognized this, as its continuing attachment to the Liberal, and later to the Labour Party indicated. The great economic complex of the South was an indissoluble link, a constant reminder of common interests with England.

For these reasons the movement for Welsh home rule is a false key to the growth of Welsh national feeling. It aroused comparatively little enthusiasm even in the hey-day of *Cymru Fydd*. Tom Ellis himself rapidly abandoned the idea when his Bala speech of 1890 fell upon stony ground. Visions conjured up amid the archaeological splendours of Luxor or the agrarian community of the Veldt dissolved when confronted with the realities of contemporary Wales, whose political fortunes rested on the turn of events at the National Liberal Federation. Without Ellis's influence, *Cymru Fydd* as organized by Lloyd George was a barren and self-contradictory movement. Far more fundamental than the desire for governmental devolution was the power of nonconformity, in some sense a national religion even more decisively than was the Roman Catholic Church in Ireland. The rise and decline of Welsh political nationalism is to be traced far more accurately in the pressure of dissent, in the campaign for disestablishment, educational equality and, to a lesser extent, temperance reform; even the land campaign originated more from social than from economic forces. It was an awareness of these limitations to the national movement that provoked much of the retrospective disillusion among many Welsh patriots, and made them suspicious of the quality of the radicalism to which they had adhered for so long.

Nevertheless, this despair, understandable and even defensible in many respects, conceals a great revolution in thinking towards Welsh affairs. The achievement of Welsh radical leaders, limited though it was, should not be minimized. In many ways, modern Wales came of age in the years after 1868, and the transformation of its status forms a not unimportant aspect of recent British history. The entire struggle for recognition had to be undertaken *ab initio*. The position of Wales was very different from that of Scotland. There the Union was of relatively recent date, while distinctive institutions survived in the form of the Kirk, the legal system and the educational structure. The Scottish squirearchy was itself the greatest patron of Scottish culture. But in Wales no significant tradition of independent statehood survived. For over two centuries, an increasingly anglicized landed class had contributed little to cultural or political life. Beneath, the residuum of native culture, as revealed in poetry and in religious expression, seemed by comparison a sterile backwater, withdrawn from the most virile forces in British life, even though here was contained all the most profound elements of the Welsh genius.

In these circumstances, Welsh politicians had to persuade the parties that there did exist a problem of Welsh nationality at all, that Wales could or should be considered separately from the affairs of England, that its culture could be regarded as valuable for its own sake, and not merely as an antiquated remnant of ignorance and backwardness as seen by the Educational Commissioners of 1847. Gradually, the Liberal Party was weaned over, culminating in Gladstone's public acknowledgement of the need for Welsh disestablishment in 1891, in direct contradiction to his earlier attitude. That the success of the disestablishment campaign was mainly due to those within the patrician circle of the party leadership, to Rendel's influence with Gladstone, to Ellis's Fabian persistence between 1892 and 1895, and perhaps to Lloyd George's growing power within the government of 1906, does not lessen the magnitude of the achievement. The mere fact of disestablishment being carried through at all, in the teeth of the indifference or the violent hostility of the greater part of English opinion, and the opposition of a powerful faction within Wales itself, was still an extraordinary feat for a tiny racial minority. As in similar movements on the Continent, the prime movers were the small body of intellectuals and *bourgeois* nationalists who gradually assumed the authority maintained by the established landed classes. Their programme appealed equally to the depressed farming community of rural Wales and to the new, first-generation professional and mercantile middle-class of the big towns of the South. They combined, therefore, the aspirations of both the rural Populists and the urban Progressives in the United States: agrarian rebellion merged with the status revolution and lent to Welsh radical-ism a nation-wide quality.[1]

The main debate took place within the Liberal Party, and most vigorously in times of opposition, with the years 1886–92 as the major formative period, when the Welsh Party could reflect opinion and prejudices in the constituencies free from the discipline of the party machine. In periods of Liberal government, such as 1892–5 and 1905–15, only a few rebellious souls maintained the pretence of 're-volt' and in time they all came to heel. The majority acquiesced submissively, leaving behind them the repeated imputation of public betrayal. But in the main these accusations were unrealistic, putting the Welsh Party in a position it could not fairly fulfil.

The Conservative or Unionist Party played a generally hostile part in this period; yet, perhaps, this was not fundamentally inspired by an innate objection to the fact of Welsh nationality. Its attitude was inevitably confused by the traditional attachment to the established Church and the landed class, who together seemed to represent the main immediate obstacles to the fulfilment of the Welsh programme. Throughout the 1880's and 1890's, in debates on a variety of issues, Conservative spokesmen monotonously maintained that 'there was no such place as Wales'. The example of Ireland seemed an ominous portent of imperial disintegration. But resistance gradually weakened. An instinctive repugnance to Welsh legislation was replaced gradually by a more intelligent appreciation of Welsh politics and even more of Welsh culture. The Welsh Intermediate Education Act of 1889, passed by the Salisbury administration, was in this respect a great landmark. By 1914 Unionists no longer questioned the propriety of separate legislation for Wales, and few doubted its claims to national status, at least in its more ceremonial aspects. In Wales, a generation of conservative nationalists seemed to be emerging, men such as Arthur Price, who conceived Welsh nationhood in the light of the heritage of medieval Catholic Christendom, and who saw in dis-establishment a means of remoulding the Welsh Church in a new national image.[2] By 1914 no newspaper was more 'Welsh' in its cover-age than the Conservative *Western Mail*, whose comprehensive sym-pathy with the religious, cultural, and sporting life of Wales enabled it to survive where even the Liberal *South Wales News* perished.

---

[1] I follow here the distinction drawn between the Populists and the Progressives by Richard Hofstadter, *The Age of Reform* (New York, 1955), chs. i–iv.

[2] Price wrote a good deal in this vein in the 1920's and early 1930's, particularly in *Y Ddraig Goch* and the *Welsh Outlook*.

In the recent past, Conservative ministries since 1951 have gone far towards acknowledgement of Welsh affairs in the central administration with the creation of a Minister of Welsh Affairs, even though episodes such as the case of the water resources of Tryweryn in Merioneth have dissipated much of the goodwill created thereby. When the Conservatives regained office in 1970, the Heath government followed Labour's lead and appointed a Secretary of State for Wales; Peter Thomas, a Welshman who sat for Hendon South, became the first Conservative holder of that post. One result of the Welsh national movement, therefore, has been the recognition by the Liberal and Conservative Parties alike that Wales possesses, not only a distinct culture, but also certain political ambitions that required adjustment, even though the parties might differ violently as to the extent of that recognition.

The Labour Party after 1900 has come to be seen as the development of a new political and sociological outlook, regarding society horizontally rather than vertically, emphasizing the uniformity rather than the diversity of the nations. Yet the early growth of the Labour movement in Wales, particularly of the I.L.P., was shot through with a recognition of the distinct needs of the Welsh industrial community. Syndicalism in South Wales was in some respects a gesture of separatism towards the government of Whitehall, and a movement towards industrial devolution. Only after 1918, with the consolidation of Labour as a national party and the cohesive effects of the depression of the inter-war years, did Labour in South Wales submerge its identity in the cause of international social democracy. Later efforts to amalgamate Socialism with Welsh nationalism in a unified organization have not been successful. The most prominent was the *Gwerin* movement, based on the University College of Bangor in the late 1930's, which was in part a reaction against the apparent sympathy of *Plaid Cymru* with European totalitarianism and the 'distributist' economics of Fascism.[1] But it failed to develop any real impetus apart from that of the Labour Party as a whole.[2]

[1] A stinging attack on *Plaid Cymru's* alleged Fascist sympathies was made by Dr. Thomas Jones in an address to the Cardiff Cymmrodorion Society on 1 Mar. 1942, later published as a pamphlet under the title 'The Native Never Returns'. Jones's main criticism was directed at the dangers of economic nationalism. During the Second World War, Germany hoped for 'fifth column' assistance from Welsh Nationalists (cf. C. Wighton and G. Reis, *They Spied on England*, London, 1958, pp. 101–2), but virtually none was found.

[2] A possible descendant of this movement was the magazine *Aneurin*, the highly ephemeral journal of the Aberystwyth students' Socialist Society, first issued in 1960 whose Welsh nationalism was more apparent than its Socialism.

After 1945 the Labour Party made only modest gestures towards local devolution in government or in industry. Measures of decentralization in the nationalized industries, such as the Wales Gas Board, made no impact. The Council for Wales, created by Herbert Morrison in 1948, was marked by increasing disillusion at the failure of governments to observe its recommendations. After nearly twenty years of fitful existence, it was finally merged into the Welsh Economic Council, another advisory body. But in the general election of 1959 the Labour Party unexpectedly announced its intention to create a Secretaryship of State for Wales, after previously announcing its hostility to such a scheme. After Labour's return to office in 1964, this new ministry was duly set up, with the veteran, James Griffiths (Llanelli), as the first Welsh Secretary of State. Eighteen months later, he was succeeded by a much younger man, Cledwyn Hughes (Anglesey), who was to be followed in April 1968 by George Thomas (Cardiff West), the first non-Welsh-speaking holder of the office. Perhaps in response to its new Welsh policies, Labour's electoral performance in 1966 was the most triumphant it had ever achieved. Thirty-two Welsh seats were won out of thirty-six, including gains in Conway, Cardiganshire, Cardiff North, and Monmouth. At that moment, Labour looked more like the national party of Wales than at any other time in its history.

However, the positive achievements of the Welsh Secretaryship of State proved disappointing to some of its erstwhile supporters: it was essentially a co-ordinating department rather than one with independent executive power of its own. Certainly, there were some useful reforms to Labour's credit. The passage of a leasehold reform bill in 1965 was widely acclaimed in South Wales. Legislation was passed to give legal status to the use of the Welsh languages in administration and the courts, as recommended by the Hughes–Parry committee. Schemes were drawn up to try to revive the sagging economy of mid-Wales by expanding its towns, while many new Board of Trade factories were brought to the mining valleys in the south. Cledwyn Hughes's white paper on local government in 1967 outlined some radical changes in the pattern of the local administrative system as it had endured since 1888. The decisive test of Labour government in Wales, however, lay in the success or failure of its over-all economic policies, and throughout 1967 and 1968 Wales appeared to be a notable victim of the restrictionist 'squeeze' policies pursued by successive Chancellors. The resultant dramatic swing of votes from

Labour to *Plaid Cymru* in the Carmarthen, Rhondda West, and Caerphilly by-elections in 1966–8 was an impressive token of popular protest at rising unemployment and industrial decay. In addition, many observers felt that Labour's concessions to the desire for popular participation in local and central government in Wales had not gone far enough. In particular, there were many Labour advocates of an elected council for Wales, instead of the nominated body proposed in the 1967 white paper on local government. Finally, in January 1970 the Welsh Council of Labour declared before the Crowther Commission inquiring into the constitution that it had indeed now been converted to the idea of an elected Welsh council which would have some executive as well as advisory powers. This was a notable advance. Yet, even after six years of the Secretaryship of State, the extent to which this new proposal represented a genuine reaction by the Labour Party against the centralization of the Webb tradition was still hard to discern. Labour's election manifesto in 1970 contained only a brief and indistinct reference to the proposal for an elected council, and the issue played little part in the campaign. In the event, Labour lost the election, regaining Carmarthen and retaining Cardiganshire, but losing four seats, Cardiff North, Conway, Monmouth and Pembrokeshire, all on the periphery of Wales, to the Conservatives. As a result, Labour returned to opposition with the extent of its commitment to the principle of national devolution in Wales during the 1970's still somewhat obscure.

Even so, one by one the more irritating slurs on Welsh nationhood have been removed since 1868. In departmental autonomy, particularly in education, in official publications and pronouncements and in general assumptions on public policy, Wales has been brought nearer its goal of national equality. No longer could the *Encyclopaedia Britannica* bear contemptuous witness to national inferiority. Monmouthshire was again received into association with the other twelve counties. All parties shared in the colourful spectacle at Caernarvon in 1911 when the new Prince of Wales was invested, a ceremonial consecration of the nationality of Wales. In the light of this, the lengthy campaigns of Richard and Gee, Rendel, Ellis, and Lloyd George were far from ineffective. Thus, to assess the political significance of Wales in the years of its greatest activity, a balance must be struck between the exaggerated hope and despair of many patriots and the sober facts of partial but genuine achievement.

Perhaps the main abiding impression that endures is of a certain sense of inferiority which for long restricted Welsh advance. The impetus which came from the Blue Books of 1847 was not calculated to generate a healthy patriotism. Welshmen had henceforth to prove that they and their culture were of moral worth, without, however, transgressing into separatism, and this balance was hard to maintain. A succession of Welsh members of Parliament politely declaimed the wrongs of their country in an empty Commons, before bored or contemptuous English audiences and departed into obscurity. Not until the rise to power of Lloyd George did Welshmen feel themselves to be fully the political equals of their English and Scottish neighbours, a feeling later reinforced by the prominence of several Welsh miners' leaders in the Labour governments of 1924, 1929, and 1945, and in the Labour Party machine. The very success of Lloyd George, his enormous advance over the position attained by any previous Welsh politician, was perhaps in itself a drawback, tending to produce an excessive identification of Welsh interests with his own personal advancement, but at least he gave confidence to his countrymen, who essentially were asking for no more than to be taken seriously. Previously the obvious obscurity of Welshmen in public life had bred disunity or an excessive and uncritical attachment to their insulated society, or, as H. A. L. Fisher harshly put it, 'the immemorial melancholy of an aggrieved people'.[1] The First World War undermined this society and the religious animosity that shrouded it, but the sense of grievance was largely removed. Welsh affairs were elevated in popular estimation, although at the expense of many of the apparent characteristics of Welsh nationality.

The national movement in Wales remains an essential and significant aspect of the political development of modern Britain. Its full significance will perhaps be revealed only by the future survival or demise of Welsh culture. Its major consequence today is that the existence of Welsh nationality is rarely in dispute. Wales it seems is unlikely now to degenerate into the status of a mere region: it can no more be compared with Yorkshire or Cornwall than can the province of Quebec with Ontario. The sense of nationality in Wales had survived during the quiescent centuries after the Union with England, but it required the long and arduous campaigns after 1868 to interpret and define that sense anew. Welshmen became aware of themselves in a new sense while Englishmen came to share in that

---

[1] *An Unfinished Autobiography*, p. 101.

awareness. There had persisted over the centuries many of the more obvious indications of nationality, a living language, a vigorous and varied literature and, in the main, a common ethnic stock. The years after 1868 gave these elements a new durability in the sense of a common struggle for recognition. The programme was at best only partially successful—against the accomplishment of disestablishment and the creation of a national educational system must be measured the continued predominance of English elements in the government and culture of Wales—but the limits of the achievement accurately reflected the limits of the aspiration. It was a facet of the struggle for a democratic society, in which a sense of regional or of national community played a significant part. The conflict was far from in vain. There were practical by-products in the form of legislation and of departmental reorganization. But of more importance was the struggle itself and the interest it rekindled in the individuality and destiny of Wales. This revived political fervour served to keep vigorous that native culture which forms the most vital possession of Wales. The years after 1868 witnessed a literary and artistic renaissance, profoundly shot through with the patriotic nostalgia of *Cymru Fydd*. In the present century, the development of Wales has presented a complete contrast to that of Ireland: whereas political nationalism has ebbed, cultural nationalism has flourished. Whether this is by itself sufficient to maintain the distinctiveness of Wales remains, however, uncertain. Whether the preservation of a common culture is possible without a comprehensive re-casting of the social order, whether a Welsh community can survive without a Welsh state, whether nationality is conceivable save in a nationalist framework, or whether the ideals of nationalism and of self-determination are fundamentally opposed, all these will depend on developments far more universal in scope than the internal fortunes of Wales. Their outcome will determine whether the concept of Welsh history will continue to be meaningful in the latter years of the twentieth century. or whether it perished with the hopes of Welsh radicals in 1914, whether the 'national awakening' represented a new and hopeful dawn or merely the flickering embers of an immemorial, dying world.

APPENDIX A

Statistics of Population and Language, 1871–1911

County	1871 Popn.	1911 Popn.	Language in 1911		
			English only	Welsh only	Bilingual
Anglesey	51,040	50,928	4,093	17,434	25,232
Brecknock	59,901	59,287	31,583	3,015	19,881
Caernarvon	106,121	125,043	14,464	42,097	59,150
Cardigan	73,441	59,879	4,966	19,497	31,580
Carmarthen	115,710	160,406	19,991	30,705	96,531
Denbigh	105,102	144,783	56,499	13,639	63,224
Flint	76,312	92,705	47,886	2,946	33,587
Glamorgan	397,859	1,120,910	608,919	31,719	361,973
Merioneth	46,598	45,565	3,340	15,857	23,119
Monmouth	195,448	395,719	314,530	1,496	33,751
Montgomery	67,623	53,146	27,003	5,367	17,039
Pembroke	91,998	89,960	55,124	6,511	20,879
Radnor	25,430	22,590	19,884	11	1,128
Totals	1,412,583	2,420,921	1,208,282	190,292	787,074

Sources: *Censuses of England and Wales*, 1871–1911 (the first linguistic census was taken in 1891).

Of the six counties where Welsh was spoken by over 50 per cent. of the population in 1911, one (Cardigan) had a rapidly declining population, two others (Anglesey and Merioneth) show a gradual decline, but three (Caernarvon, Carmarthen, and Denbigh) show a considerable advance in the period from 1871.

The totals of those able to speak Welsh (monoglot and bilingual) for the period 1891–1921 were as follows:

1891	898,914	(54·4 per cent. of total)
1901	929,824	(49·9 per cent. of total)
1911	977,366	(43·5 per cent. of total)
1921	929,183	(37·2 per cent. of total)

APPENDIX B

Comparative Statistics of Church and Nonconformist Communicants, 1905

County	Population 1901	Church	Nonconformists
Anglesey	50,606	4,807	21,251
Brecknock	59,907	7,209	15,399
Caernarvon	126,835	13,361	53,938
Cardigan	60,240	9,169	28,047
Carmarthen	135,328	18,726	59,365
Denbigh	129,942	16,922	35,339
Flint	81,700	11,621	14,016
Glamorgan	859,981	61,064	202,648
Merioneth	49,149	4,213	24,733
Monmouth	292,317	22,859	49,837
Montgomery	54,901	7,728	16,054
Pembroke	88,732	11,517	26,191
Radnor	23,281	3,885	4,861
Totals	2,012,917	193,081	551,679

Source: *Royal Commission on the Church and other Religious Bodies in Wales,* vol. v.

APPENDIX C

Statistics of Welsh Nonconformist Communicants, 1861-1913

Year	Baptists	Methodists	Independents	Wesleyans	Totals
1861	50,903	90,560	97,647	24,395	263,505
1882	81,378	122,107	116,618	32,146	352,249
1893	98,122	141,964	125,758	31,406	397,250
1895	100,534	147,297	135,108	33,741	416,680
1899	101,057	153,712	143,423	36,664	434,856
1903	116,310	165,218	148,780	35,486	465,794
1904	140,443	173,310	162,270	36,000	512,023
1905	143,385	189,164	175,313	40,811	549,123
1910	130,319	184,558	169,314	43,940	528,131
1913	127,226	183,647	168,814	43,590	523,277

Sources: *Royal Commission on the Church and other Religious Bodies in Wales,*
vols. vi and vii (nonconformist statistics).
Blwyddiadur y Methodistiaid Calfinaidd.
Baptist Handbook; Congregationalist Yearbook.
Thomas Rees, *History of Protestant Nonconformity in Wales* (2nd ed.,
1883), pp. 450-1, 461-3.

It cannot be claimed that these statistics give more than an approximate
indication of the progress of nonconformity. In some cases, the sources
used are at variance with one another: for instance, Rees's figures for the
Methodists in 1882 differ from those given in the Methodist *Blwyddiadur*
and I have therefore taken the Methodists' own figure. It should be noted
also that the totals given for the Methodists and Independents give an
exaggerated picture of their strength, as the totals of communicants of their
churches in England are included. For instance, the Independents' total
for the peak year of 1905 includes 6,261 members of Welsh Independent
chapels in England, while the Methodist total includes 18,679 members of
chapels in England, 16,749 of them in London and in Lancashire. It is,
however, extremely difficult to isolate the statistics for Wales alone in other
years.

In spite of this unreliability, the impression is that the picture presented
by the statistics is generally accurate: viz. a general, steady advance in
numbers to 1903, a dramatic increase in the two 'revival' years of 1903-5
particularly among the Baptists, followed by a recession in numbers, again
most marked among the Baptists. The year 1861 has been taken as a
starting-point as no Independent statistics are available before that year
(cf. Rev. H. Elvet Lewis, 'A Sketch of the Progress of Congregationalism,
1800-1906', *Royal Commission*, vol. vii, p. 154).

Since the First World War there has been an almost continuous decline in the numbers of communicants year by year: for instance, here are the figures given for the year 1955:

Baptists	99,750
Methodists	152,305
Independents	120,669
Wesleyans (estimated) . . .	19,000
Total	391,724

BIBLIOGRAPHY

A. Manuscript Collections
B. Official Papers
C. Periodicals, Pamphlets, and Reports
D. Works of Reference
E. Biographies
F. Other Works

A. MANUSCRIPT COLLECTIONS

1. *In Libraries, Museums, and Record Offices*

Bodleian Library, Oxford
Asquith Papers.

British Museum
Campbell-Bannerman Papers (Add. MSS., 41,206–52).
Gladstone Papers (Add. MSS., 44,086–835).
Herbert, Viscount Gladstone Papers (Add. MSS., 45,985–46,118).

Cardiff Central Library
Cardiff Liberal Association scrap-book, 1897–9.
'Cochfarf' Papers (papers of Edward Thomas, 'Cochfarf').
Pontypridd Papers (papers of Sir Alfred Thomas, first Baron Pontypridd).

Glamorgan Record Office
D/D Xes: Records of Brecon Road (Merthyr) Liberal Association.
D/D NCB: Volumes of press cuttings relating to the Tonypandy riots, 1910 (vols. vi–xvi).

London School of Economics Library
Webb Trade Union Collection (Section A).

National Library of Wales, Aberystwyth
   (i) *General Manuscripts*
       MSS. 3293E, 3470E: D. M. Richards MSS.
       MSS. 5503–5B: Henry Richard MSS.
       MSS. 5509C: Minutes of an Interview of Henry Richard and Osborne Morgan with Gladstone, 28 May 1870.
       MSS. 6411–12B: Correspondence of the Rev. Josiah T. Jones.
       MSS. 8305C–11D: Thomas Gee MSS.
       MSS. 8823–4C, 8835–8: W. J. Parry MSS.
       MSS. 9485E–7C: C. E. Breese MSS.
       MSS. 9494E: MSS. of Flintshire Elections, 1892–1910.

MSS. 15,321–3: Reminiscences of the Tithe War in West Wales, by Rev. Robert Lewis, with press cuttings.
MSS. 16,354C: T. Huws Davies MSS.

(ii) *Deposited Collections*

D. R. Daniel Papers.
T. E. Ellis Papers.
Vincent Evans Papers.
Glansevern Collection (papers of A. C. Humphreys-Owen).
Ellis Griffith Papers.
E. T. John Papers.
Herbert Lewis Papers.
Stuart Rendel Papers.
J. Bryn Roberts Papers.
D. Lleufer Thomas Papers.

University College of North Wales, Bangor

MSS. 1124–5: Correspondence relating to Caernarvonshire politics, 1880–95.
MSS. 3245: Letters to Sir John Morris-Jones.
MSS. 5446–86: William Jones Papers.
Coetmor Papers (W. J. Parry MSS.) 1B.
Sir John Lloyd Papers, MS. 314.

University College of Swansea

Minutes of Liberation Society, 1868–1914 (on microfilm).

2. *Privately Owned*

Bishop Owen Papers (transcripts). By courtesy of Miss Eluned E. Owen.
Penucha MSS. By courtesy of Professor and Mrs. Idwal Jones, Plas Penucha.
Swansea Labour Association Minute books, 1916 to date. By courtesy of Mr. J. G. Davies, secretary, Swansea Labour Association.

B. OFFICIAL PAPERS

Hansard's *Parliamentary Debates*, Third Series.
Parliamentary Debates (Authorized Edition and Official Reports), Fourth and Fifth Series.
Census of Great Britain, 1851. Religious Worship. England and Wales. Reports and Tables (1690), H.C. (1852–3). LXXXIX. 1.
Report from the Select Committee on Parliamentary and Municipal Elections (2524), H.C. (1868–9). VIII. 1.
Returns of Number and Amount of Yearly Income declared by the Church Commissioners to be payable to Curates under the 15th Section of the Irish Church Act, 1869, H.C. (1871). LV. 267.

Return of Owners of Land, 1873. England and Wales (exclusive of the Metropolis) (C. 1097), H.C. (1874). LXII.

Report of the Committee appointed to inquire into the condition of Higher Education in Wales (C. 3047), H.C. (1881). XXXIII. 1.

Second Report of the Commissioners appointed to inquire into the Elementary Education Acts (C. 5056), H.C. (1887). XXIX. 1.

Final Report of the Commissioners appointed to inquire into the Elementary Education Acts (C. 5485), H.C. (1888). XXXV. 1.

Report of the Commissioners appointed to inquire into the operation of the Sunday Closing (Wales) Act, 1881 (C. 5994), H.C. (1890). XL. 1.

Evidence, Report and *Appendices* of the Royal Commission on Land in Wales and Monmouthshire:
   Evidence (vols. 1 and 2). (C. 7439), H.C. (1894). XXXVI, XXXVII.
   Evidence (vols. 3 and 4). (C. 7661, C. 7757), H.C. (1895). XL, XLI.
   Evidence (vol. 5), *Report and Appendices, Index* (C. 8242, C. 8221, C 8222), H.C. (1896). XXXIII, XXXIV, XXXV.

List of Public Elementary Schools in Wales on 1 August 1906 (Cd. 3640), H.C. (1907). LXIII.

Report, Evidence and *Indexes* of the Royal Commission appointed to inquire into the Church and other Religious Bodies in Wales:
   Report (vol. 1) (Cd. 5432), H.C. (1910). XIV. 1.
   Evidence (vols. 2–4) (Cd. 5433–5), H.C. (1910). XV, XVI, XVII.
   Statistics and Indexes (vols. 5–8) (Cd. 5436, Cd. 5437, Cd. 5438, Cd. 5439), H.C. (1910). XVIII, XIX.

Report of the Commissioners appointed to inquire into Industrial Unrest. No. 7 Division: Report of the Commissioners for Wales, including Monmouthshire (Cd. 8668), H.C. (1917).

Conference on Devolution (a letter from Mr. Speaker to the Prime Minister) (Cmd. 692), H.C. (1920). XIII. 1.

Report of the Departmental Committee on the Organization of Secondary Education in Wales (Cmd. 967), H.C. (1920). XV. 1.

Annual Reports of the Committee of Council on Education (to 1899).

Annual Reports of the Board of Education (after 1899).

Censuses of England and Wales, 1871–1921.

C. PERIODICALS, PAMPHLETS, AND REPORTS

1. *Newspapers*

(a) English	(b) Welsh
Daily Chronicle	*Aberdare Times*
Daily News	*Baner ac Amserau Cymru*
Liverpool Daily Post	*Cambria Daily Leader*
Manchester Guardian	*Cambrian News*
Morning Post	*Cardiff Times*
The Times	*Evening Express*

Y Genedl
Glamorgan Free Press
Y Goleuad
Yr Herald Cymraeg
Llais Llafur (*Labour Voice* from 1915)
Merthyr Express
Mumbles Weekly Press and Gower News
North Wales Observer and Express
Rhondda Leader
South Wales Daily News (*South Wales News* from 1919)
South Wales Echo
South Wales Times and Star of Gwent
Tarian y Gweithiwr
Y Tyst a'r Dydd
Welsh Catholic Herald
Western Mail

2. *Other Periodicals*

(*a*) English

British Quarterly Review
British Weekly
Church Times
Contemporary Review
Guardian
I.L.P. News
Labour Leader
Liberal Magazine
Nineteenth Century
Punch
Socialist Review
Spectator
Westminster Gazette

(*b*) Welsh

Cwrs y Byd
Cymru Fydd
Y Ddraig Goch
Y Diwygiwr
Y Geninen
Labour Pioneer
Y Llenor
The Nationalist
Y Traethodydd
Wales (1894–7, ed. by O. M. Edwards)
Wales (1911–14, ed. by J. Hugh Edwards)
Welsh Leader
The Welsh Nationalist
Welsh Outlook
Welsh Review

3. *Pamphlets*

(Place of publication London, unless otherwise stated)

'ADFYR' (T. J. Hughes), *Neglected Wales*, Cardiff, 1887.
—— *The Welsh Magistracy*, Cardiff, 1887.

BENSON, Archbishop E. W., *To the Diocese of Canterbury on the Welsh Disestablishment Bill*, 1894.

BEVAN, Canon W. L., *The Case of the Church in Wales*, 1886.

BLAYDES, F. A., *The Disestablishment and Disendowment of the Church in Wales*, Bedford, 1895.

BRADLEY, Rev. J. Fovargue, *The Case against Welsh Disendowment*, 1911.

—— *Nonconformists and the Welsh Church Bill*, 1912.

BREESE, Charles E., *Welsh Religious Equality*, Portmadoc, 1892.

CAIRD, David, *Church and State in Wales*, 1912.

CECIL, Lord Robert, *Our National Church*, 1913.

CHAPPELL, Edgar L., *Wake up! Wales*, 1943.

CLAYTON, H. J., *The Church in Wales Today*, 1906.

—— *Indictment and Defence of the Church in Wales*, 1911.

CLOSS, T., *The true history of the Church in Wales*, 1890.

DANIEL, J. E., *Welsh Nationalism: what it stands for*, Cardiff, 1937.

DAVIES, D. J., *The Economics of Welsh Self-Government*, Caernarvon, 1931.

DELL, A., *The Church in Wales*, 1912.

DODD, J. Theodore, *Welsh Disestablishment*, 1912.

DOWNING, S. E., *The Church in Wales*, 1915.

EDWARDS, Bishop A. G., *The Truth about the Church in Wales*, 1889.

—— *A Handbook on Welsh Church Defence*, 1895.

EDWARDS, Dean H. T., *Church of the Cymry*, Caernarvon, 1870.

—— *Wales and the Welsh Church*, 1889.

EDWARDS, W. A., *The Welsh Church Question*, 1910.

EMERY, G. F., *People's Guide to the Welsh Church Disestablishment Bill*, 1911.

EVANS, D. Tudwal, *Sosialaeth*, Barmouth, 1911.

EVANS, H., *The Case for Disestablishment in Wales*, 1907.

GEE, Thomas, *Rhyddfrydiaeth a Thoriaeth*, Denbigh, 1896.

GIBBON, J. Morgan, *The Case for Welsh Disestablishment*, 1910.

GREEN, Archbishop C. A. H., *Disestablishment*, Cardiff, 1911.

—— *Disendowment*, Cardiff, 1911.

—— *Disestablishment and Disendowment: the experience of the Church in Wales*, 1935.

—— *Disestablishment and Disendowment in Wales*, 1937.

'GRIFFITH', *The Welsh Question, the rights of nationalities and the Conservative opportunity*, 1887.

HOWELL, Rev. David, *The Welsh Church: The Patriot's Yearning for the Prosperity of Zion*, 1890.

HUGHES, T., *Ymneillduaeth Eglwys Loegr*, Liverpool, 1903.

JAMES, J., and EVANS, W. E., *The Churchman's Shield*, 1906.

JENKINS, Sir John Jones, *Tinplates and Tariffs*, Cardiff, 1906.

JOHN, E. T., *Wales: its Politics and Economics*, Cardiff, 1919.

JOHNES, A. J., *A Prize Essay on the Causes which have produced Dissent in Wales from the Established Church*, 1835.

JONES, D., *The Welsh Church and Welsh Nationality*, 1893.

JONES, D. Lloyd, *Cynydd yr Iwerddon mewn Moesoldeb a Chyfoeth*, 1890.

JONES, Edgar, *Campaigning: my election experiences*, Cardiff, 1910.

JONES, W. Hughes, *Wales Drops the Pilots*, Caernarvon, 1937.

—— (*Elidir Sais*), *A Challenge to Wales*, Caernarvon, 1938.

JONES, Rev. J. Morgan, and JENKINS, Rev. W. L., *Passive Resistance. Liberalism and Labour*, Merthyr Tydfil, 1904.

LEWIS, J. P., *Church Plunder, State Blunder*, 1913.

LLOYD, Bishop D. L., *The Missing Link*, 1876.

—— *The Church in Wales and the Welsh People*, 1895.

'MILITIA OFFICER', *History of our Reserve Forces*, 1870.

—— *Strength and Cost of the British Army and Reserve Forces*, 1871.

MORGAN, Sir G. Osborne, *The Church of England and the People of Wales*, 1895.

MORGAN, H. A., *Church and Dissent in Wales*, Cambridge, 1895.

MORGAN-RICHARDSON, C., *Does Wales require a Land Bill? A reply to the arguments used by Mr. T. E. Ellis, M.P., in support of the proposed Land Tenure (Wales) Bill*, Cardiff, 1893.

MORRIS, Rhŷs Hopkin, *Welsh Politics*, Wrexham, 1927.

National Council of Free Churches, *Weighed in the Balance: the case for Welsh Disestablishment*, 1910.

ORMSBY-GORE, W. G. A., *Welsh Disestablishment and Disendowment*, 1912.

OWEN, Rev. D. Edmondes, *The Church in its relation to nonconformity*, 1902.

OWEN, Bishop John, *The Welsh Disestablishment Act: what it means*, 1911.

—— *Acceptance of the Welsh Church Temporalities Act*, 1919.

OWEN, Owen, *Welsh Disestablishment: some phases of the numerical argument*, 1895.

'PACIFICUS' (F. S. Oliver), *Federalism and Home Rule*, 1911.

PARRY, W. J., *The Penrhyn Lockout*, 1901.

PEROWNE, Dean, *Disestablishment and Disendowment*, 1885.

PROTHERO, R. W., *The Anti-Tithe Agitation in Wales*, 1889.

PRYCE, Rev. R., *The Working of the Education Act, 1902: its failure and future*, 1902.

REES, J. T., *Welsh Disestablishment: objections answered*, 1912.

RENDEL, Stuart, *Welsh Disestablishment*, 1887.

RICHARD, Henry, *Yr Eglwys Sefydledig ac Anghydffurfiaeth yng Nghymru*, 1882.

—— *Disestablishment of the Church in Wales*, 1883.

ROCH, Walter, *Welsh Disestablishment: the case for it*, 1912.

SPINKS, W. H., *Statement of the case for Disestablishment*, 1911.

STEAD, W. T., *The Revival of the West*, 1905.

STEPHENS, T., *Cymru heddiw ac yfory*, Cardiff, 1908.

THOMAS, W. C., *The Church in Wales*, Birmingham, 1893.

Unofficial Reform Committee, *Miners' Next Step*, Tonypandy, 1912.

VINCENT, J. E., *Tenancy in Wales*, 1889.
WILKINSON, J. Frome, *Disestablishment: Welsh and English*, 1894.
WILLIAMS, Rev. David, *Swansea and its Free Churches*, Swansea, 1909.
WILLIAMS, T. Marchant, *The Educational Wants of Wales*, 1877.
WILLIAMS, W. Llewelyn, *Cymru Fydd*, 1894.
WILSON, P. W., *Welsh Disestablishment*, 1912.
(YOUNG, E. A.), *The Penrhyn Strike*, privately printed, 1903.

There are useful collections of election addresses, leaflets, and other political literature in the National Library of Wales, the National Liberal Club, Dr. Williams's Library, Cardiff Central Library, and Swansea Public Library.

4. Reports

(i) *Annual Reports of the following organizations*
Church Congress (for 1879, 1889, 1891).
Independent Labour Party.
North Wales Liberal Federation.
South Wales Liberal Federation.
Welsh National Liberal Council.

(ii) *Miscellaneous* (place of publication London, unless otherwise stated)
Baptist Handbook.
Blwyddiadur y Methodistiaid Calfinaidd, am y flwyddyn . . ., Caernarvon.
Church of England Yearbook.
Congregational Yearbook.
Free Church Yearbook.
Independent Labour Party: Directory and Branch Returns for the three months ending 31 May 1896, Glasgow, 1896.
Report of the Welsh Land Enquiry Committee: Rural, 1914.
Second Industrial Survey of South Wales, Cardiff, 1937.
South Wales Labour Annual.
Welsh Church Congress Handbook (for 1953).

Miscellaneous publications by the Central Church Committee, the Liberation Society, and the Welsh Disestablishment Campaign Committee.

D. WORKS OF REFERENCE

(Place of publication London, unless otherwise stated)

ALLGOOD, H. G. C., *Statistics bearing upon Welsh Liberal Organization*, Cardiff, 1897.
Annual Register.
BOWEN, Ivor (ed.), *The Statutes of Wales*, 1908.
Burke's Landed Gentry.
Burke's Peerage, Baronetage and Knightage.
BUTLER, D. E., and ROSE, Richard, *The British General Election of 1959*, 1960.

CRAWSHAY, W. S., and READ, F. W., *The Politics of the Commons*, 1886.

Dictionary of National Biography.

Dictionary of Welsh Biography, 1959.

Dod's Parliamentary Companion, 1832 to date.

EVANS, J., *Biographical Dictionary of the Ministers and Preachers of the Welsh Calvinistic Methodist Body*, Caernarvon, 1907.

FOSTER, Joseph, *Alumni Oxonienses*, 8 vols., 1887–92.

HUGHES, T., *The Law Relating to Welsh Intermediate Schools*, Cardiff, 1898.

HUGHES, Thomas, *Great Welshmen of Modern Days*, Cardiff, 1931.

JENKINS, J., *The General Election, 1906. Wales and Monmouthshire: a Souvenir*, Cardiff, 1906.

JENKINS, R. T., and REES, William, *A Bibliography of the History of Wales*, Cardiff, 1931. (Second edition, 1962.)

JONES, T. I. Jeffreys (ed.), *Statutes relating to Wales, 1714–1901*, Cardiff, 1959.

JUDD, G. P., *Members of Parliament, 1734–1832*, Newhaven, Connecticut, 1955.

McCALMONT, F. H., *Parliamentary Poll Books*, Nottingham, 1910.

MAY, T. Erskine, *Law, Proceedings, Privileges and Usages of Parliament*, 15th edition, edited by G. Campion, 1950.

Newspapers Press Directory and Advertisers Guide.

RAVENSTEIN, E. G., *Census of the British Isles*, 1876.

REDLICH, J. F., *Procedure of the House of Commons*, 2 vols., 1903.

REES, T. Mardy, *Notable Welshmen (1700–1900)*, Caernarvon, 1908.

ROBERTS, T. R., *A Dictionary of Eminent Welshmen*, Cardiff, 1908.

SEYMOUR, C. T., *Electoral Reform in England and Wales, 1832–1885*, Newhaven, Connecticut, 1915.

Statesmen's Year Book.

Swansea Co-operative Congress, 1917: a souvenir, Manchester, 1917.

The Times: the New Parliament, 1868–1922.

VENN, J. and J. A., *Alumni Cantabrigenses*, 10 vols., Cambridge, 1922–54.

WHITMELL, C. T., *Elementary Education, Cardiff District*, Cardiff, 1886.

Who's Who in Wales (first ed., 1920; second ed., 1933; third ed., 1937).

Who was Who.

WILLIAMS, T. Marchant, *The Welsh Members of Parliament*, Cardiff, 1894.

WILLIAMS, W. R., *Parliamentary History of Wales, 1541–1895*, Brecknock, 1895.

E. BIOGRAPHIES

(Arranged in order of subject: place of publication London, unless otherwise indicated)

ABERDARE, 1st Lord, *Letters of the Rt. Hon. Henry Austin Bruce, G.C.B., Lord Aberdare of Duffryn*, 2 vols., Oxford, 1902.

ABRAHAM, William, 'William Abraham, 1843–1922' (unpublished University of Wales M.A. thesis, 1945), by Eric Wyn Evans.

ABRAHAM, William, *Mabon*, by Eric Wyn Evans, Cardiff, 1959.

ARNOLD, Matthew, *Matthew Arnold: Poetry and Prose*, edited by J. Bryson, 1954.

ASQUITH, H. H., 1st Earl of Oxford and Asquith, *Fifty Years of Parliament*, 1926.

—— *Life of Herbert Henry, Earl Asquith of Oxford*, by J. A. Spender and Cyril Asquith, 2 vols., 1932.

BENSON, Archbishop Edward White, *Life of Edward White Benson*, by A. C. Benson, 2 vols., 1899.

CECIL OF CHELWOOD, 1st Lord, *All the way*, 1949.

CHAMBERLAIN, Joseph, *Life of Joseph Chamberlain*, vols. 1–3 by J. L. Garvin, vol. 4 by Julian Amery, 1932–51.

—— *A Political Memoir, 1880–92*, edited by C. H. D. Howard, 1953.

CLIFFORD, Dr. John, *Life of Dr. John Clifford*, by Sir John Marchant, 1924.

DALE, the Rev. R. W., *Life of R. W. Dale of Birmingham*, by A. W. W. Dale, 1903.

DAVIDSON, Archbishop Randall, *Life of Archbishop Davidson*, by G. K. A. Bell, 2 vols., 1935.

DAVIES, David, *David Davies, Llandinam*, by Goronwy Jones, Wrexham, 1913.

—— *Top Sawyer*, by Ivor Thomas, 1938.

EDWARDS, Archbishop Alfred George, *Memories*, 1927.

—— *Alfred George Edwards, Archbishop of Wales*, by George Lerry, Oswestry, 1940.

EDWARDS, Owen M., *Cofiant O. M. Edwards*, by W. J. Gruffydd, vol. 1, Cardiff, 1936.

EDWARDS, Thomas Charles, *Letters of Thomas Charles Edwards*, 3 vols., edited by T. I. Ellis, Aberystwyth, 1952–3.

ELLIS, Thomas Edward, *Speeches and Addresses*, Wrexham, 1912.

—— *Thomas Edward Ellis*, by T. I. Ellis, 2 vols., Liverpool, 1944–8.

—— *Thomas Edward Ellis*, by Wyn Griffith, Llandybïe, 1959.

EVANS, the Rev. E. Herber, *Cofiant y Parch. E. Herber Evans*, by H. Elvet Lewis, Wrexham, 1901.

FARQUHARSON, R., *In and Out of Parliament*, 1911.

FISHER, H. A. L., *An Unfinished Autobiography*, 1940.

GEE, Thomas, *Cofiant Thomas Gee*, by T. Gwynn Jones, Denbigh, 1913.

GLADSTONE, W. E., *Gladstone's Speeches*, edited by A. Tilney Bassett, 1916.

—— *Life of William Ewart Gladstone*, by John Morley, 3 vols., 1903.

—— *Gladstone: a Biography*, by Sir Philip Magnus, 1954.

GORE, Bishop Charles, *Life of Charles Gore*, by G. L. Prestige, 1935.

GRIFFITH, Wyn, *Spring of Youth*, 1935.

GRIFFITH-BOSCAWEN, A. S. T., *Fourteen Years of Parliament*, 1907.

—— *Memories*, 1925.

GRIFFITHS, John ('Gohebydd'), *Cofiant y Gohebydd*, by Richard Griffiths, Denbigh, 1905.

GRUFFYDD, W. J., *Hen Atgofion*, Aberystwyth, 1936.

HALDANE, Richard Burdon, 1st Lord, *Haldane of Cloan*, by Dudley Sommer, 1960.

HALIFAX, Charles Lindley, Lord, *Charles Lindley, Viscount Halifax*, by J. G. Lockhart, 2 vols., 1936.

HARCOURT, Sir William, *Life of Sir William Harcourt*, by A. G. Gardiner, 2 vols., 1913.

HARDIE, J. Keir, *From Pit to Parliament: the early life of Keir Hardie*, by David Lowe, 1923.

—— *Keir Hardie*, by Emrys Hughes, 1956.

HARTWELL JONES, G., *A Celt Looks at the World*, 1946.

HENSON, Hensley, *Retrospect of an Unimportant Life*, 3 vols., 1942.

HICKS-BEACH, Sir Michael, 1st Earl of St. Aldwyn, *Sir Michael Hicks-Beach, Earl St. Aldwyn*, by Lady Victoria Hicks-Beach, 2 vols., 1915.

HODGE, John, *Workman's Cottage to Windsor Castle*, 1931.

HODGES, Frank, *My Adventures as a Labour Leader*, 1925.

HORNER, Arthur, *Incorrigible Rebel*, 1960.

HUDSON, Sir Robert A., *Sir Robert Hudson: a Memoir*, by J. A. Spender 1930.

HUMPHREYS, E. Morgan, *Gwŷr Enwog Gynt*, Aberystwyth, 1950.

—— *Gwŷr Enwog Gynt: yr ail Gyfres*, Aberystwyth, 1953.

JONES, Sir Henry, *Old Memories*, 1923.

—— *Life and Letters of Sir Henry Jones*, by H. Hetherington, 2 vols., 1924.

JONES, J. Viriamu, *Life of J. Viriamu Jones*, by K. Viriamu Jones, 1915.

—— *J. Viriamu Jones, 1856–1901: Pioneer of the Modern University*, by N. C. Masterman, Llandybïe, 1958.

JONES, Michael Daniel, *Oes a Gwaith Michael Daniel Jones*, by E. Pan Jones, Bala, 1903.

JONES, Robert Ambrose (*Emrys ap Iwan*), *Cofiant Emrys ap Iwan*, by T. Gwynn Jones, Caernarvon, 1912.

JONES, Thomas, *Welsh Broth*, 1951.

KEKEWICH, Sir George, *The Education Department and After*, 1920.

LAW, A. Bonar, *The Unknown Prime Minister*, by Robert Blake, 1955.

LEWIS, Dr. J. 'Gomer', *Darlithiwr enwocaf Cymru: sef y Parch. J. Gomer Lewis*, by the Rev. Thomas Morgan, Swansea, 1911.

LEWIS, Sir J. Herbert, *Syr Herbert Lewis, 1858–1933*, ed. by K. Idwal Jones, Aberystwyth, 1958.

LLOYD GEORGE, David, 1st Earl, *From Village Green to Downing Street: the Life of David Lloyd George*, by J. Hugh Edwards, 1909.

—— *The Life of David Lloyd George*, by Herbert du Parcq, 4 vols., 1912.

—— *The Life of David Lloyd George*, vols. 1–4 by J. Hugh Edwards, vol. 5 by J. Saxon Mills, 5 vols., 1913–24.

—— *The Life Romance of David Lloyd George*, by Beriah Gwynfe Evans, n.d. (1915).

—— *Mr. Lloyd George*, by Walter Roch, 1920.

LLOYD GEORGE, David, 1st Earl, *Mr. Lloyd George*, by E. T. Raymond, 1921.

—— *Lloyd George, 1863-1914*, by Watkin Davies, 1939.

—— *The Lloyd George I Knew*, by Alfred T. Davies, 1948.

—— *Lloyd George*, by Thomas Jones, 1949.

—— *Tempestuous Journey*, by Frank Owen, 1954.

—— *My Brother and I*, by William George, 1958.

—— *David Lloyd George: Welsh Radical as World Statesman*, by Kenneth O. Morgan, Cardiff, 1963.

—— *Better Times*, 1910.

LOCKWOOD, Sir Frank, *Sir Frank Lockwood*, by Augustine Birrell, 1898.

LUCY, Henry W., *Sixty Years in the Wilderness*, 1909.

MCKENNA, Reginald, *Reginald McKenna*, by Stephen McKenna, 1948.

MACREADY, General Sir Nevil, *Annals of an Active Life*, 2 vols., 1924.

MASTERMAN, C. F. G., *C. F. G. Masterman*, by Lucy Masterman, 1939.

MORANT, Sir Robert, *Life of Sir Robert Morant*, by B. M. Allen, 1934.

MORGAN, The Rev. J. Vyrnwy (ed.), *Welsh Religious Leaders in the Nineteenth Century*, 1905.

—— *Welsh Political and Educational Leaders in the Nineteenth Century*, 1908.

MUNDELLA, A. J., *A. J. Mundella, 1825-1897. The Liberal Background to the Labour Movement*, by W. H. G. Armytage, 1951.

OWEN, Bishop John, *The Early Life of Bishop Owen*, by Eluned E. Owen, Llandyssul, 1958.

—— *The Later Life of Bishop Owen*, by Eluned E. Owen, Llandyssul, 1961.

PARRY-JONES, D., *Welsh Country Upbringing*, 1948.

PERCIVAL, Bishop, *Life of Bishop Percival*, by William Temple, 1921.

PRICE, Dr. Thomas, *Bywgraffiadur y diweddar Barchedig T. Price, M.A., Ph.D., Aberdâr*, by B. Evans, Aberdare, 1891.

RATHBONE, William, *William Rathbone: a memoir*, by Eleanor Rathbone, 1905.

—— *Rathbones of Liverpool*, by Sheila Marriner, Liverpool, 1961.

REICHEL, Sir Harry, *Sir Harry Reichel*, ed. by John Edward Lloyd, Cardiff, 1934.

RENDEL, Stuart, 1st Lord, *Personal Papers of Lord Rendel*, ed. by F. E. Hamer, 1931.

RHONDDA, D. A. Thomas, 1st Lord, *Life of Viscount Rhondda*, by J. Vyrnwy Morgan, 1918.

—— *Life of D. A. Thomas, Viscount Rhondda*, ed. by Viscountess Rhondda, 1921.

VISCOUNTESS RHONDDA, *This was my World*, 1933.

RICHARD, Henry, *Henry Richard, M.P.*, by C. S. Miall, 1889.

ROBERTS, R. Silyn, *Silyn*, by David Thomas, Liverpool, 1956.

ROBERTS, Samuel ('S. R.'), *S. R.*, by Glanmor Williams, Cardiff, 1950.

—— *Samuel Roberts: colonizer in Civil War Tennessee*, by Wilbur Shepperson, Knoxville, Tennessee, 1961.

ROBERTS, Thomas Francis, *Thomas Francis Roberts, 1860–1919*, by David Williams, Cardiff, 1961.

ROSEBERY, 5th Earl of, *Lord Rosebery*, by the Marquess of Crewe, 1931.

SELBORNE, 1st Earl of, *Memorials*, 2 vols., 1896–8.

SMITH, F. E., 1st Earl of Birkenhead, *F. E.*, by the Second Earl of Birkenhead, new edition, 1959.

SMITH, Samuel, *My Life Story*, 1902.

SPENDER, Harold, *The Fire of Life*, n.d. (1926).

TEMPLE, Sir Richard, *Life in Parliament*, 1893.

—— *The Story of My Life*, 2 vols., 1896.

THIRLWALL, Bishop Connop, *Letters Literary and Theological of Connop Thirlwall*, edited by Dean Perowne and the Rev. L. Stokes, 1881.

—— *Letters to a Friend by Connop Thirlwall*, edited by Dean Stanley, 1881.

—— *Connop Thirlwall*, by John Connop Thirlwall, 1936.

THOMAS, the Rev. John, *Cofiant y Parch. John Thomas*, by J. Machreth Rees and J. Owen, Liverpool, 1898.

WATKINS, Sir Percy, *A Welshman Remembers*, Cardiff, 1944.

WEST, Sir Algernon, *Private Diaries of Sir Algernon West*, edited by H. Hutchinson, 1922.

WILLIAMS, W. Llewelyn, 'W. Llewelyn Williams', by the Rev. J. Seymour Rees (*Eisteddfod* prize essay).

WINTERTON, Earl, *Orders of the Day*, 1951.

F. OTHER WORKS

(Place of publication London, unless otherwise stated)

ADDIS, J. P., *The Crawshay Dynasty*, Cardiff, 1957.

ALLCOCK, G. W., *Fifty Years of Railway Trade Unionism*, 1922.

ARNOT, R. Page, *The Miners*, 1948.

—— *The Miners: Years of Struggle*, 1953.

ASHBY, W., and EVANS, I. L., *The Agriculture of Wales and Monmouthshire*, Cardiff, 1949.

ASHWORTH, W., *The Economic History of England, 1870–1939*, 1960.

AWBERY, Stan, *Labour's Early Struggles in Swansea*, Swansea, 1949.

BEALEY, F., and PELLING, Henry, *Labour and Politics, 1900–1906*, 1958.

BELL, H. Idris, *The Crisis of our Time and other Papers*, Llandybïe, 1954.

BERTHOFF, R., *British Immigrants in Industrial America*, Cambridge, Mass., 1953.

BRENNAN, T., COONEY, E., and POLLINS, H., *Social Change in South West Wales*, 1954.

BROOKE, E. H., *Chronology of the Tinplate Works of Great Britain*, Cardiff, 1944.

BUNBURY, Sir Henry (ed.), *Lloyd George's Ambulance Wagon*, 1957.

CHAPPELL, Edgar L., *Wake up! Wales*, 1943.

CLAPHAM, Sir John, *The Economic History of Modern Britain*, 3 vols., 1926–38.

COLE, G. D. H., *British Working-Class Politics, 1832–1914*, 1941.
—— *A History of the Labour Party since 1914*, 1948.
CONWAY, Alan, *The Welsh in America*, Cardiff, 1961.
COUPLAND, Sir Reginald, *Welsh and Scottish Nationalism*, 1954.
COX, Harold (ed.), *British Industries under Free Trade*, 1903.
DAVID, Islwyn, 'Political and Electioneering Activity in South East Wales 1820–51' (unpublished University of Wales M.A. thesis, 1959).
DODD, A. H., *The Industrial Revolution in North Wales*, Cardiff, 1933.
EDWARDS, Archbishop A. G., *Landmarks in the History of the Welsh Church*, 1912.
EDWARDS, Ness, *The Industrial Revolution in South Wales*, 1924.
—— *The History of the South Wales Miners*, 1926.
—— *History of the South Wales Miners' Federation*, vol. i, 1938.
ELLIS, T. I., *The Development of Higher Education in Wales*, Wrexham, 1935.
ELSAS, Madeline (ed.), *Iron in the Making. Dowlais Iron Company Letters, 1782–1860*, 1960.
ENSOR, R. C. K., *England, 1870–1914*, Oxford, 1936.
EVANS, Beriah Gwynfe, *Dafydd Dafis: sef Hunangofiant Ymgeisydd Seneddol*, Wrexham, 1898.
EVANS, D. Emrys, *The University of Wales*, Cardiff, 1953.
EVANS, Eric Wyn, 'Industrial Relations in the South Wales Coalfield up to 1912' (unpublished University of Wales Ph.D. thesis, 1952).
—— *The Miners of South Wales*, Cardiff, 1961.
GASH, Norman, *Politics in the Age of Peel*, 1952.
GEORGE, William, *Cymru Fydd: hanes y mudiad cenedlaethol cyntaf*, Liverpool, 1945.
HALÉVY, Elie, *A History of the English People in the Nineteenth Century*, new edition, 6 vols., 1949–52.
HANHAM, H. J., *Elections and Party Management. Politics in the time of Disraeli and Gladstone*, 1959.
HEINDEL, R. H., *The American Impact on Great Britain, 1898–1914*, University of Pennsylvania, 1940.
JENKINS, R. T., *Hanes Cymru yn y Bedwaredd Ganrif ar Bymtheg*, Cardiff, vol. i, 1933.
—— 'The Development of Nationalism in Wales', *Sociological Review*, 1935.
JOHN, A. H., *The Industrial Development of South Wales, 1750–1850*, Cardiff, 1950.
JONES, Ieuan Gwynedd, 'Franchise Reform and Glamorgan Politics, 1832–67', *Morgannwg*, ii (1958).
—— 'The Liberation Society and Welsh Politics, 1844–68', *Welsh History Review*, vol. i, no. 2 (1961).
—— 'The Election of 1868 in Merthyr Tydfil', *Journal of Modern History*, September 1961.

332   BIBLIOGRAPHY

KEDOURIE, Elie, *Nationalism*, 1960.
KING, C. T., *The Asquith Parliament*, 1909.
LEWIS, E. D., *The Rhondda Valleys*, 1959.
LEWIS, H. Elvet, *Nonconformity in Wales*, 1904.
LLOYD, D. Myrddin (ed.), *The Historical Basis of Welsh Nationalism*, Cardiff, 1950.
LLOYD, Sir John Edward (ed.), *A History of Carmarthenshire*, vol. ii, 1939.
LUCY, H. W., *A Diary of the Salisbury Parliament, 1886–92*, 1892.
—— *A Diary of the Home Rule Parliament, 1892–5*, 1895.
MACCOBY, S., *English Radicalism, 1886–1914*, 1955.
MAINWARING, T., *Glimpses of Welsh Politics*, Llanelly, 1881.
MINCHINTON, W. E., *The British Tinplate Industry*, Oxford, 1957.
MORGAN, J. E., *A Village Workers' Council*, Pontypridd, n.d. (1956).
MORGAN, J. Vyrnwy, *A Study in Nationality*, 1912.
—— *Wales and the Great War*, 1916.
MORGAN, Kenneth O., 'Gladstone and Wales', *Welsh History Review*, vol. i, no. 1 (1960).
—— 'Liberals, Nationalists and Mr. Gladstone', *Trans. Hon. Soc. Cymm.*, 1960.
—— 'Democratic Politics in Glamorgan, 1884–1914', *Morgannwg*, iv (1960).
MORRIS, J. H., and WILLIAMS, L. J., *The South Wales Coal Industry, 1841–1875*, Cardiff, 1958.
NICHOLSON, Ivor, and WILLIAMS, Lloyd, *Wales: its part in the War*, 1919.
O'RAHILLY, C., *Ireland and Wales*, 1924.
OWEN, Geraint Dyfnallt, *Ysgolion a Cholegau yr Annibynwyr*, Swansea, 1939.
PARES, Richard, 'A Quarter of a Millennium of Anglo-Scottish Union', *History*, October 1954.
PARRY, Owen, 'Parliamentary Representation of Wales and Monmouthshire in the nineteenth century, but mainly to 1870' (unpublished University of Wales M.A. thesis, 1924).
PELLING, Henry, *Origins of the Labour Party*, 1954.
—— *The British Communist Party*, 1958.
PRIBIĆEVÌC, Branko, *The Shop Stewards Movement and Workers' Control, 1910–22*, Oxford, 1959.
REES, Alwyn D., *Life in a Welsh Countryside*, Cardiff, 1950.
REES, Sir Frederick, 'The Welsh Political Problem', *Nineteenth Century and After*, April 1949.
REES, R. D., 'Glamorgan Newspapers under the Stamp Acts', *Morgannwg*, iii (1959).
—— 'South Wales Newspapers under the Stamp Acts', *Welsh History Review*, vol. i, no 3 (1962).
REES, Thomas, *History of Protestant Nonconformity in Wales*, 2nd edition, 1883.
RHŶS, Sir John, and JONES, D. Brynmor, *The Welsh People*, 1900.

RICHARD, Henry, *Letters on the Social and Political Condition of Wales*, 1867.

RICHARD, Henry, *Letters and Essays on Wales*, 1884.

RODERICK, A. J. (ed.), *Wales through the Ages*, vol. ii, Llandybïe, 1960.

SACKS, Benjamin, *The Religious Issue in the State Schools of England and Wales, 1902–14*, Albuquerque, New Mexico, 1961.

SELBORNE, 1st Earl of, *A Defence of the Church of England against Disestablishment* (5th edition, with supplement on the Welsh Church Commission by H. J. Clayton, 1911).

THOMAS, Sir Ben Bowen, 'Agwedd ar Wleidyddiaeth Cymru, 1900–14', *Y Llenor*, 1948.

—— 'Establishment of the Aberdare Departmental Committee, 1880. Some notes and letters', *Bulletin of the Board of Celtic Studies*, May, 1962.

THOMAS, Brinley, 'The Migration of Labour into the Glamorgan Coalfield, 1861–1911', *Economica*, 1930.

—— 'Wales and the Atlantic Economy', *Scottish Journal of Political Economy*, November 1959.

THOMAS, D. Lleufer, *Labour Unions in South Wales*, Swansea, 1901.

THOMAS, P. S., *Industrial Relations. A short study of the relations between employers and employed in Swansea and neighbourhood from about 1800 to recent times*, Cardiff, 1940.

ULLSWATER, Viscount, *A Speaker's Commentaries*, 2 vols., 1925.

VAUGHAN, H. M., *The South Wales Squires*, 1926.

VINCENT, J. E., *The Land Question in North Wales*, 1896.

—— *The Land Question in South Wales*, 1897.

WEBSTER, J. R., 'Welsh Secondary Education and Society, 1800–1918' (unpublished University of Wales Ph.D. thesis 1959).

WILLIAMS, C. R., 'The Welsh Religious Revival of 1904–5', *British Journal of Sociology*, 1952.

WILLIAMS, David, *John Frost*, Cardiff, 1939.

—— *Cymru ac America*, Cardiff, 1946.

—— *A History of Modern Wales*, 1950.

—— *The Rebecca Riots*, Cardiff, 1955.

—— 'Chartism in Wales', in Asa Briggs (ed.), *Chartist Studies*, 1959.

—— 'Rural Wales in the Nineteenth Century', *Journal of the Agricultural Society*, 1953.

WILLIAMS, Glanmor, 'The Idea of Nationality in Wales', *Cambridge Journal*, 1953.

WILLIAMS, Gwyn A., 'The Making of Radical Merthyr, 1800–1836', *Welsh History Review*, vol. i, no. 2 (1961).

—— 'Twf Hanesyddol y Syniad o Genedl yng Nghymru', *Efrydiau Athronyddol*, cyf. xxiv (1961).

WILLIAMS, H. M., 'The Geographical Distribution of Political Opinion in the County of Glamorgan for Parliamentary Elections, 1820–1950' (unpublished University of Wales M.A. thesis, 1952).

ZIMMERN, Sir Alfred, *My Impressions of Wales*, 1927.

BIBLIOGRAPHICAL NOTE TO
THE SECOND EDITION
(July 1970)

RECENT publications on Welsh history are listed in the 'supplements' to the *Bibliography of the History of Wales*, published in the *Bulletin of the Board of Celtic Studies* (vol. xx, 126–64 for the years 1959–62; vol. xxii, 49–70 for the years 1963–5; vol. xxiii, 263–83 for the years 1966–8). Complete checklists of articles relating to the history of Wales are printed annually in the December issues of the *Welsh History Review*. However, it may be helpful to other researchers to indicate some of the sources that have become available since 1962 when I completed the first edition.

MANUSCRIPTS

The most important of the new manuscript collections now available are the Lloyd George papers, housed in the Beaverbrook Library. They are comparatively sparse for the period before 1916, but contain considerable material of Welsh interest for the years of Lloyd George's premiership and the period after 1922. A major collection of Lloyd George papers, especially valuable for Lloyd George's early career in Welsh politics, has been deposited in the National Library of Wales. Two other collections of great importance in the National Library, the Thomas Jones papers and the Clement Davies papers, have not yet been generally released at the time of writing. Among the lesser collections deposited in the National Library since 1962 are the papers of Sir Hussey Vivian, Lord Swansea. Other manuscripts that I have worked on there in recent years include the D. A. Thomas papers, the Davies of Llandinam papers, the J. M. Howell collection, and various collections relating to H. Tobit Evans. In other archives, sources of value are the papers of J. J. Vaughan in the Glamorgan Record Office; the Cawdor papers in the Carmarthen Record Office; the records of the Merioneth Liberal Association in the Merioneth Record Office; and the Welsh Liberal Members Committee Minute Book, 1886–9 in the Newport Public Library. (I am grateful to Mr. W. R. Lambert for drawing my attention to this last source.) The substitution of the thirty- for the fifty-year rule has released many sources in the Public Record Office, among which the Cabinet minutes for 1919–22 have some value for this purpose.

ARTICLES

WILLIAMS, L. J. 'The First Welsh "Labour" M.P.', *Morgannwg*, vi (1962).
WILLIAMS, J. Roose, 'Quarryman's Champion', *Trans. Caernarvonshire Hist. Soc.* (1962) (and subsequent issues).

WILLIAMS, L. J., 'The New Unionism in Wales', *Welsh History Review*, vol. i, no. 4 (1963).

DAVIES, Alun, 'Cenedlaetholdeb yn Ewrop a Chymru yn y bedwaredd ganrif a'r bymtheg', *Efrydiau Athronyddol*, xxvii (1964).

JONES, Ieuan Gwynedd, 'Cardiganshire Politics in the mid-Nineteenth Century', *Ceredigion* (1964).

—— 'Dr. Thomas Price and the Election of 1868 in Merthyr Tydfil', *Welsh History Review*, vol. ii, nos. 2 and 3 (1964–5).

ELLIS, T. I., 'Premier and Chief Whip', *Trans. Honourable Society of Cymmrodorion* (1965), part I.

JONES-ROBERTS, K. W., 'D. R. Daniel', *Journal of the Merioneth Historical and Record Society* (1965).

HANHAM, H. J., 'The Creation of the Scottish Office, 1881–87', *Juridical Review* (1965), part 3.

FOX, Kenneth O., 'Labour and Merthyr's Khaki Election of 1900', *Welsh History Review*, vol. ii, no. 4 (Dec. 1965).

WILLIAMS, L. J., 'The Miners' Strike of 1898', *Morgannwg*, ix (1965).

WILLIAMS, J. E. Caerwyn, 'Syr John Morris-Jones: Rhan II', *Trans. Honourable Society of Cymmrodorion* (1966), part I.

MORGAN, Kenneth O., 'D. A. Thomas: the Industrialist as Politician', *Glamorgan Historian* (1966).

—— 'Cardiganshire Politics: the Liberal Ascendancy, 1885–1923', *Ceredigion* (1967).

PARRY, Cyril, 'The Independent Labour Party and Gwynedd Politics, 1900–20', *Welsh History Review*, vol. iv, no. 1 (June 1968).

MORGAN, Kenneth O., 'Twilight of Welsh Liberalism: Lloyd George and the Wee Frees, 1918–35', *Bulletin of the Board of Celtic Studies*, xii (1968).

JONES, Ieuan Gwynedd, 'Merioneth Politics in the mid-Nineteenth Century', *Journal of the Merioneth Historical and Record Society* (1968).

ELLIS, E. L., 'Some Aspects of the Early History of the University College of Wales', *Trans. Honourable Society of Cymmrodorion* (1967), part II.

JONES, Marian Henry, 'Wales and Hungary', ibid. (1968), part I.

ROBERTS, Brynley F., 'Sir Edward Anwyl', ibid. (1968), part II.

JONES-EVANS, Peris, 'Evan Pan Jones—Land Reformer', *Welsh History Review*, vol. iv, no. 2 (Dec. 1968).

WILLS, Wilton D., 'The Established Church in the Diocese of Llandaff, 1850–70', ibid., vol. iv, no. 3 (June 1969).

WEBSTER, J. R., 'The Welsh Intermediate Education Act of 1889', ibid.

PELLING, Henry and MORGAN, Kenneth O., 'Wales and the Boer War', ibid., vol. iv, no. 4 (Dec. 1969).

COOK, C. P., 'Wales and the General Election of 1923', ibid.

MORGAN, Kenneth O., 'The Liberal Unionists in Wales', *Nat. Lib. Wales Journal*, Winter 1969.

DAVID, E. I., 'Charles Masterman and the Swansea By-election of 1915', *Welsh History Review*, vol. v, no. 1 (June 1970).

MORGAN, Kenneth O. 'Lloyd George in Power: a Study in Prime Ministerial Government', *Historical Journal*, March, 1970.

—— 'Lloyd George's Stage Army: the Coalition Liberals, 1918–22', A. J. P. Taylor (ed.), *Lloyd George: Twelve Essays* (1970).

—— 'Welsh Nationalism: the Historical Background', *Journal of Contemporary History*, Jan. 1971.

SECONDARY WORKS

(Place of publication London, unless otherwise stated)

REES, J. F., *The Problem of Wales and other essays* (Cardiff, 1963).

ELLIS, T. I., *John Humphreys Davies* (Liverpool, 1963).

Pioneers of Welsh Education (Swansea, 1964).

JENKINS, Roy, *Asquith* (1964).

CRAIK, W. W., *The Central Labour College* (1964).

DAVIES, E. T., *Religion in the Industrial Revolution in South Wales* (Cardiff, 1965).

JONES, R. Tudur, *Hanes Annibyniaeth Cymru* (Swansea, 1966).

MORGAN, Kenneth O., *Freedom or Sacrilege?* (Penarth, 1966).

WILSON, Trevor, *The Downfall of the Liberal Party, 1914–35* (1966).

WILLIAMS, Glanmor (ed.), *Merthyr Politics: the Making of a Working-class Tradition* (Cardiff, 1966).

ARNOT, R. Page, *The South Wales Miners* (1967).

LEWIS, W. J., *The Lead Mining Industry in Wales* (Cardiff, 1967).

MORGAN, Kenneth O., *Keir Hardie* (Oxford, 1967).

PELLING, Henry, *The Social Geography of British Elections, 1885–1910* (1967).

—— *Popular Politics and Society in Late Victorian Britain* (1968).

GREGORY, Roy, *The Miners and British Politics, 1906–14* (Oxford, 1968).

KNOX, R. Buick, *Wales and Y Goleuad, 1869–1879* (Caernarvon, 1969).

MIDDLEMAS, K. (ed.), *Thomas Jones: Whitehall Diary, i, 1916–25* (Oxford, 1969).

MINCHINTON, W. E. (ed.), *Industrial South Wales, 1750–1914* (1969).

BELL, P. M. H., *Disestablishment in Ireland and Wales* (1969).

ELLIS, T. I., *Ellis Jones Griffith* (Llandybïe, 1969).

BAYLISS, G. M., 'The Outsider: aspects of the political career of Sir Alfred Mond, first Lord Melchett' (unpublished University of Wales Ph.D., 1969).

WOODHOUSE, M. G., 'Rank and File Movements among the Miners of South Wales, 1910–26' (unpublished Oxford University D.Phil., 1970).

JONES, Goronwy. J. *Wales and the Quest for Peace* (Cardiff, 1970).

LAMBERT, W. R., 'Drink and Sobriety in Wales, 1835–95' (unpublished University of Wales Ph.D., 1970).

PARRY, Cyril, *The Radical Tradition in Welsh Politics: a study of Gwynedd Politics 1900–1920* (Hull, 1970).

BIBLIOGRAPHICAL NOTE TO THE THIRD EDITION

(September 1978)

THERE have not been many major additions to the manuscript collections available for research on Welsh politics in the 1868-1922 period, since the publication of the second edition of this book in 1970. The Lloyd George Papers in the National Library of Wales, Aberystwyth, are now generally available to historians, though the Thomas Jones Papers still are not. The Glansevern and Rendel Papers there have further expanded, while the papers of Watkin Davies are a useful small collection. Elsewhere in Wales the Gwynedd Record Office, Caernarvon, has accumulated interesting materials relating to Lloyd George's early political career in Caernarvonshire, while the Clwyd Record Office, Ruthin, holds the archive of the North Wales area of the National Union of Mineworkers. For labour historians, the South Wales Miners' Library (Llyfrgell Glowyr De Cymru), attached to the University College of Swansea, is a storehouse of information. Its holdings include the private papers of such Welsh Labour MPs as S. O. Davies, George Daggar and D. J. Williams, all, however, post-1922. Still inaccessible, alas!, is the archive of the Independent Labour Party, entombed in Bristol, which contains invaluable material on the early labour movement in Wales and on Keir Hardie. To a limited extent, the gap is filled by the files of the Labour Party archive, still housed (at the time of writing) in Transport House. The Bodleian, Oxford, has recently made available the papers of Sir William Harcourt, a Welsh M.P. from 1895 to 1904. The Zimmern Papers are also of some Welsh interest. The Beaverbrook Library in London was closed in 1975; the Lloyd George Papers formerly housed in that purpose-built institution are now available in the House of Lords Record Office.

Published work on Welsh history in this period has continued to flow abundantly, reflecting the growing interest in the recent past in Welsh schools and university colleges, and in the broadcasting media. Among the more significant published works to appear since 1970 are the following:

ARTICLES

STEAD, Peter, 'Vernon Hartshorn', *Glamorgan Historian* 6 (1970)

WILLIAMS, Glanmor, 'Language, Literacy and Nationality in Wales', *History* LVI (February 1971).

ELLIS, E. L., 'Thomas Jones, C. H. and the University College of Wales, Aberystwyth', *Ceredigion* VI, No. 4 (1971).

MORGAN, Kenneth O., 'Labour's Early Struggles in South Wales', *Nat. Lib. Wales Journal* XVII, No. 4 (Winter 1972).

EVANS, L. Wynne, 'The Welsh National Council for Education, 1903-6', *Welsh History Review*, Vol. 6, No. 1 (June 1972).

MORGAN, Kenneth O., 'Lloyd George and the Historians', *Trans. Hon. Soc. Cymmrodorion* (1972).

LAMBERT, W. R., 'The Welsh Sunday Closing Act of 1881',*Welsh History Review*, Vol. 6, No. 2 (December 1972).

Llafur (Journal of the Society for the Study of Welsh Labour History) Vols. 1 and 2 (1972-8), *passim*. Concentrated attention has been paid to rank-and-file movements amongst Welsh workers, 1910-26.

Welsh History Review, Vol. 6, No. 3 (June 1973). Welsh Labour History number.

MORGAN, Jane, 'Denbighshire's *Annus Mirabilis:* the Borough and County Elections of 1868', *Welsh History Review*, Vol. 7, No. 1 (June 1974).

DAVIES, John, 'The End of the Great Estates and the Rise of Freehold Farming in Wales', ibid., Vol. 7, No. 2 (December 1974).

PRICE, R. Emyr, 'Lloyd George and Meirioneth Politics, 1885, 1886—a Failure to Effect a Breakthrough', *Journal of the Merioneth Hist. and Record Society* VII, No. 3 (1975).

———'Lloyd George and the 1890 by-election in the Caernarvon Boroughs', *Caernarvonshire Hist. Soc. Trans.* XXXVI, (1975).

WILLIAMS, L. J., 'The Coalowners of South Wales, 1873-80', *Welsh History Review*, Vol. 8, No. 1 (June 1976).

PRICE, R. Emyr, 'Newyddiadur Cyntaf David Lloyd George', *Journal of the Welsh Bibliographical Society* XI, Nos. 3-4 (1976).

HOLMES, G. M., 'The South Wales Coal Industry, 1850-1914', *Trans. Hon. Soc. Cymmrodorion* (1976).

ROWLANDS, E. W., 'Etholiad Cyffredinol 1918 yn Sir Fôn', *Anglesey Antiquarian Society and Field Club Trans.* (1976-7).

WILLIAMS, Colin H., 'Non-Violence and the Development of the Welsh Language Society, 1962-*c*. 1974', *Welsh History Review*, Vol. 8 No. 4 (December 1977).

DAUNTON, M. J., 'Jack Ashore: Seamen in Cardiff before 1914', ibid., Vol. 9, No. 2. (December 1978).

BOOKS

(Place of publication London unless otherwise stated).

MORGAN, Kenneth, O., *The Age of Lloyd George* (1971, new editions 1975 and 1978).

JONES, R. Brinley (ed.), *The Anatomy of Wales* (Cardiff, 1972).

ELLIS, E. L., *The University College of Wales, Aberystwyth, 1872-1972*, (Cardiff, 1972).

MORGAN, Kenneth O., (ed.). *Lloyd George: Family Letters, 1885-1936*, (Cardiff and Oxford, 1973).

MADGWICK, P. J., *The Politics of Rural Wales*, (1973).

GRIGG, John, *The Young Lloyd George*, (1973).

MORGAN, Kenneth O., *Lloyd George*, (1974).

HEARDER, H. and LOYN, H. R. (eds.), *British Government and Administration*, (Cardiff, 1974). Chapter on education by Gwynedd O. Pierce.

PHILIP, Alan Butt, *The Welsh Question: Nationalism in Welsh Politics*, 1945-70 (Cardiff, 1975).

HECHTER, Michael, *Internal Colonialism*, (1975).

BARKER, Michael, *Gladstone and Radicalism* (Hassocks, 1975).

MORGAN, Kenneth O., *Keir Hardie: Radical and Socialist* (1975)

KOSS, Stephen, *Nonconformity in Modern British Politics* (1975)

ROWLAND, Peter, *Lloyd George* (1976).

GEORGE, William, *The Making of Lloyd George* (1976)

COOK, Chris (ed.) *Sources in British Political History, 1900-1951*: Vol. 3. A guide to the private papers of members of parliament (1977).

SAMUEL, Raphael (ed.), *Miners, Quarrymen and Saltworkers* (1976). Chapter on quarrymen by Merfyn Jones.

HARVIE, Christopher, *Scotland and Nationalism* (1977).

DAUNTON, M. J. *Coal Metropolis: Cardiff, 1870-1914* (Leicester, 1977).

KIRBY, M. W., *The British Coalmining Industry, 1870-1946* (1977).

STEAD, Peter, *Coleg Harlech: the First Fifty Years* (Cardiff, 1977).

JONES, Beti, *Etholiadau Seneddol yng Nghymru, 1900-75* (Talybont, 1977).

WILLIAM, J. Roose, *Quarryman's Champion* (Denbigh, 1978).

HOWELL, David W., *Land and People in Nineteenth Century Wales* (1978),

SMITH, J. B. and others, *James Griffiths and his Times* (Cardiff, 1978).

OSMOND, John, *Creative Conflict: the Politics of Welsh Devolution* (Llandysul and London, 1978).

Students should also consult section XI of H. J. Hanham (ed.) *Bibliography of British History*, 1851-1914 (Oxford, 1976), and John Saville and Joyce Bellamy (eds.), *Dictionary of Labour Biography*, Vols. 1-5 (1972-   ), for Welsh entries.

INDEX

Z

Welsh political structure, 56, 245; effect of Local Government Act on, 107; in Tudor period, 300; decline of, 307–8.

Geoffrey of Monmouth, 8.

George, David Lloyd. *See* Lloyd George, David.

George, Henry, 212.

Gibbins, Frederick W., 251.

Gibbon, Rev. J. Morgan, 234, 261.

Gibbs, Viccary, 136, 156.

Gibson, John, 121 and n.

Giffard, Hardinge (1st Earl of Halsbury), 37.

Gill, 276.

Giraldus Cambrensis, 265.

Gladstone, Herbert (1st Viscount Gladstone), 67 n., 178, 209, 219.

Gladstone, Rev. Stephen, 147.

Gladstone, W. G. C., 155, 268–70.

Gladstone, William Ewart: speech at Mold *Eisteddfod*, 21, 41–42; and 1868 election, 22, 28; and see of St. Asaph, 32–33, 37; opposes disestablishment motion of 1870, 34–35; friendship with Rendel, 40; supports Welsh Sunday Closing Act, 42–43; and Welsh higher education, 44, 46–50, 52; and see of Llandaff, 59–61; and 1885 election, 63–64; and Redistribution Act, 65, 68; and first Irish home rule bill, 70–73; reasons for Welsh support for, 74–75; reserve over Welsh disestablishment criticized, 79–80, 82, 90; and tithe war, 88; announces support for Welsh disestablishment, 91–93; and 1892 election, 94, 119; and Welsh land question, 97; supports Intermediate Education Act, 99; and Welsh home rule, 106–7, 115; angered by Welsh obstruction of Clergy Discipline Bill, 117, 119; relation to Welsh members in 1892, 120–3; and appointment of Land Commission, 123–6; and University charter, 129–30, 132; attitude towards disestablishment in 1892, 133; and Suspensory Bill, 133–8; correspondence with Welsh Party, 139–40; and 1894 Disestablishment Bill, 140–1; resignation of, 142–3; attitude to 1895 Disestablishment Bill, 151,

154–5; also mentioned, 9, 160, 299, 308.

Glamorgan: industrialization of, 3, 10; immigration into, 55; and Redistribution Act, 64; tithe in, 84; and Welsh home rule movement, 110, 113, 161–2; county council elections in, 191 n.; and Welsh education 'revolt', 195; and Welsh education council, 225, 280, 294.

Glamorgan (East), parliamentary representation, 66, 244, 247, 251.

Glamorgan (Mid), parliamentary representation, 113, 210, 247, 251, 253.

Glamorgan (Rhondda), parliamentary representation, 66, 244, 304, 312.

Glamorgan (South), parliamentary representation, 65, 159, 170, 209, 219.

Glamorgan (West—Gower), parliamentary representation, 113, 169, 179, 207, 209, 211, 219, 251, 253.

Glamorgan, Vale of, 55, 65.

Glynne, Catherine, 75.

Goleuad, Y, 35, 71, 83, 156–8, 238.

Gore, Charles, Bishop of Oxford, 262–3, 266, 269–70.

Gorst, Sir John Eldon, 136, 150, 156, 183.

Goschen, Georg Joachim (1st Viscount Goschen), 82, 138, 150.

Gower, 217. *See also* Glamorgan (West—Gower).

Grady, Joe, 205.

Gray, C. M., 97.

Greaves, J. E., 233, 261.

Green, T. H., 70.

Grenfell, David R., 293.

Grey, Albert, 67.

Grey, Sir Edward (1st Viscount Grey of Fallodon), 115, 191, 192.

Griffith, Ellis Jones (later Sir Ellis Jones Ellis-Griffith): at Aberystwyth college, 51, 220; and *Cymru Fydd*, 70; in 1892 election, 118 n.; returned to parliament, 166–7; an imperialist, 179; and Welsh education 'revolt', 184, 185 n.; in 1906 parliament, 222, 241; and position of Welsh disestablishment, 232, 235–7; appointed under-secretary to Home Office, 260–1; and 1912 Disestablishment Bill, 264, 273; on First World War,